D0611632

Avoiding Nuclear Anarchy

CSIA Studies in International Security

Michael E. Brown, Sean M. Lynn-Jones, and Steven E. Miller, series editors
Teresa Johnson Lawson, executive editor
Center for Science and International Affairs (CSIA)
John F. Kennedy School of Government, Harvard University

Published by CSIA:

1. *Soviet Nuclear Fission: Control of the Nuclear Arsenal in a Disintegrating Soviet Union*, Kurt M. Campbell, Ashton B. Carter, Steven E. Miller, and Charles A. Zraket (1991)

2. *Cooperative Denuclearization: From Pledges to Deeds*, Graham Allison, Ashton B. Carter, Steven E. Miller, and Philip Zelikow, eds. (1993)

Published by Brassey's, Inc.:

3. *Russian Security After the Cold War: Seven Views from Moscow*, Teresa Pelton Johnson and Steven E. Miller, eds. (1994)

4. *Arms Unbound: The Globalization of Defense Production*, David Mussington (1994)

5. *Damage Limitation or Crisis? Russia and the Outside World*, Robert D. Blackwill and Sergei A. Karaganov, eds. (1994)

Published by The MIT Press:

6. *Shaping Europe's Military Order: The Origins and Consequences of the CFE Treaty*, Richard A. Falkenrath (1994)

7. *The Arms Production Dilemma: Contraction and Restraint in the World Combat Aircraft Industry*, Randall Forsberg, ed. (1994)

Avoiding Nuclear Anarchy

Containing the Threat of Loose Russian Nuclear Weapons and Fissile Material

Graham T. Allison
Owen R. Coté, Jr.
Richard A. Falkenrath
Steven E. Miller

CSIA Studies in International Security No. 12

The MIT Press
Cambridge, Massachusetts
London, England

UNIVERSITY OF TOLEDO LIBRARIES

Copyright © 1996 by the Center for Science and International Affairs
John F. Kennedy School of Government
Harvard University
Cambridge, Massachusetts 02138
(617) 495–1400

All rights reserved. No part of this book may be reproduced, stored in a retrieval system, or transmitted in any form or by any means — electronic, electrostatic, magnetic tape, mechanical, photocopying, recording, or otherwise — without permission in writing from the Center for Science and International Affairs, 79 John F. Kennedy Street, Cambridge, MA 02138.

Library of Congress Cataloging-in-Publication Data

Avoiding nuclear anarchy : containing the threat of loose Russian nuclear weapons and fissile material / Graham T. Allison . . . [et al.].
p. cm. — (CSIA studies in international security; no. 12)
˙ISBN 0-262-51088-X
1. Nuclear terrorism — Prevention 2. Nuclear industry — Security measures — Former Soviet republics. 3. Nuclear nonproliferation — Government policy — United States. I. Allison, Graham T. II. Series.
HV6431.A96 1995
327.1'74 — dc20   95-25376
                                                                                        CIP

10 9 8 7 6 5 4 3 2 1

Printed in the United States of America

HV
6431
·A96
1996

Contents

Acknowledgments

The fate of the nuclear arsenal left behind by the Soviet Union has been a central research focus at the Center for Science and International Affairs (CSIA) since 1991. As the Soviet Union began to slide toward dissolution in the waning months of 1991, CSIA undertook a comprehensive analysis of the nuclear challenges that would attend the collapse of the Soviet state, producing the monograph, *Soviet Nuclear Fission: Control of the Nuclear Arsenal in a Disintegrating Soviet Union*, in November 1991. Once the Soviet Union had collapsed, CSIA explored how to remove the nuclear weapons from the newly independent states, and to safely and securely consolidate them into Russia. This project produced *Cooperative Denuclearization: From Pledges to Deeds* in January 1993.

The present volume addresses the largest remaining challenge associated with the Soviet nuclear legacy: the security of the nuclear weapons and nuclear materials now largely consolidated within Russia.

This book has been a year in the making. Over the past months, we have benefited from information, comments, criticism, and corrections from dozens of government officials, some in the West, some in the former Soviet Union. We thankfully acknowledge this anonymous assistance. An early draft was read and vivisected by Robert D. Blackwill, Michael E. Brown, John Lloyd, and Philip Zelikow; they forced us to refine our thoughts and tighten our argument. Yet another draft was previewed and vetted at a brainstorming session convened by Senator Sam Nunn and Senator Richard Lugar in July 1995. We also appreciate the comments and assistance given to us at various stages by Gary Bertsch, Oleg Bukharin, Rose Gottemoeller, Robert Newman, Tom Neff, Leonard Spector, and Jeremiah Sullivan. We also wish to acknowledge the profit we have drawn from the work of others who have studied the issues raised in this volume, including Bruce Blair, Matt Bunn, Tom Cochran, Dunbar Lockwood, John Holdren, Chris Paine, and Frank von Hippel. Particular thanks are due to William Potter, who provided detailed comments on a draft of this study. Professor Potter also collaborated with CSIA in sponsoring, and took the lead in organizing, a conference on U.S. nuclear cooperation programs in the former Soviet Union that contributed greatly to our work. Finally, we offer thanks to all those upon whom we inflicted this analysis at various seminars and conferences, and whose feedback helped us sharpen our analysis.

CSIA's work on the Soviet nuclear legacy, including not only this volume but its two predecessors, has been made possible by the Carnegie Corporation of New York. For its financial and institutional support, we thank the Carnegie Corporation, whose President, David Hamburg, constantly challenges us to think as hard as we can about the most difficult problems.

It is a pleasant duty to acknowledge the contributions of our colleagues here at CSIA. We warmly thank Dawn Opstad and Jessica Hobart, who luckily for us joined the CSIA team in time to help us finish this book, and Deborah Kamen, who provided much-valued research assistance at a critical juncture. And finally, special thanks to our indispensable editor, Teresa J. Lawson, a seasoned veteran of CSIA's periodic collaborative campaigns who is unflagging in her efforts to get us across the finish line, even though she knows how hard it can be.

G.T.A.
O.R.C.
R.A.F.
S.E.M.

October 1995
Cambridge, Mass.

About the Authors

Graham T. Allison is the Douglas Dillon Professor of Government at Harvard University, and Director of the Center for Science and International Affairs (CSIA) at Harvard's John F. Kennedy School of Government. He is the former Dean of the Kennedy School (1977–89), and the founder of its Strengthening Democratic Institutions Project, now part of CSIA. Allison served in 1993–94 as Assistant Secretary of Defense for Policy and Plans in the Clinton administration, and is currently a Special Advisor to Secretary of Defense Perry. His publications include *Essence of Decision: Explaining the Cuban Missile Crisis; Fateful Visions; Hawks, Doves, and Owls: An Agenda for Avoiding Nuclear War;* and, with Russian economist Gregory Yavlinsky, *Window of Opportunity: The Grand Bargain for Democracy in the Soviet Union.*

Owen R. Coté, Jr., is Assistant Director of CSIA's International Security Program. He is an editor of the journal *International Security.* His publications include the two studies that preceded the current volume — *Soviet Nuclear Fission* and *Cooperative Denuclearization* — as well as articles in *International Security* and other journals. He was awarded the doctorate by MIT, and he is a graduate of Harvard University.

Richard A. Falkenrath is a Research Fellow at the Center for Science and International Affairs. His publications include *Shaping Europe's Military Order: The Origins and Consequences of the CFE Treaty,* as well as articles in *International Security* and *Survival.* He received his doctorate from the Department of War Studies, King's College, London, where he was a Marshall Scholar. He is a graduate of Occidental College, Los Angeles.

Steven E. Miller has been associated with CSIA in many capacities, most recently as Director of its International Security Program. He is also Editor in Chief of the journal *International Security,* and an editor of the CSIA Studies in International Security. He has been a Senior Research Fellow at the Stockholm International Peace Research Institute (SIPRI), and he has taught at in the Defense and Arms Control Studies program of the Department of Political Science at MIT. His publications include *Soviet Nuclear Fission* and *Cooperative Denuclearization,* as well as articles in *International Security, Foreign Affairs, Survival,* and numerous other journals and edited volumes. He is co-editor, most recently, of *Debating the Democratic Peace, The Perils of Anarchy: Contemporary Realism and International Security,* and *Global Dangers: Changing Dimensions of International Security.* He was awarded the doctorate by the Fletcher School of Law and Diplomacy, and is a graduate of Occidental College, Los Angeles.

Introduction

On April 19, 1995, American terrorists demolished Oklahoma City's Federal Office building, killing 162 men, women, and children. Two and one-half years earlier, international terrorists attacked New York City's 110-story World Trade Center. Had that explosion succeeded in undermining the structural foundation of that enormous building, 30,000 people might have died.

It does not require a large step to get from terrorist acts like Oklahoma City and the World Trade Center to the first act of nuclear terrorism. Suppose that instead of mini-vans filled with hundreds of pounds of the crude explosives used in Oklahoma City and New York, terrorists had acquired a suitcase carrying one hundred pounds of highly enriched uranium (HEU), roughly the size of a grapefruit. Using a simple, well-known design to build a weapon from this material, terrorists could have produced a nuclear blast equivalent to 10,000 to 20,000 tons of TNT. Under normal conditions, this would devastate a three-square-mile urban area. Much of Oklahoma City would have disappeared. The tip of Manhattan, including all of Wall Street reaching up to Gramercy Park, would have been destroyed.

Of the many extraordinary changes in the world beyond America's borders since the fall of the Berlin Wall in 1989, which change is likely to have the most profound consequences for American national security? The conventional answer is clear: Communism has expired and with it the expansionist Soviet adversary that served as the fixed point for the American foreign policy compass for four decades of Cold War. The threat is gone.

But there is a more expansive and much less comfortable answer to the question. Assessed in terms of direct consequences for American national security, the disappearance of Soviet Communism is rivaled by a much-less-noted reality: the possibility of "nuclear leakage," that is, the sale, theft, diversion, or abuse of the nuclear weapons and weapons-usable materials once securely held by the totalitarian Soviet state. As a consequence of the collapse of this command society, a vast potential supermarket of nuclear weapons and weapons-grade uranium and plutonium is becoming increasingly accessible. Absent a determined program of action to prevent nuclear leakage that is as focused, serious, and vigorous as America's Cold War strategy, nuclear terrorism against American targets or American interests is frighteningly plausible.

Awakening to the New and Unprecedented Threat: Russia in Revolution

The single most important truth about the post–Cold War security environment is that Russia is convulsed by a genuine, ongoing revolution. This revolutionary transformation of the state, the economy, and the society is as profound as the French Revolution following 1789 that led to Napoleon's challenge to European security. It is more profound than the Russian Revolution of the early decades of this century that brought Communism to power. But about the current revolution, there is one difference without precedent in human experience. Never before has a superpower arsenal of nuclear weapons and fissile material existed in the midst of an ongoing (and unavoidably turbulent) revolution.

For seven decades, the Soviet Communist government controlled, or sought to control, virtually every dimension of life: what the economy produced, what citizens did, indeed even what people thought. One of the few benign results of that system was the unquestioned control of weapons-usable nuclear materials and nuclear weapons.

With the disappearance of the Soviet Union and the death of Communism, powerful forces have torn apart the fabric of authoritarian control in the economy, the government, and the state. In this tumultuous environment, nothing valuable can be secure from loss, theft, or sale. Moreover, the systems designed by a totalitarian state to manage the Soviet Union's nuclear arsenal have been eroded or swept away by these developments. As a result, over the past three years, trickles of weapons-usable fissile materials have begun seeping out of the former Soviet Union. The current trickle could well be a harbinger of things to come. A burgeoning flow, or even a catastrophic flood, of nuclear-weapons materials, or perhaps even of weapons themselves, has become a distinct danger given the conditions in which nuclear assets are held in Russia.

The implications of this for the United States can be conveyed by asking a question: As a result of the dramatic events since the fall of the Berlin Wall, has the likelihood that a nuclear weapon will explode on U.S. territory gone up, or gone down? Our answer is unambiguous: it has gone up. Even as the probability of large-scale nuclear war between the United States and Russia has *decreased* dramatically, the probability that a nuclear weapon will detonate in Russia, or Europe, or the Middle East, or even the United States has *increased*.

With the end of the Cold War, a new conventional wisdom declares that the United States faces "no direct threat" to its security. Despite repeated assertions of this proposition by government officials, those who have come to understand the nuclear leakage threat — including many in the intelligence and policy communities — generally accept the judgment that *the risk of a nuclear detonation on American soil has increased.* But because this new threat comes in a form so unfamiliar, indeed so radically different from prior experience, and because the instruments and policies to address it are so unlike the familiar Cold War approaches that the U.S. defense establishment pursued successfully for decades, Americans have had difficulty awakening to this fact.

Coping with New Nuclear Challenges

The collapse of the former Soviet Union presented American policy-makers with three major new nuclear challenges. The first was to secure and consolidate the Soviet Union's far-flung arsenal of tactical nuclear weapons, the type which would be most useful to a terrorist group or rogue state in search of an instant nuclear capability. The second challenge was to cope with the fact that Soviet strategic nuclear weapons — principally its nuclear-armed intercontinental ballistic missiles (ICBMs) — were located in four of the Soviet successor states, raising the prospect that the demise of the Soviet Union might result in the emergence of several states with intercontinental nuclear forces. Finally, the third post-Soviet nuclear challenge was and remains to prevent the leakage of nuclear weapons or weapons-usable material from Russia and the rest of the former Soviet Union. Assessing U.S. and Russian performance in addressing these three challenges over the past several years: there has been great success in rapidly consolidating the tactical nuclear arsenal into Russia; high prospects for great success in removing the Soviet strategic arsenal from Belarus, Kazakhstan, and Ukraine; but distressingly little progress in securing the remnants of the Soviet nuclear legacy now located principally in Russia. Reducing the threat of nuclear leakage remains the great unanswered challenge of the post–Cold War nuclear agenda.

TACTICAL NUCLEAR WEAPONS

The total size of the Soviet tactical nuclear weapons arsenal has never been precisely known, but it is believed that some 15,000–30,000 tactical nuclear weapons were stationed in fourteen of the Soviet Union's fifteen constituent republics in 1991. In the context of increasing turmoil within the ranks of the Soviet military and rising instability along the Soviet periphery, especially in the conflict-ridden republics such as Armenia, Azerbaijan, Georgia, and Tajikistan, the Soviet Union's tactical nuclear weapons arsenal presented an acute risk of diversion. Scores of weapons could have come loose. If they had, could they have found their way into international black markets? Diamonds, precious metals, and virtually everything else of great value in the former Soviet Union do, so it seems unlikely that nuclear weapons would have been different. If available in international arms bazaars, would there have been buyers? Certainly, including in all likelihood both rogue states and terrorist groups. Recognizing this risk, the U.S. government undertook two unprecedented initiatives in 1991. First, in September 1991, President Bush announced the unilateral withdrawal of tactical nuclear weapons from U.S. forces around the world, a sweeping and historic initiative that vitiated in a stroke decades of U.S. military planning. President Bush successfully challenged the Soviet government (soon to be succeeded by the Russian government) to undertake a reciprocal withdrawal of tactical nuclear weapons from its military forces abroad, a process which in fact Moscow had already begun, albeit on a modest scale. Before the end of 1992, more than 10,000 tactical nuclear weapons previously stationed beyond Russia's border had been returned to Russia.

The second historic U.S. initiative was the Soviet Nuclear Threat Reduction Act of 1991, better known as the "Nunn-Lugar program" after its two principal sponsors, Senators Sam Nunn and Richard Lugar.[1] In its first year, the Nunn-Lugar program allowed the U.S. government to spend up to $400 million from the defense budget on initiatives designed to offer technical assistance to the Soviet Union (soon to be the Soviet successor states) directed toward the safe and secure transportation and dismantlement of nuclear weapons and their delivery systems, and toward the implementation of other important arms control and non-proliferation objectives. For example, one of the first Nunn-Lugar projects to yield practical results was a 1992 program in Ukraine to deliver transportation equipment that was needed to move the tactical nuclear weapons (which were in the process of being withdrawn) from their storage depots to the rail heads from which they could be shipped to Russia. Responsibility for managing the Nunn-Lugar program was assigned to the Office of the Secretary of Defense, while the process of actually negotiating Nunn-Lugar agreements with the Soviet successor states was carried out under the auspices of a specially created Safe and Secure Dismantlement (SSD) delegation.[2] Congress has authorized the Nunn-Lugar program to spend about $300–400 million each year during 1991–96, but as we explain in Chapter 3 (see esp. pp. 131–134), these authorizations have been subject to an array of problematic restrictions and requirements that have tended to reduce the effectiveness of the program as a whole. Nonetheless, the Nunn-Lugar program has played a pivotal, though often controversial, role in the U.S. government's efforts to cope with the new nuclear challenges of the immediate post-Soviet period.

STRATEGIC NUCLEAR WEAPONS

The second major challenge of the post-Soviet period concerned the ownership of the Soviet Union's strategic nuclear forces. When the Soviet Union expired, the former Soviet strategic arsenal was left in four successor states: Russia, Ukraine, Kazakhstan, and Belarus. The Bush administration and the Congress wasted no time in deciding that the United States could accept only one nuclear successor state to the Soviet Union — Russia; this was a view shared by most other states on the planet, importantly including (at least at first) the newly sovereign governments of former Soviet republics. In practice, however, the process of denuding Belarus, Kazakhstan, and Ukraine of the strategic nuclear weapons they had inherited proved to be no simple matter, particularly in the case of Ukraine. Belarus was never a serious concern because of its subservience to Moscow. Kazakhstan wavered only briefly before the pragmatic policies of President Nursultan Nazerbayev set Kazakhstan on a firm course toward total denuclearization, a status it achieved when the last nuclear warhead was removed from Kazakh territory in April 1995.[3]

With the Russian government and public at best ambivalent about Ukraine's newly acquired status as an independent state, Ukraine had a simple and intuitively appealing reason for wanting to retain a minimal nuclear deterrent. But had Ukraine retained the strategic nuclear weapons on its territory, it would instantly have become the third largest nuclear weapons power in the world. The implications of this fact for U.S. national security were grave; some 1,800 nuclear warheads on ICBMs targeted against American cities would have come under the command of a new and unstable government in Kiev, raising from one to two the number of capitals in which a unilateral decision could cause the United States to turn into a smoking, radiating ruin.

In its most consequential national security initiative, the Clinton administration moved in 1993 to establish a multi-dimensional relationship with Ukraine aimed at securing its prompt and complete denucleariza-tion. The two central strands of this strategy were an intense engagement of Russia and Ukraine designed to resolve, or at least smooth over, many of the most serious differences between Moscow and Kiev, and the exten-sive use of Nunn-Lugar assistance to coax Ukraine into fulfilling its own commitments to relinquish its nuclear warheads. Much of this diplomacy was carried out in the context of the Gore-Chernomyrdin Commission (GCC), a biannual forum convened by Russian Prime Minister Victor Chernomyrdin and U.S. Vice President Al Gore that brings together senior Russian and American officials for high-profile, and often highly techni-cal, negotiations. Vice President Gore brokered the deal that restarted the denuclearization of Ukraine at the end of 1993, an arrangement which was set forth in the "trilateral statement" issued by U.S. President Bill Clinton, Russian President Boris Yeltsin, and Ukrainian President Leonid Kravchuk at the January 1994 summit in Moscow.[4]

The trilateral statement issued at the Moscow summit was an achieve-ment of truly historic proportions: it established the framework that allowed Ukraine to begin transferring its strategic nuclear warheads to Russia for dismantlement, and to accede to the Nuclear Non-Proliferation Treaty (NPT) as a non-nuclear weapons state, which in turn allowed the START I Treaty to enter into force. In return, Russia began shipping nuclear fuel rods to Ukraine for use in civilian power reactors, and Russia and the United States together provided a formal assurance of Ukraine's independence and territorial integrity.[5] At the end of 1995, the scheduled shipments of warheads to Russia and fuel rods to Ukraine were still on schedule, and it appeared highly likely that all nuclear weapons would be removed from Ukrainian territory by mid-1997. This was the second instance in which an innovative U.S. initiative contributed to a successful outcome in dealing with the new nuclear agenda.

NUCLEAR LEAKAGE

The third nuclear challenge of the post-Soviet era is qualitatively different — and orders of magnitude more difficult — than the first two. Solutions to the first two problems have succeeded in concentrating the former Soviet nuclear arsenal — some 30,000–40,000 nuclear weapons — into Russia, which also contains the components and bulk fissile material for tens of thousands more weapons. Thus, the geographic expanse of the former Soviet nuclear arsenal has been reduced from one-sixth to one-seventh of the earth's landmass. The trouble, of course, arises from the fact that this one-seventh of the earth's landmass into which the Soviet nuclear legacy has been consolidated is a profoundly troubled society, one marked by political instability, economic distress, and rampant crime and corruption. Thousands of nuclear weapons and hundreds of thousands of pounds of weapons-usable fissile material are being held at scores of sites scattered across Russia — a fact that will hold true indefinitely. (See Appendix A, "The Russian Nuclear Archipelago.") What makes this situation an international security problem without precedent, however, is that these nuclear weapons and materials are being stored in installations that lack adequate security, which are themselves located inside a highly unstable country.

The risk is that the former Soviet nuclear weapons and materials will leak out of Russia, finding their way into the hands of rogue states or terrorist groups. American and Russian policy have not yet begun to address this problem in a manner that is commensurate with their stakes in the issue. During 1992–94, most of the U.S. initiatives designed to combat the threat of nuclear leakage were carried out in the context of the Nunn-Lugar program within the Department of Defense. As we describe in detail in Chapter 3, the effectiveness of this early effort suffered from an array of legal restrictions and bureaucratic obstacles, making the Nunn-Lugar program a problematic vehicle for improving the security of Russian fissile material quickly or comprehensively. Responsibility for implementing the various U.S. anti-leakage programs was broadened in 1994–95, but although this bureaucratic adaptation began to show a few promising results in 1995, the overall U.S. government effort was still moving too slowly. Indeed, on the current track, U.S. and Russian policies will not fully address the nuclear leakage problem for years to come, leaving U.S. interests unacceptably jeopardized for a protracted period of time.

Goals of this Study

This study has three objectives.

First, it seeks to sound the alarm about the most serious direct threat to U.S. vital interests today and for the foreseeable future. If this analysis is correct, then the prevailing view that there is today no direct threat to U.S. national security is dead wrong. If this analysis is correct, then the defining danger of proliferation of nuclear weapons is not Iran's purchase of civilian nuclear reactors that may assist Iranian nuclear ambitions a decade hence; it is the threat that today, or tomorrow, Iran will purchase nuclear weapons or fissile material from some fragment of the current Russian nuclear system. If this analysis is correct, the dominant focus of current U.S. defense plans and programs on what is called "Two Simultaneous Major Regional Contingencies" (for example, a repeat of Iraq's attack on the Persian Gulf and a North Korean attack on South Korea) is misplaced. Of even greater importance to the security of Americans at home and in various regional theaters is a global contingency: the threat of "loose nukes." Failure to properly appreciate the importance and gravity of the nuclear leakage threat is at the root of difficulties in successfully addressing it.

Second, this study seeks to define in some detail the shape of this new and not widely understood nuclear threat to U.S. territory and interests. American policy has long recognized the risks posed by additional states acquiring nuclear weapons. But the focus of traditional efforts to cope with nuclear dangers has been the preservation and maintenance of the NPT regime and the pursuit of arms control agreements. Recent success in winning indefinite extension of the NPT does indeed constitute an important victory in the international effort to prevent further proliferation. But traditional nonproliferation approaches are not sufficient for dealing with the problem of nuclear leakage, which threatens to undermine the entire NPT regime by making fissile material available to aspiring proliferators.

Nor do strategic arms control agreements suffice to confront the leakage challenge. Existing agreements between the U.S. and Russia now call for elimination of some eighty percent of the massive nuclear arsenals built during the Cold War. At the 1995 Moscow Summit, Presidents Clinton and Yeltsin sought ways to accomplish speedy ratification of the START II Treaty and to accelerate implementation. But "denuclearization" by dismantling many thousands of ready nuclear forces, though greatly important and clearly desirable in its own right, may actually exacerbate the leakage problem by producing enormous numbers of dismantled fissile weapons components.

Today, under the turbulent conditions of transformation in Russia, the defining nuclear danger is that of loss of control of tens or hundreds of pounds of weapons-usable uranium and plutonium, or, indeed, of numbers of actual nuclear weapons themselves. Weapons and weapons-usable material remain spread across hundreds of Russian sites. (See map, pp. 294–295.) At each such site, the individuals charged with assuring the security of these valuable materials are struggling to feed themselves and their families. In one highly celebrated instance, inspectors from the Russian Ministry of Defense found a battery of nuclear-armed SS-25 mobile missiles completely deserted — all the operators and guards having left to search for food. At many sites that house nuclear materials from which tens or hundreds of weapons could be fashioned, individuals can enter and leave without passing any electronic detection or alarm system. On the outskirts of heretofore "closed cities" in which the Soviet Union produced nuclear materials and weapons, expensive dachas are now appearing, built by what authorities call the "night people" — that is, criminals presumably engaged in black market activities. Vignettes such as these suggest the dynamics in Russia that could lead to nuclear leakage.

Not only is the risk of leakage substantial, but if it occurs, American territory could be at risk of nuclear attack; the likelihood of nuclear terrorism would increase; American allies, forces, and interests abroad could be jeopardized; and the norms of nuclear non-proliferation and nuclear non-use could be jeopardized. It is critically important that the enormous stakes associated with the nuclear leakage problem be widely understood.

Third, this study seeks to make the case for a more vigorous and immediate effort to tackle the challenge of nuclear leakage, to suggest what the components of such an effort might be, and to explore how the obstacles to such an effort might be overcome. There can be no doubt that an invigoration of anti-leakage efforts is necessary if progress on the nuclear leakage problem is to be commensurate with the vital national interests the United States and its allies have at risk.

The prerequisite to success is to persuade and motivate the Russian government to take the practical, concrete steps needed to improve the security and accounting systems currently guarding the Soviet nuclear legacy. To date, the Russian government has generally been unenthusiastic about international overtures in this direction, which has stymied the modest U.S. and international programs intended to improve the quality of Russian nuclear custodianship. The missing ingredient in these programs, however, has been a concerted, high-level effort to change the Russian preference structure, and to create a greater commitment to enhancing nuclear security. This can be done, as it is no less in Russia's interest than in that of the United States to prevent nuclear leakage, but it will take effort, tact, political commitment, and money.

If the requisite political will in Moscow can be nurtured or created, Russia and its international partners could begin to undertake a series of nuclear security improvements to achieve a rapid and radical increase in the security and safety of Russian nuclear weapons and fissile material. If the requisite political will can be found in Moscow and Washington, then unprecedented progress will be possible. However, if the United States government fails at the first task of persuading itself and its Russian counterpart of the importance of this endeavor, then there is essentially nothing more to do than muddle along with the existing set of slowly moving measures.

The Argument and Organization of the Study

The argument developed in this volume consists of four core propositions. Each of these propositions forms the central thesis of one of the chapters that follow.

First, the leakage of weapons-usable nuclear materials from the former Soviet Union is already occurring and could easily get worse in frequency and magnitude. This proposition is elaborated in Chapter 1.

Second, no reality of the post–Cold War international environment constitutes a more direct threat to vital U.S. national security interests than nuclear leakage. The shape of this new nuclear threat is defined in Chapter 2.

Third, the U.S. response to the threat of nuclear leakage through the fall of 1995 has been insufficient, and the level of effort has not begun to equal the U.S. stakes in the matter. This judgment derives from the discussion in Chapter 3.

Fourth and finally, if the U.S. government is to reduce the threat of nuclear leakage meaningfully in the near term, it must enlarge the political latitude available for pursuing anti-leakage efforts, and must be prepared to devote significantly greater resources to the task of safeguarding the United States and its allies from the prospects of nuclear leakage. How to advance a more ambitious anti-leakage effort is the subject of Chapter 4.

NUCLEAR LEAKAGE: OCCURRING AND LIKELY TO GET WORSE
Since 1991, the press has been filled with stories about the theft and illicit trafficking of nuclear materials and weapons from the former Soviet Union.[6] Literally hundreds of incidents have been reported, but the vast majority of the known incidents have been hoaxes or have not involved weapons-usable materials. Nevertheless, the available facts are grounds for grave concern, for at least four reasons. First, the large number of real or fraudulent efforts to sell things nuclear suggests a widespread appreciation within the former Soviet Union that such materials have market value. Second, these facts suggest a considerable effort to fill the supply side of an emerging nuclear black market.[7] Third, it is unlikely that every attempt at nuclear smuggling is detected and reported; by definition, successful transactions on black markets are covert and unnoticed. Finally, and perhaps most tellingly, buried in the large number of alleged cases are a small number of very serious incidents.

SIX KNOWN INCIDENTS. Since 1992, there have been six known cases of theft or illicit trafficking in fissile material. An employee stole approximately 3.7 pounds of HEU from the Luch Scientific Production Association at Podolsk, Russia, in mid-1992. A captain in the Russian Navy stole approximately 10 pounds of HEU from a submarine fuel storage facility in Murmansk in November 1993. German police accidentally discovered 5.6 grams of super-grade plutonium in the garage of a suspected counterfeiter in Tengen, Germany, in May 1994. In June 1994, Bavarian police in Landshut seized 0.8 grams of HEU in a sting operation. A sting operation also resulted in the seizure of almost a pound of near-weapons-grade plutonium at the Munich airport in August 1994. And approximately six pounds of HEU were seized in Prague in December 1994. To put this into historical perspective, more fissile material is known to have been stolen from the former Soviet Union than the United States managed to produce in the first three years of the Manhattan Project.

WHY LEAKAGE IS LIKELY TO GROW WORSE. Though any leakage is worrisome, a catastrophic rupture of the Russian nuclear complex, which could release a vast quantity of nuclear weapons or fissile material into international black markets, has not yet taken place. Unfortunately, there are a number of reasons to believe that nuclear leakage from Russia is likely to continue and could easily get worse: Russian society suffers from profound disorder, the result of social and economic hardship, political opportunism, and rampant criminalization; Russia's sprawling nuclear complex is in the midst of a seemingly terminal economic decline; the oppressive internal security system developed during the Soviet era has largely collapsed, and the integrity of what remains is questionable; Russia lacks a national or even a site-specific inventory system for its fissile material; Russia's nuclear installations have inadequate security against theft, particularly against insider threats; and the process of dismantling Russia's excess nuclear warheads is overwhelming Russia's capacity to store the resulting excess weapons components. Given this situation, more nuclear leakage is likely, serious incidents involving weapons quantities of fissile material are a distinct possibility, and the risk of a catastrophic rupture of the Russian custodial system remains distressingly high.

NUCLEAR LEAKAGE: THE SINGLE GREATEST THREAT TO U.S. NATIONAL
SECURITY INTERESTS

Nuclear leakage constitutes the most serious direct threat to vital U.S. interests today and for the foreseeable future. The new threat of nuclear leakage caused by the Soviet collapse has transformed the nature of the proliferation problem for the United States (and for other states seriously concerned with proliferation).[8] To appreciate this threat, four pervasive myths about nuclear weapons and fissile material must be jettisoned: first, that building a nuclear weapon is hard to do; second, that fissile materials are too hazardous or too heavy to smuggle; third, that the delivery of a nuclear weapon against the United States is a challenge; and fourth, that there is no demand for illicitly acquired nuclear weapons or fissile material. All four assumptions are dead wrong, and deeply pernicious to the extent that they inform or guide the national security policies of any state.

ONCE FISSILE MATERIAL IS AVAILABLE, WEAPONIZATION IS EASY. The denial of access to fissile material is the only reliable means of denying access to nuclear weapons. Designers of U.S. weapons have been repeating this basic truth since the early 1970s, when John Foster, a former director of the Lawrence Livermore nuclear weapons laboratory, stated that "the only difficult thing about making a fission bomb of some sort is the preparation of a supply of fissile material of adequate purity; the design of the bomb itself is relatively easy."[9] There is a consensus among U.S. weapons designers that most states and many terrorist groups could build a simple nuclear weapon given an adequate supply of fissile material.[10] The collapse of the Soviet Union and the subsequent decay of the custodial system guarding the Soviet nuclear legacy has weakened the fissile-material chokepoint, since states and possibly even sub-state groups may now be able buy or steal what they previously had to produce on their own.

TRANSPORTATION IS EASY. Many seem to draw reassurance from the belief that a weapons quantity of fissile material is too massive to be easily transported, or that nuclear smugglers would be inhibited by the health dangers associated with handling fissile materials. Both views are false. The simplest bomb design, like the one dropped on Hiroshima, requires a little over 100 pounds of HEU. A slightly more challenging but still simple implosion weapon can be constructed with less than 20 pounds of plutonium or about 40 pounds of HEU. These are weights that could be physically carried by a single human being, and because of the density of fissile material, the volumes associated with these weights are very small. Moreover, and contrary to widespread public belief, weapons-grade fissile materials can be safely handled: plutonium is radioactive, emitting alpha particles, but these particles cannot penetrate skin; HEU is hardly radioactive at all.

DELIVERY AGAINST THE UNITED STATES IS EASY. As the most open society in the world, America has borders that are exceptionally porous. The volume of people and commodities that flows through the legal points of entry into the United States is enormous and largely uninspected. Moreover, those trying to smuggle nuclear weapons, or the materials to make them, into the United States would not need to choose legal points of entry. The detection of nuclear weapons or fissile material by law enforcement officials is not easy. Technologies designed to detect nuclear materials operate over very short ranges and are presently used only at secure storage facilities and by a few special search teams. Finally, the means of delivery into or against the United States are essentially infinite. Lacking the intercontinental delivery systems preferred by the nuclear superpowers, a terrorist or rogue state would almost certainly rely on an unconventional means of delivery, such as a ship in a port, a truck bomb, or an aircraft overhead. Because they leave no clear return address, unconventional attacks are hard to retaliate against or deter.

DEMAND EXISTS. No one can doubt that there is a demand for nuclear weapons: it has been demonstrated by over a dozen states, beginning with the World War II combatants. The question some people do ask, however, is whether there is a demand for *stolen or illicitly purchased* fissile material or nuclear weapons. So far, there is little hard evidence to prove the existence of this special form of nuclear-weapons demand. This lack of evidence probably has something to do with the fact that illicit acquisition has been a feasible proliferation option only since the collapse of the Soviet Union. Since states are known to be willing to invest years of effort and billions of dollars into the acquisition of nuclear weapons, it is not plausible that they would decline to steal or purchase fissile material, or even weapons themselves, if an opportunity were to present itself. And while there is no hard evidence of a demand for nuclear weapons among terrorists or other sub-state groups, this fact gives no cause for complacency: fissile material was beyond the terrorists' reach until a few years ago, but it no longer is. Even given the heightened accessibility of nuclear weapons through nuclear leakage, some observers assert that terrorists are simply uninterested in acquiring or using nuclear weapons; people felt similarly about terrorists and chemical weapons until sarin was tasted in the Tokyo subway.

THE U.S. RESPONSE TO THE NUCLEAR LEAKAGE THREAT: INADEQUATE

The U.S. response to this new threat of nuclear leakage has not begun to equal the U.S. stakes in the matter.[11] During the first three years after the collapse of the Soviet Union, virtually no progress was made toward reducing the likelihood that a nuclear weapon or a quantity of fissile material would leak out of Russia. In 1995, a few hopeful steps were taken in a few areas of the post-Soviet nuclear archipelago. Yet most of the relevant facilities are no more secure by the end of 1995 than they were when the Soviet Union disappeared. And although several important individual successes of U.S. policy can now be identified, not enough has been done to reverse the broad-based vulnerability of Russia's nuclear custodial system.

MANY U.S. PROGRAMS, BUT PROGRESS TOO SLOW. Within the confines of current political constraints, the Clinton administration has pursued a broad range of innovative programs designed to deal with many different nuclear issues in the former Soviet Union. These programs, fully detailed in Chapter 3, fall into three basic categories: those that seek to directly improve the security of nuclear weapons and materials in the former Soviet Union; those that seek permanent disposition of fissile materials; and those that seek to "build confidence through openness" by enhancing the transparency of the Russian and American nuclear establishments. With respect to improving the security of nuclear materials, there have been a few important achievements, but in general the U.S. effort in this area has proceeded at a slow pace and on a small scale, and stands little chance of effecting a near-term reduction in the severity of the nuclear leakage threat. Similarly, the long-term disposition and transparency ne-gotiations have proceeded extremely slowly. While there have been some modest achievements on the long-term disposition question, the transpar-ency negotiations have largely been stymied by Russian intransigence.

WHY PROGRESS HAS BEEN SLOW. The U.S. effort to reduce the nuclear leak-age threat has been obstructed by Russia's reluctance to cooperate, finan-cial limits political conditions, and legal restrictions imposed by Congress, the competing priorities of the Clinton administration itself, and the meagerness of the contributions of the U.S. allies. The basic weakness in the Clinton administration's response to the nuclear leakage threat has been the absence of a concerted high-level effort to overcome these ob-stacles, especially by inducing cooperation from the Russian government and convincing the Congress, the U.S. public, and the other advanced industrial nations of the need for a more ambitious and better financed campaign against the nuclear leakage threat.

RECOMMENDATIONS

To combat the threat of nuclear leakage, the leaders of Russia, the United States, and the other major industrial powers must find a way to over-come the obstacles to faster progress that they have encountered over the past four years. At the broadest level, the president and his senior deputies should devote more time and energy to creating the political latitude that the administration must have if it is to succeed in safeguarding the United States against future nuclear threats. Since the political constraints noted above emanate principally from Moscow and Capitol Hill, the Clinton administration should aim its efforts toward these two audiences. The United States should also focus more intensely on securing the cooperation and support of its friends and allies in this effort. Assuming that such an effort does increase the political latitude needed to combat nuclear leakage, the United States should pursue programs that can contribute to the following three objectives.

PROMOTE PROGRAMS THAT DIRECTLY IMPROVE NUCLEAR SECURITY. The highest priority of U.S. non-proliferation policy must be to persuade Russia to take immediate concrete steps that reduce the near-term likelihood of nuclear leakage. To meet the urgent aim of achieving the greatest possible reduction in the nuclear leakage threat in the shortest possible time, there are at least four programs that the United States should either initiate or pursue with greater urgency. First, the U.S. should expand and accelerate the U.S. purchase of Russian HEU. Second, the U.S. government should offer to purchase Russia's excess weapons-grade plutonium. Third, the United States should do whatever is necessary to implement or accelerate security enhancement at all nuclear installations in the former Soviet Union. Finally, the U.S. government should propose to Moscow a high-priority joint inventory and site-by-site security analysis of all U.S. and Russian nuclear installations.

BUILD A CONSTRUCTIVE RELATIONSHIP WITH THE RUSSIAN GOVERNMENT, ESPECIALLY MINATOM. Rapid progress on major programs designed to reduce the threat of nuclear leakage is possible only in the context of a strong, cooperative relationship with the Russian government and, most importantly, the custodian of Russia's far-flung nuclear stockpiles. Therefore, the U.S. government should put greater emphasis on defining and advancing nuclear security programs that serve the institutional interests of key Russian actors along with U.S. national security interests. Hence, the United States should: (1) restructure the U.S. plan to purchase Russian HEU in a way that gives Minatom better economic incentives to cooperate with the United States; (2) finance joint nuclear technology projects between Minatom and Western firms; (3) fund the joint environmental clean-up of key nuclear-weapons installations in both countries; (4) expand the Industrial Partnering Program (IPP), the most successful of the U.S. programs aimed at reorienting Russian nuclear weapons enterprises toward non-military commercial activities; and (5) provide a near-term alternative energy source to the two Russian cities where weapons-grade plutonium is still being produced, so that the Russian government can shut down its three remaining plutonium- production reactors.

PROMOTE AND IMPLEMENT A LONG-TERM FISSILE MATERIAL MANAGEMENT PLAN. Finally, the United States should, in cooperation with Russia and the other key nuclear states, define a long-term plan for coping with the global surplus of excess fissile materials, and must commit the resources needed to implement this plan.[12] Long-term fissile material management is a task of global proportions that should be carried out on the basis of close international cooperation and consultation; given their unique roles as nuclear superpowers, the United States and Russia must take the lead in this area. Given the urgency of the nuclear leakage threat, a long-term strategy for coping with surplus fissile materials should be designed to reinforce near-term efforts to prevent nuclear leakage from the former Soviet Union. In this respect, the United States should (1) define and implement a staged international monitoring regime for fissile materials, beginning on a bilateral basis with Russia and gradually assuming multi-lateral characteristics; (2) establish an international plutonium bank, or "depository," as an interim plutonium disposition solution; and (3) take the lead in a concerted effort by the world's key law enforcement and intelligence agencies to develop the skills, procedures, and equipment needed to combat the illicit trafficking in nuclear materials effectively and systematically — an effort referred to in shorthand as the establishment of a "nuclear Interpol."

Act Now, Not the Morning After

Despite the serious threat of loose nuclear weapons and fissile material, and despite the existence of a panoply of measures that could help reduce the likelihood of leakage from the deadly arsenal of former Soviet weapons and fissile materials, at present there appears to be little prospect that America's leaders — whether President Clinton, or Senator Dole, or Speaker Gingrich — will take the lead in crafting a more ambitious and potentially more effective anti-leakage effort. And the reason why is clear. The "political realities," as knowing Washingtonians say, make this infeasible. No new initiative, however vital to the interests of the United States, has much prospect of getting a serious hearing in the climate of massive deficits, deep budget cuts, partisan rivalry, electoral calculations, and shrinking imagination.

Difficult as it is, identifying a new challenge is the easier part of the problem. Summoning the will and wherewithal to act effectively is harder still. This is especially so where the response requires significant changes in behavior and major exertion over a sustained period.

On the morning after the first act of nuclear terrorism, what will the president of the United States wish he had done earlier? What will the leaders of Congress be willing to support in the aftermath? What will the administration do then? What prevents us from pausing, reflecting, and summoning the wisdom to act now?

NOTES

1. Officially, the Nunn-Lugar program was named the "Cooperative Threat Reduction" (CTR) program by the Department of Defense.

2. The original head of the SSD delegation, appointed by President Bush, was General William Burns. Under President Clinton, this role was assigned to Ambassador James Goodby.

3. Another important achievement that resulted from Kazakhstan's cooperative nuclear policies was "Project Sapphire," a secret U.S. program under which 600 kilograms of newly discovered HEU was purchased from the Kazakh government and flown to the United States on U.S. military aircraft. Project Sapphire was publicly announced only after it had been completed, in November 1994. Project Sapphire is described in detail in Chapter 3 (see p. 102).

4. For a full discussion, see Richard A. Falkenrath, "The United States, the Former Soviet Republics, and Nuclear Weapons: The Problems and Policies of Denuclearization," CSIA Discussion Paper No. 94-08, September 1994.

5. Another pivotal agreement signed at the Moscow summit was the U.S.-Russian HEU purchase agreement — better known as "the HEU deal" — in which the United States agreed to buy, and Russia to sell, 500 metric tons of Russian HEU extracted from dismantled nuclear weapons over a twenty year period. The executive agents in this deal were the Russian Ministry of Atomic Energy (Minatom) and the U.S. Enrichment Corporation (USEC), a government-owned company that runs the Department of Energy's two civilian enrichment plants. This HEU deal, and the problems it has encountered, are discussed in detail in Chapter 3 and Appendix C, "The HEU Deal."

6. See, for example, John M. Rooney, "Review of Reports of Theft and Smuggling of Nuclear Material in the Former Soviet Union," United States Department of Energy Memorandum, November 29, 1994; John Barry, "Future Shock," *Newsweek*, July 24, 1995, p. 32; William J. Broad, "Moving A-Arms by Rail: Can Terrorists Be Foiled?" *New York Times*, February 18, 1992, p. 6; Steve Coll and David B. Ottaway, "U.S. Debates How to Halt Nuclear Spread," *Washington Post*, April 10, 1995, p. 1; Charles J. Hanley, "Weapons Smuggling, Nuclear Black Market: Greatest Long-Term Threat to the Security of the United States," *Cincinnati Enquirer*, March 26, 1995; Tom Masland, "For Sale," *Newsweek*, August 29, 1995, p. 30; David C. Morrison, "Heavy Metal," *Na-*

tional Journal, October 22, 1994, p. 2454; Bruce W. Nelan, "Formula for Terror," Time, August 29, 1994, p. 46; Barry Newman, "'Loose Nukes': Uranium, Plutonium, Who's Got the Goods? Nuclear Nations Ask," Wall Street Journal (European edition), May 16, 1994; Robert Wright, "Be Very Afraid," New Republic, May 1, 1995, p. 19.

7. See AP, "Top Chechen Rebel Threatens Russia with Contamination," Boston Globe, December 23, 1995.

8. Other publications have drawn attention to this threat as well, often with different emphases. See, for example, Kurt Campbell, Ashton B. Carter, Steven E. Miller, and Charles Zraket, Soviet Nuclear Fission: Control of the Nuclear Arsenal in a Disintegrating Soviet Union, CSIA Studies in International Security No. 1 (Cambridge, Mass.: Center for Science and International Affairs, Harvard University, 1991); Graham T. Allison, Ashton B. Carter, Steven E. Miller, and Philip Zelikow, eds., Cooperative Denuclearization: From Pledges to Deeds, CSIA Studies in International Security No. 2 (Cambridge, Mass.: CSIA, 1993); Robert D. Blackwill, "Russia and the West," in Robert D. Blackwill, Rodric Braithwaite, and Akihito Tanaka, Engaging Russia, Triangle Paper No. 46 (New York: Report of the Trilateral Commission, June 1995), pp. 36–40; Oleg Bukharin, "Nuclear Safeguards and Security in the Former Soviet Union," Survival, Vol. 36, No. 4 (Winter 1994–95); Thomas B. Cochran, "Nuclear Weapons and Fissile Material Security in Russia," Testimony before the Subcommittee on International Security, International Organizations and Human Rights, Committee on Foreign Affairs, U.S. House of Representatives, June 27, 1994; Leonard S. Spector, "Nuclear Weapons and Fissile Material Security in Russia," Testimony before the Subcommittee on International Security, International Organizations and Human Rights, Committee on Foreign Affairs, U.S. House of Representatives, June 27, 1994; Frank von Hippel, "Fissile Material Security in the Post–Cold War World," Physics Today, June 1995, pp. 26–31; Frank von Hippel, Marvin Miller, Harold Feiveson, Anatoli Diakov, and Frans Berkhout, "Eliminating Nuclear Warheads," Scientific American, August 1993, pp. 43–49; William Potter, "Exports and Experts: Proliferation Risks from the New Commonwealth," Arms Control Today, January/February 1992, pp. 32–37; Michael May, "Nuclear Weapons Supply and Demand," American Scientist, Vol. 82, November–December 1994, pp. 527, 530; Committee on International Security and Arms Control, National Academy of Sciences, Management and Disposition of Excess Weapons Plutonium (Washington DC: National Academy Press, 1994); International Institute for Strategic Studies, "Fissile-Material Protection: A New Challenge," Strategic Survey, 1994–1995, pp. 25–33; James Blaker, "Coping with the New 'Clear and Present' Danger from Russia," Arms Control Today, Vol. 25, No. 3 (April 1995), pp. 13–16; Bruce G. Blair, Global Zero Alert for Nuclear Forces, Brookings Occasional Papers (Washington DC: The Brookings Institution, 1995), pp. 32–43; Guy B. Roberts, "Five Minutes Past Midnight: The Clear and Present Danger of Nuclear Weapons Usable Fissile Materials," advanced research project submitted to the Naval War College, May 26, 1995; United States Congress, Office of Technology Assessment, Proliferation of Weapons of Mass Destruction: Assessing the Risks, OTA-ISC-559 (Washington DC: U.S. Government Printing

Office, 1993), pp. 111–112; United States Congress, Office of Technology Assessment, *Proliferation and the Former Soviet Union*, OTA-ISS-605 (Washington DC: U.S. Government Printing Office, 1994); Jim Hoagland, "Lots of Russian Nukes for Sale," *Washington Post*, February 23, 1993, p. 19.

9. John Foster, "Nuclear Weapons," *Encyclopedia Americana*, Vol. 20 (New York, N.Y.: The Americana Corporation, 1973), pp. 520–522; see also Chapter 2, "Nuclear Weapons" in Mason Willrich and Theodore Taylor, *Nuclear Theft: Risks and Safeguards* (Cambridge, Mass.: Ballinger Publishing Company, 1974), pp. 5–28, especially p. 6 where the authors state their central point: "If the essential nuclear materials are at hand, it is possible to make an atomic bomb using information that is available in the open literature." And see Appendix B, "A Primer on Fissile Materials and Nuclear Weapon Design."

10. See, for example, J. Carson Mark, Theodore Taylor, Eugene Eyster, William Maraman, and Jacob Wechsler, "Can Terrorists Build Nuclear Weapons?" in Paul Leventhal and Yonah Alexander, eds., *Preventing Nuclear Terrorism: The Report and Papers of the International Task Force on Prevention of Nuclear Terrorism* (Lexington, Mass.: Lexington Books, 1987), pp. 55–65.

11. *Avoiding Nuclear Anarchy* focuses primarily on the stakes and role of the United States in combating nuclear leakage. However, our assessment of the nuclear leakage threat applies equally to all other advanced industrial nations.

12. Long-term fissile material management and disposition has been the subject of several other studies, so we do not attempt to recreate a full analysis that has been thoroughly done elsewhere. The most exhaustive of these studies is the Committee on International Security and Arms Control, National Academy of Sciences, *Management and Disposition of Excess Weapons Plutonium*.

Chapter 1

Risks of Nuclear Leakage

Sitting at dozens of facilities and storage sites spread across the former Soviet Union are the makings of a nuclear proliferation catastrophe. (See map, pp. 294–295.) The new and unsettled Russian Federation possesses several tens of thousands of nuclear weapons and a vast stockpile of the fissile material necessary to make nuclear weapons, namely, plutonium and highly enriched uranium (HEU). Never before has such an enormous inventory of nuclear assets existed in such precarious circumstances: Russia's political life is unstable; its economic conditions are severe; and security at many of its nuclear installations is questionable at best, non-existent at worst. (For a detailed discussion of the latter point, see Appendix 1.)

Ever since the Soviet Union began to slide into its ultimately fatal crisis, there has been concern that Soviet (now Russian) nuclear assets might seep — or worse, flood — into the international marketplace.[1] This

---

1. See, for example, Kurt Campbell, Ashton B. Carter, Steven E. Miller, and Charles A. Zraket, *Soviet Nuclear Fission: Control of the Nuclear Arsenal in a Disintegrating Soviet Union*, CSIA Studies in International Security No. 1 (Cambridge, Mass.: Center for Science and International Affairs, Harvard University, 1991), pp. 35–47. See also United States Congress, Office of Technology Assessment (OTA), *Proliferation and the Former Soviet Union*, OTA-ISS-605 (Washington DC: U.S. Government Printing Office [U.S. GPO], 1994); William Potter, "Exports and Experts: Proliferation Risks from the New Commonwealth," *Arms Control Today*, January/February 1992, p. 32; Paul Quinn-Judge, "In Republics, an Eye on Bombs, Scientists," *Boston Globe*, June 23, 1992, p. 1. William C. Potter, with assistance of Eve E. Cohen and Edward V. Kayukov, *Nuclear Profiles of the Soviet Successor States*, Monograph No. 1 (Monterey, Calif.: Monterey Institute of International Studies, Program for Nonproliferation Studies, May 1993); Thomas B. Cochran and Christopher Paine, "Nuclear Warhead Destruction," paper prepared for the NCI/NRDC Fissile Material Workshop, Carnegie Endowment for International Peace, Washington DC, November 16, 1993; and Oleg Bukharin, "The Threat of Nuclear Terrorism and the Physical Security of Nuclear Installations and Materials in the Former Soviet Union," Occasional Paper No. 2, Center for Russian and Eurasian Studies, Monterey Institute of International Studies, August 1992.

nuclear leakage would entail the illicit sale, theft, or diversion of nuclear weapons, fissile material, nuclear design information, nuclear experts, weapons components, or even delivery systems. If it were to occur to any significant extent, such leakage would fuel the proliferation of nuclear weapons to states that covet them. It would also greatly increase the risk of nuclear terrorism, since sub-state actors would, for the first time, have ready access to nuclear weapons or the materials to make them.[2] While any form of nuclear leakage is disturbing, there is particular concern about the security of nuclear weapons themselves and the fissile material that is both the necessary ingredient in any bomb program and the most difficult to obtain. Any substantial leakage of nuclear weapons or fissile material to aspiring proliferants would deeply undermine and perhaps shatter the international nuclear nonproliferation regime. Much depends on the security of Russia's nuclear assets.

Conceptually, there are four potential sources of nuclear leakage within the Russian nuclear complex, which altogether contains some 200 tons of plutonium and 800–1,200 tons of HEU. The first is Russia's stockpile of nuclear weapons that is controlled by the Ministry of Defense. Today, this stockpile contains between 15,000 and 25,000 deployed weapons. Second, the Russian Ministry of Atomic Energy (Minatom) controls a large and growing stockpile of weapons-grade fissile material that it both produces and extracts from dismantled nuclear weapons — a task that Minatom alone is equipped to do. Russia is now dismantling some 3,000 weapons per year, which effectively shifts some 15 tons of plutonium and 45 tons of HEU from the Ministry of Defense (where the material was stored within intact weapons) to Minatom each year. Third, Minatom also has custody of an enormous amount of fissile material produced by Russian nuclear power–generating reactors, over 30 tons of which are in the form of separated reactor-grade plutonium. Finally, there is a diverse inventory of fissile material scattered across Russia in research institutes and facilities used for non-standard nuclear fuel cycles, such as the naval propulsion and space reactor programs. Custody over the material in this fourth category is not centralized, but rather is shared among the Ministry of Defense, Minatom, and a variety of other government ministries or independent agencies.

While all four potential sources of nuclear leakage are worrisome, each poses a somewhat different set of risks and dangers. The probability

---

2. On these points, see Steven E. Miller, "The Former Soviet Union," in Mitchell Reiss and Robert Litwak, *Nuclear Proliferation After the Cold War* (Baltimore, Maryland: Johns Hopkins University Press, 1994), pp. 101–103.

that an intact nuclear weapon under Ministry of Defense custody will be stolen or diverted is generally regarded as low relative to the other potential sources of leakage, but this depends on the continued organizational integrity and resilience of the Russian military. Compared to the weapons under military custody, the weapons-grade fissile material and components under Minatom custody are subject to considerably lower standards of security and accounting. The reactor-grade fissile material under Minatom custody is stored under even less secure conditions, though it is also weapons-usable.[3] Finally, the different types and amounts of fissile material used at research reactors and institutes, or in the naval fuel and space reactor programs, is subject to only the most rudimentary security standards, posing an immediate and acute nuclear proliferation risk.

To date, most of the nuclear leakage from Russia that has been detected seems to have come from the fourth category — research institutes and non-standard fuel cycle facilities. Increasingly, however, there is reason to believe that the greatest long-term risk of nuclear leakage emanates from the second category described above, the weapons-grade fissile material and components under the custody Minatom. The steady transfer of fissile material from the Ministry of Defense to Minatom in the context of the Russian nuclear weapons dismantlement program exacerbates the risk of catastrophic nuclear leakage from Russia. Minatom lacks the dedicated facilities and institutional infrastructure needed to securely store the fissile material and components that it is extracting from Russia's dismantled nuclear weapons. This under-appreciated fact is the most fundamental reason why the threat of nuclear leakage from Russia is likely to rise rather than fall over the coming years.

This next section briefly details six known instances of nuclear leakage from Russia, which unambiguously establish that leakage is already occurring. The section that follows it gives eight specific reasons why this leakage problem can be expected to grow worse over time: the sheer scale and complexity of the Russian nuclear complex preclude any "quick fix" to the problem.

---

3. On the weapons-usability of reactor-grade plutonium, see J. Carson Mark, "Explosive Properties of Reactor-Grade Plutonium," *Science and Global Security*, Vol. 4, No. 1 (1993), pp. 111–124; and Committee on International Security and Arms Control, National Academy of Sciences, *Management and Disposition of Excess Weapons Plutonium* (Washington DC: National Academy Press, 1994), pp. 32–33.

Nuclear Leakage is Happening: Six Known Incidents

Nuclear leakage is more than a hypothetical concern. Fissile material — the material necessary to make a nuclear bomb — has been stolen from storage facilities in Russia and put up for sale. This leakage has already reached alarming proportions and is likely to get much worse as more buyers and sellers of Russian fissile material join the existing black market for weapons-usable plutonium and uranium.

In the years since its collapse, there have been hundreds of alleged or reported incidents of nuclear assets spilling out of the former Soviet Union. Indeed, the German government alone has reported more than 700 cases of attempted nuclear sales between 1991 and 1994. Many such cases turn out to be frauds, but roughly half are believed by Bonn to be true instances of attempted nuclear smuggling; in the last three years there have been some sixty instances that involved seizure of nuclear materials.[4] According to another source, there were over one hundred reported instances of nuclear smuggling from the former Soviet Union during the first nine months of 1994.[5] One Russian report states that in Russia in 1993 there were 11 attempted thefts of uranium, some 900 attempts at illegal entry at nuclear facilities, and nearly 700 instances in which workers at nuclear facilities attempted to steal secret documents.[6] Hundreds of additional reports of nuclear smuggling go back to 1991.[7]

Many of these alleged incidents turn out to be untrue or unproven. Many involve fraudulent claims of possession of, or access to, weapons-usable nuclear materials. Many appear to involve efforts to sell anything

---

4. This information comes from authors' interviews in the United States, Russia, and elsewhere in 1994 and 1995. Many interviews were given on condition of anonymity. Such interviews are not cited in the rest of this book; where no source is stated, the reader can assume the source is these interviews.

5. "Nuclear Weapon and Sensitive Export Status Report: Nuclear Successor States of the Soviet Union," A Cooperative Project of The Carnegie Endowment of International Peace and the Monterey Institute of International Studies, No. 2 (December 1994), pp. 39–58.

6. Alexander Bolsunovsky and Valery Menshchikov, "Nuclear Security is Inadequate and Outdated," *The Monitor: Nonproliferation, Demilitarization, and Arms Control* (University of Georgia, Athens, Ga.), February 1995, pp. 1–2.

7. See, for example, the "Chronology of Reported Illicit Exports for 1993 and First Quarter 1994," in Carnegie Endowment for International Peace & The Monterey Institute of International Studies, *Nuclear Successor States of the Soviet Union: Nuclear Weapon and Sensitive Export Status Report*, No. 1 (May 1994), pp. 29–40; and Potter, *Nuclear Profiles of the Soviet Successor States.*

even remotely "nuclear" — such as radioactive material used for medicinal purposes — regardless of whether it has any relevance to making bombs or not. So the large number of alleged cases is not an accurate indicator of the scale of the problem.

Nevertheless, the available facts are grounds for grave concern. The large number of reported efforts to sell things nuclear, whether true or false, suggests a widespread appreciation within Russia that such materials have market value. This indicates considerable effort within Russia to fill the supply side of an emerging nuclear black market. It is unlikely that every attempt at nuclear smuggling is detected and reported; by definition, successful transactions on black markets are covert and unnoticed. Buried in the large number of alleged cases are a small number of very serious, well-documented and unequivocally dangerous incidents. The fact that a large number of the reported attempts to move nuclear materials across international borders are either failure or fiction is less important than the reality that even a tiny number of successes in transferring nuclear weapons or weapons quantities of fissile material could have disastrous consequences.

Below, we briefly describe the six unambiguous cases of nuclear leakage, each of which involved weapons-usable materials believed or confirmed to have come from Russia.

THE LUCH CASE

During a three-and-one-half month period in mid-1992, a chemical engineer named Leonid Smirnov stole approximately 3.7 pounds of HEU (90 percent enriched) from the Luch Scientific Production Association at Podolsk, Russia.[8] Smirnov, who had been employed at the Luch plant since 1968, removed HEU from the plant on over 20–25 separate occasions, each time using a 50–70 gram jar. On October 9, 1992, as he was trying to take the HEU to Moscow to find a buyer, he was apprehended at the Podolsk railway station. This is the only case of fissile material theft that the Minatom leadership has openly acknowledged.[9]

---

8.   William C. Potter, "Significant Cases of Diversion of Probable FSU-origin HEU and Plutonium," unpublished paper, Monterey Institute of International Studies, May 1995; Alexander Mytsikov, "Nuclear Security and Smuggling: What the Documents Say," *Yaderny Kontrol* (Nuclear control), PIR Center (Center for Policy Studies), Moscow, Digest No. 2 (September 1995), pp. 8–10.

9.   "Loose Nukes: Uranium, Plutonium, Who's Got the Goods? Nuclear Nations Ask," *Wall Street Journal*, May 11, 1994, p. A1.

HEU STOLEN IN MURMANSK

On November 27, 1993, Captain Alexei Tikhomirov of the Russian Navy entered the Sevmorput shipyard (near Murmansk) through an unguarded gate, broke into a building used to store unused nuclear submarine fuel, and stole three pieces of a reactor core that contained about 10 pounds of HEU (approximately 20 percent enriched).[10] Tikhomirov put the fuel in a bag and then walked out of the shipyard the way he came in.

The officer had been briefed beforehand by his brother, the civilian chief of refueling at Sevmorput, and was aware of how flimsy the security was for a substantial inventory of highly enriched uranium used as fuel for naval nuclear reactors. The shipyard was enclosed by a fence with several gates, some unguarded. The storage building containing the nuclear reactor fuel was enclosed by a smaller fence, also unguarded, with several gaping holes in it. After slipping through this inner fence, the thief had only to break a padlock and pry open a back door to get inside the storage facility. Once inside, he was able to locate the containers of reactor fuel and break off some pieces of this fuel. If he had not left the door open on his way back out, the theft would not have been detected the next day by a passing security patrol. The thief and two of his accomplices were caught and arrested eight months later in June 1994, when they sought help in selling the stolen material. Their asking price was $50,000.

SUPER-GRADE PLUTONIUM SEIZED IN TENGEN, GERMANY

On May 10, 1994, German police found 5.6 grams of super-grade plutonium (99.78 percent Pu-239) in the garage of Adolf Jäckle, a suspected counterfeiter, in Tengen, Germany.[11] This discovery was purely accidental: Jäckle was being investigated for counterfeiting. Super-grade plutonium is extremely expensive to produce and is consequently quite rare. It is believed that the material came from Arzamas-16 in Russia, or perhaps from a secret centrifuge facility in ex-Soviet Central Asia. There are some indications that an organized crime group from Bulgaria may have been

---

10. See Oleg Bukharin and William Potter, "Potatoes were guarded better," *Bulletin of the Atomic Scientists*, Vol. 51, No. 3 (May/June 1995), pp. 46–50; and Potter, "Significant Cases of Diversion." The Sevmorput shipyard contains one of three Russian storage facilities for fresh naval reactor fuel for the Northern fleet; another is nearby at Zapadnaya Litsa, and another at Severodvinsk, near Archangelsk. Pacific Fleet fuel storage is at Krashennikova Bay and Chazhma Bay, both near Vladivostok.

11. See Mark Hibbs, "Plutonium, Politics, and Panic," *Bulletin of the Atomic Scientists*, November/December 1994, pp. 24–31; Potter, "Significant Cases of Diversion"; and Gerd Rosenkranz, "Bomben für die ganze Welt," *Die Zeit*, July 22, 1994, p. 9.

involved in supplying Jäckle with the plutonium, but this has not been confirmed.

HEU IN LANDSHUT, GERMANY

On June 13, 1994, Bavarian police in Landshut seized 0.8 grams of HEU (87.5 percent enriched) as a result of a sting operation. The origin of this material is not known, but it is believed to have come from a Russian research reactor or a naval fuel assembly.[12]

PLUTONIUM SEIZED IN MUNICH

On August 10, 1994, almost a pound of near-weapons-grade plutonium (87 percent Pu-239) was seized by German police at the Munich airport.[13] The plutonium had been carried in a suitcase on a flight from Moscow. Two passengers on the flight were arrested, as was a third man in Munich who was identified as the buyer. This came about as a result of a sting operation by German law enforcement agencies. One of the two men arrested after disembarking from the plane had met earlier with undercover German police operatives, who paid him for a much smaller sample of plutonium. This man returned to Russia, where the German agencies lost track of him until he boarded the flight from Moscow with the plutonium that led to his arrest. Although there is little doubt that this plutonium originated in Russia, the original source of the material inside Russia has not been determined. Initial claims that it specifically originated in a nuclear weapon facility were disputed by Moscow.

In Germany, this episode has led to a major political controversy about the involvement of German intelligence in such sting operations.[14] Much more disturbing should be the fact that black market salesmen were able to obtain near-weapons-grade plutonium and transport it across international borders in checked luggage on a commercial flight.

---

12. Potter, "Significant Cases of Diversion"; and "Jelzin-Berater bezweifelt Existenz von Atomschmuggel," *Frankfurter Algemeine Zeitung*, August 17, 1994.

13. The plutonium probably came from reprocessed low-burnup spent fuel (from a graphite-moderated high-temperature [RBMK] reactor, for example) or from a breeder reactor "blanket." See Anton Surikov, "Munich, August 1994: New Investigation," *Yaderny Kontrol*, Digest No. 2 (September 1995), pp. 10–12; Potter, "Significant Cases of Diversion"; and Hibbs, "Plutonium, Politics, and Panic."

14. See, for example, "Germany: Back from Hades," *The Economist*, April 29, 1995, pp. 59–60. See also "Pfeile gegen Rüssland," *Der Spiegel*, April 25, 1995, p. 32; "Die Hand im Feuer," *Der Spiegel*, April 24, 1995, pp. 28–37; "Parole: 'Keine Ahnung'," *Der Speigel* April 17, 1995, pp. 18–24; and "Panik Made in Pullach," *Der Spiegel*, April 10, 1995, pp. 36–57.

HEU FOUND IN PRAGUE

On December 14, 1994, approximately six pounds of HEU (87.5 percent enriched) was seized in Prague.[15] The HEU was found in two plastic-wrapped metal containers in the back seat of a car parked on a side street. A Czech nuclear scientist, a Russian, and a Belarussian were arrested in connection with this seizure. Russian documents were found along with the nuclear material. The origin of the material is not known, although it appears to have come from the same cache as the HEU seized in Landshut, Germany, in June 1994.[16]

These six known incidents demonstrate that weapons-usable fissile material can easily be stolen or diverted from some Russian nuclear facilities and that those materials can easily be transported out of Russia.

These incidents also suggest several other disturbing conclusions. First, as the Murmansk case shows, insider information can facilitate and simplify efforts at nuclear theft. Russian nuclear facilities appear to be extremely vulnerable to insiders operating in concert. Second, the culprits in these cases were not, it appears, members of a terrorist network, an organized crime group, or a purchasing operation for a state like Iraq or Iran. Rather they seem to have been rank amateurs, yet they succeeded in getting their hands on nuclear materials and getting those materials out of Russia (although these particular smugglers did not succeed in evading capture). More organized efforts at smuggling could be even more successful. Third, in four of the six cases, there was no trail back to the source of the nuclear material. Thus it is impossible to know which nuclear leaks to plug, even if sufficient funding were available for a security upgrade, which in the Russian case it does not appear to be.

Most alarming of all, these incidents are probably only the tip of an iceberg. Western Europe is generally well policed, so it is not an ideal arena for any kind of smuggling. If weapons-usable materials are leaking into Europe from Russia, then they are probably also leaking out of Russia by other routes, such as Central Asia. The existence of multiple exit routes

---

15. Michael Gordon, "Czech Cache of Nuclear Material Being Tested for Bomb Potential," *New York Times*, December 21, 1994; Mark Hibbs, "Czech find may be re-enriched, reprocessed uranium to fuel naval or research reactors," *Nuclear Fuel*, January 2, 1995, p. 12; Charles Hanley, "Spotlight: Weapons Smuggling, Nuclear Black Market 'Greatest long-term threat to the security of the United States'," *The Cincinnati Enquirer*, March 26, 1995, p. A2; David Hughes, "Uranium Seizures Heighten Terrorism Concerns," *Aviation Week and Space Technology*, April 3, 1995, pp. 63–64; A.M. Rosenthal, "The Nuclear Smugglers," *New York Times*, January 20, 1995.

16. See Mark Hibbs, "Which Fissile Fingerprint," *Bulletin of the Atomic Scientists*, May/June 1994, pp. 10–11; and Potter, "Significant Cases of Diversion."

for nuclear smugglers constitutes a major problem in trying to cope with illicit nuclear traffic. The difference is that the probability of detection in the non-European paths is very low, and the demand for smuggled nuclear weapons or fissile material is likely to be higher.

Why Nuclear Leakage Could Get Worse

Despite the very large number of attempted or alleged incidents of nuclear leakage, so far it does not appear that there has been theft, sale, or diversion of weapons-usable fissile materials in sufficient quantities to produce a nuclear weapon. Catastrophic rupture of the Russian nuclear complex that could release a vast quantity of nuclear weapons or fissile material into international black markets has not taken place. Unfortunately, however, there are a number of reasons to believe that nuclear leakage from Russia is likely to continue and could easily get worse. We describe eight such reasons.

DISORDER IN RUSSIA

At the broadest level, Russia's nuclear assets and infrastructure exist within a society convulsed by painful transformation. The dramatic changes so far may or may not give rise to a better future, but in the interim they have produced political uncertainty, economic distress, and social dislocation. For tens of millions of Russians, hardship and deprivation are inescapable facts of life.

The difficult realities of Russian life and the turbulence associated with Russia's internal politics can reduce the likelihood of successfully containing the nuclear leakage problem. First, harsh economic conditions can create incentives for nuclear theft and smuggling. For people who are poorly housed, poorly fed, and poorly paid (when paid at all),[17] there will be a temptation to do what they can to improve their lives and secure their futures. Russia's nuclear custodians face these pressures as they preside over weapons and materials that are immensely valuable to any state or group that covets nuclear weapons.[18] It is not hard to imagine

---

17. See, for example, Frank von Hippel, Marvin Miller, Harold Feiveson, Anatoli Diakov, and Frans Berkhout, "Eliminating Nuclear Warheads," *Scientific American*, August 1993, pp. 43–49, which notes that the Russian nuclear complex was under "extraordinary stress," with staff unpaid for months and scientists encouraged to "plant potatoes" to ensure that their families had food (p. 44).

18. Saddam Hussein, for example, is estimated to have spent over $10 billion in his fruitless quest to amass weapons quantities of fissile material. No doubt he, or others like him, would be willing to spend very large sums shopping on a Russian nuclear black market. On Iraq's nuclear program, see David Albright and Mark Hibbs, "Iraq

that people leading bleak, uncertain, and difficult lives might find irresistible the prospect of wealth and security via the nuclear black market.[19]

Second, one consequence of Russia's travails has been a widespread criminalization of Russian society. Russia's organized crime syndicates (often referred to as the Russian mafia, or "mafiya") appear to be among the most powerful and effective institutions in a transforming Russian society. They control a high percentage of the Russian economy, have enormous political influence, and appear to be substantially invulnerable to the policing capacities of the current Russian state.[20] Organized crime gravitates to anything that generates large profits. In Russia, criminal activity includes drug trafficking and the illicit trade in diamonds and metals.[21] And, some accounts claim, it includes nuclear materials.[22] The former director of the CIA, R. James Woolsey, testified in 1994 that Russian organized crime could be exploiting its existing smuggling networks to facilitate nuclear trafficking.[23] For the first time in history, a state in

---

and the Bomb: Were They Even Close?" *Bulletin of the Atomic Scientists*, March 1991, pp. 16–25; and Albright and Hibbs, "Iraq's Nuclear Hide-and-Seek," ibid., September 1991, pp. 14–23.

19. For an early and pessimistic appraisal of the evolving conditions in the nuclear complex of the former Soviet Union, see Aleksander Peniagin and Boris Porfiriev, "Implications of the Soviet Union's Collapse for the Reorganization of the Nuclear Complex, and its Repercussions," in C. Wedar, M. Intriligator, and P. Vares, eds., *Implications of the Dissolution of the Soviet Union for Accidental/Inadvertent Use of Weapons of Mass Destruction* (Tallinn: Estonian Academy of Sciences, 1992), pp. 197–202. They describe the nuclear complex as experiencing a "partially uncontrolled decay"; p. 198. See also Seymour Hersh, "The Wild East," *The Atlantic Monthly*, June 1994, pp. 61–86, which describes personnel at one weapons lab as "in a state of near rebellion over the lack of such basic amenities as housing, health care, and regular paycheck"; p. 76.

20. See Stephen Handelman, "The Russian Mafiya," *Foreign Affairs*, Vol. 73, No. 2 (March/April 1994), pp. 83–96. According to Handelman, organized crime accounted for 40 percent of economic activity in Russia during 1993; p. 84. Also surveying the link between organized crime and traffic in nuclear materials is "Transnational Crime: A New Security Threat?" in International Institute for Strategic Studies (IISS), (London: Oxford University Press, May 1995), pp. 25–28.

21. "Smuggling profits have formed the foundation of postcommunist mafiya wealth." Handelman, "Russian Mafiya," p. 88.

22. Such claims are described by John Lloyd (Moscow correspondent of the *Financial Times*) in a recent review of several recent books on organized crime in Russia: "The Overcoat," unpublished manuscript. See also Hersh, "The Wild East," p. 68: "There is powerful evidence that organized crime in the former Soviet Union has been systematically seeking access to the nuclear stockpiles, with their potential for huge profit."

23. Woolsey's testimony is cited in Leonard Spector and Mark G. McDonough with Evan S. Medeiros, *Tracking Nuclear Proliferation: A Guide in Maps and Charts, 1995* (Washington DC: Carnegie Endowment for International Peace, 1995), p. 30.

possession of huge stockpiles of nuclear weapons and fissile material is plagued with rampant crime and corruption.

Third, the coherence and effectiveness of Russia's public institutions have eroded since the collapse of the Soviet Union. The central government has been weak and ineffectual. With regard to nuclear leakage, this means that Russia cannot control its own borders, making smuggling and illegal export easier. It cannot control crime within its borders; thus potential smugglers can operate with little fear of capture or legal sanction. It cannot fully control its own nuclear complex, which leaves room for uncooperative, unauthorized, or illegal behavior by institutions or individuals within that complex. In short, Russia's nuclear stockpiles exist in a weak state, with porous borders, unrestrained criminals, and unregulated institutions.

Moreover, the security of Russia's nuclear weapons and fissile material depends on the continued effectiveness of the organizations responsible for their custody, in particular, the military, Minatom, and the nuclear research institutes. Safeguards require organizational and procedural support to be truly effective. As an earlier analysis put it:

The most important safeguards are procedural, which means that groups of well-informed or well-placed individuals, acting in collusion, can certainly circumvent them. In the last analysis the custodial system for nuclear weapons is a social system. It will be strong when the society in which it is embedded is stable, and it will behave according to its intended design when organizational norms and routines are being followed by most of the people most of the time .But it is not possible to exhibit, or even to imagine, a set of safeguards on the Soviet arsenal that gives total reassurance against abuse in the midst of general social upheaval.[24]

Organizations such as the Russian military and Minatom are now operating in circumstances of great stress. Money is in short supply, paychecks are irregular, living conditions unpleasant, relations with the central government strained, and future prospects are unattractive. The Russian military, for example, is "in a shambles": "impoverished" by Russia's economic decline, "humiliated" by its loss of status and prestige, suffering an "appalling quality of life," experiencing an "exodus" of experienced officers and an "erosion of order within the ranks," not to mention a "rampant increase in corruption."[25] This is a disheartening description of the organization in custody of the world's largest inventory

---

24. Campbell, Carter, Miller, and Zraket, *Soviet Nuclear Fission*, p. 16.

25. Benjamin Lambeth, "Russia's Wounded Military," *Foreign Affairs*, Vol. 74, No. 2 (March/April 1995), pp. 86–98.

of nuclear weapons. So far, it has done a remarkably good job under extremely difficult circumstances in providing custodianship of this huge arsenal. But disorder within Russia and the resulting strains within the military could easily cause a lapse or a breakdown in the Russian military's guardianship of nuclear weapons.

By mid-1995, experts can debate whether the Russian economy has hit bottom and is now moving in the right direction, whether Russia has turned the corner in its pursuit of political reforms, and whether conditions in Russia are really as bad as they seem to the casual observer. The news from Russia is not entirely grim. But so long as Russia continues to be touched by turbulence, uncertainty, and disorder, the risk of serious nuclear leakage will persist. This seems likely to be true for years to come, even if trends in Russia are improving. But should Russia slide further in the wrong direction, the risk of catastrophic rupture of Russia's nuclear custodial system would be all the greater.

THE SIZE AND COMPLEXITY OF THE RUSSIA'S NUCLEAR INFRASTRUCTURE
The nuclear empire within Russia's troubled confines is vast and staggeringly complex. Russia's nuclear empire is a living, breathing organism that continues to function, with weapons and fissile material flowing through its veins: nuclear research continues, fissile material is still produced, nuclear power is still being generated, nuclear weapons are still deployed, large numbers of nuclear weapons are being retired and dismantled, and new nuclear weapons are probably still being produced. These activities occur at many widely distributed facilities and storage sites, and involve many institutions and many users of fissile material. The geographic and bureaucratic dispersal of the Russian nuclear complex means that weapons and materials are regularly being transported, handled, and handed off from one facility or organization to another. These activities all increase the risk of theft, and diversion.

Figure 1-1 shows the "pipeline" through which fissile material and nuclear weapons flow, from their production sites to their deployment areas and then to their ultimate destination as dismantled fissile components and bulk materials. This pipeline is complex, the chain of custody along it is not transparent, and the various destinations for the fissile material often do not meet desirable standards for safety or security, as this section explains.

FISSILE MATERIAL AND NUCLEAR WEAPONS PRODUCTION. Russia's nuclear weapons production complex is run by Minatom, from the mining of natural uranium to the hand-off of nuclear weapons to the military. There are three key phases in the production of a nuclear weapon. The first is

Warhead Production

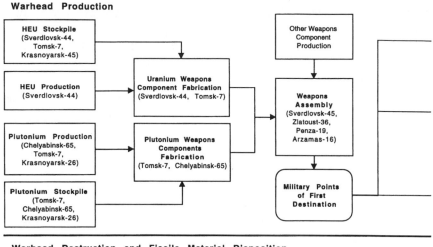

Warhead Destruction and Fissile Material Disposition

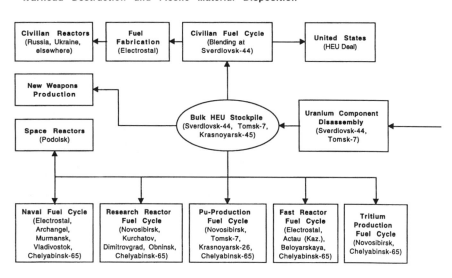

Figure 1-1. The Russian Nuclear Complex

the production of fissile material: highly enriched uranium (HEU) is produced in uranium enrichment plants, while plutonium for weapons is produced at special plutonium-production reactors and then separated at a reprocessing facility. This fissile material is transferred to a fissile material component fabrication facility, where it is molded and shaped into a form that is appropriate for use in a weapon. These components are transferred to a warhead production facility, where they are mated with the other components needed to produce a nuclear warhead, such

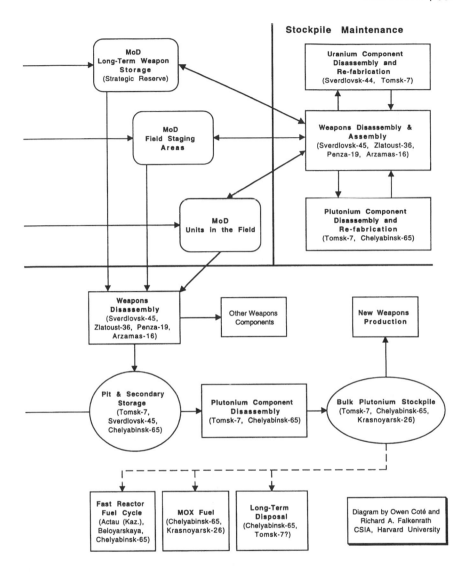

Stockpile Maintenance

MoD Long-Term Weapon Storage (Strategic Reserve)

Uranium Component Disassembly and Re-fabrication (Sverdlovsk-44, Tomsk-7)

MoD Field Staging Areas

Weapons Disassembly & Assembly (Sverdlovsk-45, Zlatoust-36, Penza-19, Arzamas-16)

MoD Units in the Field

Plutonium Component Disassembly and Re-fabrication (Tomsk-7, Chelyabinsk-65)

Weapons Disassembly (Sverdlovsk-45, Zlatoust-36, Penza-19, Arzamas-16)

Other Weapons Components

New Weapons Production

Pit & Secondary Storage (Tomsk-7, Sverdlovsk-45, Chelyabinsk-65)

Plutonium Component Disassembly (Tomsk-7, Chelyabinsk-65)

Bulk Plutonium Stockpile (Tomsk-7, Chelyabinsk-65, Krasnoyarsk-26)

Fast Reactor Fuel Cycle (Actau (Kaz.), Beloyarskaya, Chelyabinsk-65)

MOX Fuel (Chelyabinsk-65, Krasnoyarsk-26)

Long-Term Disposal (Chelyabinsk-65, Tomsk-7?)

Diagram by Owen Coté and Richard A. Falkenrath CSIA, Harvard University

as high explosives and sophisticated triggers. Once these three steps are complete, the weapon is ready to be deployed with its users, the military.

NUCLEAR WEAPONS DEPLOYED TO THE MILITARY. Between 15,000 and 25,000 deployed nuclear weapons are in the hands of the Russian military. These weapons are deployed in field storage sites near the unit responsible for their delivery or, in some cases, on their launchers ready for immediate use. Organizationally, they are spread among a number of military institutions — the army, the navy, the air force, the strategic rocket force, and the air defenses — each of which has its own distinctive operational culture, strategic and political perspectives, and standards of nuclear custody. Geographically, they are located at dozens or perhaps hundreds of nuclear storage depots scattered across Russia's enormous territorial expanse. Responsibility for the security of Russia's deployed nuclear weapons is assigned to the 12th Main Directorate of the Russian General Staff.

Since the late 1980s, nuclear operations with the Soviet and now the Russian military have been in an almost constant state of flux. The strategic nuclear modernization that began in the 1970s has now been superseded by a series of sweeping disarmament initiatives and unilateral withdrawals from service. After the Eastern European revolutions of 1989, the Soviet Union began withdrawing its tactical nuclear weapons from Europe, and after the collapse of the Soviet Union in 1991, Moscow began to withdraw its tactical and then strategic nuclear weapons from the non-Russian republics. As a result, the Russian Federation has a surplus of nuclear weapons, and is dismantling them at a rate of roughly 3,000 per year.[26] The first step in the dismantlement process is to remove the weapon from its launcher or storage position, place it in a special shipping container, and transport it to the appropriate Minatom dismantlement installation by truck and rail. When the warhead reaches the dismantlement installation, it passes into the custody of Minatom. The part of the dismantlement pipeline that is relatively transparent to U.S. eyes is the Ministry of Defense side of this bureaucratic boundary. Little is known about Minatom's dismantlement operations.

In addition to this dismantlement process, Soviet-designed nuclear weapons also require regular maintenance at the facility where they were produced, an activity which is called "stockpile maintenance."

STOCKPILE MAINTENANCE. Each year, roughly 10 percent of the deployed nuclear weapons must be returned to the installation where they were manufactured for maintenance. At a minimum, this stockpile maintenance involves dismantling the warhead and re-assembling it; it could, however, also involve dismantling the fissile material components and refabricating them at the appropriate fissile material component fabrica-

---

26. Our interview sources have indicated that the number is about 3,000 per year, and this is the number we have used in our calculations. However, Secretary of Defense William J. Perry recently cited a figure of "2000 [dismantled Russian] nuclear weapons a year in the last couple of years." See "A Legacy of Readiness: Interview with Secretary of Defense William J. Perry," *Sea Power*, October 1995, p. 11.

tion plant. Weapons requiring maintenance follow the same path as weapons destined for dismantlement, but then retrace this path back into the hands of the military. This traffic in weapons, weapon components, and fissile materials flows in both directions along the rail net that links the facilities of the Russian nuclear archipelago.

NUCLEAR WEAPONS DISMANTLEMENT AND FISSILE MATERIAL DISPOSITION. Warhead dismantlement is essentially the reverse of warhead production. First, the warhead is transferred to the weapons production facility where it was built and is taken apart, producing a number of fissile material components. The precise number depends on the weapon type and how it is dismantled.[27] Minatom then has a choice between stockpiling these fissile material components as they are, and taking them apart, which is called "below pit-level dismantlement." If it chooses the latter, the fissile material components are transferred by rail to the facility where they were fabricated.

The destruction of these components produces bulk fissile material, which can be disposed of or used in a variety of ways. Plutonium can be used to fabricate new components for new weapons, used as fuel in a special reactor, or permanently disposed of in a number of different ways. HEU can be recycled into a variety of different HEU fuel cycles, reused for new weapons production, or blended with natural uranium to produce low enriched uranium (LEU) for conventional power-generating nuclear reactors.[28] Disposition of bulk fissile material via any of these options requires further transportation between and within Russia's nuclear installations.

Public knowledge about Minatom's dismantlement decisions is quite limited. If 3,000 weapons are being dismantled at up to four sites per year, and if each weapon has on average 10 pounds of plutonium and 30 pounds of highly enriched uranium (reasonable planning figures), then 15 tons of plutonium and 45 tons of HEU are being added annually to

27. According to U.S. officials involved in the negotiations over the U.S.-funded fissile material storage facility (see Chapter 3), the Russian government's negotiating position suggests that their dismantled weapons produce three HEU components for every one plutonium component. This suggests that, on average, a dismantled Russian nuclear weapon produces four fissile material components.

28. Russia's civilian nuclear power program, also controlled by Minatom, is one of the largest nuclear power programs in the world, encompassing 29 reactors and a number of associated facilities for fabricating fuel and dealing with nuclear waste. This civilian nuclear program has never been internationally safeguarded by the International Atomic Energy Agency (IAEA), which means that Russia has no confirmed accounting of the disposition of the plutonium-laden spent reactor fuel.

Minatom's fissile material stockpile, which amounts to approximately 75 tons of plutonium and 625 tons of HEU.[29]

TRANSPORTATION. Connecting the Russian nuclear installations is a complicated transportation system. All long-range transportation of nuclear weapons, components, and fissile material in Russia is done by railroad, but trucks are used to carry them between railheads and their local destinations. The transportation of weapons is the responsibility of the 12th Main Directorate. Specially designed railcars with security troops transport weapons from the field to central military storage facilities for interim storage, or directly to one of the four Minatom facilities where weapons are assembled and disassembled. Little is known about how fissile material components and bulk fissile material are transported within Russia, but General Evgeny Maslin, the chief of the 12th Main Directorate, has stated that such shipments are handled by Minatom itself in Minatom's own railcars, not by the 12th Main Directorate.[30]

EROSION OF THE SOVIET SECURITY SYSTEM

Concerns about nuclear leakage did not arise during the Soviet period, and would not now were the Soviet nuclear security system still intact. The Soviet security system was premised on a closed and repressive society. The closed cities that formed the heart of the USSR's nuclear weapons complex were geographically remote and inaccessible. These cities were entirely circled by a perimeter of security, including fences and patrols. Travel to these cities by outsiders — Soviet citizens and foreigners alike — was forbidden. Travel from these cities was strictly regulated: members of the Soviet Union's nuclear complex were, as a general rule, not permitted to travel abroad. The Soviet Union's borders were among the most heavily policed in the world, as anyone who ever entered the USSR by car or train would know, even in the remotest of locations. As one U.S. official put it, "In the old Soviet Union, the really tough perimeter fence was the one around the border."[31] Under these conditions, there was little incentive to steal nuclear materials: the likelihood that a seller of such material would be able to meet up with a potential buyer was remote. Moreover, any nuclear theft would catch the attention of the

---

29. Authors' estimates.

30. Gen. Evgeny Maslin, comment at the conference on the Nunn-Lugar Cooperative Threat Reduction Program: Donor and Recipient Country Perspectives, Monterey Institute of International Studies, August 20–22, 1995.

31. An anonymous U.S. official, quoted in Hersh, "The Wild East," p. 69.

secret police, which was ubiquitous, effective, and ruthless. Any individual who was caught stealing nuclear materials could expect no leniency from the Soviet legal system. In the tightly controlled society of the Soviet Union, nuclear leakage was not a serious worry.

The foundations of the Soviet approach to nuclear security were swept away in the transition from a closed totalitarian state to a more open, more turbulent democratizing state. The central Russian government is now weak, the secret police is no longer omnipotent, travel is no longer restricted, borders are porous, and crime is pervasive. The system that protected weapons and fissile material during the Soviet period cannot work in the new political environment in Russia.[32]

INADEQUATE MATERIAL CONTROL AND ACCOUNTING

The disappearance of the Soviet Union's societal security system would not be cause for alarm if the USSR had supplemented its repressive approach with other security measures to safeguard against insider threats and conspiracies. Unfortunately, this is not the case at most Russian facilities possessing fissile material.[33]

The bedrock of secure custodianship of nuclear weapons and fissile materials is an effective and meticulous system of material control and accounting.[34] For a facility to meet the appropriate safety and security standards, it must be able to control and account for materials as they enter and exit the facility, or as they move within it if it is a production or disassembly facility. Material control and accounting for fissile materials requires that an accurate inventory be maintained at all times of the weights and isotopic content of safeguarded materials. Such material control and accounting systems provide a basis for determining whether a theft, diversion, or loss of material has occurred. Without a precise inventory, it may be impossible even to know that a theft has occurred, much less to assess the seriousness of any such incident.

---

32. See also "Fissile Material Security: A New Challenge," in IISS *Strategic Survey, 1994–1995*, p. 19, which similarly concludes that the Soviet approach "can no longer provide a reliable shield against the illegal diversion of fissile material."

33. A very useful and authoritative overview of this issue is Frank von Hippel, "Fissile Material Security in the Post–Cold War World," *Physics Today*, June 1995, pp. 26–31.

34. In the argot of fissile material security experts, material control and accounting is usually combined with physical protection into what is inelegantly known as "material protection, control, and accounting," or MPC&A. In Chapter 3, we follow the convention of the U.S. government by referring to MPC&A. However, this chapter, which diagnoses the nuclear security problem in the former Soviet Union, treats material control and accounting separately from physical protection.

The material control and accounting systems at Russia's nuclear installations are almost universally inadequate. The Soviet Union never developed a reliable and effective material control and accounting system because it could rely on totalitarian instruments of control to protect against insider threats. Princeton physicist Frank von Hippel reports, for example, that "until recently, the only basis for an inventory of the quantity of weapons-usable fissile material at the [Kurchatov] institute was boxes of old paper receipts in a dusty room."[35] The HEU recovered by the United States from Kazakhstan during Project Sapphire comprised 104 percent of the declared inventory. Consider the implications of a 4 percent error margin in Russian inventory accuracy: since Russia possesses on the order of 100,000 critical masses' worth of fissile material, some 4,000 weapons' worth of fissile material would be floating unaccounted for in the margins of Russia's inventory accuracy. Even if Russia's material control and accounting system were 99 percent accurate (a level of inventory accuracy almost never achieved even by Western corporations), this would leave 1,000 weapons' worth of fissile material unaccounted for.[36]

In short, until Russia's material control and accounting is improved, it is possible that great quantities of fissile material can be stolen and never missed. This is a problem that appears to be worse for fissile material than for nuclear weapons.

INADEQUATE SECURITY AT RUSSIA'S NUCLEAR INSTALLATIONS

In properly safeguarded facilities that house fissile materials, technical and procedural security systems are designed to impede access to sensitive materials, increase the likelihood that an attempted intrusion or theft will be promptly detected, and impede egress once the intrusion or theft has occurred.

In a secure installation, fissile material would be stored in locked vaults in guarded areas to which access is carefully controlled. Personnel entering or leaving the guarded areas would be searched, or required to pass through checkpoints where their identities would be checked and where they would also pass through radiation and metal detectors. The sealed material containers in the vault would be monitored by remote

---

35. Von Hippel, "Fissile Material Security in the Post–Cold War World," p. 27.

36. Material control and accounting for fissile material is inherently difficult and poses a challenge to the United States as well as Russia. For a discussion of inventory shortfalls in the United States, see Herbert Abrams and Dan Pollak, "Security Issues in the Handling and Disposition of Fissionable Material," Center for International Security and Arms Control, Stanford University, November 1993, p. 6.

television cameras, and sit upon motion detectors. The vaults and their guarded areas would be located in a building hardened against explosive attack, with fire suppression devices, anti-intrusion sensors, alarms, booby traps, and delaying devices. In addition, any building containing fissile material would be enclosed by a perimeter fence patrolled by the facility's armed guards, who would generally be able to call on a larger emergency response team.[37]

This would describe the security arrangements for few, if any, Russian facilities that have custody of fissile material. The quality of security is generally low: at its best, for weapons in Ministry of Defense custody, it approaches U.S. standards, but Minatom's military fissile material inventory is poorly secured, and its civil plutonium stockpile is even worse. The security of fissile materials used in research institutes, naval fuel cycle facilities, etc., is nothing short of terrifying.

MINISTRY OF DEFENSE WEAPONS SECURITY. Central nuclear weapon storage facilities, which are under the control of the Russian Ministry of Defense look, at least from a distance, like their American counterparts. The following description of a central weapon storage facility is based on remarks by General Sergei Zelentsov, an official of the 12th Main Directorate:

The nuclear weapons store of the Far Eastern military district [called object 645M] . . . occupies a territory of 61 square kilometers. [It] is surrounded with physical barriers with a limited number of entrances. The whole territory has a technical alarm system as well as active and passive defense means. Even authorized visits in this territory are allowed only for groups under guard surveillance. The technical measures to secure nuclear weapon stores are such that one person alone cannot unlock it. . . . The store itself is a concrete construction with armored doors. Inside, it has massive concrete screens that would form an obstacle against explosions resulting from technical accidents or hostile actions. Nuclear weapons control is so highly centralized that each nuclear device is under permanent automatic observation and any attempt to withdraw it should immediately send an alarm signal.[38]

This is an impressive description, but it is unlikely that all Russian nuclear weapons are stored in facilities like this. Some weapons may be stored in

---

37. Ibid., pp. 57–58; Herbert Abrams and Daniel Pollack, "Security Issues in the Handling of Fissile Materials," *Contemporary Security Policy*, Vol. 15, No. 3 (December 1994), p. 17.

38. Alexander Konovalov and Igor Sutiagin, "Nuclear Weapons on the Territories of the CIS States: Problems of Safety and Security," in Joachim Krause, ed., *Kernwaffenverbreitung und internationaler Systemwandel: Neue Risiken und Gestaltungsmöglichkeiten* (Baden-Baden: Nomos Verlagsgesellschaft, 1994), pp. 142–143.

improvised conventional weapon storage facilities due to shortages of dedicated nuclear weapons storage space. It would not be surprising if there were such shortages, since Russia has lost control over nuclear weapon storage facilities in Eastern Europe and the newly independent states of the former Soviet Union just as it has received the tens of thousands of tactical, and now strategic, weapons that had been deployed in those facilities. There is some evidence of shortages of storage space during the peak of the tactical weapon withdrawals in the years 1989–92. On the other hand, Russia continues to dismantle weapons at the rate of 3,000 weapons a year, and therefore almost 10,000 dedicated weapon storage positions have presumably become available in the last three years.

Moreover, the special troops that guard the Russian weapon storage facilities are exposed to the same stresses faced by other Russians. Their real incomes are steadily eroded by inflation, the housing provided them is often totally inadequate, and they do not have better conditions when they separate from the service. Over the long run, there is no guarantee that these special troops will not be compromised by the corruption that has affected the rest of Russian society.[39]

MINATOM'S MILITARY FISSILE MATERIAL INVENTORY. The lesser level of security applied to Minatom's military fissile material inventory was amply illustrated by the public report of an official Russian government investigation of the security conditions at Tomsk-7, one of Russia's largest and most sensitive nuclear weapons facilities.[40] The specific conditions described at Tomsk reflect a more general proposition about nuclear security in the closed cities of Minatom's weapon production complex:

Set up under Soviet rule for a strictly regimented closed society worried only about external threats, the security often amounts to little more than barbed wire fences and armed guards, providing scant protection against insiders

---

39. Suggestive of this concern, for example, is the report that 23 warheads are missing from the Komsomolsk-na-Amure depot. David C. Morrison, "National Security: Heavy Metal," *National Journal*, October 22, 1994, p. 2456. Morrison notes that despite Russian denials, reports of this incident "persist." Morrison also describes Russian nuclear weapons storage facilities as "hugely overburdened," though this is denied by both U.S. and Russian officials.

40. Tomsk-7 contains fissile material and weapon component production and storage facilities for both plutonium and HEU. Reportedly, more than 20,000 fissile components from dismantled nuclear weapons are stored at Tomsk-7. Testimony given by Lawrence Gershwin, House Committee on Appropriations, DOD Appropriations for 1993, Part 5, May 6, 1992, p. 498.

and their accomplices who hope to get rich by smuggling out nuclear materials for sale on the black market . . . [Russian] nuclear authorities acknowledge that their protection systems need to be updated substantially, . . . including closed-circuit cameras, coded locks, fingerprint authorization, movement sensors, . . . and effective methods for tracking their nuclear inventory during processing, a key point of vulnerability.[41]

Another Russian report noted that one of the converted warehouses at Tomsk-7 being used to store the fissile material components from dismantled weapons "was guarded by soldiers and an armored personnel carrier, and [visitors] were searched, but there was no other monitoring devices. . . . There were no electronic keys or fingerprint access that modern places have, just regular locks."[42]

The situation at Tomsk is probably fairly representative of the security arrangements at the rest of Minatom's nuclear weapons facilities. Indeed, some U.S. officials believe that not a single Russian nuclear facility of any sort, other than Ministry of Defense weapons storage bunkers, has anything close to the level of security deemed adequate for nuclear weapons. The Soviet Union, before its demise, simply was not concerned about insider threats and did not invest in the technologies, devices, and procedures designed to thwart attempted thefts under all conceivable circumstances. Hence, the Russian nuclear security system depends, to a very large extent, on the reliability of the organizations and individuals handling its nuclear materials, and is highly prone to failure whenever an individual or group of conspirators decides to exploit its vulnerabilities.

MINATOM'S CIVIL PLUTONIUM STOCKPILE. One of the largest inventories of separated plutonium in the world is that associated with Russia's civilian nuclear power program. Thirty tons of separated plutonium have accumulated at the Mayak reprocessing facility, located at Chelyabinsk-65.[43] This huge stockpile is stored not in a dedicated nuclear storage facility designed to make nuclear materials inaccessible and theft difficult, but in an ordinary converted warehouse, with windows in the walls and a

---

41. Ibid.; see also Alexander Bolsunovsky and Valery Menshchikov, "Nuclear Security is Inadequate and Outdated," *Moscow News*, No. 49 (December 9–15, 1994), p. 14.

42. Alexei Yablokov, an advisor to President Yeltsin on environmental affairs, reporting on his visit to Tomsk-7 in Margaret Shapiro, "Russia Orders Tightened Security to Protect Nuclear Materials," *Washington Post*, February 24, 1995, p. A15. See also "Russia police decry nuclear sites' security," *Boston Globe*, October 11, 1995, p. 2.

43. Details on Mayak have been drawn from von Hippel, "Fissile Material Security in the Post–Cold War World," p. 26; and interviews.

padlock on the door. Inside the warehouse are rows and rows of upright metal containers containing plutonium ingots. Mayak lies within the fenced perimeter of a closed city, but such perimeter defenses provide no protection against theft by those already inside the fence. Moreover, U.S. officials able to visit Mayak report signs of crime and corruption, including new and rather ostentatious housing construction within the main Chelyabinsk security perimeter, which the locals attributed to organized crime figures.

RESEARCH AND OTHER FUEL CYCLES. The worst situation with respect to nuclear security in Russia belongs to the fourth category of fissile material users.[44] The fissile materials used in research institutes, naval fuel cycle facilities, and other non-standard fuel cycles are stored under conditions that do not come close to meeting desired standards of nuclear custody. Just how poor the security can be at this category of facility is apparent from two illustrations.

At Building 116 of the Kurchatov Research Institute in Moscow — the oldest nuclear research facility in Russia, and essentially independent of Minatom — about 350 pounds of HEU was stored under highly insecure conditions until a major security improvement was implemented through a U.S.-Russian initiative under the "lab-to-lab" program (see Chapter 3). Building 116 had a guard at the front door, but members of the institute known to him passed freely in and out the main entrance without being searched, and without passing through metal or radiation detectors of any kind. Surrounding the building was a fence, but the fence had holes in it that the staff used often as a shortcut to the cafeteria. This building and its HEU inventory were almost completely insecure. The HEU was in a locked room but many members of the research institute had access to the room.

Similarly, about 1,000 pounds of HEU were stored under appalling security conditions at the Ulbinsky Metallurgy Plant at Ust-Kamengorsk, Kazakhstan. The HEU at the Ulbinsky Plant, covertly purchased by the U.S. government in Project Sapphire,[45] was stored not in a dedicated nuclear storage facility, but in a wooden building resembling a stable, with rusty padlocks on some of the doors. There was no security equipment of any kind behind these doors. The plant itself was enclosed by a

---

44. This conclusion is widespread among experts and officials who have examined the fissile material security issue. Concurring, for example, are Spector, McDonough, and Medeiros, *Tracking Nuclear Proliferation*, p. 30.

45. During the Soviet era, the Ulbinsky Plant served as a uranium fuel fabrication facility and as a supplier of berylium components.

fence, and a local Kazakh militia unit was assigned to guard its perimeter. Such security is no better than the security at any ordinary industrial facility.

There are many other buildings and facilities in Russia like Kurchatov or Ust-Kamengorsk, all of them housing large quantities of weapons-usable and even weapons-grade fissile material in conditions of extreme insecurity.

In sum, the nuclear security situation in Russia is very worrisome. Although nuclear weapons appear to be stored in a reasonably secure (though not foolproof) fashion, many inventories of fissile material are not. Many Russian nuclear storage facilities lack adequate security, while many stockpiles of fissile material sit in improvised storage in converted warehouses, or in lockers in unsecured buildings at various research institutes. This is an extremely undesirable state of affairs: it greatly increases the vulnerability of Russia's nuclear custodial system to leakage.[46]

WARHEAD DISMANTLEMENT IS OVERWHELMING MINATOM'S STORAGE CAPACITY

In addition to the inadequate MPC&A and security systems across the Russian nuclear complex, there is a particular problem arising from Russia's nuclear weapons dismantlement program. Every dismantled nuclear weapon results in at least two, and sometimes three, substantial chunks of fissile material: the primary, secondary, and sometimes even tertiary stages. Hence, dismantling weapons at a rate of 3,000 per year produces more than six thousand fissile components that must be stored or disposed of.[47] With many thousands of weapons still to be dismantled in coming years, this inventory will grow rapidly for some time to come.

Due to the lack of public information about the Russian dismantlement process, details of how Russia is handling the storage of fissile components from dismantled weapons are not clearly in view. However, it is clear that Minatom now has a major storage problem on its hands. The Minatom weapons production complex was never meant to function as a storage venue for huge numbers of fissile weapon components.

---

46. As one group of experts put it, "Secure storage of nuclear materials is the most critical near-term objective." Von Hippel, et al., "Eliminating Nuclear Warheads," p. 47.

47. Discussing the range of disposition options for plutonium and HEU from dismantled weapons is Brian Chow and Kenneth Solomon, *Limiting the Spread of Weapon-Usable Fissile Materials* (Santa Monica: RAND, 1993), especially pp. 61–87. Interim storage will be necessary whatever ultimate disposition options are chosen, but in the case of plutonium, storage is itself one of the long-term possibilities.

During the Soviet era, nuclear weapons production ran overwhelmingly in one direction: Minatom produced nuclear weapons and handed them over to the military. The Soviet Union did not begin to dismantle significant quantities of nuclear weapons until the mid-1980s, and only recently achieved the rate now being witnessed. This system meant that there was no need for large, dedicated facilities to store fissile components in Minatom's custody. Hence, the current dismantlement effort must be placing an unprecedented strain on available storage capacity at dismantlement sites, and this strain will continue to worsen until a new storage or disposal option becomes available or acceptable to Minatom.[48]

THE EASY TRANSPORTABILITY OF WEAPONS AND FISSILE MATERIAL
However vulnerable the Russian nuclear custodial system may be, nuclear leakage will be only a theoretical worry if nuclear weapons or the materials to make them cannot, in a practical sense, be smuggled. Many seem to draw reassurance from the belief that nuclear weapons are too large and weapons-quantities of nuclear materials too bulky or too dangerously radioactive for nuclear trafficking to constitute a serious problem. This belief is mistaken. Many nuclear weapons are easily transported by ordinary cars, trucks, and aircraft. And a weapons' worth of fissile material is not only valuable, but relatively safe to handle, easily hidden, and can be physically carried by any average person. These facts help to explain why these valuable commodities are difficult to secure in the midst of revolution.

FISSILE MATERIAL IS NOT AS UNHEALTHY AS YOU THINK. Many still seem to believe that nuclear smuggling is powerfully inhibited by the health dangers associated with the handling of fissile materials. Weapons quantities of plutonium may fit in a pocket, this view holds, but only the suicidal would actually put any there. This misconception is understandable, in view of the widespread public fears of anything nuclear. But it is false. Plutonium and HEU can be carried out of Russia with little or no danger to the nuclear smuggler.

Plutonium can be handled safely even without shielding. It is radioactive, emitting alpha particles, but these particles are unable to penetrate even the thinnest of materials, including paper and human skin. A person could indeed carry plutonium in a pocket and suffer no ill effects. Pluto-

---

48. It is worth noting that the United States has experienced a related problem as a result of its dismantlement program: there is political opposition in Texas to allowing the Pantex plant to become the only U.S. plutonium component storage site. See Kevin Cameron, "Taking Apart the Bomb," *Popular Science*, April 1993, p. 102.

nium poses grave health risks if inhaled or ingested, but there is little risk of this so long as the plutonium is not allowed to oxidize; weapon components are normally clad with metal to prevent this. One could hold such a component in one's hand for any length of time with no risk of adverse health consequences. A smuggler does not have to be suicidal to carry plutonium out of Russia.[49]

HEU is analogous to lead in terms of health risks. Swallowed in large quantities, or injected directly into the bloodstream, HEU can cause heavy metal poisoning. Otherwise, HEU is almost completely safe. One can handle it directly with little exposure to radiation.

A WEAPONS' WORTH OF FISSILE MATERIAL IS THE SIZE OF AN APPLE. The most simple gun-type weapon can produce a 15–20 kiloton yield with a little over 100 pounds of HEU. Slightly more challenging but still simple implosion weapons can be constructed with less than 20 pounds of plutonium or about 40 pounds of HEU. According to the Natural Resources Defense Council (NRDC), a nuclear explosion can be created with as little as 2.2 pounds of plutonium or 5.5 pounds of HEU in a sophisticated nuclear weapons program.[50] These are weights that could be physically carried by a single human being.

Moreover, because these heavy metals are very dense, the volume associated with these weights is very small. A quantity of plutonium the size of an apple is enough to make a simple fission weapon, and a quantity the size of a grapefruit would allow a weapon designer to use a conservative design.[51] Thus, nuclear leakage becomes a serious matter, with weapons implications, when it involves a few pounds of fissile material of a size that could readily fit in airline luggage, carry-on bags, indeed, even in the pocket of a smuggler. Several weapons worth of fissile material could be carried by a single person in a briefcase. Any commercial flight out of Russia could have aboard materials that would constitute a major breach of the Russian nuclear custodial system. The portability of weapons quantities of fissile material is part of what makes nuclear leakage such a live and worrisome possibility.

---

49. For a discussion of the dangers of plutonium which indicates that these are exaggerated in public discourse, see W. Sutcliffe, R. Condit, W. Mansfield, D. Myers, D. Layton, and P. Murphy, "A Perspective on the Dangers of Plutonium," CSTS-48-95, Center for Security and Technology Studies, Lawrence Livermore National Laboratory, April 14, 1995.

50. See Thomas Cochran and Christopher Paine, *The Amount of Plutonium and Highly Enriched Uranium Needed for Pure Fission Nuclear Weapons* (Washington DC: Natural Resources Defense Council, April 13, 1995), p. 9.

51. IISS, *Strategic Survey, 1994–1995*, p. 16.

NOT ALL NUCLEAR WEAPONS ARE BULKY MONSTERS. The old photos of the nuclear weapons produced by the Manhattan Project during World War II conjure up misleading images based on what "Little Boy" looked like: large, ponderous, and heavy. The HEU weapon that was detonated over Hiroshima was ten feet long and weighed 9,000 pounds. The plutonium weapon, "Fat Man," was ten feet long, five feet wide, and also weighed about 9,000 pounds.[52] Under the right circumstances, even these weapons could be handled by a small team of people and could be trucked or flown to some distant destination. But still, one does not imagine items of this bulk being easily "smuggled" across the border.

Therefore, it is important to realize that most of the weapons designed since those first bulky weapons are smaller, lighter, and more easily manageable by a small number of people. Nuclear weapons were, for example, fitted into eight-inch artillery shells weighing 250 pounds.[53] During the 1950s, the United States briefly introduced nuclear weapons designed to be hauled by foot soldiers in backpacks. Many modern weapons have been designed to minimize weight and volume to facilitate delivery by ballistic missiles. Many could be lifted and carried by two or three people and transported in the back of a small truck, or even in the trunk of a car. And there are few nuclear weapons in the Russian arsenal that could not be handled by conspiracies involving larger numbers of people.

All things considered, weapons quantities of fissile material are small and safe to handle, and thus easily hidden and easily transported. Transportability poses no serious limit on the nuclear leakage problem.

DEMAND FOR NUCLEAR WEAPONS AND FISSILE MATERIALS EXISTS
That there may be a supply of nuclear weapons or fissile material available for sale from Russia would matter little if there were no demand side of the market; materials that no one wants to buy pose no danger. But in fact there is a small but dangerous and highly motivated group of aspiring proliferants — including Iraq and North Korea — who have made strenuous efforts to obtain fissile materials and for whom access to Russian stockpiles would be a godsend.

Evidence is thin about the behavior of the demand side of the mar-

---

52. Information on Fat Man and Little Boy is from Thomas Cochran and Christopher Paine, *The Role of Hydronuclear Tests and Other Low-Yield Nuclear Explosions and Their Status Under a Comprehensive Test Ban* (Washington DC: Natural Resources Defense Council, March 1995), p. 4.

53. Thomas Cochran, William Arkin, and Milton Hoenig, *Nuclear Weapons Databook: U.S. Nuclear Forces and Capabilities* (Cambridge, Mass.: Ballinger, 1984), pp. 47–48.

ket.[54] There are some indications, however, of potential buyers' interest in exploiting nuclear leakage from Russia. A planeload of Russian nuclear experts, for example, was arrested shortly before taking off for North Korea where they had been hired to work in the North Korean nuclear program.[55] Iran is reported to have sent nuclear "buying teams" into the former Soviet Union in search of nuclear materials for its incipient nuclear weapons program.[56] And while hard evidence is sketchy, one must presume that states willing to invest years of effort and billions of dollars in their quest for fissile material would be willing, even eager, to buy what they can from the offerings produced by nuclear leakage from Russia. Indeed, aspiring proliferants are likely to be already familiar with operating in a covert nuclear black market, because that is often the source of the uranium enrichment or plutonium reprocessing technology necessary for their efforts to produce fissile material.[57] Moreover, efforts to strengthen the international nonproliferation regime make alternative routes to nuclear acquisition more difficult and less attractive, and thereby increase the appeal of acquisition strategies based on theft or illicit transaction.[58] The difference, in the case of nuclear leakage from Russia, is that what is involved is not fissile material production capabilities, but fissile material or perhaps even nuclear weapons themselves. It seems inevitable that this market would be irresistible to any determined proliferant.

Conclusion: More Leakage Likely, Disaster Possible

Russia's enormous nuclear complex, in all its dimensions, exists in difficult, uncertain and turbulent political and economic conditions. The previous system for protecting nuclear assets was swept away with the demise of the Soviet Union and the move toward democracy in Russia.

---

54. Some have gone so far as to suggest that the demand side of the nuclear black market simply does not exist. See, for example, "German Agents Reportedly Find No Nuclear Black Market," *Boston Globe*, May 14, 1995. We find this conclusion unconvincing.

55. "Moscow Reportedly Thwarts Plan by N. Korea to Hire Nuclear Experts," *Boston Globe*, December 20, 1992.

56. On Iran's desire for nuclear weapons, see Shahram Chubin, "Does Iran Want Nuclear Weapons?" *Survival*, Vol. 37, No. 1 (Spring 1995), pp. 86–104.

57. See, for example, Michael Klare, *Rogue States and Nuclear Outlaws: America's Search for a New Foreign Policy* (New York: Hill and Wang, 1995), pp. 187–188. Klare points out that covert transactions with Western firms have played an important role in the programs of a number of potential proliferants.

58. This point is also noted in Klare, *Rogue States and Nuclear Outlaws*, p. 187.

Most of Russia's nuclear facilities lack adequate secure storage and material control and accounting. The materials in need of protection are easily hidden and transported. Taken together, these conditions provide both the incentive and the opportunity for nuclear leakage: incentive born of economic hardship, and opportunity derived from the vulnerability of the Russian custodial system to theft or diversion. These supply-side realities are compounded by the fact that, on the demand side, there are likely to be eager and highly motivated buyers who are willing to pay for what the Russian nuclear custodians have to sell. Given this situation, more nuclear leakage is likely, serious incidents involving weapons quantities of fissile material are a distinct possibility, and a catastrophic rupture of the Russian custodial system remains distressingly plausible. This is the current state of affairs.

The United States has already experienced how a covert nuclear deal might come about. Project Sapphire began with an approach from Kazakhstan to the United States. The Kazakh authorities reported that they had found a large quantity of unprotected HEU, and they contacted the U.S. government to ask for advice on how to dispose of this material. This set in motion the chain of events that led to the purchase and removal of these materials by the United States, and their transportation to the secure storage facility at Oak Ridge, Tennessee, where the U.S. HEU stockpile is located. Project Sapphire was a great success, but it is also disturbing because one cannot help but wonder who else is receiving phone calls about supplies of fissile material.

For the average Russian engineer, guard, or scientist, the opportunity to steal and sell a cache of fissile materials could well be irresistible, as it might to any American under the same circumstances. The United States and Russia need to take immediate steps to remove these temptations. Otherwise, fissile materials will continue to leak, leaks may become torrents, and the next "Project Sapphire" will be announced not by the United States, but by Iran, Chechnya, or Hamas.

Chapter 2

Stakes:
How Nuclear Leakage
Threatens U.S. Interests

The stakes associated with the risk of nuclear leakage from Russia are enormous. A collapse of the Russian nuclear custodial system would be by far the largest disaster in the history of international efforts to prevent nuclear proliferation. All of the good done by the indefinite extension of the Nuclear Non-proliferation Treaty (NPT), by attempts to strengthen and improve the International Atomic Energy Agency (IAEA) and by efforts to deal with proliferation hot spots such as North Korea would be undermined or destroyed by nuclear leakage on a large scale. A black market in fissile material made available via nuclear leakage from Russia would eviscerate the international non-proliferation regime, since that regime depends on making access to fissile material as difficult as possible for potential proliferants. All states committed to the international non-proliferation regime ought to recognize the potentially fateful importance of the nuclear leakage problem.

The nuclear leakage problem should be one of the United States' most urgent national security concerns. Nuclear leakage would greatly increase the likelihood that forces hostile to the United States — whether states or terrorist groups — could gain possession of nuclear weapons or the means to make them. Much more than is commonly understood, this new path to nuclear proliferation constitutes a direct threat to the security of the United States. Most importantly, it could lead directly to new nuclear threats against the territory of the United States. Those who gain access to nuclear materials from the former Soviet Union may be able to fashion nuclear bombs. Such bombs could be employed against targets in the United States. For U.S. policymakers, there cannot be many issues more important than preventing the emergence of a new nuclear threat to the United States.

In this chapter, we spell out the adverse consequences of potential nuclear leakage and examine the implications for U.S. security should nuclear leakage occur.

Adverse Consequences of Nuclear Leakage

The United States, along with many of its allies, has invested decades of effort in an attempt to prevent nuclear proliferation. The imperfections of the international nonproliferation regime notwithstanding, those efforts have met with considerable success: the NPT has been permanently renewed; the overwhelming majority of states have joined the NPT as non-weapons members; a reasonably effective denial regime makes it difficult for potential proliferants to obtain the fissile material production technologies necessary to develop nuclear weapons; nuclear weapons acquisition has been relatively rare; and the number of proliferation trouble spots are few in number. But this picture could change rapidly and dramatically should nuclear leakage become a major problem.

Nuclear leakage can produce several adverse consequences. First, it is a fast, cheap route to nuclear proliferation, providing those who covet nuclear weapons with a shortcut to nuclear acquisition. Second, nuclear leakage could provide non-state actors with unprecedented access to nuclear capabilities, thereby making the threat of nuclear terrorism far more worrisome than ever before. Third, in the worst case, nuclear leakage could promote rapid, widespread nuclear proliferation and could destroy or severely damage the international nonproliferation regime. (For the technical basis of these risks, see Appendix B.)

A SHORTCUT TO NUCLEAR PROLIFERATION

Nuclear leakage can enable states seeking nuclear weapons to achieve their goal more easily, more quickly, more covertly, and more cheaply. Conceivably, nuclear leakage could also permit the acquisition of modest nuclear weapons capabilities by states that would otherwise be unable to acquire them because they lack the requisite technical or financial resources.

THE TRADITIONAL PATH TO NUCLEAR WEAPONS: SLOW, DIFFICULT, EXPENSIVE. The traditional route to the acquisition of nuclear weapons involves the purchase or development of the means of producing fissile material. With a fissile material production line, a state can build up a nuclear arsenal and steadily improve its nuclear expertise. It can start simply with crude air-delivered fission weapons and then move on to more advanced designs and delivery means. This is the route taken by every declared and undeclared nuclear weapon state to date, sometimes alone, but usually with assistance.[1]

This path to nuclear acquisition is very demanding for potential proliferants, for several reasons. First, there are the obvious technical and financial challenges. Nuclear reactors, nuclear reprocessing, and nuclear enrichment facilities are very difficult for less developed countries to design and build on their own.[2] Some uranium enrichment technologies, for example, require the construction of large facilities that consume huge amounts of electricity.[3] The necessary technologies are also very expensive whether a state attempts to develop them indigenously or buy them abroad. Iraq, for example, invested $8 billion in its calutron program alone.[4]

Second, the international non-proliferation regime has created a system of barriers designed to deny potential proliferants the means to produce fissile materials. While these barriers are not perfect, they are effective enough to make it difficult for most aspiring proliferants to develop fissile material production capabilities.

Because the technical and financial challenges are substantial and the international denial regime is in place, nuclear acquisition programs progress very slowly. Both Iraq's nuclear program and North Korea's spanned at least a decade.

Finally, the traditional route to nuclear weapons is difficult to pursue covertly. No nation has gotten very far down this path without having its intentions suspected or discovered. There has always been a substantial gap, measured in years, between the discovery of a national weapons program and its successful outcome. In some cases, this gap is exploited

---

1. For a concise discussion of all known national nuclear programs see Joel Ullom, "Enriched Uranium versus Plutonium: Proliferant Preferences in the Choice of Fissile Material," *The Nonproliferation Review*, Vol. 2, No. 1 (Fall 1994), pp. 1–15.

2. All other things being equal, it is easier to produce and separate plutonium than it is to enrich uranium. On the other hand, nuclear reactors are harder to build covertly than are uranium enrichment facilities.

3. On the requirements for pursuing various approaches to enrichment, see the useful overview in Robert F. Mozley, *Uranium Enrichment and Other Technical Problems Relating to Nuclear Weapons Proliferation* (Palo Alto: Center for International Security and Arms Control, Stanford University, July 1994). The demands imposed by enrichment will, of course, depend on which approach to enrichment is chosen. The most modern and technically challenging enrichment technologies use the least energy and are the easiest to hide.

4. David Albright and Mark Hibbs, "Iraq's Nuclear Hide-and-Seek," *Bulletin of the Atomic Scientists*, September 1991, p. 23.

by the international community to prevent such a successful outcome, as illustrated by the Israeli attack on Iraq's Osirak reactor and by the current — so far successful — efforts to halt the North Korean program. Thus, the traditional path to nuclear weapons has a built-in vulnerability, especially from the perspective of a less developed, politically isolated country that does not already possess a civilian nuclear power industry. The attempt to develop or obtain the means of producing fissile material is likely to be detected long before significant quantities of fissile material are actually produced. This means that nations seeking to prevent the spread of nuclear weapons will see clear evidence of nuclear aspirations before they are consummated. This opens a window of opportunity for the non-proliferation regime, and a window of vulnerability for the potential proliferant.

NUCLEAR LEAKAGE ELIMINATES THE FISSILE MATERIAL CHOKEPOINT. When fissile material itself is for sale, the traditional source of leverage on the nonproliferation challenge disappears. If Iraq or North Korea had been able to buy fissile material when they began their nuclear programs, they would have nuclear weapons now. Furthermore, even if they chose to develop a domestic means of producing fissile material for the longer term, the interim nuclear capability based on purchased fissile material could protect them during the period of vulnerability.

In short, nuclear leakage enables states to leap over the hardest part of acquiring nuclear weapons: accumulating weapons quantities of fissile material. Hence, it represents an enormous opportunity to any aspiring proliferant. States that relied entirely on nuclear leakage as the basis of their nuclear capability — that is, states that lacked an indigenous weapons program of their own — would, of course, have a very circumscribed capability, but they would still have nuclear weapons. States that used nuclear leakage to supplement an indigenous nuclear weapons program could protect themselves in the short term while, over the longer term, developing a more substantial, flexible, and maintainable nuclear force.

Iran may be following just such a dual path toward nuclear weapons capability. In deals with Russia and China, it seeks to buy nuclear reactors capable of producing weapons-usable plutonium. These reactors would allow Iran to develop, over the long term, a nuclear arsenal analogous to Pakistan's, India's, or even Israel's. Their operation would also train a cohort of physicists and nuclear engineers and generate a nuclear infrastructure, both of which could be indirectly used to support a weapons program based on purchased or stolen fissile material.

NUCLEAR LEAKAGE MAY CREATE INCENTIVES TO PROLIFERATE

The current world is one in which most states have promised not to possess nuclear weapons; the path to nuclear acquisition is slow, difficult, expensive, and potentially dangerous; the number of aspiring proliferants is small; and the success of their nuclear acquisition efforts uncertain. In this world, there is little incentive for most states to reconsider their decision to forgo nuclear weapons. This picture could change dramatically if nuclear leakage becomes large-scale and commonplace, producing a rapid burst of proliferation.

There are at least four major reasons why nuclear leakage is likely to affect states' decisions on proliferation questions. First, states thought to desire nuclear weapons (Iran, Iraq, North Korea, Libya, and Syria, for instance) would be able to have them in relatively short order. Neighbors of these states — Turkey, Japan, and Saudi Arabia, for example — would undoubtedly feel compelled to rethink their position on the possession of nuclear weapons; it would not be surprising if some decided that a nuclear weapons capability was necessary. Second, should the nuclear floodgates open and proliferation become widespread, those states (such as Ukraine, Taiwan, and South Korea) that have forsaken nuclear weapons, out of a concern that flouting the widely-held international norm against proliferation would damage alliance relationships and lead to international opprobrium, might recalculate, thinking that the international norm had been weakened or destroyed. Third, states that could not have nuclear weapons for the foreseeable future because they lack the financial or technical resources to obtain them might see an irresistible window of opportunity to obtain them via nuclear leakage. Fourth, in the face of widespread proliferation, states that aspire to great power or regional power status (such as Germany, Japan, or Turkey) might reconsider their decisions to renounce nuclear weapons. It is one thing to remain non-nuclear in a world where nonproliferation is the norm, quite another to remain so in a world in which numbers of smaller powers possess nuclear weapons.

A world of many nuclear powers is not an inevitable consequence of nuclear leakage, but it is a distinctly possible one. The more nuclear leakage fuels additional nuclear proliferation, the more likely it is that a wider circle of states will perceive incentives to acquire nuclear weapons.

NUCLEAR LEAKAGE INCREASES THE RISK OF NUCLEAR TERRORISM

Nuclear terrorism has been a source of concern since the beginning of the nuclear age and is certainly not an artifact of the post–Cold War, post-

Soviet era.[5] The possibility of the theft or illicit sale of nuclear weapons or fissile materials has always existed.[6] But never before has there been such acute concern about the security of thousands of nuclear weapons and enormous quantities of fissile material. The possibility that nuclear leakage from Russia will create a nuclear black market accessible to non-state actors as well as states has led to unprecedented, if underappreciated, risks of nuclear terrorism.[7]

During the Cold War, when the security of nuclear assets was not a grave concern, acquiring nuclear weapons required a substantial infrastructure devoted to producing fissile material. As we have seen, meeting this requirement was a challenge to the resources of most states. There was no concern that terrorist groups would be able to proceed successfully down this path.

Nuclear leakage would eliminate the primary barrier to nuclear terrorism because it divorces nuclear acquisition from the industrial capacity of states.[8] If a nuclear black market materializes, nuclear weapons or fissile material could be available to anyone who is able to pay the price. Obviously, the most efficient shortcut to nuclear terrorism is available if terrorists are able to purchase or steal nuclear weapons. But access to fissile material would also put terrorists over the most difficult hurdle in acquiring nuclear weapons. Substantial nuclear leakage from Russia would mean that, for the first time, non-state actors could have ready access to fissile material. Since fissile material is more vulnerable to theft

---

5. See, for example, Thomas C. Schelling, "Who Will Have the Bomb?," *International Security*, Vol. 1, No. 1 (Summer 1976), pp. 77–91; David M. Rosenbaum, "Nuclear Terror," *International Security*, Vol. 1, No. 3 (Winter 1977), pp. 140–161; Brian Jenkins, "Will Terrorists Go Nuclear?" California Seminar on Arms Control and Foreign Policy, Discussion Paper No. 64, October 1975; and Thomas C. Schelling, "Thinking About Nuclear Terrorism," *International Security*, Vol. 6, No. 4 (Spring 1982), pp. 61–77. In 1977, Rosenbaum suggested that "nuclear terrorism may be one of the most important political and social problems of the next fifty years" (p. 141).

6. See, for example, the concerns expressed in Lewis A. Dunn, "Nuclear 'Gray Marketeering'," *International Security*, Vol. 1, No. 3 (Winter 1977), pp. 107–118. Dunn was particularly concerned about the spread of civilian technologies with military implications, but also commented that "The most extreme form of 'gray marketeering' would be the sale, barter, or gift of nuclear weapons or of the 'blueprints' and special nuclear materials for their construction."

7. Specialists have been urging, without great success, that the nuclear terrorism problem be taken more seriously. See, for example, William C. Potter and Leonard S. Spector, "Nuclear Terrorism: The Next Wave?" *New York Times*, December 19, 1994.

8. See, for example, Jenkins, "Will Terrorists Go Nuclear?" p. 4: "The major obstacle to a group of terrorists going nuclear" is "lack of access to the material necessary to manufacture a bomb."

and diversion than are Russian nuclear weapons, leakage of fissile material seems the more likely scenario.

COULD TERRORISTS BUILD A BOMB? If terrorists have access to fissile material, what could they do with it? Could terrorists really make a nuclear weapon? There is an overwhelming consensus that fissile material acquisition is the major obstacle to a simple nuclear weapons capability.[9] And it has long been accepted that, given a sufficient quantity of fissile material, most states could build a simple, reliable nuclear weapon.[10] But there is also a consensus among U.S. weapons designers that many terrorist groups could build a simple nuclear weapon given an adequate supply of fissile material.[11]

A lone terrorist would not be able to fabricate a nuclear weapon, nor would most groups of terrorists or criminals have the technical wherewithal to make nuclear weapons. But *some* terrorist groups will likely be able to do so. After all, some groups that employ terror encompass large numbers of people, many of them educated; they are well organized and highly motivated; they have access to substantial financial resources; and they may have the support of states, or groups within states.[12] Given time

---

9. Michael May, "Nuclear Weapons Supply and Demand," *American Scientist,* Vol. 82 (November–December 1994), pp. 527, 530; Committee on International Security and Arms Control, National Academy of Sciences, *Management and Disposition of Excess Weapons Plutonium* (Washington DC: National Academy Press, 1994), p. 26; U.S. Congress, Office of Technology Assessment, *Technologies Underlying Weapons of Mass Destruction* OTA-BP-ISC-115 (Washington DC: U.S. GPO, December 1993), p. 3; and Peter Zimmerman, "Technical Barriers to Nuclear Proliferation," in Zachary Davis and Benjamin Frankel, eds., "The Proliferation Puzzle: Why Nuclear Nations Spread (and What Results)," *Security Studies,* Vol. 2, Nos. 3–4 (Spring/Summer 1993), pp. 345–356. See especially the "Note Added in Proof" on p. 356: "Should a nation determined to build a nuclear weapon quickly be able to purchase the fissile material, the costs for its project would probably plummet, and the time needed to construct its first weapon might decrease from years to months or weeks."

10. See, for example, Schelling, "Who Will Have the Bomb?" p. 83.

11. J. Carson Mark, Theodore Taylor, Eugene Eyster, William Maraman, and Jacob Wechsler, "Can Terrorists Build Nuclear Weapons?" in Paul Leventhal and Yonah Alexander, eds., *Preventing Nuclear Terrorism: The Report and Papers of the International Task Force on Prevention of Nuclear Terrorism* (Lexington, Mass.: Lexington Books, 1987), pp. 55–65.

12. See Steven Emerson, "The Other Fundamentalists," *The New Republic,* June 12, 1995, pp. 21–30, for an illustrative account of how well organized extremist Islamic groups are in the United States. Emerson says of Hamas, for example, that it has a "sophisticated infrastructure, complete with charitable, political, social, and even military wings." Its military network in the United States is described as "elaborate and sophisticated" (p. 25). On the risk that terrorists will gravitate to weapons of mass

and fissile material, such a group would be capable of producing a nuclear weapon, especially if it had a little help.

Nuclear weapons, after all, are a fifty-year old technology. The basic concepts are simple and well known. (See Appendix B to this volume.) While it is true that the very advanced thermonuclear weapons produced by the former Soviet Union and the United States involve extremely sophisticated technology, weapons can also be designed very simply. Many groups could build devices similar to the simple bombs dropped on Hiroshima and Nagaski. Furthermore, much has changed since 1945. Science has progressed, secrets have been declassified, military technologies have developed commercial uses, American universities have trained nuclear physicists and nuclear engineers from all over the world, and personal computers give even individuals computational capabilities undreamed of at the time of the Manhattan Project. College professors write textbooks that would have won Nobel Prizes fifty years ago, governments publish primers on simple nuclear weapon design, and companies sell neutron sources for commercial purposes.[13]

None of this means that building a nuclear weapon is trivially easy; it is not. But neither is it so mysterious and difficult that it would be impossible for a large terrorist group. By far the hardest part of acquiring nuclear weapons is gaining access to fissile material. Once fissile material is available, as it could be if nuclear leakage from Russia grows worse, nuclear weapons may become available to any group determined to have them and able to gather a modicum of technical expertise.

Gathering such expertise should not be a major obstacle, even leaving aside the possibility that expertise will also leak from Russia. As one analysis put it nearly twenty years ago, "People with the skills needed to build crude nuclear weapons are easily found in the general technical community. . . . There are thousands of people around the world with sufficient nuclear experience and tens of thousands of people with the appropriate skills in physical chemistry and explosives. Thus, most established organizations, given enough time, should be able to acquire appropriate people."[14] This is, if anything, probably even more true today than

---

destruction, see Robert Wright, "Be Very Afraid: Nukes, Nerve Gas, and Anthrax Spores," *The New Republic*, May 1, 1995, pp. 19–27.

13. On some of these points see Tom Clancy and Russell Seitz, "Five Minutes Past Midnight — and Welcome to the Age of Proliferation," *The National Interest*, No. 26 (Winter 1991/1992), pp. 3–12.

14. Rosenbaum, "Nuclear Terror," pp. 142–143. And see, for example, Jenkins, "Will Terrorists Go Nuclear?" p. 4: "Over one million persons are reported to have been trained in handling, moving, or operating nuclear weapons. The number of persons

it was twenty years ago, given the general spread of technology, the larger number of civil and military nuclear programs around the world, the increasing technical and industrial capacities of larger numbers of countries, and the mounting number of foreign scientists and engineers trained in the United States and other industrial countries. Moreover, the required number of such people is not large. As few as three to six people with requisite skills could make a nuclear weapon.[15]

SIMPLE NUCLEAR WEAPONS ARE NOT THAT DIFFICULT TO MAKE. The existence of simple designs for nuclear weapons is what puts nuclear weapons within the reach of terrorist organizations that are able to obtain fissile material. The enormous nuclear complexes of the United States or the former Soviet Union were necessary to design and produce the tens of thousands of sophisticated thermonuclear weapons that populated their arsenals during the Cold War. But terrorists would need only one or two crude devices to serve their purposes. They would undoubtedly pursue the simplest and least challenging design paths to nuclear acquisition.

The simplest way to build a nuclear weapon uses an assembly which, in principle, is nothing more than an elaborate cannon. This is known as a gun-type weapon. Such a design starts with a gun barrel. At one end of the barrel is a "bullet" of HEU. At the other end of the barrel is a larger HEU "target," screwed onto the barrel like a silencer is screwed onto the muzzle of a pistol. The bullet is fired toward the target in the same way that a cannon shell is fired in an artillery tube. The bullet rapidly accelerates to a velocity of about one thousand feet per second.[16] When it hits the target, the two pieces of HEU form a supercritical mass, and a neutron source is used to start a fast chain reaction in the HEU that releases enormous amounts of energy: an atomic explosion.

The gun-type design dates from the early days of the Manhattan

---

worldwide who have the technical expertise necessary to manufacture a crude nuclear bomb is estimated to be in the tens of thousands. Indeed, according to a recent television documentary, a bomb could be designed by a bright graduate student at MIT."

15. Mark, et al., "Can Terrorists Build Nuclear Weapons?" p. 58, say three or four is the smallest team capable of making a nuclear weapon. Schelling, "Thinking About Nuclear Terrorism," p. 64, uses the number six, citing physicist Hans Bethe's estimate of the smallest team necessary to design a bomb.

16. On required assembly velocities in a gun bomb using HEU see Robert Serber, *The Los Alamos Primer: The First Lectures on How To Build An Atomic Bomb* (Berkeley: University of California Press, 1992), pp. 56–57. A very simple gun capable of accelerating a 100-pound HEU projectile to 1000 feet per second need not weigh more than 600–700 pounds nor exceed six feet in length.

Project. From the beginning of the U.S. nuclear weapons program during World War II, it was assumed that the gun-type assembly would form the basis of the first nuclear weapons. Indeed, the design was so simple that the pacing item was the development of technology to enrich uranium in the isotope U-235. Other than the fissile material, the materials required to assemble a simple nuclear weapon of this type are not hard to obtain. The gun barrel could be ordered from any ordnance factory, as could a tungsten tamper machined to any specifications the customer desired. The charge for firing the bullet could also be fashioned by anyone with access to sophisticated firing charges and some experience in handling them.

The basic information necessary to design a simple fission weapon is available in the open literature, and has been for many years. Designers of U.S. weapons have been repeating this basic truth over and over again since the early 1970s when John Foster, a former director of the Lawrence Livermore nuclear weapons laboratory, stated that "the only difficult thing about making a fission bomb of some sort is the preparation of a supply of fissile material of adequate purity; the design of the bomb itself is relatively easy."[17] For those who still doubt the credibility of such claims, despite the credentials of their authors, it is perhaps useful to look at the problem from another angle. Would it be safe to assume that a terrorist group did not have a crude weapon if it was discovered that the group had possessed 200 pounds of HEU for a year? Who would give the president of the United States the briefing that said he need not worry about this, since only states can make and deliver nuclear weapons? What kind of reception would such a briefing receive? Viewed from this perspective, the answer seems obvious: one would have to assume at least a crude nuclear-weapons capability, and even crude weapons are weapons of mass destruction.

The first nuclear weapon used in anger was an HEU gun-type weapon called "Little Boy," which detonated over Hiroshima with a yield equivalent to 15,000 tons of TNT, or 15 kilotons.[18] Though the first and

---

17. John Foster, "Nuclear Weapons," *Encyclopedia Americana*, Vol. 20 (New York: Americana Corporation, 1973), pp. 520–522; see also Chapter 2, "Nuclear Weapons" in Mason Willrich and Theodore Taylor, *Nuclear Theft: Risks and Safeguards* (Cambridge, Mass.: Ballinger Publishing Company, 1974), pp. 5–28, especially p. 6: "If the essential nuclear materials are at hand, it is possible to make an atomic bomb using information that is available in the open literature."

18. Thomas Cochran and Christopher Paine, *The Role of Hydronuclear Tests and Other Low-Yield Nuclear Explosions and Their Status Under a Comprehensive Test Ban*, Nuclear Weapons Databook (Washington DC: Natural Resources Defense Council, March 1995), p. 4.

simplest nuclear weapon design, gun-type weapons have continued to be utilized in various ways by nuclear-armed states. South Africa's nuclear weapons, for example, used this design and its weapons had an expected yield of 10–18 kilotons.[19] Similarly, gun-type weapons of quite simple design were used in eight-inch artillery shells by the United States beginning in the early 1950s.[20] In short, gun-type designs for fission weapons may be old and simple, but they are perfectly serviceable for those whose requirement is not a modern, sophisticated thermonuclear arsenal but any functional nuclear weapon.

One limitation of the gun-type weapon is that it can only be built with HEU. For technical reasons, it is impractical to use plutonium in gun-type designs.[21] Hence, the Manhattan Project of fifty years ago came up with a second, implosion-based design. The implosion weapon was intended to exploit plutonium, which can be produced more easily than enriched uranium, though the implosion design can use HEU as well.[22] In a simple implosion weapon, like the one used on Nagasaki ("Fat Man"), the fissile material is formed into a single, solid sphere, surrounded by a tamper/reflector shell, and enclosed by a high-explosive jacket. When the high-explosive jacket is detonated, it implodes the fissile sphere, compressing it inward, and rapidly creates a supercritical mass out of a subcritical mass.

Two aspects of this design are significant compared to a gun-assembly weapon. First, because the implosion compresses the fissile core, less fissile material is required to form a supercritical mass. Simple HEU implosion weapons require only about 30 pounds of HEU to match the

---

19. David Albright, "South Africa and the Affordable Bomb," *Bulletin of the Atomic Scientists,* Vol. 50, No. 4 (July/August 1994), pp. 44–45.

20. Thomas B. Cochran, William M. Arkin, and Milton M. Hoenig, *Nuclear Weapons Databook,* Vol. I: *U.S. Nuclear Forces and Capabilities* (Cambridge, Mass.: Ballinger, 1984) pp. 47–48.

21. Several different isotopes of plutonium are produced in a reactor and these isotopes cannot be easily separated from each other. One of the plutonium isotopes, Pu-240, prevents the use of a gun-assembly design: Pu-240 nuclei fission spontaneously and emit neutrons at a rate that makes it likely that a gun assembly weapon would "pre-initiate," or fizzle.

22. Plutonium is a byproduct of irradiating uranium fuel in nuclear reactors. After several months in a reactor, the irradiated fuel will contain plutonium. By a relatively simple chemical process, plutonium can be separated from the reactor fuel. This is a simpler technology than uranium enrichment. Uranium isotope separation is generally a more complex scientific, engineering, and industrial undertaking. Indeed, Neils Bohr, the noted Danish physicist and discoverer of the fissile isotope U-235, did not believe that isotope separation was possible in practice until he saw the U.S. Oak Ridge facility in 1944.

15-kiloton yield of Little Boy. Because plutonium is a more efficient fissile material than HEU, only 12 pounds was necessary to give Fat Man a 20-kiloton yield. Second, an implosion design can use plutonium because it assembles a supercritical mass very rapidly, meaning that there is a substantially lower chance of pre-initiation than would be the case if a gun-type design were used.

The reduction in fissile material requirements and the possibility of plutonium use that an implosion design allows comes at the price of a more complex design. The implosion must be symmetrical and the high explosive jacket must be uniform in its effects when it implodes, which means that the firing system must detonate the jacket simultaneously at about fifty points spaced uniformly about its exterior. Though complicated, such a firing system can be perfected through a series of instrumented non-nuclear implosion tests using non-fissile heavy metal cores. This increase in complexity does not put a crude implosion design beyond the reach of a terrorist or organized crime group.[23] Thus, in return for a small but manageable increase in complexity, an implosion design allows designers to use fissile materials that would not be feasible in a gun-type design, such as plutonium of any isotopic composition and uranium of less than the highest levels of enrichment in U-235.[24]

Fat Man was about the same length and weight as Little Boy, but was much wider. However, these first bombs, developed during World War II, were conservatively designed and hence much bigger and heavier than necessary. Like Little Boy, Fat Man was designed to be dropped from a

---

23. In fact, a distinguished group of U.S. weapons designers, in asking whether terrorists could convert fissile material into crude bombs, began their discussion with an analysis of whether a small group could build an implosion weapon using reactor-grade plutonium. They did not consider the question of whether non-state actors could make simple implosion weapons using weapons grade plutonium worth discussing, since the answer, at least to them, was so obviously affirmative. Mark, et al., "Can Terrorists Build Nuclear Weapons?" pp. 60–61.

24. Ibid., p. 61. Advocates of plutonium use for civilian power generation often argue that only plutonium enriched to more than 90 percent in the isotope Pu-239 can be used in a weapon. See, for example, Ryukichi Imai, "Can University Students Make an Atomic Bomb?" *Plutonium* (Tokyo: Council for Nuclear Fuel Cycle, Winter 1995), pp. 2–8. This contention has been authoritatively rebutted in J. Carson Mark, "Explosive Properties of Reactor-Grade Plutonium," *Science & Global Security*, Vol. 4, No. 1 (1993), pp. 111–124. Others make the same claim about HEU, i.e., that it is useful for weapons only if it is enriched above 90 percent in U-235. See, for example, Jane Perlez, "Radioactive Material Seized in Slovakia; 9 Under Arrest," *Boston Globe*, April 22, 1995, p. 4. Others correctly note that HEU enriched to more than 90 percent is desirable for weapons, but not necessary. See Reuters, "Nuclear Contraband Intercepted," *New York Times*, April 22, 1995, p. 13.

bomber and had an extremely heavy, bullet-proof aerodynamic casing that dramatically added to its weight. An equally devastating truck bomb could be much smaller and lighter. Fat Man was also highly conservative in its use of high explosives to ensure optimal assembly of a supercritical mass. High explosives constituted almost half its weight and most of its internal volume. Relatively simple and straightforward design changes could reduce the size and weight without reducing yield and reliability or increasing design complexity.[25]

In sum, there is considerable public knowledge about relatively simple nuclear weapon designs that are straightforward enough to be within the reach of some terrorist groups. Moreover, unlike the United States and the Soviet Union during the Cold War, a terrorist or criminal organization will probably not be very concerned about the efficiency or storage life of the weapon design, the scale and predictability of the yield, or maximizing yield per unit of fissile material. Any ability to produce a nuclear explosion will give a terrorist the capacity to make threats or inflict harm far beyond anything yet experienced in the context of terrorism. As one expert puts it, "Even a weapon that is poorly constructed or is made of a large amount of lower-grade uranium could be a very messy and inefficient but incredibly destructive bomb."[26] Indeed, even a weapon that would be regarded as a dud by a U.S. weapons designer, because it did not perform to predicted effectiveness and produced only a "fizzle yield," could still, under many circumstances, produce a yield measured in kilotons. To put it more vividly, a nuclear "dud" could easily be one hundred times more powerful than the 2-ton bomb that exploded in Oklahoma City.[27] In a world in which fissile material is widely available, nuclear terrorism will be a significant and all-too-plausible worry.

LEAKAGE OF EXPERTISE CAN CONTRIBUTE TO NUCLEAR TERRORISM. The problem is compounded by a further disturbing consideration. Not only fissile material, but everything else having to do with nuclear weapons, may be available at the nuclear bazaar: expertise, secrets, design information, other weapon components, and so on. As noted in Chapter 1, Russian

---

25. This could be achieved simply by adding a beryllium reflector and several pounds of plutonium to the core, and by cutting the size and weight of the implosion assembly mechanism in half.

26. Mozley, *Uranium Enrichment and Other Technical Problems Relating to Nuclear Weapons Proliferation*, p. 4.

27. Published estimates of the Oklahoma City bomb indicate a yield equivalent to 2.5 tons of TNT. See Randolph Ryan, "Pentagon is Said to Seek Narrower Definition of Atom Test," *Boston Globe*, June 11, 1995.

sources cite hundreds of instances in which personnel in the Russian nuclear complex attempted to walk off with classified materials. There are thousands of people in the Russian nuclear complex with knowledge and experience and expertise that could be of value to a group or a state seeking to build a nuclear weapon. Thus, one cannot exclude the possibility that terrorists will be able to acquire both fissile material and the technical expertise to transform that material into nuclear weapons. Indeed, with expert assistance, terrorists might be able to produce not only crude weapons, but even more sophisticated varieties, enabling them to build smaller, more efficient bombs.[28] This is a further reason why nuclear leakage in the former Soviet Union may fuel nuclear terrorism.

NUCLEAR LEAKAGE THREATENS THE NON-PROLIFERATION REGIME
Because a heavily proliferated world is so deeply unattractive, the U.S. government has long held that the health and perpetuation of the nuclear non-proliferation regime (and other regimes restraining the spread of weapons of mass destruction) is a matter of great concern to the United States. Indeed, now that the Soviet threat has receded, the dangers associated with proliferation top the list of American security concerns. As the Department of Defense has stated, "the United States must be prepared to face new threats to its people and its interests. Of these dangers, the one that most urgently and directly threatens American interests is the proliferation of weapons of mass destruction."[29] Accordingly, the United States worked hard to ensure the permanent extension of the NPT and to address specific nuclear proliferation problems, such as North Korea and Iran.

Such efforts are necessary and commendable, but they will be insufficient if nuclear weapons or fissile materials leak out of Russia or the former Soviet Union in large quantities. The international nonproliferation regime is built upon the difficulty in obtaining weapons-quantities of fissile material; that has been the choke point that makes it hard for aspiring proliferants to produce nuclear weapons. Given an adequate supply of fissile material (10 to 25 kilograms, depending on what kind of weapon is to be produced) practically any state or well-organized crimi-

---

28. Mark, et al., "Can Terrorists Build Nuclear Weapons?" pp. 64–65, comment that state-supported terrorists might be able to build more sophisticated devices. Through the leakage of expertise, terrorists can, in effect, draw on the resources of the nuclear complex of the former Soviet Union.

29. Office of the Deputy Secretary of Defense, *Report on Nonproliferation and Counterproliferation Activities and Programs*, Washington, D.C., May 1994, p. 2.

nal or terrorist organization could fashion a primitive nuclear device that would detonate with the force of thousands of tons of TNT. The easy availability of fissile material would allow states or even non-state organizations to develop small nuclear arsenals quickly and secretly.

As we have seen, the large-scale leakage of fissile material from Russia or the former Soviet Union would provide a tremendous short cut to aspiring nuclear states; it would provide an end run around the international nonproliferation regime for potential proliferants that have been stymied until now by the current denial of fissile material production technologies. Large scale leakage would also enable the development of nuclear devices by non-state actors or by rogue organizations for the first time in the nuclear age. In all of these cases, as well as many others, the availability of fissile material, even at high prices, could transform desire for nuclear weapons into reality in short order.

Hence, a substantial flow of fissile material out of Russia or other former Soviet Union states would pose a significant, if not fatal, threat to the nonproliferation regime. This is true even though the NPT has now been indefinitely extended, even if the sale of Russian reactors to Iran is overturned, and even if the negotiations over the North Korean nuclear program are successful. Widespread success in other realms of nonproliferation policy would not compensate for the damage done by the collapse of the Russian nuclear custodial system. Large-scale nuclear leakage would result in loss of, or severe damage to, the international nonproliferation regime, an instrument that serves American interests. As we shall see below, the consequences for U.S. security, and the security of America's allies, could be devastating. Fissile material security in the former Soviet Union should be a prime concern for the international community.

New Nuclear Threats Jeopardize Vital U.S. Interests

How much does it matter to the United States that there is a considerable risk of nuclear leakage from Russia? What difference does it make to the United States that nuclear leakage from Russia could promote nuclear proliferation and boost nuclear terrorism? Judging by the complacency of the public and the unwillingness of Congress to invest more than a tiny fraction of the defense budget to help address this problem, one would conclude that this risk is of no great moment to the United States, that the stakes are low, and that U.S. interests are not centrally engaged. But that conclusion is profoundly misguided.

The United States confronts a new and different sort of nuclear threat. This threat is immediate and urgent. It consists of the possibility that leakage of nuclear weapons or fissile material from Russia will undermine the nonproliferation regime, fuel the spread of nuclear weapons, and generate unaccustomed but dangerous and potentially intractable nuclear threats to vital American interests.

There are at least three vital interests at stake: the security of the continental United States; the safety of U.S. forces deployed or sent overseas; and the security of allies and friends such as South Korea, Israel, and the European allies. The most direct and arresting new challenge that might arise as a result of nuclear leakage is the threat that nuclear weapons would be smuggled into the United States by unconventional means and used for nuclear blackmail or to inflict terror on a vast scale against American cities. Such a scenario is not implausible in a world where those hostile to the United States have ready access to Russian nuclear weapons or Russian fissile material. This threat is at least as likely as was the threat of a nuclear exchange between the United States and the Soviet Union during the Cold War, and deserves to be taken just as seriously.

Current national security policies are focused on preparing to fight two major regional contingencies, on persuading potential new nuclear nations to abandon attempts to develop or obtain reactors or enrichment technologies, and on developing counterproliferation measures to deal with new nuclear nations. These are important issues, but they are dwarfed by the danger that the trickle of fissile materials out of Russia and the former Soviet Union might become a torrent. The damage to American vital interests should the nuclear leakage problem grow more severe is such that coping with this problem ought to be regarded as another contingency that U.S. defense policy should be equally prepared to meet.

THE THREAT OF NUCLEAR DETONATION IN THE UNITED STATES
Imagine that the next truck bomb that goes off in New York or Oklahoma City is a nuclear weapon. Is this just a morbid but unrealistic fantasy? Unfortunately, this scenario becomes all too plausible if nuclear weapons or nuclear materials begin to flow out of Russia in significant quantities.[30] Many of the states and terrorists that may be shopping in the Russian nuclear bazaar are deeply hostile to the United States. Such adversaries have shown no reluctance to engage in terrorism against the United States, nor have they shown qualms about striking civilian targets and

---

30. "As horrible as the tragedies in Oklahoma City and the World Trade Center were, imagine the destruction that could have resulted had there been a small-scale nuclear device exploded there." "Remarks by the President at U.S. Air Force Academy Graduation Ceremony," Office of the Press Secretary, The White House, May 31, 1995, p. 5.

harming innocent people.[31] The acquisition of one or more nuclear weapons by such enemies immediately and massively increases the threat that they pose to the United States and the urgency and difficulty of dealing with them. The intense reaction of the United States to the small and incipient North Korean nuclear program is a clear indication of the impact nuclear leakage could have on American perceptions and policy.

DELIVERY AGAINST THE UNITED STATES IS POSSIBLE. If rogue states or terrorist groups make bombs from leaked fissile material, could these weapons actually be delivered against targets in the United States? Unfortunately, the challenge of bringing nuclear materials into the United States and there to fabricate weapons is not great. In part, this is true for some of the same reasons that it is not difficult to get fissile material out of Russia: dangerous quantities of fissile material are small, safe, and easily portable. But several other factors also come into play.

First, America's borders are porous. The volume of people and commodities that flow through the legal points of entry into the United States is enormous and largely uninspected. There are 301 ports of entry and fewer than 10,000 customs inspectors, that is, roughly thirty inspectors per port of entry, none of whom are trained or equipped to detect nuclear materials. Each day, roughly 1.25 million people arrive in the United States. Each day, some 1.36 billion kilograms of cargo from abroad arrive by sea at U.S. ports and 4.66 million kilograms arrive by air. Fewer than 5 percent of the entries into the United States are physically inspected, and then only after they have arrived at ports in or near major U.S. cities.[32] Given the size of the daily inflow of people and material into the United States, the U.S. Customs Service cannot prevent the entry of fissile material and other weapon components.

A case in June 1995 involving black market activity in specialized material for nuclear reactors illustrates the point. Seven tons of zirconium, a metal used as cladding for nuclear fuel, was brought from Ukraine into the United States, from which it was intended to be shipped to Iraq in violation of the trade embargo against Iraq. Five tons of the zirconium was discovered in a warehouse in Queens, New York. As an FBI agent commented, "That an ordinary warehouse in Woodside, Queens, could

31. For a general discussion of America's vulnerability to terrorism, see Stephen Sloan, "Terrorism: How Vulnerable is the United States?" in Stephen C. Pelletiere, *Terrorism: National Security Policy and the Home Front* (Carlisle, Penn.: U.S. Army War College Strategic Studies Institute, May 1995), pp. 61–76. So-called "super-terrorism" involving weapons of mass destruction is discussed in ibid., pp. 72–74.

32. Figures from private communication, U.S. Customs Service, May 15, 1995.

be used as a trans-shipment point for five tons of nuclear-grade zirconium, originating in Ukraine and destined for Iraq, should serve as a wake-up call as to the ease with which such material is available."[33] While this episode did not involve fissile material, it does suggest the difficulty of preventing the influx of sensitive or dangerous material into the United States. If seven tons of zirconium can be brought illegally into the United States, how likely is it that seven pounds, or 70 pounds, of plutonium can be stopped? And had the seven tons been plutonium or HEU rather than zirconium, it would have been many hundreds of weapons' worth of fissile material.

Moreover, those trying to smuggle nuclear weapons or the materials to make them into the United States need not choose legal points of entry. There is ample evidence that illegal entry into the United States is possible. For example, strenuous efforts have failed to keep either drugs or illegal immigrants out of the United States.[34] At most, 10 percent of the flow of drugs is seized by government agents (though even this estimate is little more than a guess since no one knows the aggregate total of drugs smuggled into the United States every year).[35] There is no reason why a nuclear weapon is less likely to make it into the United States than a bale of marijuana, a packet of heroin, or a farm worker from Latin America. If nuclear terrorists are as successful at smuggling as drug dealers, the United States will have a terrible problem on its hands.

---

33. Grant McCool, "Three Held in Alleged Nuclear Black Market Deal," *Washington Post*, June 9, 1995.

34. For a discussion of the illegal flow of criminal activity across international boundaries, see "Transnational Crime: A New Security Threat?" in IISS, *Strategic Survey, 1994–1995*, pp. 25–33. The internationalization of organized crime is discussed in Phil Williams, "Transnational Criminal Organizations: Strategic Alliances," *The Washington Quarterly*, Vol. 18, No. 1 (Winter 1995), pp. 57–72; the implications of international crime for international security are treated in Phil Williams, "Transnational Criminal Organizations and International Security," *Survival*, Vol. 36, No. 1 (Spring 1994), pp. 96–113. The failure of U.S. efforts to prevent the flow of drugs into the United States makes this a perennial issue on the U.S. policy agenda. See, for example, House Committee on Judiciary, Subcommittee on Crime and Criminal Justice, *International Drug Supply, Control, and Interdiction* (Washington DC: U.S. GPO, 1994). Reflecting the extent of U.S. efforts to prevent international drug smuggling is a recent compilation of international agreements on that subject that runs more than 700 pages. See U.S. Congressional Research Service, *International Narcotics Control and U.S. Foreign Policy: A Compilation of Laws, Treaties, Executive Documents, and Related Materials* (Washington DC: U.S. GPO, 1994). The literature on the international "war on drugs" is vast. One recent example is T.J. Dunn, *The Militarization of the U.S.-Mexico Border: Low Intensity Conflict Doctrine Comes Home* (Austin: University of Texas, 1995).

35. Williams, "Transnational Criminal Organizations and International Security," p. 102.

Second, detection of nuclear weapons or fissile material is not easy. Technologies designed to detect nuclear materials operate over very short ranges and are used only at secure storage facilities and by a few special search teams. Some materials in nuclear weapons can be detected at a range of 30–300 feet using existing technologies, but only if the material is not shielded.[36] If drug dealers are willing and able to ship cocaine in lead ingots,[37] it would be foolish to assume that nuclear smugglers cannot similarly find ways of shielding their goods. In any event, sensors capable of detecting nuclear materials are absent from U.S. ports of entry. Moreover, some nuclear weapons, especially those using HEU, can be designed to be all but undetectable. Thus, to detect a nuclear weapon or component hidden in a freight container, the container must be physically searched by personnel who know what to look for.

Highly enriched uranium is so inert that it has a very low radiation signature and is extremely hard to detect. Outside of a few feet, even the most sophisticated passive radiation detectors would fail to detect HEU. With any kind of shielding, passive detection becomes impossible. Since it is a heavy material, HEU, whether shielded or not, shows up in an X-ray, but it shows up in ways that are indistinguishable from any other dense material, like lead, iron, or steel. Passive sensors are unlikely to be the solution to the nuclear smuggling problem.

There is a different approach to detection, based on active sensors that bombard unshielded HEU with an active radiation source designed to induce fission; the resulting neutron emissions can be detected at ranges of a few feet. However, active radiation detectors that rely on induced fission to detect and identify fissile materials are dangerous to operate near people and they are not — and as a practical matter, they could not be — used at ports of entry in the United States.

X-rays and metal detectors can detect metal but cannot identify it as HEU. HEU can also be shielded from detection by passive radiation detectors that could only identify it upon very close examination. Most international airlines do not X-ray baggage checked at curbside. Even if they did, there currently is no policy requiring that all metal objects flown into the United States on commercial airlines be identified by an X-ray operator, removed from checked or carry-on luggage, and exposed at close range to ultra-sensitive (and expensive) radiation detectors. Nor would such a policy be practical. The density of plutonium is comparable

---

36. Steve Fetter, et al., "Detecting Nuclear Warheads," *Science & Global Security*, Vol. 1, Nos. 3–4 (1990), pp. 225–302.

37. This episode is reported in Williams, "Transnational Criminal Organizations and International Security," p. 102.

to that of HEU, but plutonium is significantly more radioactive than HEU. This makes passive detection of plutonium by sensitive radiation detectors in the absence of heavy shielding more feasible, but the distances involved are still short. Plutonium is no less detectable than HEU by X-rays, but can be induced to emit neutrons, making plutonium more detectable by active detection means. However, if the plutonium were surrounded by a 25-pound tungsten shield, it would weigh no more than and be no more detectable than the HEU component.

Unfortunately, other means of transporting smuggled nuclear materials are even less amenable to serious security measures aimed at preventing fissile material from being smuggled into the United States. Imagine, for example, that five shipping containers with Russian HEU weapon components inside them were stolen by the guards at Tomsk and "exported" from Russia. Inside each of the containers, a buyer could find a solid cylinder of HEU, eight inches long, three inches in diameter, and weighing about 30 pounds: picture a heavy baton. Each cylinder would provide more than enough HEU for a simple Fat Man weapon, and four would provide more than enough for a Little Boy weapon. These five cylinders of HEU could be shipped in five different 40-foot commercial shipping containers. Some 40,000 such commercial containers are routinely stacked up at the SeaLand terminal in Bayonne, New Jersey. Only about 5 percent of these are opened before they clear customs, and the ones that are opened receive only cursory inspection. Needless to say, there is no policy to run all the metal that passes through Bayonne through a radiation detector.

The story is not much different for plutonium. If, for example, the five containers stolen from Tomsk contained plutonium weapon components, the effect on delivery probabilities would differ only in the details. Each of the plutonium components would be in the form of a hollow, spherical shell weighing about 10 pounds. The diameter of the outside surface of the sphere would be about four inches, and the shell wall would be about one inch thick: picture a heavy tennis ball. The surface of the plutonium would have a thin layer of nickel, aluminum, or steel plating or cladding. Three of these heavy tennis balls would provide enough plutonium to make two simple Fat Man implosion weapons.

Thus, both plutonium and HEU are easy to smuggle and hard to detect. There is no way to make it impossible for fissile material to be smuggled into the United States. At present, in fact, there is only a small risk of detection for smugglers even if they pass through legal ports of entry; any seizure of nuclear material by customs authorities would result from luck as much as anything. Given the huge volume of people and goods that flow into the United States every day, even a large investment of resources is unlikely to render the risk of nuclear smuggling negligible.

Third, the means of delivery are essentially infinite. Americans are accustomed to thinking in terms of long-range bombers and intercontinental missiles, but these will not be the delivery means of choice for terrorists or rogue states. Because they do not possess and cannot afford the intercontinental delivery systems preferred by the nuclear superpowers, they will almost certainly rely on unconventional means of delivery.[38] For example, nuclear weapons could be shipped by sea and exploded in a harbor, or driven by truck to any location in the continental United States. Nuclear weapons or components could be flown into the United States in private aircraft or smuggled across the border on foot. A criminal or terrorist group could even ship a weapon into the United States in pieces small and light enough to go by Federal Express, UPS, or even the postal service. If it possessed enough fissile material for several weapons, such a group could even afford to fail once or twice before getting the material for a weapon into the United States.

Certainly, every effort should be made to police America's borders, but policing will remain imperfect whatever level of resources are invested. The nuclear smuggling threat against the United States depends on the probability of success of an attempt to bring 12 pounds of plutonium or 30 pounds of HEU into the United States. Efforts to detect and interdict nuclear smugglers are extremely unlikely to reduce the likelihood anywhere close to zero. Thus, nuclear leakage must be prevented or kept to an absolute minimum in the first place if this threat is to be avoided.

In sum, there are genuine grounds for concern that, if nuclear leakage makes fissile material available to terrorists, the United States could find itself subjected to new and unorthodox nuclear threats, or worse, experience a nuclear detonation on its territory. Considering this conclusion,

---

38. There is remarkably little literature on unconventional means of delivery, especially in comparison to the attention lavished on other nuclear threats. Even the still remote threat of ballistic missiles in the Third World has a fairly substantial literature associated with it, while next to nothing has been written about a threat that already exists. Some discussion of the unconventional delivery threat can be found in Albert Carnesale, "Defenses Against New Nuclear Threats," in Robert D. Blackwill and Albert Carnesale, eds., *New Nuclear Nations: Consequences for U.S. Policy* (New York: Council on Foreign Relations Press, 1993), pp. 204–209. See also the brief discussion in Robert W. Marrs, "Nuclear Terrorism: Rethinking the Unthinkable," Naval Postgraduate School, December 1994, pp. 66–67. See also Irving Lachow, "GPS-Guided Cruise Missiles and Weapons of Mass Destruction," Lawrence Livermore National Laboratory Director's Series on Proliferation, June 1, 1995.

nuclear leakage ought to be among the small number of highest priorities in American security policy. Nothing is more vital to the United States than protecting its territory and citizens from nuclear attack.

OTHER U.S. INTERESTS ARE THREATENED BY NUCLEAR LEAKAGE
The potential nuclear threat to the continental United States should be all the reason Washington requires to treat nuclear leakage as an issue of utmost importance. But other vital U.S. interests are potentially threatened by nuclear leakage as well. Indeed, since nuclear leakage represents, in effect, simply an easier, quicker path to nuclear proliferation, all of the reasons why the United States regards it as in its interest to strongly oppose nuclear proliferation are reasons for serious concern about nuclear leakage.[39] Indeed, since it is widely believed that nuclear proliferation represents the primary threat to American security in the post–Cold War world, nuclear leakage too ought to be regarded as a major challenge to U.S. interests.

U.S. FORCES DEPLOYED OR SENT ABROAD ARE THREATENED BY NUCLEAR LEAKAGE. In a proliferated world, U.S. forces overseas would be vulnerable to nuclear attack. For example, U.S. forces deployed in defense of South Korea, Japan, Kuwait, or Saudi Arabia could come under nuclear attack if North Korea, Iraq, or Iran succeed in getting nuclear weapons. U.S. military bases and installations abroad could become targets of nuclear terrorists. U.S. intervention forces being sent abroad could be jeopardized by nuclear weapons in the hands of hostile forces. A world of nuclear plenty is not a world congenial to American military power, which is precisely why America's adversaries pursue nuclear weapons.

Many of the military countermeasures necessary to deal with this threat are part of the Clinton administration's counterproliferation initiative. This initiative is sensible and well-conceived, but the challenges facing it are daunting. Imagine, for example, that by the summer of 1990

---

39. For a fuller discussion, see Lewis A. Dunn, "New Nuclear Threats to U.S. Security," in Blackwill and Carnesale, eds., *New Nuclear Nations*, pp. 20–50. A brief but thorough assessment of U.S. interests in preventing proliferation can be found in Jerome H. Kahan, "Nuclear Threats from Small States," Center for Naval Analyses, April 1995, pp. 4–7. Reflecting the wide consensus that proliferation is the major danger confronting the United States is Michael J. Mazarr, *North Korea and the Bomb: A Case Study in Nonproliferation* (New York: St. Martin's Press, 1995), p. 205. Mazarr concludes: "The Secretary of Defense, the Joint Chiefs of Staff, and, it appears, the American people have all identified proliferation as the chief threat facing the United States in the post–Cold War world."

Iraq had designed and built several simple nuclear warheads for its Scud missiles.[40] During Desert Storm, the probability of delivery of a Scud against Israel or Saudi Arabia was essentially equal to its reliability which, fortunately, was low, but this might not be the case in the future. U.S. efforts to destroy Scuds prior to launch and to shoot them down after launch were close to useless.[41] Even if future efforts to counter Scuds became as effective as current U.S. efforts to counter manned aircraft, some leakage is inevitable if the attacker is determined. There are no easy or obvious answers to the military threats that could arise should nuclear leakage lead to nuclear acquisition by forces hostile to the United States.

Consequently, the nuclear leakage issue has enormous implications for U.S. military forces. Failure to contain the nuclear leakage problem would lead to a world of greater operational risks and difficulties; in many conceivable scenarios, one could not employ U.S. forces without exposing them to the possibility of nuclear attack.

NUCLEAR LEAKAGE THREATENS U.S. REGIONAL SECURITY INTERESTS. The challenge to U.S. regional interests posed by nuclear leakage is also great. U.S. allies such as Israel and South Korea are confronted by hostile regional opponents that are actively seeking nuclear weapons. The U.S. stake in the security of these states is high. The prospect of a nuclear-armed Iraq played a large role in U.S. decision-making prior to Desert Storm. The prospect of a nuclear-armed North Korea is a major issue today. In the latter case, an additional concern is the consequence for regional stability in Asia of the nuclear domino effect. South Korea and Japan are easily capable of developing nuclear weapons. U.S. alliance policies there and in Western Europe are motivated partly by a desire to eliminate the nuclear temptations faced by these advanced countries, by keeping their neighborhoods as nuclear-free as possible. Nuclear leakage would guarantee proliferation in a number of areas of regional instability that are now nuclear-free.

Once such proliferation occurs, U.S. interests could be engaged and threatened in a number of ways. Countries that the United States has committed to defend can be threatened or attacked by nuclear weapons. In fulfilling its treaty obligations, the United States could easily be drawn

---

40. This hypothetical scenario is vividly elaborated in Robert D. Blackwill and Albert Carnesale, "Introduction: Understanding the Problem," in Blackwill and Carnesale, *New Nuclear Nations*, pp. 3–19.

41. On the latter point, see Theodore A. Postol, "Lessons of the Gulf War Experience with the Patriot," *International Security*, Vol. 16, No. 3 (Winter 1991/92), pp. 119–171.

into a war that included the use of nuclear weapons, for example, if North Korea were to strike South Korea with nuclear weapons. Regional nuclear wars involving U.S. allies could escalate to draw in the United States, for example, if Israel were to go to war with a nuclear-armed rival.[42] Nuclear use in regional wars could have massive economic consequences. For example, a war in the Persian Gulf area that involved Iran, Iraq, Kuwait, and perhaps Saudi Arabia could enormously disrupt world energy markets and plunge the United States and the industrial world into a severe economic downturn. Thus, directly and indirectly, U.S. interests would be adversely affected should nuclear leakage fuel regional nuclear proliferation.

Conclusion: Nuclear Leakage is a Major Threat

Large-scale nuclear leakage would sweep away the main barriers to nuclear proliferation. Rogue states, terrorists, and criminals would gain access to nuclear weapons or the materials to make them. Major nuclear leakage constitutes a shortcut to a much more proliferated world, considerably more dangerous than the current international environment. Vital American interests would be jeopardized and could be severely damaged. In particular, the threat of nuclear use against U.S. targets would be frighteningly real. Forces hostile to the United States, whether states, terrorists, or criminals, could bring weapons into the United States by unconventional means, and threaten or destroy targets on American territory. Thus, nuclear leakage from Russia can raise the risk of nuclear detonations or nuclear blackmail in the United States. Indeed, although the likelihood of all-out nuclear war has declined as a result of the end of the Cold War, the risk of a nuclear detonation in the United States might well be higher than ever if nuclear terrorists gain access to Russian nuclear materials. Leakage raises stakes for the United States that are enormously important.

During the Cold War, the United States invested hundreds of billions of dollars to insure itself against various "worst-case scenarios" involving Soviet surprise nuclear attacks. What is the worst-case scenario in the context of the nuclear leakage threat? It would involve the full collapse of the Russian nuclear custodial system. This would result in a flood of nuclear weapons, fissile materials, and design expertise into the international black market. This would bring a nuclear weapons capability

---

42.   For a fuller discussion of regional nuclear wars and means of averting them, see Lewis A. Dunn, *Containing Nuclear Proliferation*, Adelphi Paper No. 263 (London: IISS, Winter 1991), pp. 46–58.

within the reach of essentially anyone who had the money to pay for it. Because the supply of weapons and materials would be plentiful, the price, while not likely to be cheap, would not necessarily be exorbitant. In short order, any state that wanted nuclear weapons — Iran, Iraq, North Korea, Libya, Serbia — would be likely to have them. Many other states that practice nuclear abstinence in the context of the present nuclear regime would probably conclude that they too needed nuclear weapons. Terrorist groups would be able to shop at the Russian nuclear bazaar. Consider Hamas with nuclear weapons; the Red Brigade with nuclear weapons; the Islamic Jihad with nuclear weapons; the Chechens with nuclear weapons. This is plausible if Russian nuclear leakage becomes a torrent. The risks to the United States of living in such a world would be great. So it is worth asking: Is the United States doing enough to try to contain the nuclear leakage threat? Is it allocating resources to this problem at a level commensurate with the threat? How much should the United States be prepared to spend to fend off this worst-case scenario?

The answers to these questions are fateful, because the stakes could hardly be higher.

Chapter 3

Response: Inadequacies of American Policy

The risk of nuclear leakage is immediate and urgent. The stakes associated with nuclear leakage are high. These realities should compel the United States (as well as Russia and other interested parties) to undertake strenuous efforts to prevent nuclear leakage from Russia and other former Soviet republics. Indeed, the potential jeopardy to American interests warrants large-scale investments of political capital and financial resources. If a leakage disaster should occur, history will be harsh on those who failed to make every reasonable effort to address the problem while it was still treatable.

Unfortunately, so far U.S. policies and programs have not produced a dramatic reduction in the risk of nuclear leakage. To be sure, a multitude of efforts to address the leakage problem have been made and some progress has been achieved. Many in the Clinton administration and some in Congress have recognized the threat of nuclear leakage and have labored hard to push forward anti-leakage initiatives. Indeed, in 1995, after several years in which very little progress occurred, promising beginnings were made in the implementation of several key anti-leakage programs. As a result, at a handful of nuclear facilities in Russia, security systems have been improved and the vulnerability to theft or diversion of hundreds of pounds of fissile material has been significantly reduced. These are welcome and hard-earned indications that, at long last, steps are being taken in the right direction. Should this pattern continue, the result will be a steady, if gradual, diminution of the nuclear leakage threat — a point which U.S. officials emphasize with justifiable pride, given the difficulties in getting to this point. And no doubt, slow progress is better than no progress.

The problem is that, at the current rate of progress, substantial risk of nuclear leakage will persist for years to come. The fact of progress at some buildings in some Russian nuclear installations is heartening, but most of the relevant Russian facilities are no more secure today than they were when the Soviet Union disappeared; improving the security of hundreds of pounds of fissile material is worthwhile, but the large majority of Russia's vast inventory — tens of thousands of pounds — remains stored under inadequate security at dozens of facilities. By a wide margin, there is more undone than done. As President Clinton's science advisor, John Gibbons, has said of fissile material security in Russia, "the scope of this problem is awesome."[1] Accordingly, America's strong national security interest in reducing the nuclear leakage threat as much as possible as quickly as possible cannot be adequately served by programs advancing at a modest, or even an ordinary, pace. There is an urgent imperative to try to do better. Even the most ardent defenders of existing policies wish it were possible to do more and to move forward more quickly. In short, U.S. policies and programs aimed at reducing the risk of nuclear leakage, extensive and well-intended as they are, have not produced results commensurate with U.S. stakes in the issue: they do too little to remove the risk of serious nuclear leakage and eliminate the possibility of a catastrophic rupture.

Why has this been the case? Responsibility for this state of affairs is shared between Russia and the United States, but it lies most fundamentally in Moscow. No progress can be made if the relevant authorities in Russia are not prepared to acknowledge and address the problem and if they are unwilling to cooperate with the United States in doing so. To date, key players in Russia — particularly including Minatom and its head, Viktor Mikhailov — have been unenthusiastic about and often unwilling to engage in cooperation with the United States to improve nuclear security. In fact, they have been reluctant even to concede that there is a problem (since such acknowledgment amounts to self-condemnation).[2] While Russia's erratic, sluggish, and often unforthcoming responses to U.S. proposals for cooperative programs have not precluded all progress, they have generally meant that progress is slow, small-scale,

---

1. John H. Gibbons, "Managing Nuclear Materials in the Post–Cold War Era," Keynote Address to the Second International Policy Forum: Management and Disposition of Nuclear Weapons Materials, March 22, 1995, p. 1.

2. See, for example, Vladimir Orlov, "Interview with Gennedy Evstafiev, Chief of the Office on Arms Control and the Non-Proliferation of Weapons of Mass Destruction of the Foreign Intelligence Service," *Yaderny Kontrol* (Nuclear control), PIR Center, Moscow, 1995 (English version); Vladimir Orlov, "Interview with Victor Mikhailov, Minister of Atomic Energy for the Russian Federation," *Yaderny Kontrol*, 1995; "Stop Worrying About Nuclear Smuggling," *The Jamestown Foundation Monitor* (e-mail news service), May 31, 1995; and "Moscow Denies Existence of Nuclear Smuggling," *The Jamestown Foundation Monitor*, May 25, 1995.

and arduously achieved — and they cast doubt on the prospects for future progress. Thus, for example, to the extent that Russia has been willing to cooperate with the United States in the area of nuclear security, it has been primarily at the level of individual laboratories and autonomous institutes, not in the sprawling industrial enterprises that are central to the Russian nuclear weapons complex.[3] According to many U.S. officials, the increasingly anti-Western political climate in Russia in general, and Minatom's reluctance to cooperate in particular, suffice to explain the slow progress in improving nuclear security in Russia.

It is indisputable that there is little Washington can do if Russia will not cooperate with the United States to improve nuclear security. But this does not mean that U.S. anti-leakage policies should be exempt from scrutiny or regarded as inherently blameless. Quite the contrary: since the United States cannot directly and unilaterally tackle the nuclear security problem in Russia, one of the primary goals of its policy must be to affect Russian behavior. The United States must attempt to encourage and facilitate the desired steps in Russia. It can do this only by creating incentives that induce Russian authorities to move in the right direction and by providing means that allow them to do so. Thus, while the root of the problem is in Moscow, it is still the case that current U.S. policies have largely failed to meet these objectives. Minatom's recalcitrance suggests that U.S. policy has been insufficient in motivating the required actions on the part of Russia.

Several characteristics of U.S. policy may help explain why this has been true. First, the U.S. Congress has never treated this issue as a high-priority national security problem and hence has never appropriated more than small sums of money to address it — even while insisting that extra billions be spent on the defense budget. Much larger sums, which could easily be justified given U.S. interests in preventing nuclear leakage, might be more effective at motivating and facilitating the desired steps in Russia, but they have simply not been available. Indeed, the Clinton administration has had to battle simply to preserve existing funding levels, even though the amounts involved are a tiny fraction of the defense budget. Second, much of the money appropriated by Congress for addressing this issue has been subject to a web of constraints and conditions that has made it difficult to spend quickly and flexibly, and that has directed most of the money to U.S. contractors and consultants.

---

3. This point is developed in Oleg Bukharin, "Minatom and Nuclear Threat Reduction Activities," paper presented to the conference on the "Nunn-Lugar Cooperative Threat Reduction Program: Donor and Recipient Country Perspectives," Monterey Institute of International Studies, August 20–22, 1995.

Giving contracts to large American firms may be good pork-barrel politics, but not surprisingly it has not had the necessary positive impact on Russian incentives to cooperate. Third, that Congress has treated a critical national security program as if it were just another failing foreign-aid program suggests that the Clinton administration has been unpersuasive in explaining the seriousness of the problem and the extent to which it threatens U.S. interests. Fearful of offending Russian sensibilities, and thereby damaging the prospects for Russian cooperation, the administration has been reluctant to advertise the imperfections and vulnerabilities of the Russian custodial system. Finally, even while pursuing extensive cooperation with Russia on nuclear security, the Clinton administration has pressed other issues — NATO expansion and the Iran reactor deal, for example — that were certain to antagonize many Russians and damage the climate of U.S.-Russian relations. In short, while the Clinton adminstration has tried hard, with some limited successes, to advance a quite comprehensive set of anti-leakage initiatives, it has done so in a manner heavily constrained by Congress and in a worsening political context damaged at least in part by its own policies.

The aim of this chapter is to describe the various and extensive programs aimed at reducing the nuclear leakage threat, to assess their progress, and to explore in greater detail why their progress has been so slow. In the sections that follow, the specific U.S. programs designed to reduce the threat of nuclear leakage from the former Soviet Union are outlined.[4] It is impossible for these accounts to be completely up-to-date, but they do fully convey the range of effort and the rate of progress so far. These programs fall into three broad categories: those intended to improve directly the security of fissile material and nuclear weapons; those designed to halt the accumulation of fissile material or actually dispose of existing material and weapons; and those that aim to increase the transparency of the Russian nuclear complex, which the Clinton administration calls "building confidence through openness." Within these categories, some programs have been unsuccessful, while others have achieved considerable success against long odds.

Overall, however, although the trends are moving in the right direction, the pace is too slow, the serious risk of leakage persists, the potential threat to American interests remains high, a catastrophe is still possible, and the need to fashion more effective policies is both urgent and critically important. In the final section of this chapter, therefore, we analyze in

---

4. These descriptions of U.S. programs draw extensively from interviews with current and former U.S. officials conducted between October 1994 and September 1995.

detail the root causes of the slow progress made in combating the nuclear leakage threat.

Enhancing Nuclear Security: Not There Yet

One of the main sources of the nuclear leakage risk is inadequate security at many Russian facilities that contain nuclear weapons or fissile material. Accordingly, an urgent priority — for both the U.S. and Russian governments — should be to enhance security at facilities where inadequacies exist. While no detailed and authoritative public accounting of the failings of Russian nuclear security has been made available, it appears that security improvements would be desirable in hundreds of buildings at dozens of facilities in Russia. Until security upgrades have been implemented at every inadequate site, the Russian nuclear custodial system will remain vulnerable to nuclear leakage.

The United States has tried to encourage and facilitate improved nuclear security in Russia through a number of sensible initiatives. Unfortunately, the majority of these programs have gotten off to a very slow start. Only in 1995, in fact, did any of the U.S. programs targeted at improving Russian nuclear security begin to show appreciable signs of success. Only a few Russian facilities of concern have been significantly improved, and worrisome vulnerabilities will remain for years to come.

While bureaucratic sluggishness in Washington may account for some of this delay, the largest part of the problem appears to be lack of cooperation from the relevant parties in Russia. It is, however, hardly surprising that enthusiastic cooperation from Minatom has not been forthcoming, since Minatom has little incentive to let American contractors make good money swarming around their facilities, identifying and correcting Minatom's "alleged" security deficiencies, and offering Minatom itself little in the way of direct economic benefit.

Whatever the correct explanation for the meager cooperation so far, by the end of 1995 nothing more than promising beginnings had been made in advancing nuclear security in Russia. Many of the most vulnerable facilities are yet untouched by security enhancement programs, and the largest part of the effort lies ahead. Without an acceleration and expansion of existing initiatives, the nuclear leakage problem will persist. As U.S. Undersecretary of Energy Charles Curtis has observed, until such time as nuclear security in Russia has been improved, "we're going to have to be lucky."[5] There will inevitably be an interim period in which

---

5. Quoted in Matthew L. Wald, "Today's Drama: Twilight of the Nukes," *New York Times*, July 16, 1995.

the potential nuclear threat to the United States is acute. A central goal of U.S. security policy must be to make this period as brief as possible.

The most alarming inadequacies of the Russian nuclear custodial system are those associated with inventories of fissile material located outside the nuclear weapons complex. In addition, the safe and secure storage of nuclear weapons and weapon components on either end of the dismantlement process is another worry. Most of the U.S. programs directed toward the proliferation risks in Russia fall outside the boundaries of the production facilities dedicated to Russia's nuclear fuel cycles and weapons production program, which is managed by the 4th Main Directorate of Minatom and is where the bulk of Russia's fissile material stockpile resides.[6] Rather, what progress has been made by the various U.S. programs has occurred primarily in institutes that are independent of Minatom, such as the Kurchatov Institute, or within Minatom's 5th Main Directorate, which is responsible for nuclear weapons research and development.[7] The distinction between the 4th and 5th Main Directorates is an important one because it makes clear the fact that security improvements in one area of the Russian nuclear complex — its research centers and design labs — will not necessarily translate into similar progress in the fissile material and weapons production facilities. To do this will require a qualitative shift in the U.S. approach to the nuclear leakage problem, one which must recognize and respond to the challenging social and economic needs of Minatom's largest nuclear cities.

In the following section, we survey the U.S. initiatives and programs intended to reduce the risk of nuclear leakage. These programs fall into six categories: those designed to improve fissile material protection, control and accounting (MPC&A); those designed to increase the safety and security of intact nuclear warheads, particularly during transport; those targeting the "brain drain" or otherwise seeking to address the human

---

6. "The 4th Main Directorate and its giant production facilities [Chelyabinsk-65, Tomsk-7, Krasnoyarsk-26, and Sverdlovsk-44] are under much greater economic stress [than the 5th Main Directorate], and have strong dependence on Minatom's political leadership and industrial infrastructure. Managers of the production facilities are less interested in [U.S. cooperative] projects because these projects do not bring tangible benefits, but interfere in day-to-day operations." Bukharin, "Minatom and Nuclear Threat Reduction Activities," p. 5.

7. "The 5th Main Directorate of Minatom is represented by research institutes which are less dependent on Minatom's administrative and production structures, and have diverse technical and intellectual capabilities. The [cooperative] projects [with the United States] stabilize the directorate and its institutes, help to carry out their strategic mission (safety and security of the nuclear arsenal, warhead dismantlement) and to expand work to new areas (safeguards, commercial activities)." Bukharin, "Minatom and Nuclear Threat Reduction Activities," p. 5.

element of the nuclear leakage problem; those that seek to improve the export control capabilities of the former Soviet republics; those that seek to facilitate the creation of a sound nuclear regulatory regime in the former Soviet republics, especially Russia; and those that seek to improve the ability of domestic and foreign law enforcement agencies to combat nuclear smuggling. In concluding this section, we discuss the gaps in the U.S. response, and assess its effect so far.

MATERIAL PROTECTION, CONTROL AND ACCOUNTING: FIRST STEPS FINALLY TAKEN

Material protection, control, and accounting (MPC&A) is one of the greatest weaknesses in the Russian nuclear custodial system, and its improvement is one of the most important non-proliferation tasks on the agenda today. It is a problem both within sites and between them, as there is no site-specific or national system for fissile material tracking in Russia. Most of the known leakage of fissile materials from Russian nuclear installations can be attributed to failures of the Russian MPC&A system.

Until 1996, the U.S. government had two MPC&A programs underway. The first was a Nunn-Lugar program that was carried out at the government-to-government level, which is represented by Minatom in the case of fissile material security. The second was a lab-to-lab program that was initiated by the Los Alamos National Laboratory but is now managed by the Department of Energy. In late 1994, however, the Clinton administration decided to transfer the management of the Nunn-Lugar MPC&A program from the Department of Defense to the Department of Energy, which faces fewer institutional obstacles to successful implementation. The government-to-government and lab-to-lab programs are described separately below.[8]

GOVERNMENT-TO-GOVERNMENT. On September 2, 1993, after over a year of frustrating negotiations, the United States signed a $10 million Nunn-Lugar agreement with the Russian government to assist in the development of a model MPC&A system at the Electrostal fuel fabrication facility outside of Moscow.[9] Both low enriched and highly enriched uranium are fabricated into fuel rods at Electrostal, but at the Russians' insistence, the

8. These accounts are based primarily on interviews with U.S. and Russian officials.

9. Similar but slightly smaller material control and accounting programs are also being run in Kazakhstan and Ukraine.

original MPC&A agreement applied only to the civilian LEU fuel fabrication line.[10]

Not satisfied with an MPC&A effort that focused solely on LEU, the U.S. government decided in early 1994 to allocate another $20 million from the Nunn-Lugar account. The U.S. side proposed to use the money to upgrade the MPC&A at the Sverdlovsk (now called Yekaterinburg) facility for blending HEU to LEU, which would be done on a large scale because of the U.S. plan to purchase 500 tons of Russian HEU over 20 years (described below), and at whichever sites the Russians themselves determined to pose the greatest risk of diversion. To begin these site-specific security evaluations, the U.S. government invited a Russian delegation to visit the Department of Energy's Hanford, Washington, installation to see how the plutonium is secured and accounted for in the United States; this visit took place in July 1994. Reciprocally, a U.S. delegation was invited to the Mayak reprocessing facility at Chelyabinsk-65 to do a sample joint security assessment; this visit took place in October 1994.

Minatom declined, however, to allow the United States to build an MPC&A system at the Sverdlovsk blending facility, or to supply a list of the installations most in need of security upgrades. At the Russian-American summit meeting in Washington in September 1994, however, the Russian government started to show some new flexibility, and offered to allow the United States to assist in the creation of MPC&A systems at three non-military sites that work with large quantities of weapons-usable material: Electrostal (the HEU fuel fabrication line), the Mayak complex at Chelyabinsk-65,[11] and the Institute of Physics and Power Engineering at Obninsk. Since these facilities were on the U.S. government's own classified lists as high-risk Russian installations,[12] it agreed to fund the MPC&A upgrades, but asked to go to three more sites as well: the Luch Scientific Production Association (Podolsk), the Scientific Research Institute for Atomic Reactors (Dmitrovgrad), and the nuclear fuel rod and

---

10. The Russians offered to allow the United States to build model MPC&A systems at the Novosibirsk LEU fuel fabrication line as well as the one at Electrostal. The U.S. government declined to build two such MPC&A systems, because LEU is not a proliferation threat.

11. The British government also has a promising MPC&A program underway at the reactor-grade plutonium reprocessing facility at Chelyabinsk-65.

12. These facilities had in common relatively large amounts (over 200 pounds) of bulk HEU or plutonium, and locations outside of the closed cities of the weapons complex, in which security concerns have historically been taken more seriously than elsewhere in Soviet society.

pellet fabrication plant at Novosibirsk. After further negotiations, the Russians agreed to this expansion of the Nunn-Lugar MPC&A program, though they deferred a final decision on Novosibirsk.

On January 20, 1995, the two states signed a government-to-government agreement on using the $20 million from the Nunn-Lugar fund to improve the MPC&A at Electrostal, Mayak, Obninsk, Podolsk, and Dmitrovgrad.[13] For half a year, however, the Russian government stalled on allowing U.S. specialists to visit these installations to perform the necessary site-security surveys. It was only at the June 1995 meeting of the Gore-Chernomyrdin Commission that Minatom granted the specific approval needed to begin work under the second Nunn-Lugar MPC&A contract.[14] The Russian government's agreement to allow U.S. work to commence at the five new nuclear installations coincided conspicuously with a U.S. offer to make a $100 million advance payment to Minatom under the troubled U.S.-Russian HEU purchase agreement (described in Appendix C).[15]

In the summer of 1994, the Russian side also asked for assistance in establishing a national MPC&A training center at Obninsk, which the U.S. government later agreed to provide from the original $10 million Nunn-Lugar agreement.

In late 1994, responsibility for implementing the two Nunn-Lugar MPC&A agreements was transferred from the Department of Defense to the Department of Energy. This was a sensible change for at least four reasons. First, this shift helped to insulate the MPC&A program from some of the political criticism that the Nunn-Lugar program was then beginning to receive, particularly for spending its money too slowly and for deviating from the original Nunn-Lugar mandate. Second, the Department of Energy is responsible for fissile material security and accounting in the U.S. nuclear complex, so it makes sense that it should also have this responsibility in the former Soviet Union. Third, it was believed — rightly, it has so far turned out — that by being shifted to the Department of Energy, the MPC&A program could avoid most of the more problematic requirements of the Nunn-Lugar program, such as being conditioned

---

13. "Russians Agree to U.S. Help in Protecting Nuclear Facilities," *Open Market Research Institute (OMRI) Daily Digest*, No. 20, Part I (January 27, 1995).

14. U.S. Secretary of Energy Hazel R. O'Leary and Russian Minister of Atomic Energy Viktor Mikhailov, "Joint Statement on Protection, Control and Accounting of Nuclear Materials," June 30, 1995.

15. Numerous U.S. officials have privately expressed their view that the $100 million advance under the HEU deal was pivotal in persuading Minister Mikhailov to allow work to begin under the second Nunn-Lugar MPC&A agreement.

on Russia's arms control compliance, being subject to rigorous audit and inspection, and being required to "buy American" whenever possible.[16] Finally, the Department of Energy was achieving quick results with a smaller lab-to-lab program in 1994, so it was hoped that this success could carry over to the government-to-government program were it handed over to the Department of Energy.[17]

LAB-TO-LAB.   While the government-to-government MPC&A program languished in 1994, surprisingly quick results in the MPC&A area emerged from a prior relationship between Russian and U.S. nuclear-weapons labs. The lab-to-lab program started in February 1992, when the directors of the Los Alamos and Lawrence Livermore National laboratories met with the directors of Arzamas-16 and Chelyabinsk-70 in Russia. Beginning in June 1992, scientists from the weapons labs began an unprecedented series of U.S.-funded collaborative research projects on scientific topics such as internal confinement fusion, lasers and optics, metallurgy, and high-explosive driven pulsed power generators.[18] According to Sig Hecker, the director of Los Alamos, these collaborations bought the Russian scientists "support from the Russian government, since funding was very difficult to come by and the government had to make tough choices."[19]

In April 1994, in response to a growing number of nuclear smuggling reports, Undersecretary of Energy Charles Curtis directed the U.S. labs to extend the lab-to-lab scientific collaborations to include "joint work on nuclear material protection, control, and accounting."[20] This proved to be an intelligent initiative: leaders from the two labs quickly worked out an

---

16.   The "buy American" and audit and inspection requirements (see pp. 132–134) were particularly troublesome in the negotiations with Minatom on the two MPC&A contracts, since the Russian side did not view the program as fully reciprocal or fair.

17.   In practice, there was nothing simple about the "handing over" of the Nunn-Lugar program to the Department of Energy. Tales of counterproductive bureaucratic in-fighting abound.

18.   See Gary Taubes, "Cold War Rivals Find Common Ground," *Science*, Vol. 268 (April 28, 1995), pp. 488–491.

19.   Ibid., p. 488.

20.   Mark Mullen, et al., "U.S.-Russian Laboratory-to-Laboratory Cooperation in Nuclear Materials Protection, Control, and Accounting," paper presented to the 36th Annual Meeting of the Institute of Nuclear Materials Management, Palm Desert, California, July 11, 1995, p. 2. Mullen, who is on the staff at Los Alamos, also reports that Arzamas-16 "had informally suggested in previous discussions with Los Alamos that the lab-to-lab approach should be explored for MPC&A cooperation, and these ideas had been reported to Under-secretary Curtis."

initial program of action by telephone, and within six weeks of Curtis's request, contracts had been signed for a joint project to develop an indigenous Russian MPC&A system at Arzamas-16 and a model physical protection system at the Kurchatov Institute.[21] The Department of Energy made $2 million available to the labs for this joint MPC&A project in fiscal year 1994, and then increased the budget for the lab-to-lab program to $15 million in fiscal year 1995.[22] These funds were not subject to the stringent procurement rules of the Department of Defense, and could legally be spent on Russian goods and services; this aspect of the lab-to-lab program has been central to its success.

The program at the Kurchatov Institute was led by the Sandia National Laboratory and focused on upgrading the security system at Building 116, which contains over 150 pounds of HEU in two critical assemblies that are used to study the physics of civilian reactors.[23] In September 1994, a joint Russian-American team conducted a detailed site security assessment and developed a preliminary design for the upgrades. In November and December the security upgrades were implemented, which involved clearing the areas around the building; conducting a physical inventory of the building's fissile material;[24] and installing a new fence with sensors to detect intrusion, a portal control and monitoring system, remote cameras, new lighting fixtures, interior alarms, a central alarm station, and a computerized system for material control and accounting.[25] The improvements to the security of Building 116 were in place by February 1995, when the new physical protection system was demonstrated to 75 officials from the United States and the former Soviet Union. The total cost of these upgrades was about $1 million, which was split three ways between the Sandia National Laboratory, the Kurchatov Institute, and a quasi-

---

21. Taubes, "Cold War Rivals Find Common Ground," p. 489.

22. The $2 million in FY94 came from reprogramming, which was also supposed to be the source of the $15 million in FY95. However, the Department of Energy could not agree on where to take these funds from, so they were given to the Department of Energy out of the Nunn-Lugar budget.

23. For a more detailed description of the Kurchatov improvements, see N.D. Bondarev, et al., "U.S./Russian Laboratory-to-Laboratory MPC&A at the RRC Kurchatov Institute," paper presented to the 36th Annual Meeting of the Institute of Nuclear Materials Management, Palm Desert, California, July 11, 1995.

24. The procedures used in this physical inventory were developed in cooperation with specialists from Euratom, and used portable high-resolution gamma-ray spectrometry equipment and data-analysis software that was supplied by the Lawrence Livermore National Laboratory. Bondarev, et al., "U.S./Russian Laboratory-to-Laboratory MPC&A at the RRC Kurchatov Institute."

25. Ibid.

commercial Minatom institute called Eleron, which manufactures nuclear security equipment. Most of the technical equipment that went to Kurchatov was purchased from Russian suppliers. Over 1995–96, it is planned that the MPC&A enhancements to Building 116 will be extended throughout the Kurchatov Institute.

The lab-to-lab program at Arzamas-16 focused on jointly developing model MPC&A methods and technologies that could be disseminated throughout the most sensitive sites in the Russian nuclear complex. This began with MPC&A training at Los Alamos for Russian scientists in August 1994, then turned to the construction of a model MPC&A system at a "relatively non-sensitive location at Arzamas-16 using small samples of nuclear materials."[26] Most of the technical equipment in this model facility was of Russian origin, and was purchased with U.S. funds from the lab-to-lab program. This testbed system was demonstrated twice in early 1995 to Russian and American scientists, and later to managers of Russian nuclear enterprises; in May 1995, by order of Minister Mikhailov, the equipment from the testbed facility was moved to Minatom headquarters in Moscow, where it was shown to a large number of government officials and nuclear plant managers.[27] On the basis of these exhibits, over a dozen major Minatom institutes or enterprises expressed an interest in participating in the program, though it remains to be determined what the nature of that participation will be, which facilities within which installations will be upgraded, how quickly these upgrades will be carried out, and where the financing for these upgrades will come from.[28] By mid-1995, however, security equipment was purchased and installed at Obninsk and Chelyabinsk-70.[29]

---

26. Mullen, et al., "U.S.-Russian Laboratory-to-Laboratory Cooperation in Nuclear Materials Protection, Control, and Accounting," p. 7.

27. Vladimir Yuferev, et al., "Demonstration of Safeguards Technology at the Russian Institute of Experimental Physics (VNIIEF), Arzamas-16," paper presented to the 36th Annual Meeting of the Institute of Nuclear Materials Management, Palm Desert, California, July 11, 1995, p. 2.

28. Reportedly, the institutes and enterprises that have expressed an interest in receiving some or all of the Arzamas-16 MPC&A system are: Arzamas-16 (presumably for the more sensitive facilities), Chelyabinsk-70 (another weapons lab), Tomsk-7, Mayak, Avangard, Penza, Sverdlovsk-45, Krasnoyarsk, the Luch Scientific Production Association at Podolsk, the Institute of Automatics, Eleron, the Bochvar Institute of Inorganic Materials, and the Institute of Physics and Power Engineering at Obninsk. Mullen, et al., "U.S.-Russian Laboratory-to-Laboratory Cooperation in Nuclear Materials Protection, Control, and Accounting," p. 7.

29. See Igor P. Matveenko, et al., "Collaborative Russian-U.S. Work in Nuclear Material Protection, Control, and Accounting at the Institute of Physics and Power Engineering," paper presented to the 36th Annual Meeting of the Institute of Nuclear

An important goal of the lab-to-lab program was to encourage the development of a locally designed and produced MPC&A system that is appropriate for the unique needs of the Russian nuclear complex, and in so doing, to create an indigenous lobby of nuclear security advocates who have vested interests in deploying and maintaining an effective MPC&A system throughout Russia. This was a politically savvy approach to the nuclear leakage problem, and it appears to have worked so far, producing a generally enthusiastic Russian response. For example, according to Victor Murogov, the director of the Institute of Physics and Power Engineering at Obninsk:

The Americans have provided us with a wonderful system — a video camera with software and a line-operated station that records changes in the position of the materials in storage. At the end of the day you have a full trajectory of the material movement (this gram of material has moved from this point to that one). This is the latest technology, and they have already brought it to us, which is a great achievement in Russian-American cooperation. It is also important that the Americans are establishing a portal [monitor] that makes it impossible to steal even a microscopic amount of fissile material.[30]

Murogov was similarly upbeat about the U.S.-funded center for national MPC&A training at his institute:[31]

The [Institute of Physics and Power Engineering] has set up a center to train Minatom specialists in ensuring the non-proliferation of fissile materials. It is based on the nuclear security departments of companies in this industry. In this respect foreign institutes and centers have helped us a lot: they have provided us with software, data banks, computer facilities. They have taught our specialists how to handle machinery. There is unique technology in the West. There are also very simple and common machines, like a portal [monitor], which is, as a matter of fact, like an airfield gate that should be at any entrance checkpoint. But we don't have them (*and without the Western aid I don't know when we would have received them*); we do everything slowly and rely on the intuition of those who check.[32]

Materials Management, Palm Desert, California, July 11, 1995; and Vladimir Teryohin, et al., "U.S./Russian Laboratory-to-Laboratory MPC&A Program at the VNITF Institute, Chelyabinsk-70," paper presented to the 36th Annual Meeting of the Institute of Nuclear Materials Management, Palm Desert, California, July 11, 1995.

30. Vladimir Orlov, "Interview with Victor Murogov," *Yaderny Kontrol*, September 1995, p. 5.

31. The Russian MPC&A training center at Obninsk is being funded through the first Nunn-Lugar MPC&A contract, not the lab-to-lab program.

32. Orlov, "Interview with Victor Murogov" (emphasis added).

Murogov's testimony is a heartening dividend from a very worthwhile investment, but it is important to remember that his institute holds less than one percent of the total Russian stockpile of fissile material. His statement also gives evidence of how poorly the other 99 percent is guarded.

A central goal in any U.S. strategy to combat nuclear leakage must be to build on the success of the lab-to-lab program by encouraging and funding the production and installation of the jointly developed MPC&A system at as many Russian nuclear installations as possible, as quickly as possible. Current U.S. plans aim to do so between 1996 and 2002 with a total budget of about $415 million.[33] For fiscal year 1996, the Department of Energy has asked for $70 million for its nuclear materials security program, of which $40 million would be devoted to further MPC&A improvements through the lab-to-lab program. The real test for the lab-to-lab program lies in disseminating the new MPC&A system beyond the sphere of weapons laboratories and research institutes, into the large, troubled industrial enterprises associated with the Russian nuclear fuel cycles and weapons program, a task which is likely to require an even greater commitment of U.S. resources and effort.

The political challenge in building on the success of the lab-to-lab program will be to preserve the elements that have made it successful in the first place. In this respect, three issues are critical. First, lab-to-lab funds must continue to be spent freely on Russian goods and services; a change in this rule could easily bring the entire program to a grinding halt, particularly since the equipment used in the model Arzamas-16 system is largely of Russian manufacture. Second, the lab-to-lab program must not be subjected to a stringent audit and examination requirement like that faced in the Nunn-Lugar program. To date, the program has done well with joint technical demonstrations. Given the sensitivity of the facilities into which it is hoped the lab-to-lab MPC&A system will be installed, a U.S. insistence on non-reciprocal audit and examination rights would severely hamper the program, if not kill it off entirely.[34]

---

33. Kenneth Luongo, "U.S. Program on Nuclear Material Security in Russia and the Newly Independent States," presentation to the conference on the "Nunn-Lugar Cooperative Threat Reduction Program: Donor and Recipient Country Perspectives," Monterey Institute of International Studies, August 21, 1995.

34. In the summer of 1995, the Senate Armed Services Committee introduced a provision into its draft fiscal year 1996 defense authorization bill that would require the executive branch to reach a government-to-government agreement on audit and examinations for the Department of Energy's expenditures like the agreement for Department of Defense expenditures under the Nunn-Lugar program. Although not yet law when this report was written (the provision could still be dropped in confer-

Finally, the implementation of the lab-to-lab MPC&A program must continue to be seen as advantageous to each individual Russian nuclear enterprise and to the Russian government as a whole. Care must be taken to ensure that the program does not become an easy target for opportunistic political attacks in Russia, particularly by ensuring that there is no public impression that Russian state secrets are being given away. More importantly, however, the U.S. government will have to take concrete steps to ensure that Minatom's large nuclear enterprise — rather than just the relatively small research institutes and weapons labs — are persuaded that the installation of a new MPC&A system is economically beneficial. This will require a more sympathetic U.S. approach to the social and economic problems of Russia's nuclear cities.

The lab-to-lab program has proven effective on a small scale. It is beginning to expand, and the Russian reaction has been more forthcoming than is the case in other instances. But it remains to be seen whether it can move far enough and fast enough before it is too late. The results achieved so far deserve much praise, but they represent only the first small step toward the completion of a very large project.

SAFE AND SECURE WARHEAD TRANSPORTATION

The first form of U.S. nuclear-safety assistance offered to the former Soviet republics under the Nunn-Lugar program was designed to reduce the risks of theft and accidents while the nuclear weapons of the former Soviet Union were being transferred back to Russia. This assistance consisted of armored blankets, rail-car conversion kits, communication equipment, and emergency response equipment. Designed to reduce the risk of a nuclear-weapons accident during transportation, this equipment was purchased from U.S. suppliers and, beginning in late 1992, transferred directly to the former republics.[35] This program was too late to affect the inter-republic tactical nuclear weapons transfers, since the last tactical nuclear weapons were withdrawn from Ukraine in May 1992. However, the equipment did arrive in time to be used in the transfer of strategic warheads from Ukraine and Kazakhstan to Russia, and in the transfer of warheads of all kinds among their designated storage facilities and dismantlement sites within Russia. This is a valuable form of assistance, since transportation is "one of the most vulnerable points" along

---

ence, or President Clinton could veto the entire bill), if retained this requirement would do great harm to real U.S. national security interests by crippling an exceptionally successful program.

35.   "CTR Semi-Annual Report," September 30, 1994.

the warhead chain of custody, according to General Evgeny Maslin, the chief of the 12th Main Directorate of the Ministry of Defense (which handles Russian nuclear warheads).[36]

The program was expanded in 1995 with the signing of a new $42 million "Warhead Technical Exchange" agreement between the Department of Defense and the Russian Ministry of Defense.[37] This agreement aims at improving the security of nuclear warheads along the entire military chain of custody, which falls outside of Minatom's jurisdiction. Under this contract, the United States will supply additional equipment for secure warhead transportation, special containers for transporting warheads, and computers for keeping track of nuclear charges. It is also possible that the U.S. government will provide equipment for guarding nuclear weapons storage sites, but this is not yet certain. Although there seems to be a good working relationship between the Russian Ministry of Defense and the U.S. Department of Defense, the openness between the two military establishments does not yet seem to have extended to showing each other their nuclear weapons storage facilities. Given the nearly catastrophic consequences that would follow the loss of a Russian nuclear weapon, these programs are worth building upon, and the U.S. government should work toward upgrading the security of Russia's weapons depots as well as the transportation systems that link them.

The Russian military has received warhead-safety assistance from other countries as well. Great Britain and France have delivered warhead containers to Russia, and Great Britain has also apparently given Russia 18 special trucks for carrying nuclear weapons.

INCOMPLETE EFFORTS TO ADDRESS THE "BRAIN DRAIN," AND OTHER NEGLECTED PERSONNEL ISSUES

The personnel of the Russian nuclear empire — military and civilian — are critical to any nuclear security effort in at least two respects.[38] First, they are responsible for safeguarding Russia's nuclear weapons and fissile materials. If they are negligent in meeting these responsibilities or, worse,

---

36. Vladimir Orlov, "Interview with Gen. Maslin," *Yaderny Kontrol*, March 6, 1995, p. 2.

37. Comments by General Roland Lajoie at the conference on the "Nunn-Lugar Cooperative Threat Reduction Program: Donor and Recipient Country Perspectives," Monterey Institute of International Studies, August 21, 1995.

38. For a cogent discussion of the "human element" in the nuclear leakage problem, see Dorothy S. Zinberg, "The Missing Link? Nuclear Proliferation and the International Mobility of Russian Nuclear Experts," paper presented to the conference on the "Nunn-Lugar Cooperative Threat Reduction Program: Donor and Recipient Country Perspectives," Monterey Institute of International Studies, August 20–22, 1995.

tempted to participate in theft or diversion, the nuclear leakage problem will be insoluble. Second, many of them possess expertise that could be of great value to aspiring proliferants or potential nuclear terrorists. For these reasons, an enlightened nuclear security policy would attempt to minimize the incentive of these personnel to defect from their responsibilities by finding ways of contributing to an adequate quality of life for them, and by trying to create opportunities that make their future prospects look less bleak.

Largely due to domestic political constraints within the United States, U.S. policy has not been very effective at addressing these concerns. Most of the Nunn-Lugar funding has been directed at American contractors, making it impossible to expend resources in ways that improve the standard of living of Russian personnel. And while the champions of Nunn-Lugar in the Congress have understood the need for a comprehensive nuclear security policy, the Congress as a whole has been skeptical and unreceptive when the Clinton administration has sought to spend money on items such as housing for retiring Russian missile officers, much less for underemployed technicians at Russian plutonium production reactors. Thus, American policy has not done much so far to promote the living standards of the average member of the Russian nuclear empire; indeed, it has been growing more and more difficult to spend U.S. tax dollars for these purposes.

THE INTERNATIONAL SCIENCE AND TECHNOLOGY CENTER. The most significant and visible program in this category is focused specifically on the "brain-drain" problem. It is the International Science and Technology Center (ISTC), which began operation in Moscow on March 3, 1994.[39] The ISTC is intended to provide funding to ex-Soviet nuclear scientists and weapon technicians for non-military projects,[40] and to reduce their financial incentives to steal nuclear materials for profit.[41] The United States has provided $25 million toward the initial operating budget of the ISTC, with

39. A parallel center was set up in Ukraine, the Science and Technology Center in Ukraine (STCU), on July 16, 1994. The United States has committed $10 million to the STCU, Canada $2 million, and Sweden $1.5 million.

40. One of these projects is to develop an MPC&A system for Tomsk-7, which is being funded at a few hundreds of thousands of dollars.

41. For a good overview of the ISTC, see R. Adam Moody, "A Case Study of the Cooperative Threat Reduction Science Center Initiative," paper prepared for the conference on the "Nunn-Lugar Cooperative Threat Reduction Program: Donor and Recipient Country Perspectives," Monterey Institute of International Studies, August 20–22, 1995.

other contributions coming from the European Union, Japan, Sweden, and Switzerland; the United States allocated a further $24 million of the ISTC in fiscal year 1995.[42] The establishment of this facility, which was long delayed by political and bureaucratic obstruction in Moscow, is a success for the U.S. government, and the ISTC is already yielding important benefits in the Western effort to engage the Russian nuclear establishment on a cooperative basis. The United States expects to sponsor several thousand scientists and engineers from the weapons complex during 1994–97.[43]

The ISTC is a worthwhile program. However, it will be able to fund only a small fraction of the hundreds of thousands of individuals who work in the Russian nuclear empire. It is not even able to support all those who possess high scientific or technical expertise. Moreover, the beneficial effects of the ISTC should not be exaggerated, since no amount of Western research-related grant money is going to be able to equal the enormous financial gain that an aspiring proliferant could offer to a sought-after individual. More significantly, the ISTC does little or nothing for the guards and administrators of nuclear installations, who probably pose even worse security risks than scientific personnel. Hence, the ISTC is an example of a well-conceived program aimed directly at an aspect of the nuclear leakage threat that got off to a slow start and, as implemented, only incompletely addresses the problem.

DEFENSE CONVERSION EFFORTS. Working over a longer time horizon than the ISTC are a number of U.S. programs aimed at "converting" the former Soviet military-industrial complex, that is, at providing former weapons workers and enterprises with viable non–weapons related employment. These programs started within the Department of Defense's Nunn-Lugar program, which decided to provide the seed capital for a limited number of joint ventures between U.S. companies and defense enterprises in Russia, Belarus, Kazakhstan, and Ukraine.[44] These projects were selected to serve highly specific demilitarization needs in order to advance larger

---

42. Of this $24 million in fiscal year 1995, $9 million was earmarked for Kazakhstan and $5 million for Belarus. The Ukrainian STCU received an additional $5 million in fiscal year 1995. In fiscal year 1996, U.S. contributions from the ISTC and STCU will come from the Department of State's "Freedom Support Act" fund.

43. "CTR Semi-Annual Report," September 30, 1994.

44. Through fiscal year 1994, the Department of Defense proposed to spend $40 million on defense conversion in Russia: $10 million in Belarus; $15 million in Kazakhstan; and $40 million in Ukraine. This money goes primarily to U.S. companies who are in the process of establishing joint ventures in the four eligible states.

U.S. national security aims related to denuclearization and the implementation of strategic arms reduction.[45] The Nunn-Lugar defense conversion projects proved politically unpopular, however, and no new Nunn-Lugar conversion contracts are planned for fiscal year 1996 or beyond. Partly as a substitute, however, the Department of Defense set up the Defense Enterprise Fund in 1994, which is essentially a quasi-official investment fund for military conversion projects.[46] The Defense Enterprise Fund has its own management and budgetary line item, and it makes grants to U.S. companies that wish to invest in creating joint ventures with enterprises of the former Soviet military-industrial complex.

Another U.S. conversion project is the Department of Energy's "Industrial Partnering Program" (IPP), created at the initiative of Senator Pete Domenici in 1994 with an initial funding level of $35 million.[47] The IPP seeks to match former Soviet weapons labs, institutes, and scientists with private U.S. companies, with the U.S. laboratories acting as intermediaries.[48] The hope behind the IPP is that these joint ventures will eventually become self-sustaining, profitable, non-military enterprises that do not require the direct involvement of the U.S. government. The IPP seems to have achieved good results so far, with over 180 joint venture projects initiated in the program's first year.[49] A multinational seminar series run by the U.S. Arms Control and Disarmament Agency (ACDA) complements the IPP. The IPP specifically targets Russia's nuclear weapons complex, in contrast to the Defense Enterprise Fund, which applies to the post-Soviet military-industrial complex broadly defined.

In general, defense conversion is a good technique for dealing with the "human element" of demilitarization and denuclearization, especially

---

45. For example, the first defense conversion contract in Ukraine (for $5 million) was awarded to Westinghouse to fund a joint venture with a Ukrainian enterprise that made ballistic missile guidance systems; the joint venture would make control equipment for nuclear reactors.

46. The initial funding for the Defense Enterprise Fund was $7.67 million in fiscal year 1994.

47. See Katherine E. Johnson, "U.S.-FSU Nuclear Threat Reduction Programs: Effectiveness of Current Efforts and Prospects for Future Cooperation," paper presented to the conference on the "Nunn-Lugar Cooperative Threat Reduction Program: Donor and Recipient Country Perspectives," Monterey Institute of International Studies, August 20–22, 1995, pp. 24–25.

48. The U.S. companies involved in the IPP are associated as a consortium known as the U.S. Industrial Coalition (USIC), which has around 80 members. The industrial members of USIC contribute to the costs of running IPP projects.

49. Department of Energy, "Program Summary: New Independent States Industrial Partnering Program," May 1995.

when it is targeted at key sectors, such as former Soviet weapons labs, and when U.S. industry is closely involved in the project. However, defense conversion programs are sometimes politically vulnerable, as evinced by the severe political criticism elicited by the use of Nunn-Lugar funds from defense conversion programs that provide housing for demobilized officers of the Strategic Rocket Forces. Moreover, while we support the defense conversion programs that have been pursued by the U.S. government so far, it remains to be seen whether or not they can make a positive impact across the breadth of the post-Soviet defense sector.

LITTLE EFFORT AND LITTLE PROGRESS ON EXPORT CONTROLS

At the June 1992 summit of the G-7 in Munich, the leaders of the seven largest industrial democracies declared that they "attach the highest importance to the establishment in the former Soviet Union of effective export controls on nuclear materials, weapons, and other sensitive goods and technologies and will offer training and practical assistance to help achieve this."[50] This statement was an exaggeration: to date, Western assistance to the states of the former Soviet Union in the area of export controls has been trivial.

An effective export control system would consist of an appropriate legal and bureaucratic framework integrated with a capable enforcement mechanism. The laws regulating a state's exports should impose severe penalties on those who are caught trafficking in nuclear materials. A state's export control system must be able to monitor and control state-sanctioned exports of dual-use items as well as illicit exports (smuggling). The enforcement mechanism should include not only an efficient bureaucratic process for authorizing or denying specific export requests, but also effective policing at border crossings and points of entry and exit. Policing against the smuggling of nuclear materials is no easy task, but the odds of detecting illicitly exported nuclear materials can be improved significantly through adequate staffing at border posts, special training for border guards and customs inspectors, and special equipment for detecting nuclear materials at all points of entry and exit. Even if border policing against nuclear smuggling can never be completely effective, the presence of numerous trained officers equipped with modern detection devices should deter many potential nuclear smugglers — assuming, of course, that the penalties of detection are high and that border guards cannot be easily bribed.

---

50. Quoted in Gary K. Bertsch, "Introduction," in Gary K. Bertsch and Igor Khripunov, eds., "Russia's Nonproliferation Export Controls: 1994 Annual Report," Center for East-West Trade Policy, University of Georgia, Athens, Georgia, 1994, p. 8.

The borders of the former Soviet republics have become exceptionally and dangerously porous since the collapse of the Soviet police state, a situation which has led to a boom in smuggling not only of nuclear materials, but also of drugs, precious metals, and conventional weapons.[51] Of the states of the former Soviet Union, only Russia inherited a set of export control laws that was even close to adequate.[52] Russia's implementation of export controls, however, is seriously deficient. Russia's many border posts and points of entry lack even the most rudimentary equipment for detecting nuclear materials, and the underpaid officials who staff these posts have received no special training in the identification and detection of nuclear materials. (This is also true, it should be noted, of the U.S. Customs Service.) The situation in the other former Soviet republics is even worse: not only do they lack trained officials and special detection equipment, but as new states they also generally have inadequate export control laws and regulations, and little if any centralized means for authorizing or denying legitimate export requests.[53]

The United States has held negotiations with the Russian government since 1992 about strengthening Russia's export control laws and enforcement capabilities.[54] In January 1995, the Russian and U.S. governments

---

51. According to Nikolai Arsipov, the head of the anti-drug squad of the Russian Ministry of Interior, "the turmoil that followed the collapse of the Soviet Union left Russia's borders virtually open to smugglers traveling via former Soviet Central Asia." Paraphrased in "Dramatic Increase in Drug Smuggling," *OMRI Daily Digest I*, No. 159 (August 16, 1995).

52. See William C. Potter, "Nuclear Exports from the Former Soviet Union: What's New, What's True," *Arms Control Today*, Vol. 23, No. 1 (January/February 1993), pp. 6–7. For a thorough analysis of Russia's export control laws, see Bertsch and Khripunov, "Russia's Nonproliferation Export Controls: 1994 Annual Report."

53. For an early call for international export control assistance to the new states of the former Soviet Union, see William C. Potter, "Exports and Experts: Proliferation Risks from the New Commonwealth," *Arms Control Today*, Vol. 22, No. 1 (January–February 1992), pp. 32–37. The difference between the export control systems in Russia and the other former Soviet republics is discussed in William C. Potter, "Viewpoint: Nuclear Insecurity in the Post-Soviet States," *The Nonproliferation Review*, Vol. 1, No. 3 (Spring–Summer, 1994), pp. 63–64, reprint of testimony given to the Subcommittee on International Security, International Organizations, and Human Rights of the Committee on Foreign Affairs of the U.S. House of Representatives, June 27, 1994. According to Potter, there has been a small amount of progress in Ukraine's development of an export control system since 1994. See William C. Potter, "Cooperative Threat Reduction: Progress in Export Control and Safeguarding Naval Fuel," paper presented to the Third Meeting of the U.S.-German Study Group on Nonproliferation, Bonn, Germany, June 12– 23, 1995, pp. 3–6.

54. For a good discussion of the export control problem, see William C. Potter,

signed a Memorandum of Intent to use the $2.26 million in CTR funds, designated for export control assistance to Russia, to pay for seminars, personnel exchanges, and conference travel.[55] Needless to say, even after the U.S. government manages to spend this money, Russia's borders are unlikely to be significantly less open to the free flow of nuclear materials. There are no plans to purchase nuclear materials detection equipment for Russia, in part because the Russian government refused to accept U.S. audits and inspections of U.S.-procured equipment. And, although there has been some discussion of U.S.-funded training for Russia's border guards, to date this has not focused on the nuclear smuggling threat. (See the discussion of law enforcement cooperation below.)

The U.S. government has been more successful at disbursing export control aid to Belarus, Kazakhstan, and Ukraine. The United States has signed and begun implementing export-control assistance agreements with Belarus for $16.26 million, Kazakhstan for $7.26 million, and Ukraine for $13.26 million.[56] These funds are being used for training programs for licensing and enforcement personnel; policy consultations and personnel exchanges; computer systems for automating the states' export licensing systems; and some border enforcement equipment, such as hand-held radiation detectors and six patrol boats for the Kazakh Customs service to use in the Caspian Sea. Although most of this aid had not been delivered by mid-1995, it will doubtless improve the export control systems in Belarus, Kazakhstan, and Ukraine.

Finally, there are small U.S. export control assistance programs underway with the three Baltic states, coordinated by the State Department and funded out of the Nonproliferation and Disarmament Fund. This money has been used to finance contacts between the U.S. Customs Service and the Baltic border services, and is planned to be used to supply computer equipment needed to automate the Baltic states' export licensing systems. There are no formal U.S. export-control assistance programs

---

"Cooperative Threat Reduction: Progress in Export Control and Safeguarding Naval Fuel," pp. 2–7; more generally, see also the Center for International Trade and Security, "Non-Proliferation Export Controls," a report from the workshop on "U.S. and Japanese Nonproliferation Export Controls: Interests and Initiatives," University of Georgia, Athens, Georgia, March 27– 28, 1995.

55. Potter, "Cooperative Threat Reduction: Progress in Export Control and Safeguarding Naval Fuel," p. 2.

56. Responsibility for export-control assistance to the Soviet Union was transferred from the Department of Defense to the Department of State in 1995, and in fiscal year 1996, the Department of State plans to spend $15 million on export-control assistance out of its Nonproliferation and Disarmament Fund.

with the other former Soviet republics: the four central Asian states, the three Caucasian states, or Moldova.

U.S. export-control assistance programs to the states of the former Soviet Union deserve greater emphasis and priority than they have so far received. Moreover, this is an area in which the involvement of other states should be most welcome: the Scandinavian states, for example, should be encouraged to adopt much larger assistance programs with the Baltic states. The focus must be on results, not minor bureaucratic and procedural achievements. A truly focused and committed U.S. policy against nuclear leakage would aim to ensure that there are enforcement officials trained and equipped to detect nuclear materials at every single point of exit and entry in the entire former Soviet Union. The current U.S. policy does not aim for anything close to this standard.

HIGH HOPES FOR NUCLEAR REGULATION

In late 1991, the Russian nuclear regulatory agency, Gosatomnadzor (GAN), approached the U.S. Nuclear Regulatory Commission (NRC) and asked for assistance in developing a nuclear regulatory regime for Russia. Although President Yeltsin has made GAN responsible for "maintaining a system of accounting and control for nuclear materials,"[57] the agency has no power to regulate Minatom's policies, behavior, or public disclosures. A further problem is that there is no independent mechanism by which nuclear plant managers who violate official security and safety standards can be punished or fined for their laxity.

Recognizing the potential usefulness of a non-Minatom Russian regulatory agency, the United States offered to provide assistance for GAN out of the first Nunn-Lugar MPC&A contract with Russia.[58] Minatom originally resisted this, but when the contract was signed it was agreed that $1 million of the $10 million contract would go to the NRC to fund a regulatory assistance program. Minatom argued that these funds could only be spent on activities with Russian nuclear inspectors who are directly involved in regulating the LEU fuel line of the Electrostal fabrication plant near Moscow. Nonetheless, the NRC has used this $1 million

57. "On the Priority Measures for Improving the System of Accounting and Safety for Nuclear Materials," Decree of the President of the Russian Federation No. 1923, September 15, 1994, para. 2; reprinted in *The Monitor* (University of Georgia), February 1995, p. 18.

58. Some $300,000 has also been given to the NRC by the U.S. Agency for International Development (AID) to fund regulatory assistance work with GAN as a result of a mid-1992 plan by the Bush administration, the "Lisbon Safety Initiative," to offer nuclear safety assistance to the former Soviet republics.

to fund training programs and exchange visits with Russian nuclear regulators.[59] The NRC has also assisted GAN in developing policies and plans for local, regional, and national nuclear regulations, which Russia now wholly lacks.

In late June 1995, the Department of Energy signed a major new agreement with the Russian government under which Energy hopes to provide $10 million in regulatory assistance to GAN and Minatom in fiscal year 1996 and beyond. Although the action plans for this program were still under development in September 1995, the Department of Energy expects to offer four kinds of assistance: continued funding of the work of the NRC to assist in the writing of Russian nuclear regulations; establishing and providing equipment for a central Russian nuclear material tracking system; providing technical equipment needed to carry out inspections, such as hand-held non-destructive assay (NDA) devices; and continued training courses for Russia's nuclear regulators and inspectors.

NEW TERRITORY FOR LAW ENFORCEMENT

Of all senior officials in the Clinton administration, the one who articulated the earliest and the clearest assessment of the threat of nuclear leakage from the former Soviet Union was Judge Louis Freeh, the director of the Federal Bureau of Investigation (FBI). In May 1994, several months before the sensational seizure of plutonium at the Munich airport, Judge Freeh made the following statement to Congress:

We must focus on the possibility of organized crime, rogue nations, or bands of terrorists obtaining nuclear weapons or weapons-grade plutonium and uranium from Russia or any other source. There are vast amounts of nuclear weapons and nuclear materials in the former Soviet Union. *It is the greatest long-term threat to the security of the United States.* This is a priority we must work on jointly with Russia.[60]

The strength of this statement suggests that the FBI would be moving decisively to enhance its ability to combat the international trafficking in nuclear materials. Unfortunately, only the first, most tentative steps have

---

59. In October 1994, for example, Russian nuclear inspectors from Electrostal observed a week-long NRC inspection in Missouri.

60. Testimony by Louis J. Freeh in U.S. Congress, *International Organized Crime and its Impact on the United States,* Hearing before the Permanent Subcommittee on Investigations, Committee on Governmental Affairs, U.S. Senate, 103rd Cong., 2nd sess. (Washington DC: U.S. GPO, May 25, 1994), p. 16 (emphasis added). Interestingly, Freeh's assertion appears in the transcript of his oral remarks, but not in his prepared statement, which in fact plays down the threat of fissile material smuggling.

been taken by U.S. law enforcement and intelligence agencies — of which the most important are the FBI, the Central Intelligence Agency (CIA),[61] and the Customs Service — to address the threat of nuclear leakage.[62]

The law-enforcement response to the nuclear leakage threat should have three components. First, it should involve a priority diplomatic effort to pool and coordinate the efforts in this area being made by the law enforcement and intelligence agencies of other countries. Second, it should involve aggressive programs to train and supply equipment to the law enforcement and intelligence agencies of other countries that are currently inadequately prepared to combat nuclear materials trafficking. Third and most importantly, the law enforcement and intelligence agencies of the United States must train and equip themselves to combat nuclear smuggling and protect the United States from terrorist attacks involving weapons of mass destruction (WMD).

In the area of coordinating international law-enforcement efforts to combat nuclear smuggling, no real progress has been made and the issue lacks priority status for the Clinton White House. There has been some consultation among some international law enforcement agencies, but no systematic coordination of their efforts or pooling of data. The Russian government has stated that it is willing to address the nuclear smuggling issue within the context of the G-7+1. The chairman's statement from the July 10, 1994, meeting of the eight heads of state in Naples, Italy, resulted in a call for cooperation in the area of combating nuclear smuggling and terrorism, but by September 1995, the U.S. government was still working on draft language for a successor communiqué. No practical steps had been taken in the intervening 14 months.

In the area of international training efforts, the FBI has taken some useful and interesting steps forward. In July 1994, Judge Freeh went to Moscow to establish an FBI liaison office and develop a program of cooperation with the Ministry of Interior (MVD), the Russian counterpart to the FBI. In August 1994, Congress provided $30 million to the FBI to fund law enforcement training courses in the states of Eastern Europe and the former Soviet Union. This has led to a large number of FBI training courses in Russia for Russian law enforcement officers and, in April 1995, the opening of the International Law Enforcement Academy in Buda-

---

61. Understandably, little is publicly known about the role of the CIA in the U.S. response to nuclear leakage, proliferation, and terrorism.

62. See also R. Jeffrey Smith, "Bid to Curb Nuclear Smuggling Lags," *International Herald Tribune,* August 29, 1994, p. 7.

pest.[63] The training courses for Russian officers are without precedent and deserve much praise. However, these courses have not focused on combating nuclear trafficking and terrorism; instead, they have concentrated on "organized crime investigations, financial crime investigations, and management science."[64] To date, there have been only preliminary discussions of special courses to train law enforcement officers to combat nuclear smuggling. The lack of FBI courses in the former Soviet Union focused on nuclear trafficking has two main causes: first, the Russian government has been hesitant to publicly acknowledge that there is in fact a serious nuclear smuggling problem on its territory;[65] and second, the FBI and other U.S. law enforcement agencies, such as the Customs Service, have no particular expertise in combating nuclear trafficking or WMD terrorism to share with their Russian counterparts.

Finally, U.S. law enforcement agencies are themselves less than well prepared to deal with the new threats of nuclear trafficking and terrorism. The FBI has a few special training courses for its officers on topics related to WMD proliferation, but the real priorities of the FBI lie in other areas such as organized crime, drugs, and white-collar crime. There is no special FBI office that focuses on tracking and combating trafficking in nuclear materials, nor is there a special unit devoted to protecting U.S. territory from WMD attack. Similarly, the Customs Service is the primary enforcement agency at U.S. borders, but its main mission is to enforce U.S. trade laws, not to detect and locate nuclear materials or weapons, a task for which its officers are neither trained nor equipped. In 1995, Congress allocated $10 million from the defense budget to fund a joint training program between the Defense Nuclear Agency and the FBI to "expand and improve United States efforts to deter the possible proliferation and acquisition of weapons of mass destruction by organized crime organizations in Eastern Europe, the Baltic countries, and states of the former Soviet Union." By the end of 1995, the FBI and the Department of Defense had not worked out the details about how this $10 million should be spent, but the purpose of this program had been refined to

---

63. "FBI Training Academy Opens in Budapest," *OMRI Daily Digest II*, No. 81 (April 25, 1995).

64. Freeh, Statement before the Senate Judiciary Committee, February 14, 1995 (from Federal News Service Washington Package [on-line]).

65. In this respect, Judge Freeh's candor about the threat of nuclear leakage from the former Soviet Union may have been counterproductive. See Wendy Sloane, "FBI's Moscow Mission: The Mob, Nuclear Theft, Keeping the Order in Russia," *Christian Science Monitor*, July 5, 1994.

consist of the establishment of a "training program jointly carried out by FBI and Department of Defense to expand and improve [U.S. government] efforts to deter proliferation and acquisition of WMD by organized crime in Eastern Europe, [the] Baltic nations, and former Soviet Union states."[66] This potential collaboration between the Department of Defense and the FBI is the sort of sensible thing that the government should be doing more urgently, more often, and more extensively. To date, however, the effort to integrate the resources and expertise of the U.S. law enforcement community into the fight against nuclear smuggling has been at best disorganized.

The law enforcement aspects of the effort to reduce the threat of nuclear leakage urgently need to be examined from top to bottom, and to be imbued with the energy, resources, and sense of purpose that might allow positive results to be achieved.

IN SUMMATION: WHAT'S MISSING?

Taken together, the programs and initiatives described above represent a sensible and fairly comprehensive response to the nuclear leakage threat. They include efforts meant to enhance security at Russian nuclear facilities, improve material control and accounting, and inhibit brain drain. If these programs were well established, widely applied in Russia, and moving forward vigorously, the need for concern about U.S. approaches to the nuclear leakage threat would be much reduced. However, some four years after the end of the Soviet Union, several of the key programs involved had just gotten off the ground.

Moreover, there are particular gaps in these programs' coverage of the nuclear leakage problem in Russia. First, the Russian naval fuel cycle has been almost totally ignored, for reasons having to do primarily with the strong opposition from the U.S. Navy to any sort of cooperative or reciprocal program in this area. The Clinton administration has now decided to talk about the security of the naval fuel cycle with Russia, and the Department of Energy has asked for $5 million in its fiscal year 1996 budget request to address the Russian naval fuel cycle, but it remains to be seen how far or how fast this program will move. Securing the Russian naval fuel cycle is an exceptionally large task, since there are many storage sites around Russia used for storing fresh naval fuel, which contains HEU.

Second, the intra-Minatom nuclear transportation system has been completely untouched. Minatom has its own rail cars and special guards assigned to the task of ferrying Russia's fissile material and nuclear

---

66. "FBI Support Program," Briefing by the Defense Nuclear Agency, U.S. Air Force Academy, Colorado Springs, Colo., June 5, 1995.

weapon components between Minatom's key nuclear installations. These rail cars travel on the same tracks as do the rail cars of the 12th Main Directorate of the Ministry of Defense, which has received a considerable amount of Nunn-Lugar aid to increase the security and safety of these shipments. But Minatom does not use the 12th Main Directorate's rail cars, and thus has seen no security improvements in its transportation system. Given the acute vulnerabilities of fissile material during transportation, the U.S. government should act quickly to remedy this situation.

Third, as noted already, Minatom's largest facilities for handling weapon components and weapons-grade fissile material remain untouched by U.S.-sponsored MPC&A improvements. Improving MPC&A at the research and design laboratories like the Kurchatov Institute, Obninsk, Arzamas-16, and Chelyabinsk-70 is a much smaller challenge than doing so at the sprawling industrial sites like Tomsk-7, Krasnoyarsk-26, and Chelyabinsk-65, but it is here where the greatest concentration of proliferation danger resides.

Finally, U.S. progress on the "softer" aspects of enhancing nuclear security — export controls, law enforcement, nuclear regulation, countering the brain drain — pale compared to the achievements of the lab-to-lab MPC&A program. The lab-to-lab program is impressive not only because of its results, but also because of its clear focus and sense of mission. Without downgrading the importance of site security in any way, the rest of the agenda for combating nuclear leakage deserves upgrading, particularly in the form of access to resources, high-level political support, and interagency cooperation within the U.S. government.

Fissile Material Disposition: Promising Ideas, Troubled Implementation, Irrelevant Timetables

The previous section described efforts to enhance security at and among existing Russian facilities that handle, store, and transport nuclear weapons and fissile materials. A second strand of American policy takes a different approach: it aims at removing fissile material from Russia and elsewhere in the former Soviet Union; providing Russia with secure, long-lasting fissile material storage facilities; and ending the production of new fissile material. As with the initiatives described above, these are appropriate and potentially effective responses to the nuclear leakage challenge. But implementation has been slow and troubled, and the timetables are much too protracted for the immediate nuclear leakage threat.

We should note that the question of fissile material disposition — particularly of plutonium — is a controversial subject within the United States itself, which is beset by competing interest groups dedicated to their own particular economic or environmental concerns. That the U.S. government has had some difficulty coming to terms with the fissile material disposition problem in the former Soviet Union should therefore be less than surprising.

PROJECT SAPPHIRE: SUCCESS IN REMOVING HEU FROM KAZAKHSTAN

One way to deal with insecure fissile material in the former Soviet Union is for the United States to buy the material and move it to a secure location in the United States. One of the few unqualified successes for U.S. nuclear security policy involved just such a transaction: the purchase and removal of an inventory of HEU from Kazakhstan.

In late November 1994, approximately 600 kilograms of HEU (over 90 percent enriched) was flown out of the Ust-Kamenogorsk fuel fabrication facility in eastern Kazakhstan on American military aircraft and brought to the United States. This material, which had been produced as fuel for a prototype nuclear-powered submarine, was discovered by the Kazakh government in 1993, and was being stored under highly insecure conditions. Kazakhstan brought the problem to the attention of the United States and asked for assistance in securing this material. After highly secret internal deliberations, the United States decided to purchase the HEU from Kazakhstan and fly it to the United States for final delivery to the Y-12 plant at Oak Ridge, Tennessee.[67] The agreement of the Russian government was necessary for this operation to take place, however, and there were concerns that Minatom would object to the sale, claiming the material as its own. Ultimately, however, the Russian government acquiesced. The operation was delayed for several months by U.S. domestic politics and the stringent environmental and legal requirements involved with transporting nuclear materials, but in the end the operation proved to be a major non-proliferation achievement.

In this case, in a matter of months an inventory of HEU, stored under distressingly insecure conditions, was entirely removed from the former Soviet Union to a highly secure facility in the United States. It is hard to imagine a more effective response to the nuclear leakage threat. This transaction is justifiably regarded as a great success, and it is one that provided mutual benefit: the United States eliminated a potential leakage

---

67. The price paid by the United States in Project Sapphire was in the low tens of millions of dollars, half in cash, half in aid-in-kind. Both the Kazakh and U.S. governments are keeping the precise purchase price of this HEU secret, Almaty because it does not want to be accused of receiving too little for the material, Washington because it does not want to reveal how much it is willing to pay for excess fissile material.

problem and gained possession of valuable HEU; Kazakhstan earned much-needed capital.

THE HEU DEAL: UNREALIZED POTENTIAL

One of the most promising elements of American policy toward nuclear leakage involves the purchase of a very large quantity of HEU from Russia — the "HEU deal," which could, in effect, become Project Sapphire on a grand scale. However promising, the HEU deal suffers from three significant drawbacks. First, even if the HEU deal goes as planned, it will take two decades to implement, which does not solve the immediate pressing need to secure Russia's HEU. Thus we argue for a drastically accelerated timetable. Second, implementation is limited by Russia's ability to blend LEU; our solution is for the United States to buy the HEU before it is blended. Finally, the HEU deal has been entrusted to an organization, the U.S. Enrichment Corporation (USEC), whose underlying mission and incentive structure are contradictory to the goals of the HEU deal. Thus without constant administration oversight, the HEU deal may not even be implemented as planned.

In the HEU deal with Russia, the United States could purchase and remove hundreds of metric tons of HEU, rather than hundreds of kilograms. In August 1992, the United States and Russia agreed on the U.S. purchase of Russian HEU extracted from dismantled nuclear weapons for use as civilian reactor fuel.[68] An initial agreement was signed on February 18, 1993; the formal HEU purchase contract was signed in January 1994, during President Clinton's trip to Moscow. In this deal USEC, a government-owned corporation that runs the U.S. civilian uranium enrichment facilities, and which was then in the process of being privatized, contracted to purchase up to 500 tons of Russian HEU over the next twenty years.[69] This HEU is to come from dismantled nuclear weapons, but Russia will blend it down to a 4–5 percent U-235 fuel mixture before delivery to USEC. This uranium is then to be sold on the world market by USEC. The original contract specified a price of $780 per kilogram of 4.4 percent enriched uranium delivered to USEC, which would give the deal a total value of approximately $12 billion, but the purchase price is

---

68. For a full discussion of the HEU deal, see Appendix C of this study; Thomas L. Neff, "Integrating Uranium from Weapons into the Civil Fuel Cycle," *Science and Global Security*, Vol. 3 (1992), pp. 55–62; and Oleg Bukharin, "Weapons to Fuel," *Science and Global Security*, Vol. 4 (1993), pp. 179–188.

69. Russia is to supply 10 tons per year for the first five years of the contract, and 30 tons per year thereafter.

to be renegotiated annually "in accord with international economic and market conditions."[70] The HEU deal was intended to be budget-neutral for the U.S. government.

If implemented, the HEU deal would serve several objectives simultaneously. It would give Russia an incentive to dismantle its de-activated warheads to below the pit level. It would reduce the total amount of weapons-usable fissile material in Russia. It would provide work — paid for in hard currency — to the Russian nuclear establishment, thus reducing the incentives for emigration and theft, in exchange for a good with real economic value. However, although the HEU deal is undoubtedly a net "winner" for the United States and Russia, there might be some adverse effects in terms of nuclear leakage. While the arrangement reduces leakage risks by encouraging warhead dismantlement, by requiring the de-enrichment of the highly enriched uranium contained within those warheads, and by removing the material from Russia, the HEU deal could also produce some interim risks in Russia if the likelihood that bulk HEU will be stolen from storage or during transport is greater than when the HEU is stored in assembled weapons.[71] Even when this possibility is considered, though, a successfully implemented HEU deal should make a major contribution to reducing the overall threat of nuclear leakage.

However, the procedure for implementing the HEU deal that was set up in 1994 is unsound. Most importantly, the agency given responsibility for implementing the purchase, USEC, has conflicting objectives with respect to purchasing HEU from Russia. On the one hand, USEC as a wholly-owned government enterprise is implementing an important U.S. foreign policy objective by buying excess Russian HEU. On the other hand, because USEC was in the process of being privatized, its executives had a responsibility to maximize the market value of USEC shares, which would go to the Treasury. Not wanting to assume any obligations for itself that are not profitable, USEC sought a significantly lower purchase price from Russia, which Minatom was unwilling to accept, as well as a subsidy from the U.S. government equal to the "non-proliferation premium" paid to buy HEU from Russia. At the same time, USEC also does not want to give up executive authority over the HEU deal, since if Russian uranium is to be brought to the U.S. market, USEC wants to ensure that it controls

---

70. Wilson Dizard III and Mark Hibbs, "HEU Deal Signed in Moscow by Timbers, Mikhailov; Terms Unchanged," *Nuclear Fuel*, Vol. 19, No. 2 (January 17, 1994).

71. This risk is suggested in Oleg Bukharin, "U.S.-Russian Cooperation in the Area of Nuclear Safeguards," *The Nonproliferation Review*, Vol. 2, No. 1 (Fall 1994), pp. 30–37. Russia's HEU blending facility at Yekaterinburg should be an obvious priority candidate for a U.S.-funded MPC&A upgrade.

when, how, and at what price this uranium is resold. USEC will buy Russia's HEU only reluctantly so long as it fears that it could lose executive authority over the deal, but the U.S. government has effectively established an implementation system in which the executive agent must constantly be policed.

In addition to this quite fundamental problem with the HEU deal, at least two other issues have complicated its implementation. The first is its problematic status under U.S. trade law, particularly U.S. anti-dumping laws (as applied to non-market economies), the North American Free Trade Act (NAFTA), and the General Agreement on Tariffs and Trade (GATT). The second complication is the transparency agreement attached to the HEU deal, which is supposed to ensure that the uranium comes only from newly dismantled weapons in Russia, and is used only for non-military purposes in the United States. These issues are described in detail in Appendix C.

In sum, the core concept of the HEU deal is terrific, but in practice, its implementation has been badly flawed in several ways. First, and perhaps most fundamentally, the Bush and Clinton administrations handled the HEU deal not as an urgent national security program but as a commercial transaction. As a consequence, its fulfillment has been delayed by disputes over price and bickering over trade law. Second, and following from the first, the Bush administration gave responsibility for implementing the HEU deal to an entity — USEC — whose primary considerations are commercial, whose incentives to speed or delay the deal are heavily influenced by market forces and price calculations, and whose interests are not served by the importation of large quantities of de-enriched HEU from Russia.

Third, implementation of the deal depends on annual agreement between USEC and Russia on a purchase price. As originally structured, USEC — not the White House — had the power to decide how much, if any, Russian HEU is purchased in any given year. This arrangement virtually guaranteed that the U.S. executive agent in the HEU deal would oppose any expansion or acceleration of the HEU purchase, even though this would clearly serve U.S. national security interests. Finally, the HEU deal involves fixed amounts of HEU to be purchased over a twenty-year period, which, from a national security perspective, makes no sense whatsoever. In the context of the nuclear leakage threat, the United States should be concerned with any excess HEU that exists at any time. That the United States might, if USEC and Minatom can agree on a price, buy a fixed quantity of HEU twenty years from now is utterly irrelevant to the current predicament. Thus, the HEU deal as currently configured does disappointingly little to redress the immediate nuclear leakage threat, and may do nothing at all in the future if USEC and Minatom stay at a stalemate over the price issue.

If the HEU deal could be implemented quickly, it would represent enormous progress in reducing the risk of nuclear leakage. If the United States were able to buy large amounts of HEU at a rapid pace, excess inventories of HEU would not accumulate in insecure facilities in Russia, while Russia would have an incentive to continue, or even to accelerate, the dismantlement of nuclear weapons in order to profit from selling the HEU removed from the weapons, while the infusion of U.S. dollars would be improving the fortunes of personnel within the Russian nuclear empire. Unfortunately, as presently configured, the HEU deal is far less useful than it might be and its future status is very much in doubt. (In Chapter 4, we detail our ideas about how the HEU deal should be restructured to serve U.S. national security aims better.)

THE PLUTONIUM STORAGE FACILITY: TOMORROW'S SOLUTION FOR TODAY'S PROBLEM

In 1991 negotiations with the Russian government over the pace of START I implementation and nuclear-warhead dismantlement, Moscow asserted that the principal bottleneck in this process was insufficient storage space for the pits and secondaries from dismantled weapons. To address this need, on October 5, 1992, the United States signed a $15 million Nunn-Lugar contract with the Russian government for design work on a new storage facility.[72] A further $75 million was later authorized for providing "material, training, and services related to the construction and operation" of the facility; this equipment has been procured and delivered. Furthermore, in 1995 bilateral talks with Russian Prime Minister Chernomyrdin, Vice President Gore expressed a willingness to commit a second $75 million to the storage facility project, to be made available once the construction of the facility had begun. This money is now scheduled to be spent in fiscal year 1996 or later. (The United States later agreed that some of this money could be spent on construction expenses in Russia.)

The plutonium storage facility has encountered serious difficulties.

---

72. The $15 million for design work on the Russian plutonium storage facility went to the U.S. Army Corps of Engineers. Minatom chose a Russian design, but the Russian design bureau refused to release the plans until it received an additional $1 million. Minatom refused to provide this money out of its own budget, threatening to delay the construction of the facility still further. The Department of Defense also refused to provide this additional funding, arguing that it had already met the terms of its contract, while the Russian side had not. In the end, the Department of Energy gave the $1 million to Minatom out of its general budget, and the blueprints were released.

The United States government hoped that this new facility would meet or exceed Western standards for safe and secure warhead and weapon component storage; that Russia would store all or the vast majority of its excess weapons-grade fissile material and warhead components there; and that the United States would be granted extensive inspection rights to verify that the components sent to the facility are not recycled into new weapons. Correspondingly, the U.S. government has sought to negotiate detailed and binding agreements with the Russian government on the quantity and type of components and fissile material that will be stored in the facility, on U.S. inspection rights at the facility, and on the irreversibility of the dismantlements. Minatom has been reluctant to provide firm commitments on any of these points.

There have been other problems as well. Initially, Minatom was unable to secure the necessary construction permits at the first site it designated for the storage facility, near Tomsk-7, and had to settle on an alternative locale, at Chelyabinsk-65, where construction began in the fall of 1994.[73] The storage facility will not begin operations until 1998 at the earliest, which raises questions about the wisdom of spending the largest single amount of money devoted to fissile material security from a very limited budget on a project that does nothing to meet the immediate needs for secure storage. For all these reasons, there is some disillusionment with the plutonium storage facility project, and its cancellation has been considered.[74]

If it is built, the Nunn-Lugar plutonium storage facility in Russia would offer a significant improvement to the safety and security of excess weapons-grade fissile materials and weapon components. But because it will not become operational before 1998 at the earliest, it does nothing to

---

73. Russia has announced its intention to build a second storage facility at Tomsk, reportedly with assistance from Japan.

74. One of the reasons why the storage facility contract might be canceled is that there is a possibility that the funds earmarked for the project will be revoked by Congress if they are not spent quickly enough. Unspent Nunn-Lugar funds are a serious political liability for the Cooperative Threat Reduction (CTR) program, since the program has been criticized for being too slow by some members of Congress and some commentators outside of the government. (Some $300 million of the first $800 million of the reprogramming authorization granted by the FY91 and FY92 Nunn-Lugar bills was lost when the Department of Defense was unable to spend it in time. A smaller amount was rescinded in FY95.) The Nunn-Lugar office, therefore, might prefer to cancel the storage-facility contract itself, thereby keeping control of the funds, rather than let Congress do it, which would in all likelihood transfer the funds outside of the CTR program.

address the immediate proliferation risks arising from the deficit of safe and secure storage facilities.[75]

PLUTONIUM PRODUCTION CUT-OFF: VICTORY BY 2000?

In addition to preventing the leakage of fissile material from post-Soviet stockpiles, the United States would also like both to stop new additions to this stockpile and to reduce its total size. With respect to these objectives, plutonium and HEU present different difficulties and require different programs. The production of new HEU for weapons has already ceased both in the United States and the former Soviet Union.[76]

According to Western estimates, Russia is producing 1.5 tons of weapons-grade plutonium per year, and separating one additional ton of reactor-grade plutonium per year.[77] Weapons-grade plutonium production is occurring at three dual-purpose reactors, two at Tomsk-7, and one at Krasnoyarsk-26. The Russian government has announced on several occasions an interest in halting its weapons-grade plutonium production, but has delayed doing so because these three reactors also supply heat and electricity to nearby cities. The separation of reactor-grade plutonium, on the other hand, is going on because Minatom is committed to eventually adopting a plutonium-based fuel cycle, preferably one that relies on fast breeder reactors.

Russia's continued production of plutonium, particularly weapons-grade plutonium, is problematic for a number of reasons. First, the production of weapons-grade plutonium is inconsistent with the joint Russian-American support for a multilateral convention banning the production of fissile material for weapons purposes. Second, it aggravates the proliferation risks in Russia by adding to the already massive stock

---

75. In a related program, the United States signed a contract to supply Russia with 32,000 specially designed fissile material storage containers under a $50 million Nunn-Lugar contract. The purpose of this program is to provide "safe and protective transport and storage of fissile material in connection with the expeditious destruction of nuclear weapons." The canisters will presumably be used in the U.S.-financed fissile material storage facility. These special canisters were designed by Sandia National Laboratories in consultation with Russian experts, but the containers originally supplied by the U.S. contractor did not meet their design specifications and could not be shipped to Russia. New canisters were later manufactured. "CTR Semi-Annual Report," September 30, 1994.

76. Russia is still producing HEU for its naval fuel cycle. There is, however, considerable variation in the enrichment level of Russian submarine fuel, ranging (most experts believe) from 30 percent to 90 percent.

77. Thomas B. Cochran and Robert S. Norris, *Russian/Soviet Nuclear Warhead Production* (Washington DC: Natural Resources Defense Council, September 8, 1993), pp. 109–110.

of bulk weapons-usable fissile material. Third, it complicates the global non-proliferation effort by lending credibility to the argument that the nuclear-weapon states are not serious about the disarmament responsibility contained in Article VI of the Nuclear Non-proliferation Treaty (NPT). Finally, it can create domestic political problems for the Clinton administration and the CTR program. In 1994, for example, the U.S. Congress attached a condition to the fiscal year 1994 Department of Defense authorization bill, the Markey amendment, stipulating that no Nunn-Lugar funds could be obligated or expended for the plutonium storage facility in Russia unless the president could certify that Russia was "committed to halting the chemical separation of weapons-grade plutonium from spent fuel and is taking all practical steps to halt such separation at the earliest possible date."[78]

The plutonium production issue was first brought up in the U.S.-Russian Joint Commission on Economic and Technological Cooperation in late 1993, not least because of the Markey amendment[79] and President Clinton's September 1993 proposal at the United Nations to negotiate a global ban on the production of new fissile material for weapons.[80] In March 1994, Secretary of Energy O'Leary and Minister for Atomic Energy Mikhailov reached a preliminary understanding on phasing out Russia's production of weapons-grade plutonium, and agreed to conduct a joint feasibility study on developing alternative energy sources for those cities now relying on power from the dual-purpose reactors.[81] After additional expert-level negotiations in May 1994, Vice President Gore and Prime Minister Chernomyrdin signed a formal agreement in Washington on

---

78. Cited in Dunbar Lockwood, "U.S., Russia Reach Agreement for Plutonium Site Inspections," *Arms Control Today*, Vol. 24, No. 4 (April 1994), p. 22.

79. See the statement by Dr. Harold P. Smith, Jr., Assistant to the Secretary of Defense (Atomic Energy), before the Armed Services Committee of the House of Representatives, 103rd Cong., 2nd sess., April 28, 1994, p. 11.

80. The proposal appears in the "Joint Statement by the President of the Russian Federation and the President of the United States of America on Non-Proliferation of Weapons of Mass Destruction and the Means of their Delivery" made by Bill Clinton and Boris Yeltsin on January 14, 1994, in Moscow. For a good discussion of the multilateral fissile material production cut-off proposal, see Frans Berkhout, Oleg Bukharin, Harold Feiveson, and Marvin Miller, "A Cutoff in the Production of Fissile Material," *International Security*, Vol. 19, No. 3 (Winter 1994/95), pp. 167–202; and Wolfgang Liebert, "Managing Proliferation Risks from Civilian and Weapon-Grade Plutonium and Enriched Uranium: Comprehensive Cutoff Convention," paper presented to the 45th Pugwash Conference on Science and World Affairs, Hiroshima, Japan, July 23–29, 1995.

81. Lockwood, "U.S., Russia Reach Agreement for Plutonium Site Inspections."

June 23, 1994 to halt weapons-grade plutonium production. Russia agreed to shut down the three reactors still producing weapons-grade plutonium by the year 2000, though the agreement also stipulated that both states would "take all practical steps" to shut the reactors down before then. This could involve U.S. assistance in developing new power-generation capabilities to replace those of the three reactors, as envisaged in the O'Leary-Mikhailov statement, but the U.S. government has avoided making any commitment to this effect.[82]

In a side agreement, the United States and Russia promised not to resume plutonium production at any previously shut-down reactor.[83] In October 1994, Russian President Yeltsin announced that Russia would no longer put new plutonium into weapons. This pledge was followed by a Clinton-Yeltsin joint statement at the May 1995 summit committing both states never again to build weapons from excess fissile material from dismantled weapons, newly produced fissile material, or civilian material.[84]

The plutonium production cut-off is a valuable agreement despite its limitations, the worst of which is its long implementation period, which means that it will have no immediate effect on the Russian proliferation risks, and that up to 8 tons of new weapons-grade plutonium could be added to the Russian surplus before the cut-off goes into effect. The agreement satisfies the Markey amendment condition, and it will make it somewhat easier for the United States to promote the idea of a worldwide cut-off of the production of fissile material for weapons. More importantly, the joint feasibility study on replacement energy production options at Tomsk-7 and Krasnoyarsk-26 establishes the principle of direct American technical involvement in two of Russia's most sensitive nuclear installations, which could well result into greater transparency and better technical collaboration in the future.

Serious disagreements remain, however, on how to finance the alternative energy sources Tomsk-7 and Krasnoyarsk-26, and whether new facilities (if any) should be nuclear or non-nuclear. Minatom is committed to a nuclear solution, and has suggested a joint advanced reactor devel-

82. At the time the plutonium production shut-down agreement was signed, Minatom proposed a joint program to develop a new high-temperature gas reactor (HTGR) that could burn weapons-grade plutonium, transforming it into spent reactor fuel, which poses a markedly reduced proliferation risk. The U.S. government rejected this request.

83. Dunbar Lockwood, "U.S., Russia Agree to Phase Out Nuclear Weapons Reactors," *Arms Control Today*, Vol. 24, No. 6 (July/August 1994), p. 24.

84. "Joint Statement on the Transparency and Irreversibility of the Process of Reducing Nuclear Weapons," May 1995.

opment program to this end. So far, however, the U.S. government has rejected this approach, and this standoff continues.

LONG-TERM PLUTONIUM DISPOSITION: A LONG-RUN DISAGREEMENT?

In January 1995, the United States and Russia agreed to begin a joint study of long-term plutonium disposition. The intentions of this joint study are to ensure that, whatever the two states do on the question of plutonium disposition, they do it with transparency and in a cooperative environment; to develop joint criteria for making decisions on long-term disposition; and to analyze the options according to these criteria.

There is little reason for optimism that the two sides will reach similar conclusions about how ultimately to dispose of their weapons-grade or reactor-grade plutonium. The two sides approach the problem from quite different perspectives: Minatom regards plutonium as a valuable asset that should be used as reactor fuel, while most American experts consider plutonium a waste product and a serious security hazard. For instance, the United States would like Russians to stop reprocessing the spent reactor fuel, which they are now doing at a rate of one ton per year. The Russians reject this idea completely, and President Yeltsin has in fact announced plans to build a new reactor and a large new reprocessing plant at Krasnoyarsk. Furthermore, Minatom wants to finance this project with private, international contracts, and has proposed a change in Russia's atomic laws that would end the requirement that high-level waste be shipped back with separated plutonium, which would differentiate Russian commercial reprocessing from that offered by other states in the business, such as Britain and France. Thus, on the long-term plutonium disposition question, the only progress that has been made is a commitment to a joint study.

RESEARCH REACTOR CONVERSION: GOOD FOR THE LONG RUN

Finally, the Argonne National Laboratory has a small program to develop techniques for using low-enriched uranium (LEU) fuel in research reactors currently using HEU fuel.[85] If such conversions were widely implemented, they would reduce the long-term proliferation risks posed by the roughly twenty HEU-based research reactors in the former Soviet Union.[86] This program is a useful component of a long-term policy for

---

85. This is the RERTR program, which stands for "reduced enrichment for research and test reactors."

86. See Carnegie Endowment for International Peace and the Monterey Institute of International Studies, *Nuclear Successor States of the Soviet Union: Nuclear Weapon and Sensitive Export Status Report*, No. 1 (May 1994), Table 1-D, pp. 14–18.

minimizing proliferation risks in the former Soviet Union. Although this program does not bear centrally on the current concerns over nuclear leakage, it is interesting to note that recent reports from the International Atomic Energy Agency (IAEA) indicate that Iraq tried to extract HEU from the cores of the two Iraqi research reactors — one Soviet-designed and the other French-designed — in its crash program to build a nuclear weapon just prior to the Gulf War.[87] Immediate reduction of such a risk can come only from prompt improvements in the MPC&A systems at the reactor sites, or from the physical removal of the HEU. Funding for this project is currently sufficient only to develop LEU fuels, not to implement the switch to the new fuel types at the relevant reactors.

Transparency: Much Discussion, Little Progress

In 1994, the Clinton administration developed an ambitious agenda for Russian-American nuclear transparency, which it called "building confidence through openness" but which is sometimes also referred to as "nuclear glasnost."[88] At the January 1994 summit in Moscow, Presidents Yeltsin and Clinton directed their experts to explore practical means of making the two states' nuclear reductions more transparent to one another and irreversible. Through a variety of proposals and programs that have now been partially integrated, the Clinton administration has tried to reach agreements with Russia on the exchange of restricted data on each other's nuclear weapons programs, on reciprocal inspections of each other's surplus nuclear stockpiles, and on the verification of the HEU deal and the plutonium production cut-off agreement. This agenda is bold indeed by the paranoid standards of the Cold War, and the Clinton administration deserves credit for going further than any administration has gone before.

Transparency is important for four main reasons. First, as President Clinton's science advisor has put it, "you need to know how big a problem is before you can solve it."[89] This remark suggests a larger point:

---

87. See Steven Pagani, "IAEA Says Iraq Planned Short Cut to Nuclear Device," *Reuter News Agency*, August 29, 1995.

88. Transparency with the non-Russian republics is less of an issue because these states have acceded to the NPT as non–nuclear weapons states, have negotiated comprehensive safeguards agreements with the IAEA, and are in the process of implementing these safeguards, which provide for a high degree of transparency of a state's nuclear complex. Russia, as a nuclear-weapons state, falls outside of this normal IAEA transparency regime.

89. Gibbons, "Managing Nuclear Materials in the Post–Cold War Era," p. 4.

there are significant deficiencies in the U.S. government's understanding of the Russian nuclear security problem, a fact which should come as no surprise since the Russian government itself is incapable of monitoring its enormous static and dynamic inventories of fissile material. Second, transparency is vitally important if Russia and the United States are going to establish a genuinely cooperative effort to deal with their shared nuclear proliferation risks. Without openness, the permissible extent of cooperative nuclear security projects will be sharply circumscribed by the need to keep relevant information secret.

Third, transparency will make it easier to sustain U.S. domestic political support for cooperative nuclear security projects in Russia, since transparency makes it possible to verify that Russia is following through on its commitments and that U.S.-provided funds are being used in appropriate ways.[90] If the transparency achieved is fully reciprocal, it should also make it easier to create and sustain Russian domestic political support for controversial joint projects with the United States inside sensitive nuclear installations. Finally, a legally codified transparency regime would also lend credence to the "irreversibility" — another goal of the Clinton administration's nuclear security agenda — of the nuclear disarmament and dismantlement achievements of the early 1990s. If Russia and the United States have the right to monitor each other's stockpiles of surplus nuclear weapon components and weapons-usable materials, each will have greater confidence that these inventories have been permanently removed from the other state's arsenals. At a minimum, an effective transparency regime would allow them to know if and when a state began to tap into its surplus nuclear stockpile.

For these four reasons, the importance of the transparency agenda should not be underestimated, but neither should the challenge of putting it into effect. Habits of secrecy are strong in the Russian and American nuclear complexes, and not without reason. General John Shalikashvili, the Chairman of the U.S. Joint Chiefs of Staff, noted in 1993 that "a country's nuclear secrets are probably its most prized possessions."[91] During the Cold War, the United States and Russia each were preoccupied with keeping the other's spies out of its own nuclear installations. Elaborate laws, regulations, institutions, and procedures were developed for

---

90. On congressional pressure for more transparency into the Russian weapons dismantlement process, see John Deni and Dunbar Lockwood, "DOD Plan Calls for More Transparency in Managing U.S.-Russian Plutonium," *Arms Control Today*, Vol. 24, No. 3 (April 1994), p. 23.

91. Quoted in Thomas B. Cochran, Robert S. Norris, and Oleg A. Bukharin, *Making the Russian Bomb: From Stalin to Yeltsin* (Boulder: Westview, 1995), p. xii.

the sole purpose of keeping nuclear secrets. Breaking down the Cold War habits of extreme nuclear secrecy is no easy task, but it is a vital one is the post–Cold War era.

Perhaps understandably, the pace of progress at the working level on specific nuclear transparency programs has not matched the general ambition of the Clinton administration's objectives. Much of the delay comes from the Russian side, but the U.S. inter-agency process bears much blame as well. Thomas B. Cochran observes that the "painfully slow pace" of the transparency effort is due in part to "the reluctance of the Department of Defense to relinquish militarily useful fissile materials and open U.S. weapons facilities to safeguards."[92] The main deficiencies in the Clinton administration's mutual inspections proposal are that it excludes the nuclear weapons "that will remain in the enduring stockpile" along with naval reactor fuel,[93] and that it does not provide for perimeter monitoring of the two sides' nuclear materials and weapons installations. While we recognize that some nuclear weapons-related information, and much of the U.S. Navy's nuclear propulsion technology, clearly should not be shared with the Russian government, we believe that technical procedures could be designed that would permit reciprocal access to sensitive nuclear installations without revealing excessive amounts of information with real military relevance.

Below, we describe the specific programs being pursued and the problems they have encountered. In each case, serious negotiations with the Russian government began only in 1994–95, and legally codified results are still lacking.

BILATERAL DATA EXCHANGE: DISCUSSIONS CONTINUE
During the Washington summit of September 1994, Presidents Yeltsin and Clinton informally agreed on a confidential, bilateral exchange of data on each other's aggregate warhead and fissile material stockpiles. They then directed a joint working group to negotiate the details of the agreement in time for the data exchange to take place at the December 1994 meeting of the Gore-Chernomyrdin Commission (GCC). By September 1995, however, no formal agreement had been reached and no data exchange had taken place.

One of the key sources of delay on the U.S. side was the requirement

---

92. Thomas B. Cochran, "Dismantlement of Nuclear Weapons and Disposal of Fissile Material from Weapons," paper presented to the 45th Pugwash Conference on Science and World Affairs, Hiroshima, Japan, July 23–29, 1995, pp. 1–2.

93. Gibbons, "Managing Nuclear Materials in the Post–Cold War Era," p. 4.

(specified in a 1994 amendment to the Atomic Energy Act of 1954) that the United States conclude with Russia an Agreement for Cooperation, such as those which control the sharing of restricted U.S. data with Great Britain and France. Congress specifically amended that act to permit such an agreement with Russia, but its details still had to be laboriously worked out at the inter-agency level. For this reason, the United States was not able to table its opening proposed draft for an Agreement for Cooperation with Russia until the December 1994 GCC, which was when the data exchange was supposed to take place. At this meeting, the United States also tabled a "comprehensive" transparency and irreversibility concept that would tie the data exchange agreement to a newly proposed reciprocal monitoring and inspection regime (discussed below).[94] If accepted by the Russians, this exceptionally ambitious, comprehensive concept would mandate that the two sides exchange data on their total fissile material and warhead stockpiles; receive inspections of virtually every facility in their nuclear complex except those where active weapons are stockpiled or naval fuel is fabricated; and accept inspections of all warheads awaiting dismantlement, and all components removed from dismantled weapons.

Since December 1994, the U.S. government has tabled several different proposals about the kind and extent of the data on nuclear weapons and fissile materials that the two sides should exchange. The Russian government was unprepared to negotiate seriously on these proposals until April 1995, and even then the Russian officials at the working level displayed a noticeable hesitancy in following through on their president's commitment to an exchange of data. This lack of progress prompted President Clinton to raise the issue with President Yeltsin at the May 1995 Moscow summit, which resulted in a new joint statement that "express[ed] the desire of the United States of America and the Russian Federation to establish as soon as possible concrete arrangements for enhancing transparency and irreversibility of the process of nuclear arms reduction."[95] The crucial issue, of course, concerns the signing of the Agreement for Cooperation, without which no further progress on the transparency agenda will be possible. The Clinton administration and the Russian government failed to complete the Agreement for Cooperation

---

94. For a description of this "comprehensive" concept, see ibid., pp. 4–5.

95. "Joint Statement on the Transparency and Irreversibility of the Process of Reducing Nuclear Weapons."

in time for the Russian-American summit in October 1995. The exchange of data can occur only when the Agreement for Cooperation is in place.

MUTUAL RECIPROCAL INSPECTIONS: A TECHNIQUE FOR VERIFICATION

An inspection technique that could be used to verify a bilateral data exchange has been demonstrated in another U.S.-Russian openness program, the so-called the "Mutual Reciprocal Inspections" (MRI) program. This is a Department of Energy initiative that was agreed to by Minister Mikhailov and Secretary O'Leary in March 1994.[96] The idea behind MRI is to provide a relatively non-intrusive means of verifying the existence and measure the extent of both sides' stockpiles of fissile material components extracted from dismantled nuclear warheads.

The first practical steps in the MRI program were two bilateral "familiarization visits" to the U.S. facility at Rocky Flats, Colorado, in July 1994, and then to the Russian facility at Tomsk-7 in October 1994.[97] During these visits, the two sides demonstrated radiological techniques for determining that a fissile material canister contains a nuclear weapons component, without revealing the exact mass or geometry. Although no actual nuclear weapons components were used during these familiarization visits — doing so would require an Agreement for Cooperation — the demonstrations were carried off successfully, and the MRI verification technique is generally regarded as viable. In the fall of 1995, negotiations were underway toward a second set of demonstration visits that would inspect actual plutonium and HEU components taken from dismantled nuclear weapons. The success of these negotiations, of course, is linked to the completion and entry into force of the Agreement for Cooperation.

The hope is that the MRI technique will become widely used as a way for the two sides to inspect each other's stockpiles of stored fissile material and nuclear weapon components. To this end, the U.S. government built the MRI technique into the comprehensive transparency concept it presented at the GCC meeting in December 1994 , though at this time the Russian government had not yet agreed in principle to allow regular inspection of its weapons dismantlement process. An important achievement of the May 1995 summit in Moscow, however, was that President Clinton secured President Yeltsin's pledge that Russia and the United

96. See Michael R. Gordon, "Pentagon Offers New Way to Verify Disarmament," *New York Times*, March 10, 1994, p. A6; "U.S. and Russians Agree to Nuclear Dismantling Inspections," *New York Times*, March 17, 1994, p. A16.

97. See Dunbar Lockwood, "U.S., Russia Begin Detailed Talks on Fissile Materials," *Arms Control Today*, Vol 24, No. 5 (June 1994), p. 25.

States would negotiate an agreement that would establish "a cooperative arrangement for reciprocal monitoring at storage facilities of fissile materials removed from nuclear warheads and declared to be excess to national security requirements."[98] (This pledge had not been part of the joint statement of September 1994, which referred only to a data exchange, not to the means of verifying that data exchange.)

TRANSPARENCY PROVISIONS IN THE HEU DEAL

The HEU deal also contains a protocol stipulating that the United States will have the right to verify that the uranium supplied under the deal will be drawn only from newly dismantled weapons, rather than existing stockpiles or newly produced uranium. This is a challenging task, for technical and political reasons.[99] An initial HEU deal transparency protocol was signed in April 1994, but it provides insufficient access to Russia's weapons dismantlement and HEU blending processes to determine that the uranium purchased by the United States comes only from blended-down HEU, much less from newly dismantled warheads. Specifically, the United States currently does not have adequate inspection rights at the source of the HEU — the weapons dismantlement site — or at the blending facility, where uranium from weapons could be diluted with other stocks. As one analyst put it, "in order to prevent cheating via use of hidden internal piping, it would be necessary to either do repeat design verification [at the blending facility] or to implement some technical means to verify that there is no valve, flange, or penetration in the product pipe between the blending point and the container in which the product is collected."[100] To date, the Russian government has refused to allow this level of intrusion at its HEU blending facility.

The weaknesses in the HEU deal's transparency regime are politically sensitive since the conclusion that the United States cannot verify that the purchased uranium comes only from dismantled weapons might reduce the level of U.S. support for the program. Negotiations to increase the transparency of Russia's implementation of the HEU deal have proceeded discreetly during 1995, and the subject was discussed at the June 1995

---

98. "Joint Statement on the Transparency and Irreversibility of the Process of Reducing Nuclear Weapons."

99. See Oleg Bukharin and Helen Hunt, "The Russian-U.S. HEU Agreement: Internal Safeguards to Prevent Diversion of HEU," *Science & Global Security*, Vol. 4 (1993), pp. 198–212.

100. Helen M. Hunt, "Promoting Nuclear Safeguards and Security in Russia," paper presented to the European Safeguards Research and Development Association (ESARDA) Symposium, Aachen, Germany, May 1995, p. 4.

GCC. The hope is that the issue can be dealt with in the context of a larger U.S.-Russian agreement on transparency, which would include inspections along the warhead dismantlement pipeline, and that the Russian government will eventually agree to U.S.-assisted MPC&A.

TRANSPARENCY PROVISIONS FOR THE PLUTONIUM STORAGE FACILITY

The plutonium storage facility to be built with Nunn-Lugar funds at Chelyabinsk-65 is supposed to have inspection provisions associated with it that would allow the United States to confirm that it is being used for its intended purpose, and to verify that the weapons components or fissile material placed there is not later used for new weapons construction.[101] The early negotiations on this issue did not go well, and the topic has now been subsumed within the negotiations on the bilateral data exchange and reciprocal monitoring arrangements.

VERIFYING THE WEAPONS-GRADE PLUTONIUM PRODUCTION CUT-OFF

The Russian government agreed in June 1994 to shut down its three remaining weapons-grade plutonium production reactors by the year 2000 or earlier. The two governments agreed at that time to negotiate a verification protocol within six months (i.e., by December 1994). This deadline was not met, but the negotiations are continuing. Reportedly, the basic outlines of the verification agreement have already been agreed to, but the Russian negotiating team has delayed signing the agreement in order to put more pressure on the United States to supply an alternative energy source for Tomsk-7 and Krasnoyarsk-26.

Why Progress Has Been Slow

As we have shown, the United States has already created a fairly comprehensive set of proposals, initiatives, and programs seeking to reduce the threat of nuclear leakage. In its outlines, this is an impressive array that covers most aspects of the problem in one way or another. A few areas in the post-Soviet nuclear complex remain untargeted. However, the main problem is that progress, where it has been achieved at all, has occurred at a pace that is not commensurate with the U.S. stakes in the matter. In even the most successful U.S. programs to date, the pace of progress has been too slow to effect a meaningful reduction in the worldwide risk of nuclear proliferation arising from a theft or diversion in the former Soviet Union. After the first instance of nuclear terrorism or

---

101. See Dunbar Lockwood, "U.S., Russia Reach Agreement for Plutonium Site Inspections," *Arms Control Today,* Vol. 24, No. 3 (April 1994), p. 22.

proliferation caused by nuclear leakage, the United States will draw little comfort from the fact that the Russian nuclear stockpile was on track to become fully secure in the early years of the twenty-first century.

The question posed now, therefore, is not so much what new initiatives and proposals the U.S. government could or should make, but rather how the best of the initiatives and proposals already on the table can be dramatically accelerated. This requires exploration of why progress to date has been so fitful and so slow in the area of improving nuclear security in Russia.

Progress in the U.S. effort to improve nuclear security in the former Soviet Union has been slow for four reasons. First, and most importantly, Russia has been largely unable to enact the needed improvements on its own, and not always willing to cooperate with the United States or other states to this end. Second, the U.S. Congress has failed make available the resources that are sufficient to motivate and to underwrite the necessary improvements in Russia; for the most part, even those programs that the Congress has funded have been too laden with restrictions to induce substantial cooperation on the Russian side. Third, the executive branch has been slow to come to grips with the severity of the nuclear leakage threat, and the competing objectives of the Clinton administration have seriously undermined the efficacy of the U.S. attempt to induce Russian cooperation. Finally, the rest of the world, and most importantly the other major industrial — and nuclear — powers such as France, Japan, Germany, and Great Britain, have for the most part failed to carry their weight with respect to the widely shared threats of nuclear leakage, terrorism, and proliferation. Each of these points is discussed further below.

RUSSIA: THE HEART OF THE PROBLEM

The most important reason for the poor record of cooperative efforts to improve nuclear security in Russia has been political resistance in Moscow, particularly within Minatom. Many Russian officials, particularly those within Minatom, refuse to admit that there is a problem with Russia's nuclear security and accounting systems. Minister Mikhailov states that "as far as weapons-grade materials are concerned, the [Russian] accounting system ensures their absolute security. They cannot be stolen."[102] Evegeny Mikerin, a deputy minister for Atomic Energy, states baldly that "not one gram of plutonium" is missing in Russia.[103] In the

---

102. "Interview by Vladimir Orlov with Victor Mikhailov," *Yaderny Kontrol* (1995), p. 2 (English version).

103. "Pfeile gegen Russland," *Der Spiegel*, April 25, 1995, p. 32.

aftermath of the August 1994 discovery of plutonium on a plane from Moscow in Munich airport, most Russian officials strenuously denied that it was even possible that the material was of Russian origin, as alleged by the German government and amplified by the international media. In fact, the most common reaction in Moscow was to accuse the German intelligence service of manufacturing the incident to assist Chancellor Kohl in his election campaign, to gain commercial advantages over Russia, and to weaken the Russian state.[104]

Russian cooperation is essential if containment of the leakage threat is to succeed. The overwhelming majority of insecure weapons and fissile material are in Russia. Since Russia is a sovereign state, neither the U.S. government nor the international community as a whole can step in and make direct improvements to the security of nuclear weapons and fissile material in Russia. Successful anti-leakage policies, therefore, depend on motivating Moscow to immediate improvements in the security of Russian nuclear weapons and fissile material, whether unilateral or cooperative. Russia is at least as threatened by nuclear leakage as the United States is, and therefore should have an incentive to improve its nuclear security and accounting on its own, without any international prodding. This is not a case in which Russia is being pressed to act against its own best interests. But the Russian government has failed to invest political or financial resources into introducing significant improvements in the Russian nuclear security and accounting system.

There is some evidence, however, the Russian elite is aware that Russian fissile material and nuclear weapons are not as secure as they should be, or as they were during the Soviet era. Reports of lax fissile material security, theft, and smuggling have received wide coverage in the Russian press.[105] Despite the blanket assertions of Minatom and some

---

104. These accusations were echoed by the influential German weekly *Der Speigel* in a series of cover stories about the so-called "plutonium affair," which led to calls for the resignation of Bernd Schmidbauer, the coordinator of the German intelligence services. See "Die Hand im Feuer," *Der Spiegel*, April 24, 1995, pp. 28–37; "Parole: 'Keine Ahnung'," *Der Speigel*, April 17, 1995, pp. 18–24; and "Panik Made in Pullach," *Der Spiegel*, April 10, 1995, pp. 36–57.

105. One of the most detailed of these Russian press reports is Alexander Bolsunovsky and Valery Menshchikov, "Nuclear Security is Inadequate and Outdated," *Moscow News*, No. 49 (December 9–15, 1994), p. 14. Admittedly, however, much of the apparent demand for nuclear materials during 1991–94 appears to have been generated by reckless Russian journalists seeking a story. See Kirill Belyaninov, "Nuclear Nonsense, Black-Market Bombs, and Fissile Flim-Flam," *Bulletin of the Atomic Scientists*, March/April 1994, pp. 44–50.

officials in the Russian security services, a few Russian officials are willing to acknowledge that Russian nuclear security and accounting is inadequate. In September 1994, President Yeltsin issued a decree calling on the Russian government to "raise additional money to fund priority measures for developing and introducing a state system of accounting and control for nuclear materials and implementation of the state specific program for the physical protection of nuclear materials and facilities."[106] In February 1995, Prime Minister Chernomyrdin ordered tighter security of all Russian nuclear facilities, following a report by the Ministry of the Interior (MVD) that 80 percent of these facilities lack equipment to detect nuclear materials.[107] Undercover MVD officers have also conducted sting operations in the closed nuclear cities to evaluate the security of Minatom's installations, acts which Minister Mikhailov dismisses as "provocations."[108]

The issue of fissile material security has also been raised repeatedly by world leaders in their meetings with President Yeltsin, Prime Minister Chernomyrdin, and other high-level Russian officials. The issue is discussed periodically at the regular meetings between Vice-President Gore and Prime Minister Chernomyrdin, was the subject of two letters sent to Yeltsin in August 1994 by German Chancellor Kohl, and was raised by President Clinton during the September 1994 and May 1995 summit meetings with President Yeltsin. Moreover, since the summer of 1994, international law enforcement officials including Bernd Schmidbauer, the head of the German intelligence services, and Louis Freeh, the director of the FBI, have traveled to Moscow to discuss the threat of nuclear leakage and trafficking with Sergei Stepashin, the head of the FSB (the Federal Security Service, successor to the KGB), and other Russian officials. Yet, while it seems that the Russian government is aware that the security of Russian fissile material and nuclear weapons is an issue of considerable global concern, these high-level expressions of concern have yielded little in terms of results.

At least some Russian leaders also understand that nuclear leakage threatens Russian security. At the beginning of the war in Chechnya,

---

106. "On the Priority Measures for Improving the System of Accounting and Safety for Nuclear Materials," Decree of the President of the Russian Federation No. 1923, September 15, 1994, para. 4; reprinted in *The Monitor*, February 1995, p. 18.

107. Margaret Shapiro, "Russia Orders Tightened Security to Protect Nuclear Materials," *Washington Post*, February 14, 1995, p. A15; "Chernomyrdin Orders Tighter Nuclear Security," *OMRI Daily Report*, Part 1, No. 40 (February 24, 1995).

108. "Interview by Vladimir Orlov with Victor Mikhailov," *Yaderny Kontrol*.

Prime Minister Chernomyrdin reportedly phoned Minister Mikhailov to demand "all information on radioactive wastes left on the Chechen territory and on the possibility of their use by the enemy."[109] Mikhailov denied that any nuclear materials remained in Chechnya, but "an official from the Foreign Intelligence Service hinted at the possibility of a connection between the thefts of radioactive materials and General Dudayev's announcement of 'Chechnya's holy nuclear war against Moscow'."[110] Similarly, Foreign Minister Andrei Kozyrev has stated that safeguarding fissile material is an important priority in Russian foreign policy, and argued that Russia is more threatened by nuclear leakage than the United States or Germany because Russia, unlike these two states, is near nations that have nuclear ambitions or that have not acceded to the NPT.[111] The misconception that "only a huge, well-developed industry" could build a nuclear weapon, as Minister Mikhailov puts it,[112] appears to be accepted in Russia even more widely than in the West. There is, however, an appreciation in Moscow that stolen nuclear materials could be used for extortion or as radiological weapons.

EXPLANATIONS FOR RUSSIA'S UNRESPONSIVENESS. There are many explanations for the lack of progress or urgency in Russia's efforts to improve the security of its fissile material. One is lack of money: as General Evgeny Maslin, the head of the 12th Main Directorate of the Ministry of Defense, concedes, "the technical security equipment used at Russian nuclear installations is out of date; but Russia is currently incapable of upgrading it for lack of financial resources."[113] Another explanation is that the Russian government has too many other problems and crises on its hands to give the nuclear leakage issue the attention that it deserves. Economic reform, domestic political instability, NATO expansion, Chechnya, the problems with Ukraine over Crimea and the Black Sea Fleet, the rise of criminal activity since the collapse of the Soviet Union, and many other issues probably rank ahead of insecure fissile material on the agendas of Russia's most important leaders. Although these factors have certainly

---

109. "Nuclear Terrorism: The Problem that Will Soon Become Urgent," *Yaderny Kontrol* (1995), p. 4.

110. Ibid.

111. Yuri Kozlov, ITAR-TASS, August 30, 1994; translated in FBIS-SOV-94-168, August 30, 1994, p. 5; reported in "Nuclear Developments," *The Nonproliferation Review*, Vol. 2, No. 2 (Winter 1995), p. 108.

112. "Interview by Vladimir Orlov with Victor Mikhailov," *Yaderny Kontrol*, p. 3.

113. "Interview with Eugene Maslin, head of the 12th Department of the Ministry of Defense of the Russian Federation," *Yaderny Kontrol*, March 6, 1995, p. 4.

had an effect on Moscow's ability to focus on the nuclear leakage problem, there are deeper explanations for the lack of urgency in the Russian government's response.

Many Russians view their nuclear complex as one of Russia's last legitimate claims to great-power status, and are understandably reluctant to admit to a humiliating inferiority to the West in the nuclear area, as they have had to do in so many other areas. Even if pride were not a factor, however, most Russian politicians also do not know just how inadequate the security and accounting systems at Russian nuclear facilities really are. Minatom has jealously guarded its monopoly on information about what goes on inside the closed cities. While a great deal of information about these installations has been released since the breakup of the Soviet Union, Minatom is its own oversight agency. Gosatomnadzor (GAN), the agency that President Yeltsin has made responsible for "maintaining a system of accounting and control for nuclear materials,"[114] has no power to regulate Minatom's policies, behavior, or public disclosures. Moreover, many knowledgeable observers, both inside and out of Russia, have played down the threat of nuclear leakage by arguing that the leakage that has occurred is innocuous, since it has involved only small amounts of material that are not usable in weapons; that there is no demand for fissile material or nuclear weapons except among enterprising journalists, petty criminals, and Western governments that wish to suborn Russia and its nuclear industry;[115] and that only highly developed states could build a nuclear weapon out of smuggled fissile material.

Compounding these internal reasons for Russia's complacency about the leakage problem is the fact that much of the international effort to persuade the Russian government to take the threat of nuclear leakage more seriously have been poorly planned or executed. The German government's handling of the fallout from the sting operation that led to the seizure of plutonium in Munich is the best example of a counterproductive international approach to the question of Russian nuclear security and accounting. The Russian government resented having been an indirect target of a sting operation run by the German intelligence service, and reacted very badly to the international media hype that followed. Similarly, the effectiveness of the Nunn-Lugar program has been under-

---

114. "On the Priority Measures for Improving the System of Accounting and Safety for Nuclear Materials," Decree of the President of the Russian Federation No. 1923, September 15, 1994, para. 2; reprinted in *The Monitor*, February 1995, p. 18.

115. Minister Mikhailov has also argued that the Russian "oil and gas complex is involved in the campaign against the Russian atomic industry." "Interview by Vladimir Orlov with Victor Mikhailov," *Yaderny Kontrol*, p. 3.

mined by the complex and demanding sequence of negotiations and paperwork that needed to be take place before Nunn-Lugar funds could be spent; by the fact that these funds had to be spent on U.S. contractors; and by the reluctance of the U.S. government to offer Russia the same access to U.S. nuclear facilities and operations that Washington has required Moscow to accept.

In addition, there was a general deterioration of the political climate between Russia and the United States in 1993–95. Many Russians have become disillusioned by what they perceive as the ungenerous response of the United States and the West to Russia's troubles. Many Russians seem to believe that the West both helped to cause the Soviet Union's downfall and is now exploiting Russia's weakness. Many Russian politicians see domestic advantage in being anti-Western and anti-American. A number of difficult issues — Chechnya, NATO expansion, and so on — have arisen to complicate U.S.-Russian relations. None of this means that cooperation between Russia and the United States is impossible, but clearly the political environment is much less conducive to such cooperation than it was several years ago. Indeed, a common refrain of officials in the Clinton administration is that they are now dealing with a different Russia than that which existed when President Clinton entered office in January 1993, a Russia with which it is more difficult to deal. Prospects for cooperative anti-leakage efforts are unlikely to be completely separated from the wider fabric of U.S.-Russian relations, and the trends are not particularly favorable.

MINATOM: CRUCIAL BUT RELUCTANT. At the center of the difficulties the United States has encountered in its past attempts to improve the security and accounting systems at Russian nuclear installations, however, lies Minatom and its head, Victor Mikhailov. The process of negotiating with Mikhailov and his deputies on the implementation of Nunn-Lugar contracts has been extremely frustrating for all of the U.S. officials involved, in marked contrast to the business-like relationship these same officials have developed with the Russian Ministry of Defense. Relations with Minatom are so strained, in fact, that the Nunn-Lugar office in the Department of Defense reportedly considered canceling its $175 million plutonium storage facility project with Minatom,[116] and in early 1995 permitted responsibility for fissile-material security programs in the former Soviet Union to be transferred to the Department of Energy, which

---

116. Joseph Albright, "U.S. Close to Abandoning Russian Plutonium Storehouse Project," *Washington Times*, October 21, 1994, p. 17.

has had somewhat greater success with Minatom through the lab-to-lab program.

Minatom, however, is the key to making nuclear containment work. Minatom owns or controls the vast majority of the fissile material that is at greatest risk of leaking out of Russia. Unless Minatom substantially improves the way it handles, accounts for, and secures the fissile material in its possession, the vulnerability of the United States and its allies to nuclear proliferation and terrorism will continue unabated. A priority of U.S. foreign policy must, therefore, be to find a way to motivate and enable Minatom to improve its nuclear security and accounting systems. To do this, Western leaders must understand and accommodate the institutional interests of a collapsing nuclear-industrial empire within a collapsing political-industrial empire, no mean feat.

Minatom's vested interests explain its hostility toward allegations of lax security and accounting of fissile material, as well as its unwillingness to accept non-reciprocal intrusions by the United States into Russia's most sensitive nuclear installations. Beset with excess capacity, the Russian nuclear complex faces a very uncertain future: there are no new orders for nuclear weapons; nuclear weapons testing has been halted; funding for the construction of major new facilities such as reactors, reprocessing plants, or fuel fabrication facilities is extremely limited; research budgets have been slashed; the graduates from the best scientific departments in Russia can no longer be attracted to work in the closed cities; and some of the world's worst ecological disasters pollute the environment in which Minatom employees and their families live and work. Against this backdrop, Minatom knows that if it were to concede that it is unable to safely and securely store the fissile materials and nuclear weapons in its custody, it would risk a further reduction of its complex, or the transfer of some of its operation to another agency. Minatom wants to market its reactor fuel and reprocessing services abroad, but it knows that its competitive position will suffer if it comes to be perceived as a troubled industry in need of foreign assistance rather than as a responsible international supplier of nuclear products and services. For all these reasons, therefore, it is unsurprising that Minatom has been less than cooperative with the international efforts to improve the security of Russian nuclear facilities.

The central Russian government has not made a priority of compelling Minatom to upgrade its nuclear security and accounting systems, or to cooperate with the United States or other international actors. The main reason for this is that Minatom, despite all its problems, is an extremely important fixture in the Russian economy and society. In addition to maintaining Russia's arsenal of nuclear weapons, Minatom employs or supports over one million people, supplies 15–20 percent of Russia's electricity, and has the capacity to generate more hard currency than almost any other single actor in the Russian economy. Victor Mikhailov, moreover, is a powerful political figure in Moscow in his own right: he is a member of the parliamentary bloc formed by Prime Minister Chernomyrdin in April 1995 to counter the expected strength of right-wing parties in the December elections to the Duma. As a well-known Russian "hawk," Mikhailov is believed to be crucial to Chernomyrdin's strategy for the December election of attracting the support of the Russian nationalists and communists from fringe parties to the centrist coalition that comprises the current government. In July 1995, Mikhailov was appointed to the Russian Federation's Security Council.[117]

Although Russia must ultimately be held accountable for its own nuclear security problem, circumstances in Russia make it unlikely that Moscow, on its own, will have the political capacity or the financial resources to tackle the nuclear leakage problem promptly and vigorously. As described above, there are a number of reasons why key figures and institutions in Russia have not been eager to cooperate with the United States to address the problem. This does much to explain the slow progress in improving fissile material security in Russia. Unfortunately, American national security interests will remain threatened by nuclear leakage so long as Russia is unwilling or unable to take the practical steps needed to contain its own nuclear weapons and fissile materials within the boundaries of its nuclear installations.

CONGRESS: PART OF THE SOLUTION, PART OF THE PROBLEM

The U.S. Congress is an absolutely crucial player in shaping U.S. efforts to cope with the nuclear legacy of the former Soviet Union — including efforts to address the nuclear leakage threat. It determines how much money can be spent on these endeavors, how easily the appropriated monies can be spent, to whom the funds can be directed, and on what they can be spent. Via the annual budget process, it necessarily revisits these questions every year, and hence the judgments of Congress about the importance and effectiveness of U.S. anti-leakage efforts — and of other cooperative initiatives in the nuclear realm — play a central role in influencing the scale and character of the American effort. To a very large extent, it is Congress that shapes the political and budgetary context within which U.S. anti-leakage policies are crafted and pursued. Congress must therefore bear much of the responsibility for the fact that American

---

117. "Yeltsin Names Nuclear Power Minister to Security Council," *The Jamestown Monitor*, Vol. 1, No. 50 (June 12, 1995).

policy has so far been insufficient to produce the necessary nuclear security improvements in Russia.

Congress has behaved paradoxically in the U.S. effort to reduce the threat of nuclear leakage. On the one hand, several of the key U.S. programs now seeking to improve Russian nuclear security originated as congressional initiatives, sometimes with only lukewarm support from the executive branch. The Nunn-Lugar program is, of course, the archetype of such an initiative, but the Industrial Partnering Program — the brainchild of Senator Domenici of New Mexico — is another good example. But, on the other hand, the Congress has done much to make it harder for the U.S. government to successfully come to grips with the problem of nuclear insecurity in the former Soviet Union. In particular, Congress has been unwilling to allocate more than small amounts of money to this problem, has provided funds in forms that are difficult to spend quickly or flexibly, and has prevented or discouraged expenditure of this money in places and on things that matter to the Russians. Having thus constrained and circumscribed the U.S. effort, Congress has responded to the slow and halting progress by becoming increasingly critical of the Clinton administration's programs, skeptical of their value, and reluctant to spend money on them.

The ways in which Congress has limited, even hamstrung U.S. anti-leakage efforts are explored in the discussion that follows. If there is to be a significant reinvigoration of U.S. policy, in the hope of producing better results more rapidly, there must be major changes in Congress's approach to this issue.

SPENDING TOO LITTLE. The risk of nuclear leakage is one of the major challenges to American security at present. One should expect this to be reflected in U.S. defense spending. Even in the post–Cold War era, the United States routinely spends tens of billions of dollars annually to counter major threats. Strangely, and inappropriately, this has not been the case with the nuclear leakage threat. Congress has never authorized more than minor sums of money to address the nuclear legacy left behind by the Soviet Union, and an even smaller fraction is allocated specifically to efforts at minimizing nuclear leakage. Even these sums have been provided grudgingly: the Clinton administration has had to struggle to preserve these modest funding levels and has been fearful of Congress's wrath should it ask for significantly more, however useful or necessary more funding might be. The level of funding for Nunn-Lugar and associated programs has not generally been set according to judgments about how much it will take to get the job done. Rather, budget requests have been pegged at levels directly linked to estimates about what the Congress was willing to fund. Accordingly, should U.S. anti-leakage efforts fail, Congress will have a lot to answer for.

The sums of money the United States has devoted to its overall effort to cope with the Soviet nuclear legacy are mere pittances relative to the magnitude of the stakes involved or to the size of the U.S. defense effort. The United States is spending many tens of billions annually for the capability to cope with two major regional contingencies. It is spending several billion dollars per year trying to develop missile defenses that, all agree, will be imperfect at best. But during the period from 1991 to 1995, only $400 million per year — less than two-tenths of one percent of the defense budget — has been devoted to a program aimed at permanently eliminating most of the nuclear weapons that once threatened targets in the United States, and at preventing the spread of Russian nuclear weapons and materials to hostile forces that might use them against the United States.

Moreover, only a fraction of this annual $400 million has been allocated to enhancing nuclear security in Russia. Table 3-1 shows the amount of money the U.S. government allocated toward nuclear security projects in the former Soviet Union between fiscal years 1992 and 1995, and the amounts requested for fiscal year 1996. The total for five years is about $500 million, of which only a fraction is devoted to programs directly related to fissile material security, and far less than this sum was actually spent by mid-1995. In contrast, the Department of Energy has spent between $800 million and $1 billion per year to secure and account for the U.S. stockpile of weapons-grade fissile material, which poses a lesser proliferation risk than the post-Soviet nuclear stockpiles. A highly secure U.S. stockpile does little to reduce the threat of nuclear leakage if the post-Soviet stockpiles remain untouched. If U.S. expenditures on the security of U.S. nuclear assets are a guide, the level of U.S. expenditure of nuclear security abroad, where it matters most, is clearly less than is warranted. Yet, should nuclear leakage occur on a large scale, countless billions will undoubtedly be spent coping with its consequences.

There would be no cause for complaint about the present level of funding if the available resources sufficed to meet the core U.S. objective: reducing the leakage threat as much as possible as quickly as possible. But, as we have seen, this is simply not the case. It is stunning that there exists a major threat to American interests and a (perhaps ephemeral) opportunity to address and reduce that threat, that the current program has proven insufficient, and that Congress is unprepared to spend any significant fraction of the defense budget on this problem. Obviously, it is undesirable to spend more than necessary, but a program that actually succeeded in rapidly and substantially reducing the risk of nuclear leakage would be a great bargain at many times the present levels of funding. It is odd that a Congress that so often has had the attitude that in matters of defense it is better to spend too much than too little should be so tight-fisted when it comes to the nuclear leakage threat.

How much should the United States be willing to spend on nuclear security and accounting programs in the former Soviet Union? Imagine a program that could directly purchase former Soviet nuclear warheads from Russia for $1 million each. If there were 30,000 nuclear weapons to buy, this would cost the United States government $30 billion. This would indisputably be a worthwhile expenditure of U.S. taxpayer dollars, especially against the scale of the other U.S. national security programs. For comparision, the operation in Haiti is costing the American taxpayer about $2 billion per year. The United States, Japan, and South Korea were willing to pay $4.5 billion for a freeze in the North Korean nuclear program. The United States has spent around $36 billion on ballistic missile defense since 1983, even though it has yet to deploy a system other than the Patriot, a converted 1970s anti-aircraft missile. The international community spent $60 billion to eject Saddam Hussein from Kuwait. And the government says it needs a defense budget of $250 billion per year to prepare for two simultaneous medium regional wars. In comparison, the United States has spent merely tens of millions of dollars to acquire 600 kilograms of highly enriched uranium — enough for about 15 primitive bombs — being insecurely stored in Kazakhstan in Project Sapphire.

Another way to think about the value of nuclear security and accounting in the former Soviet Union is to calculate the economic loss that would result from a singular nuclear attack against a U.S. city. The present discounted value of lower Manhattan is at least $2 trillion, about one-third of the country's total annual GNP.[118] Rationally, therefore, the U.S. government should be willing to spend $2 billion per year on nuclear security and accounting programs if these programs reduced the probability of a nuclear detonation in lower Manhattan by only 0.1 percent (i.e., one in a thousand) per year.

The unfortunate truth, of course, is that the United States has little

---

118.   The $2 trillion estimate assumes a $260 billion gross product for lower Manhattan, a discount rate of 5 percent, and an expected life span of the existing productive assets in lower Manhattan of ten years. These are very conservative assumptions, and ignore the environmental implications, the wider regional damage, and the consequences of the collapse of the international monetary system which would almost certainly follow the destruction of the world's financial center.

Table 3-1. Combating Nuclear Leakage: Summary of U.S. Allocations (in millions of dollars).

Program	FY92–95	FY96[1]
Department of Defense programs		
Plutonium Storage Facility	91.00[2]	29.00[3]
Fissile Material Storage Containers	50.00	
Accident and Emergency Response Equipment	56.50[4]	
Weapons Security and Transportation	32.00	42.50
Department of Energy programs		
Gov't-to-Gov't MPC&A — Russia	30.00[5]	10.00[6]
Gov't-to-Gov't MPC&A — Belarus	3.00[7]	
Gov't-to-Gov't MPC&A — Kazakhstan	8.00[8]	
Gov't-to-Gov't MPC&A — Ukraine	22.50[9]	
Lab-to-Lab MPC&A — Russia	17.00[10]	40.00
Nuclear Regulatory Assistance		10.00
Naval Fuel Cycle Security		5.00
MPC&A upgrades in Latvia, Georgia, and Uzbekistan		
Industrial Partnership Program (IPP)	35.00[11]	10.00[12]
Department of State programs		
Export Controls	39.04[13]	15.00[14]
International Science Centers (ISTC & STCU)	64.00[15]	18.00[16]
Total	448.04[17]	184.50
Project Sapphire	n.a.[18]	

SOURCE: Information from relevant executing and budgeting offices.

[1] FY 96 funds shown as requested (9/95); not yet authorized or appropriated.

[2] From Nunn-Lugar budget: $15m for design; $75m for construction equipment. From DoE budget: $1m for additional payment for Russian design work.

[3] Up to $75m has been considered for FY96 and beyond, but not yet committed or obligated.

[4] Russia: emergency response equipment $15m; rail car conversion kits $21.5; armored blankets $5m; Belarus, Kazakhstan, and Ukraine: emergency response equipment, $5m each.

[5] From Nunn-Lugar funds in DOD budget. First $10 million contract was for MPC&A work on the LEU line at Electrostal, the MPC&A training center at Obninsk, and including $1m for regulatory work with GAN and Minatom. Second $20m contract is for MPC&A work at Electrostal, Obninsk, Podolsk, Mayak, and Dmitrovgrad.

[6] Part of the FY96 DOE budget request, to be used for continued work at five sites and possibly also Novosibirsk.

[7] Funds from Nunn-Lugar funds in DOD budget.

[8] Funds from Nunn-Lugar funds in DOD budget. $15m more may be made available from prior year DOD funds.

[9] Funds from Nunn-Lugar funds in DOD budget.

[10] Funding in FY94 ($2m) came from DOE budget; funding for FY95 ($15m) came from Nunn-Lugar funds in DOD budget.

[11] From the FY94 Foreign Operations Appropriations Act.

[12] DOE is seeking additional funds ($30m) for FY96.

[13] Funding for FY92–95 ($39.04m) came from Nunn-Lugar funds in DOD budget: Russia: $2.26m; Belarus: $16.26m; Kazakhstan: $7.26m; Ukraine: $13.26m.

Continued

[14] Funds to come from the Department of State's Nonproliferation and Disarmament Fund (NDF).

[15] Funding for FY92–95 ($64m) came from Nunn-Lugar funds in DOD budget: ISTC (general): $35; ISTC (Kazakhstan): $9m; ISTC (Belarus): $5m; STCU: $15m.

[16] Funds to come from the Freedom Support Act.

[17] Of this total amount for FY92–95, all but $2m for lab-to-lab and $35m for IPP came from the Nunn-Lugar program in the DOD budget.

[18] Exact amount not available. U.S. expenditures related to Project Sapphire are classified. Funds were drawn variously from the DOD, DOE, and DOS budgets. U.S. officials describe the expense as in the "low tens of millions of dollars."

---

trouble spending billions on weapons produced by American industry, but has great difficulty organizing itself to expend similar sums on unconventional programs with an even greater impact on U.S. national security interests. To paraphrase Senator Sam Nunn, how much would the United States pay for a weapon that could destroy a nuclear weapon already in the hands of the Hezbollah? The answer is surely in the billions. A similar willingness should motivate spending to keep that weapon out of its hands in the first place. Relative to expenditures aimed at other major threats to U.S. security, the level of effort associated with anti-leakage policies is low by an enormous margin.

In sum, more money might produce better results, but Congress has been unwilling to make more money available, even though larger sums are clearly warranted by U.S. stakes in the issue. This may be part of the explanation for why progress has been so slow, and clearly indicates an area in which the United States could try to do much better. Congress's parsimonious approach to this issue will appear remarkably short-sighted in retrospect if the United States ends up with a serious security problem caused by nuclear leakage.

COUNTERPRODUCTIVE CONDITIONS AND RESTRICTIONS. The effectiveness of U.S. tax dollars appropriated for the purpose of addressing the leakage threat depends not only (and perhaps not even primarily) on the amount of money made available. It also matters when and how the money may be spent, and on whom. Here too, Congress has been neither generous nor far-sighted. Rather than provide ample sums that can be flexibly spent in the service of an urgent U.S. national security interest, Congress has enmeshed many of the U.S. programs designed to improve the security of nuclear weapons and materials in the former Soviet Union in a web of conditions and restrictions, seriously reducing the ability of these programs to achieve their stated aims. This has been particularly true of the Department of Defense's Nunn-Lugar program, which until 1995 was the primary source of financial support for U.S. anti-leakage efforts. Responsibility for funding anti-leakage programs is being shifted to Department of Energy (DOE) accounts, which so far have been less shackled by Congressional limitations, but it remains to be seen whether the DOE budget will remain immune from harmful Congressional intervention.

Four sets of constraints are particularly salient in understanding the slow progress achieved in the overall U.S. effort to reduce the threat of nuclear leakage, particularly those initiatives carried out under the auspices of the Nunn-Lugar program.

The "Buy American" Restriction. Of the conditions that Congress has imposed on Nunn-Lugar funding, one of the most crippling has been the injunction that wherever possible these funds should be spent on U.S. suppliers of goods and services. Specifically, the legislation specified that these funds "should, to the extent feasible, draw upon United States technology and United States technicians."[119] In effect, Congress has treated Nunn-Lugar not as an urgent response to an immediate national security challenge, but as another opportunity for pork-barrel politics. As a consequence, all but a tiny fraction of the Nunn-Lugar funding has gone to American contractors.[120] Indeed, adminstration officials with responsibility for selling Nunn-Lugar programs to Congress stress the importance of being able to say that the taxpayers' money allocated to Nunn-Lugar is going to American recipients. This may produce highly motivated American companies. Predictably, it has had little positive impact on attitudes in Russia. If anything, it may have made matters worse (at least with Minatom) because Russian actors and agencies that hoped to benefit from Nunn-Lugar have grown cynical and disillusioned. Since the goal of U.S. policy must be to influence Russian behavior, there ought to be an emphasis in structuring Nunn-Lugar (and other anti-leakage programs) to create financial incentives for desired Russian action. What is needed is appropriately motivated Russian institutions and individuals, not happy American corporations or grateful congressional districts.

If the available Nunn-Lugar funds were used to purchase goods and services in Russia, rather than to reward American contractors, it is even possible that the current magnitude of funding would suffice. But the record seems clear that the leaders of Minatom have not been swayed by the present configuration of the program.

The Application of Defense Acquisition Guidelines. Money appropriated

---

119.   22 U.S.C. § 212(b) (1991).

120.   As one House staffer noted of American aid to Russia more generally, "By deliberate intent, Russia and Ukraine didn't see a single dollar— the money went to foreign consultants and contractors." Charles Flickner, "The Russian Aid Mess," *The National Interest*, Winter 1994–1995, p. 14.

for Nunn-Lugar falls under defense acquisition guidelines. This means that a complex matrix of legal provisions and procurement rules govern the expenditure of Nunn-Lugar funds, putting them in a regulatory context that is famously slow and inflexible. As officials responsible for Nunn-Lugar frequently explain, the legal complexities associated with spending this funding make the Pentagon's lawyers important players. The Department of Defense acquisition process may be appropriate for procuring weapons that take years or decades to develop and manufacture, but it hardly allows for quick and agile reactions necessary to respond to an immediate policy challenge.

Stringent Inspection and Audit Requirements. The purchases and activities funded by the Nunn-Lugar program must be audited and inspected by an appropriate U.S. agency. In normal circumstances, this is a perfectly reasonable and desirable requirement. In this instance, however, the requisite inspections and audits must take place at some of the most sensitive military and nuclear installations in Russia. This has been a bone of contention in many of the negotiations with Russia on specific Nunn-Lugar projects and has been the source of considerable delay. It might facilitate progress if Congress could find some more flexible way to fulfill its oversight responsibility.

The Demand for Certifications of Certain Russian Behavior. The U.S. government may provide Nunn-Lugar assistance in a given year only if the president certifies for that year that Russia is meeting a number of conditions, including being "committed to complying with all relevant arms control agreements."[121] Given the ambiguity of Russia's compliance with the 1972 Biological Weapons Convention,[122] the inability of Russia to meet

---

121. Specifically, the first Nunn-Lugar bill specified that the president must certify to Congress that the aid recipient "is committed to: (1) making a substantial investment of its resources for dismantling or destroying such weapons; (2) forgoing any military modernization program that exceeds legitimate defense requirements and forgoing the replacement of destroyed weapons of mass destruction; (3) forgoing any use of fissionable and other components of destroyed nuclear weapons in new nuclear weapons; (4) facilitating United States verification of weapons destruction's carried out under section 212; (5) complying with all relevant arms control agreements; and (6) observing internationally recognized human rights, including the protection of minorities." 22 U.S.C. § 211(b) (1991).

122. See Vladimir Orlov, "The Bomb for the Poor (Russian Biological Weapons)," *Moscow News,* February 4, 1994, p. 14; and Michael R. Gordon, "U.S. Asking Russia to Show It has Ended Germ Weapons Program," *New York Times,* September 1, 1992, p. A4. In the fiscal year 1996 budget deliberations, for example, the House National Security Committee slashed Nunn-Lugar funding to $171 million, and then the full House voted to withhold all Nunn-Lugar funding out of concern over allegations about continuing Russian work on biological weapons. (Ironically, on the same day,

that chemical weapons destruction commitments,[123] and Russia's violation of the flank ceilings of the Treaty on Conventional Arms Forces (CFE),[124] by 1996 the certification requirement threatened to paralyze the Nunn-Lugar effort entirely. U.S. officials working on Nunn-Lugar programs commonly note that months are lost every fiscal year awaiting the completion of the certification process.

The United States should expect and encourage Russia to comply with its arms control commitments, but the national security benefits of destroying Russian nuclear weapons and securely storing Russian fissile material are independent of whether or not Russia complies with the CFE flank ceilings or reveals all information about its past and present biological weapons program. Moreover, since Nunn-Lugar funds are generally spent on U.S. contractors, the threat that this assistance will be denied to Russia provides little if any leverage over Russian behavior. It is a peculiar logic to suggest that if Russia fails to comply with all of its international treaty obligations, the United States should respond by refusing to pursue its own national security interests.

These restrictions made the Nunn-Lugar program politically viable in the U.S. Congress, but they damaged the ability of the program to achieve the critically important aims it set for itself — especially in the area of securing nuclear weapons and fissile materials. Not only were the sums of money involved quite modest, but they were difficult to spend quickly and it was a domestic political liability to spend them in Russia on things Russian. All things considered, this seems a meager response to a large threat, and a ponderous response to a situation in which moving swiftly is essential.

Moreover, as a consequence of the constraints outlined above, it took about three years after the passage of the original legislation before large amounts of Nunn-Lugar money actually began to be spent.[125] These delays provoked much criticism of the Nunn-Lugar program, despite the

the House voted in favor of an extra $553 million for the B-2 program that had not been requested by the Pentagon.) See John Mintz and Bradley Graham, "House Sustains B-2 Funds, Blocks Aid to Destroy Soviet Nuclear Arms," *Washington Post*, June 14, 1995.

123. See Michael R. Gordon, "Moscow is Making Little Progress in Disposal of Chemical Weapons," *New York Times*, December 1, 1993, p. A1; and Elizabeth A. Palmer, "The Slow Road to Destruction (Chemical Weapons)," *Congressional Quarterly*, Vol. 52, No. 36 (September 17, 1994).

124. See Richard A. Falkenrath, "The CFE Flank Dispute: Waiting in the Wings," *International Security*, Vol. 19, No. 4 (Spring 1995), pp. 118–144.

125. See, for example, Dunbar Lockwood, "Dribbling Aid to Russia," *Arms Control Today*, July/August 1993, pp. 39–42.

fact that they were due in no small measure to the onerous reporting and disbursement procedures dictated by Congress (exacerbated by the bureaucratic disarray found in many of the former Soviet republics). These delays also generated cynicism and disillusionment among recipient governments, compounded by the requirement that Nunn-Lugar funds be spent on U.S. companies rather than in the recipient country itself.

CONGRESS'S UNWILLINGNESS TO ALLOW EXPENDITURES TO REFLECT RUSSIAN PRIORITIES. This analysis has emphasized that a major goal of U.S. anti-leakage policies must be to influence Russian behavior by creating incentives for Russia to move in desired directions. One significant step in this direction would be to provide funding to Russian recipients rather than American contractors. Efforts to influence Russia are also more likely to be successful if the United States is prepared to provide funding for projects that matter to the Russians. This, Congress has been increasingly unwilling to do.

The Russians have been worried about housing for officers decommissioned as a result of the denuclearization process, about the quality of life for members of its nuclear complex, and about cleanup of the often terrible environmental problems caused by its nuclear programs. Moscow has been eager for U.S. help in addressing such problems. The Clinton adminstration has tried to be responsive, and some such help has in fact been provided. Congress, however, has not been sympathetic.

Because the Nunn-Lugar program was the product of a delicate political compromise in the U.S. Congress shortly after the failed Soviet coup attempt in August 1991, its appropriate scope has been controversial. Those in favor of a broader scope have supported using Nunn-Lugar funds to help convert the post-Soviet defense industries into non-military enterprises, to supply housing for newly unemployed officers of the Strategic Rocket Forces, and to improve the security systems at Russia's many nuclear installations. But increasingly the predominant mood in Congress favors a narrow scope for the program, supporting only those projects that contribute directly to the destruction of weapons of mass destruction, the improvement of the safety and security of nuclear weapons while being transported, or the elimination of bottlenecks in the implementation of the Soviet Union's nuclear arms control commitments. Unfortunately, some of the programs of great interest to Russia — such as the provision of housing to demobilized former Soviet officers — have made the Nunn-Lugar program a target for political attack.[126]

---

126.   Arguing that the Nunn-Lugar mandate should include assistance for demobi-

CONGRESS'S FAILURE OF UNDERSTANDING. The unhelpful and occasionally counterproductive aspects of Congress's engagement with this issue seem rooted in two misunderstandings. First, with a few notable (and vital) exceptions, many — apparently a majority — in Congress remain oblivious to the potential threat that resides generally in the Soviet nuclear legacy and specifically in the risk of nuclear leakage. Congress simply could not behave the way that it has on this issue if America's stakes were widely and properly understood. After the House Appropriations Committee approved a supplemental defense appropriations bill in January 1995 that rescinded $80 million of Nunn-Lugar funding, for example, members of the Committee insisted that the rescissions had come from programs "not essential" to the defense of the United States.[127] Indeed, strong supporters in Congress of the Nunn-Lugar and related programs openly lament the political impossibility of gaining Congressional support for more ambitious programs.

Second, many U.S. legislators and legislative assistants — including many who do in fact recognize the threat of nuclear leakage — treat cooperative nuclear security projects in the former Soviet Union as if they were foreign aid. Foreign aid is generally unpopular, and foreign aid to Russia is especially unpopular in the United States and in Congress. Hence, this characterization of cooperative nuclear security and disarmament programs is not only fundamentally wrong but politically damaging to U.S. anti-leakage efforts — and more than a little ironic, in view of the fact that American contractors have been the primary beneficiaries of most U.S. expenditure for nuclear cooperation so far. The insecurity of nuclear materials in the former Soviet Union poses a direct threat to vital U.S. national security interests, but it so happens that this threat can most effectively be reduced in the near term by spending money in Russia on Russian goods and services, which superficially resembles foreign aid. So far, U.S. lawmakers have had trouble getting over their reflexive dislike of anything that resembles foreign aid, and appear largely to have failed to grasp the link between the security of their constituents and the security of the Russian nuclear complex. If Congress does not comprehend that U.S. anti-leakage efforts are not foreign aid but a crucial national security program, it is unlikely ever to act appropriately with respect to this issue.

---

lized officers, see Ashton B. Carter, "How to Reduce Nuclear Risk," *Miami Herald*, May 10, 1995, p. 17. For a critique, see Flickner, "The Russian Aid Mess."

127. See Kerry Gildea, "House Appropriators Pass $3.2 Billion DOD Supplemental," *Defense Daily*, January 30, 1995, p.138.

ASSESSMENT: CONGRESS'S DISAPPOINTING ROLE IN SHAPING U.S. POLICY. Some members of Congress — notably Senators Nunn and Lugar — have played decisively important roles in furthering U.S. efforts to cope with the Soviet nuclear legacy. Moreover, as the Soviet Union collapsed in 1991, Congress showed bold and commendable initiative in taking the lead to fashion an American response to the nuclear challenges arising from the disintegration of a nuclear superpower. Congress deserves credit for continuing to support Nunn-Lugar and DOE nuclear cooperation programs throughout the period since the demise of the Soviet Union. In these ways, Congress has contributed to such progress as has been made.

Nevertheless, Congress is also primarily responsible for the fact that the U.S. anti-leakage effort is much skimpier than U.S. stakes warrant; that U.S. programs have been U.S.-centric — funneling money to American recipients to address American concerns — rather than Russian-centric, as they must be if they are to be more successful; and that U.S. efforts have been slow and ponderous rather than quick and agile. Nuclear leakage is an immediate challenge that deserves the most rapid possible remedies. But Congress has not made it possible to move swiftly, and has done much that slows things down. Thus, Congress is a significant part of the explanation for the disappointing progress so far.

THE CLINTON ADMINISTRATION: COMPETING PRIORITIES
The Clinton administration's room for maneuver on post-Soviet nuclear issues has been shaped by erratic cooperation from Russia, on the one hand, and by constraints imposed by Congress, on the other. Operating in this difficult political landscape, it has pursued an ambitious nuclear agenda, and has achieved some historic successes, especially the denuclearization of Ukraine and the accelerated implementation of the START Treaty. As we have seen, even in the area of fissile material security, the Clinton administration has made some progress down an obstacle-strewn path.

Nevertheless, its broad and fairly comprehensive set of proposals designed to reduce the threat of nuclear leakage have moved slowly and fitfully forward, producing progress at a pace not nearly fast enough in view of the risks and stakes associated with the issue. And while much of the responsibility for this slow progress belongs to Russia and the Congress, the administration must be accountable for failing to be more persuasive with Congress and for causing some difficulties in relations with Russia.

THE LEAKAGE THREAT HAS NOT HAD THE PRIORITY IT DESERVES. At the working levels of the Clinton administration, officials responsible for anti-leakage efforts appear to have pursued their agenda seriously and persistently, with some positive results to show for their efforts. Moreover, these same officials note that the president, vice president, and other high officials give extensive attention to the fissile material security issue, to a remarkable degree it is said, given the arcane and technical nature of the subject.

Still, there are reasons to believe that at the highest levels of the U.S. government, this issue has not received the sustained attention and priority that it deserves. Indeed, until 1995, it would have been safe to say that nuclear security in the former Soviet Union received little attention from top officials in the Clinton White House. In 1994, for example, the Deputy Secretary of State gave a speech in which he identified 13 arms control priorities of the Clinton administration; fissile material security was not one of them.[128] This, at least, appears no longer to be true: over the first half of 1995, senior Clinton administration officials began to recognize and to appreciate properly the seriousness of the threat of nuclear leakage.

Prompted by a rash of nuclear smuggling incidents in 1994, the White House commissioned a report on the matter from the President's Committee of Advisors on Science and Technology (PCAST).[129] Drawing from a number of classified intelligence estimates, the report concluded that "the global problem of nuclear theft and nuclear smuggling is among the most serious and urgent national security threats the United States faces in coming decades."[130] According to several U.S. officials involved, the PCAST report resulted in a significant elevation of the nuclear security issue on the Clinton national security agenda. One contributor to the PCAST study reports that the president and vice president are now "clearly seized"[131] by the subject of nuclear weapons and fissile material security in the former Soviet Union. As a result, some useful bureaucratic realignments have been implemented,[132] and the security of Russian

---

128.   Strobe Talbott, "U.S. Interests and Russian Reform," *Arms Control Today*, Vol. 25, No. 3 (April 1994), pp. 3–8.

129.   The PCAST panel that wrote the report was chaired by John Holdren, and its other members were Norman Augustine, General William Burns, C. Ruth Kempf, and Sally Ride. Matthew Bunn was the chief staffer for the panel.

130.   John P. Holdren, Testimony before the Subcommittee on Europe of the Senate Foreign Relations Committee, August 23, 1995, p. 3.

131.   Ibid., p. 12.

132.   As a result of the increased attention given to the nuclear leakage threat in late 1994 and 1995, the U.S. fissile material security programs for the former Soviet Union

nuclear installations reportedly has become a regular item on the agenda of most meetings between high-level Russian and American officials.[133]

Nuclear leakage now appears to be attracting attention from the highest officials in the land, but what really matters is results, and these are still disappointing. Several considerations suggest that senior administration officials could be doing better.

First, nuclear security is now on the agenda of high-level meetings, but it is never at the top of the agenda, judging by headlines, official commentary, and the reaction of officials at the working level. Such officials often complain, some bitterly, about the way that their issues and concerns are overshadowed at high-level meetings. It is not enough to say that fissile material security is a top priority; it is necessary to behave as if it is. This, it seems, is not the case.

Second, in contrast to other difficult issues pressed hard by senior administration officials in interactions with Moscow, there have been few tangible results — and certainly no dramatic improvements — as a consequence of consideration of the issue at summits or other high level meetings. It raises suspicion about how vigorously the administration is really pushing on this issue when meeting after meeting, and summit after summit, produce no significant change in the situation.

Third, and perhaps most fundamentally, if the threat of nuclear leak-

---

were consolidated into the Office of Arms Control and Nonproliferation of the Department of Energy; a new National Security Council staffer was hired to work full-time on fissile material security issues; the president ordered the drafting of a presidential decision directive on fissile material security; Ambassador James Goodby was appointed as the president's personal representative for Nuclear Security and Disarmament; the Department of Energy created a new Nuclear Materials Security Task Force; and overall oversight responsibility for the administration's fissile material security effort was given to a high-level standing committee on nonproliferation that is co-chaired by the president's special advisors for the former Soviet Union, Coit D. Blacker, and for nonproliferation, Daniel Poneman.

133. For example, President Clinton is known to have discussed the issue of Russian nuclear security with President Yeltsin at the September 1994 meeting in Washington, their May 1995 meeting in Moscow, and at the G-7+1 meeting in June 1995 in Halifax, where it was agreed to hold a follow-on G-7+1 meeting in Moscow in March 1996 that will be devoted to nuclear issues. Likewise, Vice President Gore and Russian Prime Minister Victor Chernomyrdin regularly discuss nuclear security at the biannual meetings of the Gore-Chernomyrdin Commission. While these high-level meetings have produced some concrete results, the issue of nuclear security has tended to be overshadowed by other, more topical concerns: at the May 1995 summit in Moscow, for example, an important agreement was reached on transparency, but this agreement went virtually unnoticed against a barrage of media reports on U.S.-Russian disagreements over the reactor sale to Iran and the Russian operation in Chechnya.

age were accorded high-priority status as one of the major threats to U.S. security, this would be reflected throughout U.S. policy toward Russia. An administration that gave primacy to reducing the nuclear leakage threat as much as possible, as quickly as possible, would avoid any policies or steps that would interfere with the intimate nuclear cooperation necessary to meet that objective. The Clinton administration, however, has chosen to pursue some policies that were certain to antagonize Moscow, inflame the Russian debate, and cloud U.S.-Russian relations. For example, the decision to press for NATO enlargement has clearly undermined the cooperative spirit in Russian-American relations.[134] From the perspective of the fissile material security issue, it would have been wiser to postpone the question of NATO enlargement and to work to keep it off the active policy agenda. Another even more perplexing illustration is the administration's severe reaction to the Russian sale of nuclear reactors to Iran. This deal, if consummated, *might* turn out to be a proliferation problem in a decade or so; it would take years to build the reactors. Fissile material security is, on the other hand, an urgent and immediate proliferation problem. Yet Secretary of State Christopher appears to have invested far more energy trying to stop the Iran reactor deal than to advance the fissile material security issue, and has done so at the cost of some aggravation in U.S.-Russian relations. Choices like these make it difficult to sustain the argument that the Clinton administration really has given priority to establishing an effective, cooperative relationship with Moscow that is focused on combating nuclear smuggling, proliferation, and terrorism. Cooperation with Russia on the nuclear security front cannot be expected to proceed unaffected by discord in other dimensions of U.S.-Russian relations.

Fourth, by all accounts, the time and energy of senior officials has been regularly distracted by issues of lesser importance to U.S. national security interests. Officials working on nuclear security often find their

---

134. According to Sergey Rogov, a leading Russian foreign policy specialist, "Russia takes the problem of NATO enlargement as a major challenge for its foreign policy. For the first time in years we have a consensus in the country — from the left-wing to the right-wing forces — at least none of the major political forces in Russia supports NATO's enlargement without Russia's participation. . . . No matter how NATO expansion is packaged it will be treated as a threat to Russia. It will inevitably provoke the creation of a CIS military block. Then the two defense blocks would probably start to compete and enlarge, and that would trigger a new Cold War type rivalry." Sergey Rogov, "NATO Enlargement: The Unresolved Issues," paper presented to the 11th Annual Strategic Studies Conference, Knokke-Heist, Belgium, September 7–10, 1995, p. 12.

superiors preoccupied with Haiti or Rwanda or Somalia or Bosnia. Such issues, though tragic and challenging, are not nearly as important to U.S. security interests as the nuclear leakage threat. As one official commented, if there is a nuclear disaster from Russia, people will wonder why Haiti commanded so much attention.

In short, while the administration can hardly be accused of ignoring this issue and while it has made some progress in difficult circumstances, it has clearly been in the grips of competing priorities that have impeded its ability to make maximum progress on nuclear leakage. It has not always subordinated less important issues that distract from the overall mission of motivating and facilitating all necessary improvements in the Russian nuclear custodial system. It has not consistently sacrificed in areas of lesser importance to the national security of the United States in order to promote the prospects for progress on nuclear leakage. And it has not placed the problem at the top of the bilateral agenda.

THE ADMINISTRATION HAS NOT PERSUADED CONGRESS. The behavior of Congress suggests that the seriousness of the nuclear leakage threat has not been communicated by the administration in a clear and convincing way. Rank-and-file lawmakers (and the public that they represent) are largely unaware of the severity of the nuclear leakage threat and the importance to the United States of addressing it effectively. If the administration wishes for more latitude on this issue from Congress, it needs to convince a winning majority within Congress of the urgency of the nuclear leakage threat. At best, judging by Congressional attitudes, this has only partially been done: Congress is worried enough to support a modest and constrained program, but not a more ambitious and flexible program.

Administration officials protest that it is difficult to mount a compelling case without offending important counterparts in Russia, who are described as extraordinarily sensitive about the United States trumpeting their inadequacies and shortcomings.[135] This is a legitimate concern. But most of the necessary facts are already in the public domain, and some Russian sources have themselves catalogued the problems and vulnerabilities of the Russian nuclear complex. Moreover, it may be worthwhile to risk offending some in Russia rather than run the risk of failure with

---

135. As one U.S. diplomat in Moscow put it, "Trust that took thousands of hours to build can be destroyed in a 10-minute speech." Quoted anonymously by John P. Holdren in his Testimony before the Subcommittee on Europe of the Senate Foreign Relations Committee, August 23, 1995, p. 12.

a policy that is not producing progress rapidly enough. Perhaps most important, it is not obvious why it is necessary to publicly humiliate Russia in order to persuade Congress. But whether for this or other reasons, a sufficient effort to persuade Congress has not been made.

For these reasons, the Clinton administration too has its place in an explanation of the slow pace of progress on fissile material security.

THE OTHER INDUSTRIAL POWERS: NOT CARRYING THEIR WEIGHT

This study has focused on the threat of nuclear leakage to U.S. security interests and the U.S. role in combating the threat of nuclear leakage, and intentionally so: the United States has played by far the largest role in trying to tackle nuclear leakage. Furthermore, as a nuclear superpower and as Russia's partner in strategic affairs, the United States has a particular responsibility and natural capacity to do so. This does not mean that no other states have a stake in this problem or that others should not try to contribute to its solution. Quite the reverse: many states — Germany, Japan, France, Great Britain, Canada, Italy, Israel — are at least as threatened by nuclear proliferation and terrorism, and hence by nuclear leakage, than the United States. Germany has already experienced fissile material smuggling on its territory; Japan has already experienced terrorist attacks with weapons of mass destruction; and France, Great Britain, and Italy have serious domestic terrorism problems. The leaders of these states should be exercised about the threat of nuclear leakage, and should be deeply committed to combating it. The intellectual, political, and financial resources of the allies should be brought to bear on the problem as well.

At its outset, the Clinton administration sought to collaborate with the U.S. allies in cooperating with Russia to address the dangers associated with the Soviet nuclear legacy. Unfortunately, this effort met with so little positive response, and required so much diplomatic energy to pursue, that it was soon abandoned in favor of more unilateral initiatives to promote denuclearization and enhance nuclear security in Russia and the rest of the former Soviet Union. Hence, the efforts of leading states to combat the global threat of nuclear leakage have proceeded with little high-level coordination and a very uneven commitment of resources. The Clinton administration's programs designed to combat nuclear leakage have not gone as far or as fast as desirable, but it has at least advanced a concerted and comprehensive set of initiatives addressing many different aspects of this problem. The same cannot be said of America's friends and allies: with a few exceptions, the other major industrial powers have contributed little to reducing the dangers arising from the degradation of the nuclear custodial system in the former Soviet Union.[136]

Conclusion: Right Ideas, Wrong Pace

The Clinton administration has launched a multitude of programs, initiatives, discussions, and negotiations to deal with the threat of nuclear leakage from the former Soviet Union. On its current trajectory, it is impossible to know precisely when the U.S. response to the nuclear leakage threat will start having a major impact. We only know that it could easily be too late.

That the progress of most U.S. programs directed at the nuclear leakage threat has been inadequate and slow is not for want of trying. The Clinton administration, caught between the constraints imposed by Congress and the absence of cooperation in Moscow, has struggled to push forward on nearly every path that might redress some aspect of the problem. Within the context of readily available resources, existing domestic political constraints, and a U.S.-Russian relationship that has grown steadily less healthy since 1991–92, it has not proven possible to structure a policy that induces widespread cooperation in Russia. Instead, as the previous discussion indicates, key players in Russia have been recalcitrant, and critically important initiatives have been slowed or stymied by the absence of cooperation from Moscow.

Initial U.S. attempts to cope with the nuclear leakage problem were carried out in the context of the Nunn-Lugar program, but without much success. During 1993–94, the Department of Defense made some gains in the area of improving the safety and security of former Soviet nuclear weapons during transport, an important achievement that had much to do with the businesslike relationship established with the 12th Main Directorate of the Russian Ministry of Defense, which is responsible for handling Russia's active nuclear weapons. But the Nunn-Lugar pro-

---

136. The principal exceptions are a British program supplying special containers and trucks for transporting warheads (a program which partially duplicates a U.S. effort); a British program assisting in the improvement of the MPC&A system at the civilian fuel reprocessing plant at Chelyabinsk-65; a Euratom program to help the former Soviet republics improve their nuclear assaying and regulatory capabilities; contributions to the international science centers (the ISTC and the STCU) from the European Union, Sweden, and Japan; and assistance for the Baltic states from several Scandinavian countries in the area of export controls. Japan has also said that it would provide financial assistance for the construction of plutonium storage in Russia. Other programs may exist, but if so, they are not well publicized.

gram's initial attempt to improve the security of Russia's dismantled warhead components and fissile material stockpile — which required the cooperation of Minatom — met with frustration and achieved little. This fact resulted in a major restructuring of the U.S. effort for dealing with nuclear leakage in late 1994. At this time, lead responsibility for improving the security of Russian fissile material was consolidated into the Department of Energy, and the Department of State took over the implementation of the Department of Defense's small programs having to do with export control assistance and the international science centers in Moscow and Ukraine.[137] This bureaucratic adaptation appears to have improved the effectiveness of the U.S. effort to combat nuclear leakage while simultaneously making the key programs less vulnerable within the Congress.

In the area of enhancing the security of fissile material in the former Soviet Union, important results have been achieved in 1995, particularly by the lab-to-lab program. But far more remains to be done. We do not believe that the threat of nuclear leakage has so far been appreciably reduced by the U.S. effort. And it remains to be seen whether the initial successes of the lab-to-lab program can be continued, much less scaled up to affect the entire Soviet nuclear complex. Building on the apparent success of the lab-to-lab program will require more American commitment, more American leadership, and more American resources.

On the question of the long-term disposal of fissile material in the former Soviet Union, the U.S. government has acted with the necessary alacrity only once, in Project Sapphire. On the U.S.-Russian HEU purchase agreement, the White House has allowed peripheral issues such as the commercial interests of USEC to undermine a vitally important national security initiative. With respect to the long-term disposition of Russian plutonium and the production cut-off, the U.S. government has acted with a lamentable lack of boldness and urgency. The United States appears just as incapable of dealing with the Russian plutonium problem as it is of dealing with the American plutonium problem — but, unfortunately, the Russian plutonium problem poses a much greater national security threat.

In building "confidence through openness," the Clinton administration has advanced a commendable set of proposals that go almost far enough, but the implementation of these proposals has been allowed to

137. Expressing opposition to this "balkanization" of the Nunn-Lugar program is Rose Gottemoeller, "Icon and Tool: The Benefits, Problems, and Future of the Nunn-Lugar Program," paper prepared for the conference on the Nunn-Lugar Cooperative Threat Reduction Program: Donor and Recipient Country Perspectives, Monterey Institute of International Studies, August 20–22, 1995, pp. 5–7.

slip and suffer from unacceptable temporizing in Washington and Moscow alike. It is on the issue of transparency that the lack of cooperation on the Russian side is most apparent — specifically, in the unwillingness of lower level officials to follow through quickly on commitments made by President Yeltsin. Heightened attention and effort from the White House, which should include a rethought and restructured U.S. policy toward Russia, is necessary to ensure that the transparency agenda does not become a good idea whose time never came.

Chapter 4

The Challenge: A Response Commensurate with the Stakes

During the first three years after the collapse of the Soviet Union, virtually no progress was made in reducing the likelihood of nuclear leakage from Russia. In 1995, after considerable exertion, progress was visible for the first time. But while the picture has improved, progress is still much too slow. At the current pace, the United States and other concerned parties will be exposed to the risk of nuclear leakage for years to come. Because nuclear leakage can be so threatening to vital U.S. interests, and because it will be so much more difficult to cope with the global nuclear proliferation problem if fissile materials escape from Russia into an international nuclear bazaar, addressing the nuclear leakage problem gradually is highly undesirable. Hence, the progress witnessed so far, while commendable and heartening, does not reduce the imperative to try to do better.

What is required is a dramatic acceleration and intensification of anti-leakage efforts. The impediments to such an acceleration appear to be almost entirely political. For the most part, it is clear what needs to be done to improve security at vulnerable sites in Russia. The problem in Russia is large and challenging but finite and solvable. As we have seen in the previous chapter, a sensible and comprehensive set of cooperative initiatives to enhance nuclear security has already been put forward. The amounts of money required may be considerably more than is currently being spent (though not necessarily so), but it is unimaginable that the cost would be unaffordable in the context of a $250 billion defense budget in which major programs are allocated billions or tens of billions of dollars annually. In short, the nuclear leakage threat is not one of those intractable public policy problems where answers are elusive, effective responses are unavailable, or the necessary funding is unaffordable. In the proper political context, rapid progress in addressing the nuclear leakage threat would be possible.

Therefore, what is most important at this point is to consider how to create a more supportive political environment, one more conducive to rapid progress. Unfortunately, over the last several years, a pattern of behavior has emerged in interactions among the four critical players — the Russian government, Minatom, Congress, and the Clinton administration — that permits only slow and grudging progress and appears to obstruct rapid movement. As we have seen, Minatom has not been an enthusiastic and willing partner in cooperation with the United States on nuclear security, not least because it derives little direct benefit from existing programs. The Russian government has been willing to endorse summit communiqués proclaiming the importance of fissile material security, but has not been willing to compel its own ministry, Minatom, to be more cooperative. The Congress has been willing to support only a modest, inflexible, and substantially constrained program configured to reward American contractors rather than create inducements for Russian cooperation. Finally, the Clinton administration has earnestly pursued an impressively ambitious agenda of nuclear cooperation with Russia even as it pushed prominent policy initiatives — such as NATO expansion — destined to damage the climate of cooperation in U.S.-Russian relations, and it has never persuaded Congress to provide a level of support that would promote swift and successful implementation of that agenda. The unhelpful aspects of the behavior of these four key players can be mutually reinforcing, and combine to limit the political latitude available for pushing forward with the anti-leakage agenda. This is the logjam that must be broken.

How might that be done? Obviously, if the wave of a magic wand could cause all four of these actors to behave more appropriately with respect to the fissile material security issue, the problem would be easily solved. If the key players would consistently and coherently pursue paths that seem justified by the importance of the problem and their stakes in its solution, the nuclear leakage threat would be much more amenable to rapid solution. It is easy enough to urge that the players should act in a manner more consistent with their interests, and our concluding discussion urges that they do so.

But the reality is that they have not been doing so, and this shows little sign of changing. Hence, the challenge for American policy is to find some way to alter the political landscape so that the latitude for rapidly pursuing the anti-leakage mission is enlarged. In this context, it is Congress that occupies center stage. Congress alone seems in a position to make changes in its approach to this issue that affect either the room for maneuver or the incentives of all the other key players. It can permit the Clinton administration, or any successor administration, to move more aggressively with a larger and more flexible program. If Congress were willing to allow U.S. funding for cooperation on nuclear security to flow more freely into Russia and be spent on Russian goods and services, it could significantly influence the incentives for cooperation on the part of the Russian government and Minatom. Because Congress might be able to break the political logjam that has prevented rapid progress in enhancing nuclear security in Russia, it is crucially important that the leakage threat and its implications for American security come to be more widely understood in that body.

This chapter has two purposes. First, and most importantly, it seeks to describe how the relevant parties should change their behavior to act in a manner that better reflects their interest in the nuclear leakage issue. The purpose of encouraging such changes is to increase the political latitude for pursuing the anti-leakage agenda. This subject is addressed in the opening section of the chapter.

Second, this chapter outlines the steps and measures that ought to be vigorously undertaken for more progress in an altered political environment. Two considerations have governed their selection. First, because the danger is immediate and a nuclear leakage catastrophe could easily happen in the near future, priority should be placed on those programs that will quickly and directly improve the security of fissile material in Russia. Further delay in implementing such enhancements simply prolongs the period in which the threat of nuclear leakage jeopardizes U.S. national security interests. Second, rapid progress on major programs designed to reduce the threat of nuclear leakage requires a strong cooperative relationship with the Russian government and, most importantly, intimate nuclear cooperation with the custodian of Russia's far-flung nuclear stockpiles, Minatom. Emphasis must be given to programs that contribute to such a relationship and that promote sustainable, mutually beneficial nuclear cooperation, including programs that serve the institutional interests of key Russian actors as well as U.S. national security interests. Such programs may not themselves contribute directly to near-term improvement of nuclear security in Russia, but they are nevertheless an important element of the near-term policy agenda if they help create a political environment in which rapid security enhancements are possible. This is true even of long-term issues, such as the disposition of fissile material. Working now with Russia (and the other key nuclear states) to define and begin implementation of a long-term plan for coping with the global surplus of excess fissile materials not only addresses a big issue that has been repeatedly stalled for political and bureaucratic reasons, but can also reinforce nuclear cooperation and thereby buttress efforts to prevent nuclear leakage from the former Soviet Union in the short term. If the United

States is not willing and able to build such relationships, the odds of successfully eliminating the nuclear leakage problem are slim.

In short, the most important programs are those that directly and rapidly enhance nuclear security and those that promote the nuclear cooperation necessary for rapid treatment of the nuclear leakage threat. The programs that best meet these criteria — many of which have already been proposed or pursued by the Clinton administration — are discussed in the remaining sections of this chapter.

To do any of this, however, the leaders of Russia, the United States, and the other major industrial powers are going to have to find a way to overcome the obstacles to faster progress that they have been encountering over the past four years. It is to this subject that we turn first.

Creating Political Latitude for a More Effective Response to the Nuclear Leakage Threat

The previous chapter outlined the obstacles that have so far prevented rapid progress in the international efforts to cope with the threat of nuclear leakage. These obstacles were mostly political in nature, and had to do with preferences, perceptions, choices, and political calculations of Russia, the U.S. Congress, the Clinton administration, and the other major industrialized states. They arise from the paradox that most of the relevant parties — possibly excepting Minatom — are not acting in a manner consistent with their own best interests.

The following discussion sketches what Russia, Congress, the Clinton administration, and America's allies could do to contribute to a more favorable political environment for cooperative nuclear security programs. At least one of them will have to modify its behavior substantially for the current logjam to be broken.

RUSSIA'S VITAL INTEREST IN PREVENTING LEAKAGE
No state has a greater stake in combating nuclear leakage than Russia, but Russia has to date been surprisingly reluctant to undertake unilateral or cooperative measures sufficient to make a difference. Nuclear weapons and special nuclear materials are among the most valuable assets of the Russian state, and deserve to be carefully guarded. Even more importantly, Russia's geostrategic position and fragile internal composition make it almost uniquely vulnerable to the threats of nuclear terrorism and proliferation. Finally, cooperating in the area of nuclear security would provide Russia with an opportunity to give tangible expression to the attempt to form a genuine strategic partnership with the United States, and to confirm Russia's special responsibilities as a nuclear superpower.

A Russian government that acted in a manner that was commensurate with its interests would do more than make well-meaning promises at high-level meetings that are not implemented, or only reluctantly implemented, by recalcitrant bureaucracies in its own ministries, predictably resulting in glacial progress or outright impasse. A Russian government that acted in a manner that was commensurate with its interests would unilaterally take the initiative on the question of nuclear security, eliminating bureaucratic obstacles to rapid security improvements as they arise. A Russian government that was eager to redress the leakage problem and enthusiastic about doing so in a cooperative manner, as it ought to be, would fundamentally change the situation. So far, however, Moscow has done little more than pay lip-service to American concerns about the problem.

CONGRESS: IMPEDIMENT OR CATALYST?

Congress has been a big part of the explanation for the slow progress so far, but it could also be the key to doing better in the future. Heretofore, Congress has acted in a manner at odds with U.S. interests in this issue, circumscribing and constraining the U.S. effort; congressional leaders who do understand the nuclear leakage threat have had to spend large amounts of time and effort battling for programs that they know to be necessary but still not sufficient. This state of affairs has jeopardized U.S. national security.

A Congress which properly appreciated the risk of nuclear leakage, and the threats that flow therefrom, would behave differently in a number of respects. First, it would be willing to spend what it takes to successfully address the nuclear leakage threat. Congress is not normally stingy when it comes to coping with major threats to U.S. security, and it should not be so in the case of nuclear leakage. Helping Russia eliminate nuclear weapons that were once aimed at the United States and seeing to it that the resulting nuclear materials are safely and permanently disposed of should be regarded as an extremely effective form of strategic defense. No ballistic missile defense system, however expensive and elaborate, can ever work as well as a policy that promotes the destruction of nuclear weapons before they are ever used and that prevents any possible re-use of the fissile components by Russia or other nuclear aspirants. Congress is enthusiastic about spending significant sums of money to defend the United States against nuclear attack; if it spent equivalent sums on this much better form of strategic defense, it would increase the Nunn-Lugar program and the other anti-leakage funding by roughly ten-fold.

Second, Congress should be willing to allow anti-leakage funding to be spent in Russia. Making Nunn-Lugar a "buy American" program probably made it easier for members of Congress to support and defend this program. But this convenience for Congress undermines the effectiveness of the program. As we emphasize, a main aim of U.S. policy must be to influence Russian behavior by creating incentives for cooperative behavior, but giving contracts to American businesses provides little inducement for Moscow. Congress could help create constituencies for nuclear cooperation in Moscow by permitting expenditure of U.S. tax dollars on Russian goods and services. As a bonus, utilizing Russian labor, technologies and companies may be the quickest and cheapest way to make progress.

Third, also for the sake of seeking to influence Russian behavior and to create Russian incentives for cooperation, the Congress should allow money to be spent on matters of concern to Russia. Expenditures on housing for Russian officers, or for food and medicine for the Russian nuclear complex, or for conversion and retraining of those enterprises and individuals dislocated by nuclear dismantlement, can, if they contribute to the resolution of the nuclear leakage problem, justifiably be regarded as money well spent to further the national security interests of the United States. Self-interest, not misguided altruism, provides grounds for allowing U.S. spending to reflect, to some reasonable degree, the priorities of the Russian government. It will probably be politically difficult for members of Congress to endorse what looks like welfare spending in Russia while painful cuts are being made on programs at home. But in this case the demands of U.S security ought to prevail over political expediency. The merits of the case for a vigorous and effective anti-leakage effort are so compelling that Congress ought to be able to do what the national interest requires without running large domestic political risks.

Fourth, Congress should resist the temptation to make U.S. anti-leakage efforts conditional on Russian behavior in other areas, such as arms control and relations with the "near abroad." Russian arms control violations and misbehavior in the near abroad cannot be condoned, but at the same time it makes little sense to cancel programs that independently advance U.S. national security aims because Russia is doing something that affronts U.S. sensibilities. The U.S. interest in preventing nuclear leakage is strong no matter what Russia is doing in other domains.

Fifth, because time is an enemy in the context of fissile material vulnerability, Congress should appropriate money for anti-leakage efforts that can be spent quickly and flexibly. This means providing money that is not subject to cumbersome defense acquisition guidelines. Nor is it desirable to insist on stringent audit and inspection requirements when these impede the effectiveness of the program; it will matter little that the accountants are satisfied if the policy fails. Congress has every right to hold the executive branch accountable for these expenditures and to fulfill its oversight obligations. But it ought to work with the administration to find ways of meeting appropriate accountability concerns that do not diminish the prospects for success.

Many observers, not least members of the Clinton administration who have struggled for several years to defend the Nunn-Lugar program in the face of growing Congressional skepticism, will regard this set of recommendations as politically infeasible. Congress's instincts have been moving in the other direction, toward a less well-funded and more tightly constrained program. Others doubt that a Republican-dominated Congress will provide the needed funds and flexibility to a Democratic president, especially with an election coming into view. And these predictions may be correct.

But the case for regarding nuclear leakage as a major threat to American security is overwhelming. It does not seem beyond the bounds of the feasible that a majority of Congress could be persuaded to see it that way if they were exposed more fully to the issue. When President Clinton and Vice President Gore were given a detailed briefing on this problem in the spring of 1995, they were "clearly seized" by the issue.[1] The problem is so arresting that it seems likely that many members of Congress would react similarly if provided the same information. A Congress "clearly seized" by this issue, able to put it in its proper context as a major national security challenge, might well rise to the occasion and stir itself to advance some or all of the recommendations suggested here. Congress is not in the habit of shirking its responsibility when it comes to national security, and acts of bipartisan statesmenship are possible when high national interests are at risk. Should Congress be so inclined, it could make a huge difference to the size and character of the U.S. anti-leakage effort, and that in turn could produce a marked change in Russian attitudes.

THE CLINTON ADMINISTRATION MUST WORK FOR MORE LATITUDE
Many Clinton administration officials have worked energetically to advance a broad agenda of cooperative nuclear security programs with Russia and the other former Soviet republics within the confines of existing political constraints, and the Clinton administration has done reasonable well within these constraints. What it has been unable to do is to expand the range of what is politically feasible in the realm of enhancing nuclear security. The political constraints imposed upon the administra-

---

1. John P. Holdren, Testimony before the Subcommittee on Europe of the Senate Foreign Relations Committee, August 23, 1995, p. 3.

tion by Moscow and the Congress seriously limit the possibilities for rapid progress in improving the quality of nuclear security within the former Soviet Union. Therefore, if the Clinton administration wishes to do significantly better, it needs to do more than just work hard within the context of existing political constraints. It must attempt to alter the political landscape on which it operates by forging a different relationship with Congress and Moscow with respect to the nuclear leakage threat.

This diagnosis of the weaknesses in the Clinton administration's basic strategy for dealing with the threat of nuclear leakage suggests an obvious prescription: the president and his senior deputies must devote more time and energy to creating the political latitude that the administration must have if it is to succeed in safeguarding the United States against the future nuclear threats that will arise if nuclear leakage takes place.

First, since extensive cooperation in the nuclear sphere cannot be expected to occur outside of the context of a healthy U.S.-Russian relationship, the administration should work to minimize the number and severity of problems in U.S. relations with the Russian government and, in particular, with the leaders of the Russian nuclear complex. More generally, the Clinton administration should focus on programs that serve not only U.S. national security interests, but also the Russian national interests and the institutional interests of Minatom. Some issues will unavoidably complicate U.S.-Russian relations — Chechnya, for example, or the delicate Bosnian diplomacy — but in a number of instances the Clinton administration has pursued policies that could harm U.S.-Russian relations, such as NATO expansion and the campaign to stop the Russian reactor sale to Iran. In many cases, the U.S. government will have no choice but to walk a very fine line between the promotion of U.S. national interests and its distaste for some of Russia's behavior, but these trade-offs should be consciously weighed and continually re-assessed. The quality of the Russian-American political relationship has deteriorated since 1992–93, even as the U.S. government has tried to come to grips with the one issue in Russia — the insecurity of nuclear materials — that most directly threatens U.S. national security. A change in U.S. policy toward Russia along the lines suggested above could do much to slow or reverse this deterioration, and to expand the political latitude for cooperative nuclear security programs in Russia.

Second, the Clinton administration should make a sustained, high-level effort to inform and persuade the Congress of the dangerous realities of insecure nuclear weapons in the former Soviet Union. This need not be done publicly or in a way that the Russian government would find humiliating or insulting. Since the administration finds its key programs unduly constrained by funding or legislative restrictions, the president should invite key congressional leaders to the White House for the same threat assessments that he himself receives. This effort should be handled by the president and vice president — not by departmental officials, whose counsel may be easier to dismiss as institutional fund-raising. Only the president and the vice president have the personal authority, prestige, and wide responsibility needed to make a truly persuasive case for a more ambitious U.S. response to the threat of nuclear leakage, and for the creation of a more productive relationship with Minatom. Persuading the Congress of these realities will make it easier for the United States to pursue its interest in improving fissile material security in the former Soviet Union even as new disputes with Russia arise, a virtual inevitability in the current international climate. A failure to convince the Congress of the seriousness of the nuclear leakage problem will handicap the U.S. effort to deal with this threat. Congress is extremely unlikely to change its approach to the nuclear leakage problem in the absence of an effective campaign of education and persuasion, and the Clinton administration ought to be powerfully motivated to play a central role in such a campaign, given its understanding of the true stakes associated with the nuclear leakage threat and its commendable desire to do something about it. Indeed, it is somewhat mystifying that more along these lines has not been attempted already.

THE OTHER INDUSTRIAL POWERS SHOULD HELP

The interest of the other members of the G-7 in preventing nuclear leakage is fully equal to that of Russia and the United States, but the gap between their interests and their behavior has been wide. If the actions of Germany, Japan, France, Great Britain, Canada, and Italy were commensurate with their interests in preventing nuclear leakage, then they would make nuclear security one of the highest items on the agenda of their relations with Russia and the other states of the former Soviet Union, as well as an important common pursuit with the United States. Moreover, they would be prepared to commit considerably more resources to reducing the threat of nuclear proliferation. While several of the industrial states have made modest contributions to this endeavor, in the main it seems that the allies have either seriously underestimated the threat of nuclear leakage to their own security, or have been content to sit it out and hope that the Americans and Russians would take care of the problem. Ideally, this would change, and preferably at the allies' own initiative rather than through pressure from U.S. diplomats and politicians, whose efforts are often viewed as annoyances in allied capitals. Several of the specific programs outlined below would best be pursued with greater involvement by the other key industrial states.

NEEDED: POLITICAL LATITUDE FOR RAPID PROGRESS

In sum, the most urgent prerequisite for doing better in addressing nuclear leakage is a political environment that facilitates rapid progress. It is not hard to conceive why and how the various key parties to this issue might act so as to produce more political latitude for swift forward movement. That they are not now acting in such a manner is the core of the problem; should the status quo persist, the best that can be hoped for is gradual, and often grudging, progress, leaving in place for an uncomfortably long period the haunting possibility of nuclear leakage. Were Russia to attach higher priority to nuclear leakage and were it to become more willing to engage in immediate cooperative efforts with the United States to reduce the nuclear leakage threat, this would immediately transform the situation. But such Russian behavior has not been forthcoming; the United States cannot assume that it will be forthcoming; and Washington does not control or determine the Russian foreign policy debate or the direction of its policy on this issue. Hence, from the perspective of U.S. policy, it must be assumed that the initiative for breaking the political logjam must come from Washington. The crucial nexus lies in the interaction of the administration and Congress. If they can work together on the basis of a shared perception of the gravity of the leakage problem and the threat it can pose to core U.S. interests, it may be possible to fashion an American effort much more effective than the current policy, one that produces the desired reactions in Russia. That appears to be the most promising path by which the United States can more effectively pursue its high aim of reducing the nuclear leakage threat as much as possible as quickly as possible.

And if more progress becomes possible, what should be done? This question is addressed in the sections that follow. The first examines programs that can quickly and directly reduce the vulnerability of fissile material in Russia. The second discusses programs that have the potential to contribute to the emergence of a more constructive relationship with the custodians of the Russian nuclear complex. The third advances proposals for collaboratively managing the long-term disposition of fissile material, relevant in the short run because they would reinforce the habit of nuclear cooperation and give additional substance to U.S.-Russian nuclear collaboration.

Promote Programs that Directly Address the Nuclear Leakage Threat

The highest priority of U.S. non-proliferation policy must be to persuade Russia to take immediate concrete steps that reduce the near-term likelihood of nuclear leakage. No other non-proliferation objective is as urgent as improving the security of fissile material in the former Soviet Union. Stopping the Russian-Iranian reactor deal, shutting down the North Korean reactor program, signing a multilateral fissile material production cut-off convention — all of these worthwhile aims pale in comparison to the importance of reducing the likelihood that a nuclear weapon or quantity of fissile material will be stolen and diverted to a nuclear aspirant.

To meet the urgent aim of achieving the greatest possible reduction in the nuclear leakage threat in the shortest possible time, there are four key programs that the United States should initiate or pursue with greater urgency.

EXPAND AND ACCELERATE THE U.S. PURCHASE OF RUSSIAN HEU

One simple way to reduce the threat of nuclear leakage is to buy excess fissile material in the former Soviet Union and transfer it to a secure locale. This has already been done on a small scale in Project Sapphire, with great success. Purchasing fissile material also has the collateral benefit of injecting hard currency into troubled nuclear establishments, which frees up funds for salaries and security improvements. This general strategy for dealing with the nuclear leakage threat deserves to be used more aggressively by the United States.

The U.S. government agreed in 1992 to purchase up to 500 tons of highly enriched uranium from dismantled Russian warheads over twenty years (see Chapter 3 and Appendix C); this material is to be blended down and used as reactor fuel. The HEU deal was set up as a commercial transaction rather than a vital national security program.[2] For a complicated set of bureaucratic, political, and legal reasons — the most important of which is that USEC, the U.S. executive agent in the agreement, has an economic incentive to buy as little Russian uranium as possible, as slowly as possible — the United States is not now buying as much Russian HEU as quickly as it should. Politically influential groups, including USEC and U.S. uranium mining companies, have an interest in minimizing the amount of Russian uranium that is sold on the domestic and worldwide nuclear fuel markets. To date, the White House has been unwilling to challenge these interests by accelerating the rate of the U.S. purchase of Russian HEU, or by buying more than 500 tons.

The United States government should stop treating the HEU deal as a normal business transaction and start treating it as one of the most

---

2. See Appendix C for a full discussion.

critical and intelligent national-security initiatives of the post–Cold War era. The United States should aim to purchase as much Russian HEU as possible, as quickly as possible, given capabilities for secure and safe transportation. There are a number of ways to achieve such an acceleration and expansion of the HEU purchase. For example, the United States could take Minatom up on its offer to sell this excess HEU directly to the United States, rather than purchase the HEU only after it has been blended down to LEU in Russia; this would greatly accelerate the removal of this material from Russia.[3] Alternatively, Russia could be given the right to sell its blended-down warhead HEU on the U.S. market without restriction. Or the U.S. Treasury could buy the HEU directly and add it to the U.S. reserve for future use as civilian reactor fuel when needed. To date these options have been neglected by the White House.

An expansion and acceleration of the HEU purchase agreement would not necessarily entail a major new expense for the United States government, but it would allow the United States to quickly remove vast quantities of HEU directly from Russia for future use in civilian power generation while simultaneously transferring to the Russian government $1–2 billion per year. The offer of so much up-front hard currency would give the United States enormous leverage over Russia's nuclear security policies and programs, and might go a long way toward creating in Minatom the cooperative attitude that has been so noticeably absent. As evidence, Russian Deputy Prime Minister Oleg Davydov suggested in April 1995 that if "the U.S. proves willing to buy Russian uranium," Russia might reconsider its proposed reactor sale to Iran.[4] Not only does an HEU deal structured along these lines serve an urgent national security purpose, but it is sensible on economic grounds as well, since the United States would be getting a valuable marketable commodity in return.

BUY RUSSIA'S EXCESS PLUTONIUM

Plutonium, unlike HEU, is not economically viable as nuclear fuel given current market conditions. Plutonium does, however, pose acute proliferation risks, especially if it is weapons-grade and neatly clad in conveniently transportable forms. Because of the proliferation risk posed by Russia's stockpile of excess weapons-grade plutonium, the United States

---

3. The Russian Minister of Atomic Energy, Viktor Mikhailov, made this offer in a June 6, 1994, letter to Vice President Gore. The United States government has not yet responded to this proposal. Wilson Dizard III, "Matek Teams Russian, U.S. Entities to Implement HEU Deal, Courts USEC," *Nuclear Fuel*, Vol. 19, No. 13 (June 20, 1994).

4. Reported by ITAR-TASS, cited in "Davydov Hints of Possible Deal on Iran," *OMRI Daily Digest I*, No. 78 (April 20, 1995).

should offer to buy it — or at least some of it — for a combination of cash, aid in kind, and possibly even debt relief. In the absence of sound market indicators, the price paid for the plutonium would be essentially arbitrary (though unfortunately, many Russians think the material actually has great economic value).

A U.S. purchase of Russian plutonium could cause a number of serious technical, legal, and political problems, but it would yield a major national security benefit. If bringing the plutonium to the United States were politically impossible, then the purchased material could be held in Russia or a third country under U.S. or international safeguards pending a viable permanent disposal option. This arrangement could then form the basis of an international plutonium bank (described below) which would be part of the much needed long-term fissile material management strategy.

ACCELERATE SECURITY ENHANCEMENTS ACROSS THE FORMER SOVIET UNION

In parallel with buying as much of Russia's fissile material as possible as quickly as possible, the United States should take all steps necessary to ensure that the conditions in which Russia's fissile material and nuclear weapons are held are brought to internationally acceptable standards as quickly as possible. This should involve four specific steps.

First, the United States should underwrite the accelerated mass production and dissemination throughout the Minatom complex and the former Soviet Union of the MPC&A system developed through the lab-to-lab program. The United States should pay the Russian enterprises to produce Russian-made security equipment to be installed at Russian (and non-Russian) nuclear installations.[5] This project has in fact already begun, but it should be accelerated. The Department of Energy requested $70 million for its fissile material security program in fiscal year 1996, and plans to use about $40 million of this request for MPC&A production and dissemination. Because of domestic political constraints in Russia, the Department of Energy may be able to spend only $70 million in fiscal year 1996, but it is imperative that this program not be constrained by limits on resources.

Second, the United States must focus its efforts and resources on the

---

5. In addition to quickly improving the security at the sites containing fissile material, this measure would also have the valuable side-effect of injecting new activity and money into at least some of the Russian weapons laboratories, thereby reducing the Russian weapon scientists' incentives to emigrate to jobs with aspiring nuclear proliferators.

task of extending the successes of the lab-to-lab program beyond Russia's labs and into Minatom's industrial centers for handling nuclear weapons and fissile materials, including Tomsk-7, Chelyabinsk-65, Sverdlovsk-44, and Krasnoyarsk-26. These city-sized installations have suffered severe economic and social losses over the last five years. They contain the bulk of Russia's total fissile material stockpile, but remain virtually untouched by internationally motivated security enhancements. To overcome the political and bureaucratic obstacles to expanding the scope of the U.S. fissile material security programs into Minatom's industrial centers, the U.S. government should devise a package of economic and social inducements that is tailored for the particular needs of each nuclear installation that is resisting security cooperation with the United States. Several ideas for these packages appear below, but the basic point is that the institutional needs of Russia's research institutes and laboratories are different from those of Minatom's large industrial installations, so one cannot expect the apparent successes of the lab-to-lab program to be easily duplicated throughout the entire Russian nuclear complex.

Third, the United States should encourage and facilitate the transfer from Minatom's storage facilities at the dismantlement sites of any dismantled weapons components or excess fissile materials whose security cannot be quickly improved *in situ* to converted Ministry of Defense bunkers.[6] These military bunkers may require some technical modification to house fissile material containers (rather than weapons), but because the basic structures are already present, these modification are probably relatively minor and affordable. The transfer could be described as temporary, reversible as Minatom builds larger, more secure fissile

---

6. Extreme security precautions should be taken during this transfer, since the process of moving a large amounts of fissile material from one site to another would temporarily raise the risk of a diversion. The first step should be to implement immediate enhancements to the physical security of the warhead-component storage facilities, and to conduct the comprehensive inventory proposed above of the components now in storage at Minatom sites. The transfer should then be conducted with extremely careful accounting before and after the shipment. The warhead components should be placed in containers designed especially for fissile component storage, if they are not already, and a system of seals should be employed to verify that the contents of the canisters have not been tampered with since their initial packaging. American observers should be involved in this process from the start, but this preference should not distract from the central objective of the transfer, which is to move thousands of fissile-material components from less secure to more secure conditions. This transfer could be carried out very quickly— in a matter of months—if the relevant bureaucratic actors were committed to it.

material storage facilities.[7] The key obstacles to this move are bureaucratic and political in nature. The Ministry of Defense, for instance, might not want to assume responsibility for these dismantled warhead components. Minatom will show even greater reluctance. Both bureaucracies' objections should be overcome by direct and indirect forms of payment: the direct payments would be used to enact security improvements at the relevant installations and to carry out the transfer,[8] while the indirect payments would be channeled through the programs described below.

Fourth and finally, the United States and its allies should invest in the procurement of remote detection equipment to be delivered to as many border crossing points and police stations within the former Soviet Union as possible, and in providing appropriate training to those who would use this equipment. (It would also be prudent for the states of the West to undertake programs of this kind domestically, with their own border guards and law-enforcement agencies.) This is an expensive task, but it is a worthwhile one. While there is no "silver bullet" for the nuclear smuggling problem, the knowledge that remote detection equipment might be present at a given border crossing should discourage many would-be nuclear traffickers.

CONDUCT A JOINT U.S.-RUSSIA NUCLEAR INVENTORY AND SITE-BY-SITE
SECURITY ANALYSIS

Since the Russian government does not know exactly how much or what types of nuclear materials and components are now held at its nuclear installations, it cannot reliably detect an insider theft or diversion after it has occurred.[9] Therefore, Russia and the United States should immedi-

---

7. The United States should encourage but not require that the material shipped to Ministry of Defense bunkers be declared "permanent excess," and be accompanied by a pledge not to reuse it for weapons purposes. However, since insisting on such a pledge is likely to reduce the amount of material that Minatom would agree to store in Ministry of Defense bunkers, this should not be regarded as an essential element of the package.

8. Implementing this proposal would require funds to conduct an inventory of dismantled weapons components and fissile material; to provide for heightened security during the packaging and shipment of these components and materials; and for technical improvements and security enhancements at the military bunkers to which the components and materials are to be transferred.

9. According to a former chief inspector of GAN, "Russia does not have clear national policies for the safekeeping of radioactive substances. Moreover, Russia does not have a complete list of the radioactive substances in the nation." Reported in *Asahi Shimbum* (in Japanese), August 28, 1994; reported in Carnegie Endowment for International Peace and Monterey Institute of International Studies *Nuclear Successor States of the Soviet Union: Nuclear Weapon and Sensitive Export Status Report*, No. 2 (December 1994), pp. 41–42.

ately begin a joint and reciprocal inventory of their total fissile material stockpiles and a joint site-by-site security analysis at each of their nuclear installations. The inventory and site-by-site security analysis should be comprehensive so that no sensitive but potentially insecure stockpile of fissile material is left unaccounted for. Moreover, the inventory should be jointly conducted so that it reinforces the overall sense of a shared Russian-American mission in the area of nuclear security, and assists the cause of "building confidence through openness." The reciprocity of the proposal should reduce some of the obstacles now being encountered in the area of installing nuclear security equipment at Russian nuclear installations. Under the current political realities, the Russian government is no more likely to agree to such a venture than the United States is to make such a proposal, but a breakthrough might be possible if a revised U.S. policy on nuclear leakage created a climate conducive to cooperation and progress. (However, if a joint inventory and site-by-site security analysis remains politically non-viable, then the United States should proceed with dispatch along its current track of trying to equip and train Russian teams to do nuclear inventories and security analyses on their own. The most important point is that the job get done, not that the United States be directly involved in it.)

Joint teams of Russian and American experts would inspect, assay, and measure all of the bulk fissile material and weapons components in each other's custody. In the case of items containing sensitive design information, existing and demonstrated techniques for remote measurement can be used.[10] This would be an enormous and expensive task — in Russia alone there are hundreds of tons of fissile material stored at dozens of sites — but it would serve several important objectives at once.[11] First, and most importantly, it would allow the Russian government to determine exactly how much fissile material and of which types are being stored at all of its nuclear installations. This would complement the site-by-site security analysis, providing conclusive evidence that huge amounts of fissile material are held under insecure conditions. It would also improve deterrence against insider theft, since an accurate inventory of existing stocks would increase the likelihood that a theft would be promptly detected. A joint inventory could also contribute to a mutual

---

10. See Theodore B. Taylor, "Verified Elimination of Nuclear Warheads," *Science & Global Security*, Vol. 1, Nos. 1–2 (1989), pp. 1–26; and Steve Fetter, et al., "Detecting Nuclear Warheads," *Science & Global Security*, Vol. 1, Nos. 3–4 (1990), pp. 225–302.

11. Specifically, this proposal would require U.S. funds to conduct a one-time inventory of fissile materials at a very large number of installations in Russia, as well as to conduct a Russian-American inventory of nuclear sites in the United States.

effort to reduce the aggregate number of installations containing special nuclear materials, since both governments could use the occasion of the inventory to re-evaluate which of their installations really must contain fissile material. Finally, the inventory could help strengthen Russia's nuclear regulatory regime and offer the United States an opportunity to work closely with Minatom. It is far from certain that the Russian government would agree to any or all of these programs under current circumstances; this is why we focus in the next section on specific programs that would increase Russia's incentive to cooperate with the United States across the breadth of an ambitious nuclear security agenda.

Build a More Constructive Relationship with the Custodians of the Russian Nuclear Complex

Rapid progress in improving the security of Russia's nuclear weapons and materials is not likely to occur without a positive Russian-American political relationship, and is even less likely to occur without a cooperative relationship with the authorities in Russia's nuclear complex, principally Minatom and Victor Mikhailov, the Minister for Atomic Energy. By late 1995, the Russian-American political relationship could still be described as reasonably positive, but few knowledgeable observers would argue that the United States had managed to achieve a good cooperative relationship with Minatom. Indeed, the U.S. government has not done much in attempting to build a constructive relationship with Minatom, and this fact has jeopardized U.S. national security interests because of its implications in the area of enhancing the security of Russia's nuclear installations.

If one tries to see the world through the eyes of a top Minatom official, it appears as though most of what the United States has done during 1991–95 has been a direct challenge to the institutional interests of the Russian nuclear complex. From Minatom's perspective, the United States has denied Russia access to its nuclear fuel markets; maligned the safety of Soviet-design reactors; pried into Russia's most secret installations; purveyed myths about inadequate security at Russia's nuclear installations; created a phony nuclear black market by running provocative sting operations; tried to frustrate international efforts to close the nuclear fuel cycle through the use of reprocessed plutonium as fuel; and campaigned to halt a billion-dollar reactor sale to Iran that violates no international law. Not all of these views are justified, but the point is that most senior Minatom officials believe that U.S. policy has tended to threaten rather than to support the interest of the institution they represent. This must change if the United States is to have any serious hope of effecting a near-term reduction in the threat of nuclear leakage.

Building a constructive relationship with Minatom requires an appreciation of its institutional interests, and a willingness to accommodate those interests in tangible ways.

First, nuclear power is Minatom's sole remaining *raison d'être*. With the nuclear arms race over, Minatom is effectively out of the business of building weapons. Environmental clean-up has not yet become a central mission for Minatom. This leaves only the civilian nuclear fuel cycle to absorb Minatom's productive potential and to justify its existence. It should not, therefore, be surprising that Minatom officials are among the most ardent proponents of nuclear energy, and in particular of closed fuel cycles based on reprocessed plutonium.[12] But the future of nuclear power in Russia is not particularly bright: little money is available to construct new reactors, much less design and develop the advanced reactor types that Minatom officials covet, and Russia has plentiful supplies of oil and gas that compete with nuclear power in Russia's distorted energy market.

Second, Minatom is responsible for the lives of about one million people, most of whom live within cities that exist solely to produce or process nuclear materials. Most of these one million people do not enjoy high standards of living, and their futures are generally quite bleak: the weapons production process is now being run in reverse, and there is little money in the former Soviet Union for new reactor construction. Their economic well-being depends on the future of nuclear energy in Russia, and their physical well-being depends on the adherence to reasonable standards of safety in the day-to-day operations of the plants near their homes. Caring for these people is more important to Minatom than complying with the wishes of the United States as regards modern MPC&A equipment.

Third, the internal prestige and strength of Minatom depends to a certain extent on its ability to export nuclear goods and services abroad for hard currency earnings. U.S. cooperation with Minatom, therefore, requires an understanding that it can be motivated by offers that bring new resources, new business, and new expansion opportunities to the Russian nuclear complex. Minister Mikhailov is a serious negotiator when real money is on the table, but he is dismissive and obstructionist when it is not. There is more to this pattern of behavior than a base desire for self-enrichment. Mikhailov sees himself as the steward of one of Russia's

---

12. The U.S. government, on the other hand, has officially discouraged the use of plutonium as fuel since the 1970s and is generally anti–nuclear energy in orientation.

most precious resources, its sprawling nuclear industry; recognizing that this industry is under threat from several different directions, he is dedicated to ensuring that it remains viable and strong.

This section considers five programs that the United States and its allies could pursue to put their relationship with Minatom on a far more positive footing. A positive relationship is not an end unto itself, but has value only insofar as it leads to a rapid reduction in the threat of nuclear leakage. All of the programs proposed below should be viewed in this light, since they will not seem nearly so compelling or attractive if they are divorced from the paramount national security aim of preventing nuclear leakage. They aim to give Minatom a major incentive to improve the quality of the security and accounting systems at its nuclear installations. At present, such an incentive, to the extent that it exists at all, is only weakly felt. Moreover, the programs outlined below would begin to mitigate some of the underlying causes of the nuclear leakage threat: the economic duress of Russia's nuclear industry, its bleak future, and the environmental hardships endured by the people within this complex. Ironically, American national security has become intertwined with the health and viability of the Russian nuclear energy industry.

The programs envisioned here are almost certainly infeasible in the current political context. So long as the political landscape remains constrained, ambitious and innovative proposals are very unlikely to find favor. But in an atmosphere more conducive to progress, an agenda like the one outlined below may become more tenable and would certainly contribute to the sort of relationship with Minatom necessary if anti-leakage efforts are to prosper.

RESTRUCTURE THE HEU DEAL

The HEU deal could be restructured in a number of ways so that it better serves the interests of Minatom, by generating more money faster, as well as the national security interests of the United States. This is in no way a question of holding the HEU deal hostage to a particular course of Russian behavior; it is instead a way to reward constructive changes in the Russian attitude toward cooperative nuclear security ventures. The cost of any of the options for restructuring the HEU deal is that they conflict with the commercial interests of politically influential U.S. groups and companies (especially the U.S. Enrichment Corporation). The fact remains, however, that if the U.S. government really wants to establish a more constructive relationship with Minatom, a vehicle for doing so is already at its disposal.

JOINT NUCLEAR TECHNOLOGY DEVELOPMENT

As part of a strategy of building a constructive relationship with Minatom, the United States should finance selected joint development projects with Russia of new nuclear technologies that both countries need. For example, the two countries share a common interest in the safe long-term disposition of weapon-grade plutonium. Another area of shared interest lies in advanced thermal reactor development to serve future commercial nuclear power generation requirements, especially in rapidly industrializing countries like China. In both areas, strong joint-technology development partnerships should begin that resemble the deep cooperation that already exists between the American and Russian manned space programs.[13] More rapid near-term progress toward cooperatively improving the security and accounting systems at Russian nuclear installations would be possible if Russian installation managers had confidence in longer-term cooperation between the U.S. and Russian nuclear complexes.

A joint nuclear technology development program could serve U.S. national security interests in at least five ways. First, it could significantly improve the quality of the relationship between Minatom and the U.S. government, tangibly demonstrating that the United States understands and supports Minatom's institutional interests. This could help shift the terms of the relationship between Minatom and the U.S. government, perhaps leading to a breakthrough in the area of nuclear security. Second, joint technology projects would provide work for Russia's nuclear scientists and engineers and, if the development project results in a new commercially competitive product (such as an advanced thermal reactor), perhaps even a new long-term source of export earnings. This could help stem the "brain drain" and reverse the socio-economic decline of Russia's nuclear cities. Third, the program would increase the involvement of U.S. and other Western firms in the fate of Russia's nuclear cities, leveraging the U.S. investment and laying the basis for a long-term cooperative relationship. Fourth, in the case of advanced thermal reactor projects, the new reactor might contribute to a long-term plutonium disposition op-

---

13. The NASA manned space station was saved from a near-death experience in Congress by the prospect of Russian cooperation. Russian involvement in what is now International Space Station Alpha will be absolutely crucial to its success for three reasons. Russian involvement gives NASA access to technologies it does not possess, reduces costs, and gives the space station a foreign-policy rationale. On the high degree of U.S.-Russian cooperation on this project, see Craig Covault, "Russian FGB 'Space Tug' Leads Station Alpha," *Aviation Week & Space Technology*, September 4, 1995, pp. 48–51.

tion. Finally, if an advanced reactor development project is successful, it might result in new, safer, more efficient, and more proliferation-resistant thermal power reactors.

Considerable research has been done on options for the long-term disposition of plutonium from weapons.[14] An exhaustive report by the U.S. National Academy of Sciences[15] narrows the options to two: burning the plutonium as fuel in existing light water power reactors, or mixing and vitrifying the plutonium in glass with existing high level wastes. In either case, plutonium from weapons would be made as proliferation-resistant as the vastly larger stockpiles of reactor-grade plutonium in the form of spent fuel from commercial reactors. On balance, vitrification is probably the preferred option in the United States, while Russia prefers the reactor option.

Whatever disposition options are eventually chosen, the United States and Russia should cooperate in their development and implementation. The specific technical areas in which cooperation could be pursued are myriad, ranging from research into different vitrification techniques, building or expanding fuel fabrication plants, modifying existing reactors to burn fuel with varying percentages of plutonium in it, or building new reactors. Furthermore, the overall plutonium disposition mission could be combined and a division of labor established that would exploit each country's comparative advantages. Thus, if a reactor disposition option were pursued, U.S. and Russian plutonium might be fabricated into reactor fuel at a U.S. plant, burned in existing Russian light water power reactors, and stored as spent fuel pending ultimate disposition at a third site under international safeguards. This level of cooperation, which sounds outlandish under current political circumstances, is actually no more dramatic than the cooperation that now exists between the U.S. and Russian space programs.

Another potentially fruitful area of nuclear cooperation between the United States and Russia is advanced power reactor development.[16] Re-

---

14. The definitive study is from the Committee on International Security and Arms Control, National Academy of Sciences, *Management and Disposition of Excess Weapons Plutonium* (Washington DC: National Academy Press, 1994).

15. This is the "Reactor Panel" study, a follow on report to the National Academy study, ibid. See Panel on Reactor-Related Options for the Disposition of Excess Weapons Plutonium, Committee on International Security and Arms Control, National Academy of Sciences, *Management and Disposition of Excess Weapons Plutonium: Reactor-Related Options* (Washington DC: National Academy Press, 1995).

16. Analysts and industry groups often combine the development of advanced reactors with the plutonium disposition mission, thereby linking together progress on

gardless of the future of nuclear power generation on American and Russian soil, there is a growing view that global energy and environmental concerns will require further development of nuclear energy as less developed regions of the world enter periods of intense industrial development.[17] There will be a demand for safe, clean, efficient, and proliferation-resistant power reactors, if not in the United States and Russia, then in China, India, and elsewhere. Both U.S. and Russian companies currently lack the necessary resources to develop and export such reactors by themselves. A joint development program, partially financed by the U.S. and Russian governments, would circumvent this obstacle.

General Atomics, a U.S. company, has already proposed a joint advanced development program with Minatom using modular high-temperature gas reactor (MHTGR) technology. This proposal was presented in the context of the plutonium disposition mission but need not remain limited to that context. Gas reactors use small fuel pellets that encapsulate the highly radioactive fission products that other reactors must contain within heavy, external pressure vessels.[18] This technology could make MHTGRs safer and cheaper than existing thermal power reactors. For these reasons, gas reactor development for commercial power generation seems to make more sense for the foreseeable future than do advanced light water reactors or breeder reactors.[19]

Plutonium disposition and advanced reactor development are just two of the areas in which fruitful, cooperative technical development

---

these two issues. We delink these two missions, as does the National Academy, because the cheapest and fastest reactor option for plutonium disposition involves using existing light-water reactors, not new, advanced reactors.

17. For example, Patrick E. Tyler, "China's Inevitable Dilemma: Coal Equals Growth," *New York Times*, Wednesday, November 29, 1995, p. 1.

18. Because fission products are contained within the fuel pellets, the high-temperature gas that transfers heat from the fuel can be used directly to drive a power generating gas turbine. Direct cycle power generation eliminates complicated heat exchangers and reduces inefficiencies in the conversion of heat to electricity. Also, fission product containment in the fuel eliminates the need for expensive high-pressure containment vessels, reducing construction costs and simplifying site location. These economic advantages are accompanied by inherent safety improvements over existing thermal reactors. A final added advantage of a gas reactor is that it allows very high "burn ups." In other words, it burns a higher percentage of the fissile isotopes in its fuel than does any other thermal reactor design.

19. Advanced light water reactors do not provide as much improvement in inherent safety as do gas reactors. Fast breeder reactors add the nonproliferation issues of a plutonium fuel cycle to an already daunting set of technical challenges. For an introduction and overview of various reactor technologies, see Anthony V. Nero, Jr., *A Guidebook to Nuclear Reactors* (Berkeley, Calif.: University of California Press, 1979); and Committee on Future Nuclear Power Development, National Research Council, *Nu-*

could be pursued by the United States and Russia. The prospect of such cooperation in the future, made tangible by steps that could be taken immediately, could induce a higher degree of cooperation by Minatom on matters of fissile material security and accounting at their storage sites.

UNDERTAKE JOINT ENVIRONMENTAL CLEAN-UP AT KEY NUCLEAR WEAPONS SITES

In addition to possessing the world's greatest concentration of fissile material and nuclear weapons, Russia also contains the world's greatest concentration of ecological disasters caused by nuclear accidents and the deliberate discharge of nuclear wastes. Even more than its U.S. counterpart, the Soviet Union built its nuclear-weapons industry with little regard for the damage these activities were causing the environment, and bequeathed to Russia an ecological problem of staggering proportions. For example, according to the Natural Resources Defense Council, the area around Chelyabinsk-65 is "arguably the most polluted spot on the planet — certainly in terms of radioactivity."[20] Each of Russia's large installations for handling fissile materials and nuclear weapons has a history of deadly accidents, some catastrophic in scale, and in addition its decaying facilities pose a distinct risk for still more accidents and contamination. Russia's nuclear installations pose a substantially more severe environmental hazard than do their U.S. equivalents (which are also fewer in number). Thus, the daily custodians of Russia's nuclear stockpiles live not only under profound economic duress, but also in an environmentally dangerous situation that is for most Westerners simply unimaginable.

In 1992, George Perkovich and William Potter urged the Bush administration to "launch an effort to put Soviet nuclear experts to work cleaning up the enormous environmental damage caused by 40 years of nuclear weapons production."[21] Perkovich and Potter noted that Russian scientists have considerable expertise in the area of nuclear clean-up and

---

clear Power: Technical and Institutional Options for the Future (Washington DC: National Academy Press, 1992). On gas reactors in the context of plutonium disposition, see National Academy, Reactor-Related Options, pp. 181–189.

20. Thomas B. Cochran, Robert S. Norris, and Oleg A. Bukharin, Making the Russian Bomb: From Stalin to Yeltsin (Boulder: Westview, 1995), p. 117. See also Robert Darst, "Environmental Restoration and Research," Chapter 8 of Graham Allison, Ashton B. Carter, Steven E. Miller, and Philip Zelikow, eds., Cooperative Denuclearization: From Pledges to Deeds, CSIA Studies in International Security No. 2 (Cambridge, Mass.: Center for Science and International Affairs, 1993).

21. George Perkovich and William C. Potter, "Cleaning Up Russia's Future," Washington Post, January 5, 1992, p. C2.

accident management, and that this expertise could be productively shared with the West. The Perkovich-Potter proposal deserves to be revisited by the Clinton administration, and adapted to the particular needs of 1995 and beyond. Specifically, the proposal should be integrated into the overall U.S. effort to induce cooperation from Minatom in the area of improving Russia's nuclear security and accounting systems. The U.S. should develop a comprehensive and ambitious environmental assistance program for Russia's nuclear cities, one which would focus on retraining, funding of activities, and the purchase of clean-up equipment, but condition the provision of this assistance on the rapid implementation of modern MPC&A systems at the relevant nuclear facilities. Russians, of course, have grown cynical about Western promises of assistance and aid because past promises have frequently turned out to be less than they originally seemed, so an initial up-front unconditional grant would do much to allay Russian cynicism. Ideally, the allies should be persuaded to participate in the program as well.

The great virtue of an environmental assistance proposal of this kind is that it can be targeted at specific nuclear installations in Russia that pose high proliferation risks but that have so far proven impervious to the current approach for implementing MPC&A upgrades. Most importantly, a program of this kind would give the local plant managers, workers, and people in the relevant cities a vested interest in cooperating with the West in the area of MPC&A upgrades. In some cases, it might even provide them with new business opportunities in the area of environmental clean-up, perhaps even to be exported. Although the United States could not underwrite the full cost of nuclear-environmental clean-up in Russia, if used properly even a relatively small financial contribution — perhaps in the low tens of millions of dollars per city — could create significant goodwill.

Initial political opposition to this program would surely be high. The United States has environmental problems of its own at the key U.S. facilities for producing fissile material and components for weapons, at Rocky Flats, Colorado, Hanford, Washington, and Savannah River, South Carolina; in the current fiscal climate, a proposal to spend U.S. taxpayers' dollars on environmental clean-up in Russia would probably meet with derision in the Congress. But the president has never made a serious effort to shift the nature of the political debate on this issue by clearly linking such a program to the introduction of nuclear safeguards and security systems at the Russian facilities that pose the greatest threat of nuclear leakage to U.S. national security interests. Given the severity of this threat and the limited success of the current approach, such an attempt is worth a try.

EXPAND THE INDUSTRIAL PARTNERING PROGRAM

The Department of Energy's Industrial Partnering Program (IPP), created at the initiative of Senator Pete Domenici, deserves continued support and, indeed, expanded resources. The IPP should be used as the principal U.S. vehicle for encouraging private sector involvement in converting Russia's nuclear weapons enterprises and rechanneling the talents of Russia's weapons scientists to domestic purposes. The White House and the Congress should put greater emphasis on attracting the best of U.S. industry into the IPP, and encouraging private firms to invest their own resources into forming joint ventures with entities inside Russia's nuclear cities. Where appropriate, special trade exemptions should be granted for goods produced and exported as a result of IPP projects. Funds from the IPP should be used as seed money for the joint ventures, with the greatest possible amount going to the Russian partner.

The goal of the IPP is to create as many commercially viable, non-military joint ventures inside Russia's nuclear complex as possible, thereby increasing the number of Russians with a vested interest in the continuation of cooperative nuclear security projects with the United States and other Western countries. This background of private activity could then come to form the commercial basis for a broader nuclear partnership between Russia and the United States.

PROMOTE ALTERNATIVE ENERGY AT TOMSK AND KRASNOYARSK

Russia is still producing an estimated 1.5 tons of weapons-grade pluto-nium at three dual-purpose production reactors, two at Tomsk-7 and one at Krasnoyarsk-26. The Russian government has agreed to shut these reactors down by the year 2000, or sooner if an alternative source of heat and energy is found for the surrounding areas. Minatom would like these alternative energy sources to be new nuclear reactors, but only non-nuclear power plants could become available before 2000.[22] The United States has an interest in halting the accumulation of plutonium in Russia, but this interest is generally regarded as insufficiently compelling to finance the provision of alternative power and heat generators for Tomsk-7 and Krasnoyarsk: this position is understandable given that the addition of 5–10 more tons of fresh weapons-grade plutonium will have minor impact on the proliferation risks posed by the 170 tons of plutonium already produced and stored in Russia. The United States, therefore, has so far agreed only to assist Russia in finding an alternative energy option from these two cities, not to pay for it.

---

22. The non-nuclear alternative power options are a gas-fired power plant, a coal-fired power plant or, in the case of Krasnoyarsk, hydropower.

However, paying for a short-term alternative energy source for Tomsk and Krasnoyarsk assumes a different character if it is viewed in terms of an overall strategy aimed at building a constructive, positive relationship with Minatom and at inducing prompt cooperation on the question of installing modern security equipment at Russia's most sensitive nuclear installations. Would $100 million spent in Tomsk-7 and Krasnoyarsk on a new heat and electricity supply, chosen and produced by Russians, be a worthwhile investment if the authorities at these cities agreed to immediately shut down the plutonium production reactors and install effective MPC&A equipment at all of their nuclear installations? The answer is clearly yes.

Agree on a Comprehensive Program from the Long-Term Management of Fissile Material

Long-term fissile material management and disposition has been the subject of many other studies, so there is no need to recreate analysis that has been thoroughly done elsewhere.[23] There is little dissent among experts in the field that the international community is in dire need of a strategy for dealing with its accumulated stockpiles of weapons-usable material. Even more important than a sound strategy, however, is the political will needed to implement it, which to date has been largely absent.

The question of long-term fissile material management and disposition is a task of global proportions that should be carried out on the basis of close international cooperation and consultation. Given their unique roles as nuclear superpowers, it is incumbent upon the United States and Russia to take the lead in this area. In doing so, both governments should organize their efforts in a manner that reinforces the urgent task of preventing nuclear leakage in the short term.

DEFINE AND IMPLEMENT A COMPREHENSIVE LONG-TERM

MANAGEMENT SCHEME

There are many different visions for how excess fissile materials should be managed over the long term.[24] One attractive scheme, derived from the recent U.S. National Academy of Sciences study of plutonium dispo-

---

23. The best of these studies is the Committee on International Security and Arms Control, NAS, *Management and Disposition of Excess Weapons Plutonium*.

24. For one particularly strong call for an international plutonium regime, see George Perkovich, "The Plutonium Genie," *Foreign Affairs*, Vol. 72, No. 3 (Summer 1993), pp. 153–165.

sition, calls for a staged process that begins bilaterally and then assumes multilateral characteristics as and when appropriate.[25] From a national-security perspective, the foremost purpose of any long-term management strategy must be the permanent denial of weapons-usable materials to states and sub-state groups contemplating the acquisition of a weapon; environmental and financial considerations are of secondary importance. An effective long-term management scheme would have at least four main stages.

First, the accumulation of new fissile material for weapons should be halted as soon as possible. This involves shutting down Russia's three plutonium production reactors and concluding a multilateral fissile-material production cutoff convention.[26] Both items are already on the Clinton administration's foreign policy agenda but deserve heightened attention and a greater commitment of resources.

Second, the United States and Russia must continue their nuclear weapons dismantlement programs, and should agree as a matter of urgency on the details of the reciprocal data exchange originally pledged by President Yeltsin and Clinton in September 1994. Even more importantly, the two governments should designate a much larger portion of the resulting fissile material as "permanently excess" to the national security needs of their two countries. President Clinton announced in March 1995 that he had "ordered that 200 tons of fissile material, enough for thousands of nuclear weapons, be permanently withdrawn from the United States nuclear stockpile. Two hundred tons of fissile material will never again be used to build a nuclear weapon."[27] However, most of this fissile material has never been inside a real nuclear weapon, and the total U.S. stockpile of separated plutonium and HEU is believed to be approximately 1,100 tons.[28] The United States should go beyond this first step by declaring all fissile material that the government does not plan to use in

---

25. Committee on International Security and Arms Control, NAS, *Management and Disposition of Excess Weapons Plutonium.*

26. For an excellent discussion of the multilateral fissile material production cutoff, see Frans Berkhout, Oleg Bukharin, Harold Feiveson, and Marvin Miller, "A Cutoff in the Production of Fissile Material," *International Security*, Vol. 19, No. 3 (Winter 1994/95), pp. 167–202.

27. President Clinton, "Remarks to the Nixon Center for Peace and Freedom Policy Conference," *Weekly Compilation of Presidential Documents*, March 1, 1995, p. 343.

28. According to the Natural Resources Defense Council, the total U.S. plutonium inventory is about 100 tons, of which 86 tons are weapons grade. According to the Department of Energy, the United States produced 994 tons of HEU between 1945 and 1992. Cochran, "Dismantlement of Nuclear Weapons and Disposal of Fissile Material from Weapons," pp. 4–5.

active nuclear weapons as permanent excess, and promptly offering to allow Russia to inspect and monitor this material on a reciprocal basis. Russia, in turn, should be strongly encouraged to declare a comparable portion of its fissile material stockpile as permanent excess, and to accept the U.S. offer of reciprocal inspections.

Third, the United States and Russia should pursue permanent disposal options for their permanent excess stockpiles on an urgent basis and under continued reciprocal monitoring. There is no need for the two states to pursue identical permanent disposal strategies, and neither state should delay its own long-term disposal program until the other state is prepared to begin.[29] As a general rule, the U.S. and Russian governments should endeavor to transform their excess weapons materials at as high a rate as possible into forms that pose a proliferation risk comparable to spent reactor fuel: the so-called "spent fuel standard" defined by the National Academy study.

Fourth, Russia and the United States should agree to the reciprocal monitoring of all of their key nuclear installations and activities. The Clinton administration's transparency and irreversibility proposal of December 1994 is a step in the right direction, but the U.S. government would do well to seek permanent portal monitoring at all nuclear installations and to expand its proposal to encompass the naval fuel cycle. The two states should also agree on security standards for nuclear weapons and various forms of weapons-usable fissile materials, and should establish routines for monitoring each other's compliance with these standards. The main current obstacle is the unwillingness of the Russian government to accept such an intrusive arrangement; surmounting this difficulty will require the creation of a constructive relationship with the Russian government and especially with Minatom.

These four steps would establish a sound bilateral regime for managing the excess fissile materials of Russia and the United States. The final stage in the process would involve the gradual internationalization of the

---

29. The United States has struggled without great success to address its own long-term disposition problem; how it chooses to handle this challenge has international implications. As President Clinton's science advisor has put it, "we must keep in mind that while our own excess plutonium poses little direct security risk, the actions we take in managing it will have a major impact on the international scene. What we do with our plutonium in the United States will inevitably affect what Russia does. And what we do with the basic building blocks of our Cold War nuclear arsenal will inevitably affect how other countries manage their plutonium, and how they view our seriousness about arms reduction and nonproliferation." John H. Gibbons, "Plutonium and International Security," Statement before the Committee on Energy and Natural Resources, United States Senate, May 26, 1994, p. 3.

Russian-American regime. First, the United States and Russia could try to draw in the other three nuclear-weapons states — China, France, and Great Britain — making it a five-way regime. These states could work to harmonize their fissile material management regimes with the nuclear safeguards systems that apply non-nuclear weapons states. As an ultimate step, the nuclear states of the world could then begin to work together to store their fissile material stockpiles in conditions more secure than the spent fuel standard, a step that is rational only if performed on a global scale.

ESTABLISH AN INTERNATIONAL PLUTONIUM BANK

The idea of establishing some sort of international plutonium depositary is not a new one.[30] Such a plutonium bank "would consist physically of existing facilities, suitably upgraded, and of newly constructed facilities, located on the territory of the depositing nation. These facilities would have to meet international standards of safety and security. The resulting storage facility would be designated International Plutonium [Bank] facilities and would come under the custody of an international guard force. Any nation that deposited a kilogram of plutonium into internationally safeguarded custody in this fashion would receive a payment of perhaps $20,000 from an International Plutonium [Bank] Fund, which would be capitalized by the international community, . . . principally the United States, Japan, Britain, France, and Germany." This idea now deserves to be revived as part of the long-term U.S. strategy for dealing with the fissile material overhang of the Cold War.

The immediate objective of the International Plutonium Bank would be to give the Russian government a major financial incentive to store its excess plutonium under secure conditions in the near term and in a way that could be easily integrated with the long-term fissile material management scheme discussed above. If the International Plutonium Bank could be set up quickly, this program would partially supplant our proposal that the United States directly purchase some or all of Russia's excess weapons-grade plutonium. The financial implications of the International Plutonium Bank for the United States are difficult to determine: the United States would contribute substantially to its initial capitalization, but would also deposit some of its own excess plutonium into the Bank, thereby recouping some or all of its initial costs. The allies should be persuaded to contribute to the initial capitalization of the International

---

30. See, for example, Ashton B. Carter and Owen Coté, "Disposition of Fissile Materials," chapter 3 in Allison, Carter, Miller, and Zelikow, *Cooperative Denuclearization,* pp. 125–127.

Plutonium Bank, and over time it may be possible to increase the scope of the Bank to include civilian spent fuel, fees for which would significantly increase the financial base for the Bank.

ESTABLISH A "NUCLEAR INTERPOL"

To date, the response of the world's law enforcement and intelligence agencies to the phenomenon of nuclear leakage has been inadequate. But any comprehensive long-term management scheme for fissile material must include a component focused on policing. To rectify this deficiency, the leading industrial states, including Russia, should establish a "Nuclear Interpol" that is dedicated to detecting and disrupting all illicit activities related to nuclear proliferation and other weapons of mass destruction.[31] States and terrorists groups that might contemplate the acquisition of a nuclear capability through the illicit purchase of fissile material should be put on notice that there exist many well-trained and well-funded organizations working in concert to prevent them from doing so, and to punish them if they try.

Since nuclear smuggling, terrorism, and proliferation are necessarily international in character, combating nuclear leakage can be done most effectively through careful international coordination and advanced planning. Although it might have some formal institutional structure, "Nuclear Interpol" is really shorthand for an urgent, concerted effort by the world's key law enforcement and intelligence agencies to develop the skills, procedures, and equipment needed to combat the illicit trafficking in nuclear materials effectively and systematically. A multilateral databank of nuclear "fingerprints" would also be useful, since this could decrease the amount of time required to determine the origin of a recovered nuclear sample or residue. The "Nuclear Interpol" initiative should also involve the strengthening of national laws concerning nuclear smuggling, the Nuclear Suppliers Group export-control guidelines, and possibly even the revival of the COCOM export-control regime.[32] Information on state-sanctioned exports of dual-use items should be systematically shared and processed so as to increase the likelihood of detecting a pattern of purchases indicative of an illicit nuclear-weapons program.

---

31. The phrase "Nuclear Interpol" is attributed to Frank Barnaby in John Roberts, "Disarmament: 'Nuclear Interpol' Needed to Combat Trafficking," *Inter Press Service,* February 16, 1995.

32. On the Nuclear Suppliers Group, see Tadeusz Strulak, "The Nuclear Suppliers Group," *The Nonproliferation Review,* Vol. 1, No. 1 (Fall 1993), pp. 2–10; and Leonard S. Spector, Mark G. McDonough, and Evan S. Medeiros, *Tracking Nuclear Proliferation: A Guide in Maps and Charts, 1995* (Washington DC: Carnegie Endowment for International Peace, 1995), Appendix D, pp. 180–183.

Finally, considerably more should be done in the area of international planning and preparation for responding to acts of nuclear terrorism. The United States and Russia should develop coordinated contingency plans for dealing with thefts of nuclear materials or weapons and with terrorist nuclear threats and attacks. An institutional basis for such cooperation has already been established with the Nuclear Risk Reduction Centers, established and promoted by Senators Nunn and Warner in the mid-1980s specifically to allow the superpowers to coordinate their responses to third-party nuclear threats.[33] The United States should also encourage and assist its key allies to develop their special teams for dealing with nuclear incidents, like the U.S. Nuclear Emergency Search Teams (NEST).[34] This effort should be internationally coordinated to the maximum extent possible.

Conclusion: Must We Wait for a Catastrophe?

Clearly there is much more that can and should be done to reduce the nuclear leakage threat as much as possible as quickly as possible. However, so long as the current political logjam over nuclear leakage exists, it will not be possible to advance any ambitious agenda for rapidly abating the nuclear leakage threat, whatever its details. Given the stakes associated with this problem, it is not appropriate to treat it in a business-as-usual fashion, subjecting it to the normal vagaries of domestic politics, allowing the national interest to be subordinated to institutional interests and bureaucratic squabbles, treating anti-leakage policy as an opportunity for pork barrel politics, and allowing it to slip in and out of the purview of senior authorities. This is a problem that deserves sustained attention from U.S. leaders, bipartisan understanding in Congress, and a concerted and substantial investment of U.S. political capital and financial resources to enlarge the political latitude available for pressing foward swiftly with an ambitious anti-leakage effort.

All this will be perfectly clear the day after a catastrophe results from nuclear leakage. The challenge now is to achieve that clarity on the basis of an awareness that catastrophe is possible, and to act accordingly to prevent it.

---

33. See Sam Nunn and John W. Warner, "U.S.-Soviet Cooperation in Countering Nuclear Terrorism: The Role of Risk Reduction Centers," in Paul Leventhal and Yonah Alexander, eds., *Preventing Nuclear Terrorism* (Lexington, Mass.: Lexington Books, 1987), pp. 381–393.

34. On NEST, see Mahlon E. Gates, "The Nuclear Emergency Search Team," in Leventhal and Alexander, *Preventing Nuclear Terrorism*.

Appendix A

The Russian Nuclear Archipelago

By Owen R. Coté, Jr.

A major theme of this report is the danger of nuclear weapons and fissile materials leaking from Russia. This appendix gives a more detailed look at the sources of this problem (see also map, pp. 294–295, and Figure 1-1 on pp. 32–33). A vast nuclear complex developed in the former Soviet Union during forty years of Cold War. Today, this complex remains charged with the task of safeguarding the more than 1,200 metric tons of weapons-usable fissile materials under its control. These materials reside in three complexes within the Russian nuclear archipelago, each described below: the Ministry of Defense (MOD) weapons complex; the Minatom weapons design and production complex; and the complex of various non-weapon users of weapon-usable materials, such as for naval reactors and research reactors. Next, I describe the inadequacies in material accounting and physical security that characterize that complex as it continues to operate in the midst of revolution. Finally, a comparison of the Russian nuclear complex to its American counterpart shows that it is larger, more active in terms of ongoing operations, and less advanced along the road to denuclearization.

The MOD Weapon Complex

The MOD weapon complex contains weapon launchers, weapon storage facilities, and the weapon transportation system interlinking these facilities into one unified complex.

WEAPON DEPLOYMENTS

The Soviet nuclear stockpile grew steadily from 1949 until it reached its greatest size in 1986. Victor Mikhailov, the head of Minatom, has stated that the stockpile then contained 45,000 weapons. According to one western estimate, this stockpile could be subdivided into two categories. Operational strategic, theater, and tactical weapons numbered 33,000, while older weapons held in reserve numbered 12,000.[1] Launchers for tactical nuclear weapons were deployed by the Army, Navy, Air Defense Forces, and Air Forces, and were located in Poland, Czechoslovakia, Hungary, East Germany, Mongolia, all three Baltic Republics, all or almost all of the republics of the former Soviet Union (FSU), and aboard deployed ships and submarines of all four Soviet Fleets. Strategic and theater launchers were deployed only in Russia, Ukraine, Kazakhstan, and Belarus, under the control of the Air Forces, the Navy, and the Strategic Rocket Forces. The nuclear weapons themselves were under the control of the Soviet General Staff. This control was exercised through direct physical custody by the 12th Main Directorate at storage facilities or in transit, and by coded use-control devices or locks on weapons deployed on launchers.[2]

Within MOD's custody, depending on the type and age of the weapon, deployment might be to a central, reserve storage area (numbering in the tens or dozens), more dispersed and smaller field storage sites collocated with the delivery units (hundreds), or actual deployment on a launcher such as an ICBM, a ship, or a submarine (thousands).

CONSOLIDATION AND DISMANTLEMENT OF EXCESS WEAPONS

The weapon complex has been contracting since the mid-1980s. One can identify three relatively distinct phases of this contraction. Beginning in 1986 or 1987, the Soviet Union began dismantling weapons at a rate of 2,000 to 3,000 a year.[3] For the first time, the Soviet stockpile began a net

1. Robert Norris and William Arkin, "Estimated U.S. and Soviet/Russian Nuclear Stockpiles, 1945–94," *Bulletin of the Atomic Scientists* (November/December 1994), pp. 58–59.

2. Special MOD nuclear security troops, perhaps under the control of the 12th Directorate, are located at nuclear bases. The FSB, the successor to the KGB, also has a role in nuclear weapons security, both operationally as the security force for storage installations, and technically as the source of use-control devices and their codes. More recent reports indicate a weapons security role for Interior Ministry troops as well. The exact division of labor between these entities remains somewhat unclear.

3. Considerable confusion reigns in the open literature concerning past Soviet stockpile management practices. Many authors claim that the Soviets never dismantled weapons before 1986, and that the stockpile simply grew from 1949 to 1986 without any recycling of fissile materials from the oldest to the newest weapons. Others assert that some dismantlement and recycling occurred, but at a much reduced rate compared to the United States. By one estimate, the Soviets produced a total of 55,000 weapons, with a maximum stockpile size of 45,000. Thus, one might assume that the first 10,000 warheads were recycled. By contrast, the United States produced a total of

decline. Next came the consolidation effort resulting from the end of the Cold War. In this phase, as dismantlement of older weapons continued, newer weapons were withdrawn by the thousands from Eastern Europe, and then from the former Soviet Union and consolidated in Russia. Finally, since 1992, Russia has struggled to dismantle the backlog of excess weapons created by this consolidation campaign even as new arms control obligations add more weapons in need of dismantlement.

From its peak of 45,000 warheads in 1986, the Russian weapon stockpile fell to approximately 33,000 weapons in 1992, a decrease of 12,000 weapons.[4] The Russian dismantlement effort has continued since 1992 at roughly this rate, which slightly exceeds the U.S. rate, and there are no plans to increase these dismantlement rates.

Beginning in the late 1980s and by August 1991, all tactical nuclear weapons (approximately 4,000) were removed from Eastern Europe (East Germany, Poland, Czechoslovakia, and Hungary), all three Baltic Republics, and Mongolia. By May 1992, all tactical nuclear weapons (approximately 5,800) had been removed from the newly independent, non-Russian states of the FSU (all the non-Russian republics of the FSU except Moldova). By June 1991, the FSU had also complied with its Intermediate-range Nuclear Forces (INF) Treaty obligations, dismantling the launchers associated with some 3,000 theater weapons. Thus a total of 12,000–13,000 weapons were moved from launchers or forward deployment areas and consolidated in central storage facilities in Russia in the space of about three years. Thus, between 1986 and 1992, approximately 12,000 weapons were dismantled and, during the latter half of this period, approximately 12,000–13,000 other weapons were consolidated at Russian storage facilities.

Starting in 1992, as dismantlement continued at the rate of 2000 weapons a year (with an emphasis on weapons consolidated from Ukraine[5]), other consolidation efforts loomed on the horizon. START I treaty obligations require that the Russians remove or destroy the launchers associated with approximately 4,000 strategic weapons. START II will require launcher reductions resulting in the consolidation of 4,000 further

---

70,000 weapons to create a stockpile that never exceeded 30,000 weapons. This analysis assumes the second scenario where Soviet dismantlement occurred before 1986, but at a low rate (i.e., 10,000 weapons between 1949 and 1986).

4. For the purposes of this analysis, assume that none of the 12,000 weapons dismantled were from the operational stockpile as it stood in 1986, but that they were the older, inactive weapons mentioned above.

5. Oleg Bukharin, "Nuclear Safeguards and Security in the Former Soviet Union," *Survival*, Vol. 36, No. 4 (Winter 1994–95), p. 62.

weapons. Finally, the Bush/Gorbachev and Bush/Yeltsin initiatives of 1991–92 imply Russian commitments to consolidate and eliminate (remove from launchers or forward storage areas and dismantle at least to pit level, explained in note 20) approximately 4,000 of its remaining tactical nuclear arsenal of 8,000 weapons.[6] Thus, in the decade from 1993 to 2003, Russia will dismantle a further 15,000–20,000 weapons and consolidate another 12,000, leaving an operational stockpile of 3,000 strategic weapons and 4,000 tactical weapons, and a reserve stockpile of 4,000 weapons, assuming no new production.[7]

The numbers of already consolidated and dismantled weapons are a manifestation of the tremendous progress achieved by the Russian MOD's denuclearization campaign. They also reflect the magnitude of the challenges still facing that complex as it continues to consolidate and dismantle weapons in the midst of social and political upheaval.

MAINTENANCE REQUIREMENTS FOR DEPLOYED WEAPONS

Weapons move around as part of the process of denuclearization, and weapons and weapon components also move back and forth in order to receive scheduled maintenance. Unlike their U.S. counterparts, Soviet weapons were not designed to have long shelf lives.[8] Instead, deployed Soviet weapons are continuously cycled back to their place of assembly for maintenance and refurbishment. In many cases, the components are in turn shipped back to their assembly sites for further maintenance. Then, the process is reversed: refurbished components flow from compo-

---

6. I define "remaining tactical arsenal" as follows: In 1986, at its peak, the Soviet stockpile contained 18,000 active tactical weapons. 10,000, or more than half of these weapons, have since been removed from Eastern Europe, the Baltics, Mongolia, and the non-Russian FSU and consolidated in Russia where 8,000 active tactical weapons were already deployed. This consolidation, along with eventual dismantlement of the non-Russian tactical weapons, could be said to meet the requirements of the unilateral initiatives of 1991–92, and one might consider the 8000 Russian weapons as the "remaining tactical arsenal." I would argue that budget-driven force reductions and security concerns will make it highly desirable for Russia to also remove approximately half of the 8000 operational tactical weapons in this arsenal from their deployment areas and to consolidate them in central storage areas if they have not yet already done so. Interviews with senior officials from the Office of the Secretary of Defense confirm that there is a Russian tactical nuclear weapon consolidation effort.

7. Production of weapons continues in Russia without interruption, although the types and rates are not discussed in the open literature.

8. U.S. weapons are designed to last up to thirty years with nothing but field-level maintenance. A stockpile surveillance program ensures the reliability of deployed weapons by periodically bringing a small, random sample of each weapon type back to the Pantex plant in Texas for analysis. Only if major unanticipated problems are discovered would an entire class of weapons be recalled to Pantex for modification.

nent assembly facilities back to the weapon assembly facilities; the weapon assembly facilities reassemble the weapons; and the refurbished weapons flow back out into the field and return to MOD custody.

One account estimates that weapons need such depot-level maintenance every seven years.[9] In a stockpile of tens of thousands of weapons, this maintenance cycle creates a continuous, two-way traffic in fissile materials and assembled weapons between fissile material production facilities, component assembly sites, weapon assembly sites, weapon storage sites, and weapon deployment areas. These sites are not separate buildings within one industrial facility. Rather, they are spread across the length and breadth of Russia, an area comprising one-seventh of the world's landmass. Thus, the "pipelines" of fissile material, weapon components, and assembled weapons that link these sites to each other are vast.

Weapon maintenance also occupies a considerable portion of the overall capacity of the assembly/disassembly facilities (four for weapons and three for weapon components) that could otherwise be used to accelerate dismantling operations. Maintenance activities also add to the burdens already placed on weapon transportation and storage activities by the consolidation and dismantlement campaigns described above.

WEAPONS TRANSPORTATION

Weapons transportation over any distance is done exclusively by rail. Special MOD rail cars designed to protect the weapons from external attack are combined into trains, and these trains move the weapons between forward storage areas, rear storage areas, and the weapon assembly/disassembly facilities. Trains also move weapon components and fissile materials between Minatom facilities, but these trains are under Minatom's control. Over short distances, as between a railhead and an operating base, weapons are transported on special trucks in convoy with service vehicles and several armored cars. Russia has never used aircraft for weapon transportation (unlike the United States).

Minatom and the Weapon Production Complex

When weapons enter weapon assembly/disassembly facilities they cross a custodial boundary and pass from MOD control to Minatom control.

---

9. See Alexander Konovalov and Igor Sutiagin, "Nuclear Weapons on the Territories of the CIS States: Problems of Safety and Security," Joachim Krause, ed., *Kernwaffenverbreitung und Internationaler Systemwandel: Neue Risiken und Gestaltungsmöglichkeiten* (Baden-Baden, Germany: Nomos Verlagsgesellschaft, 1994), p. 138.

Minatom's weapon design and its material and component production facilities are the heart of the Russian weapon production complex. Some of these facilities also support other non-weapon nuclear activities, which I discuss below.

THE CLOSED CITIES

These facilities are contained in ten closed cities.[10] Each city is a set of laboratory or industrial facilities for material, component, or weapon research and production and a collocated city where the employees and their families live. The cities are "closed" in that travel to and from them is restricted, and they are enclosed by a fence guarded on the inside by FSB (former KGB) troops and patrolled on the outside by MVD (Interior Ministry) troops. During the Cold War, these cities were also secret in that their names and locations were absent from official maps, and they were assigned phony post office box numbers in the larger Russian cities of Arzamas, Penza, Zlatoust, Sverdlovsk (now Yekaterinburg), Chelyabinsk, Tomsk, and Krasnoyarsk. Sverdlovsk, Chelyabinsk, and Krasnoyarsk each had two separate closed cities assigned them.

Arzamas-16 was the Soviet Union's first weapon design laboratory, and like its U.S. counterpart, Los Alamos, Arzamas is also reputed to have some weapon assembly/disassembly capabilities. Other weapon assembly/disassembly facilities are located at Sverdlovsk-45, Zlatoust-36, and Penza-19. Some reports list these latter two facilities as non-nuclear component assembly/disassembly facilities.[11] Taken together, these facilities are reputed to have a capacity of 7,000 weapons per year, compared to the 1,500–2,000 weapons per year capacity of the sole U.S. weapons assembly/disassembly facility at the Pantex plant in Amarillo, Texas.[12]

The FSU's second design laboratory is located at Chelyabinsk-70 and its first major plutonium production facility at Chelyabinsk-65. Chelyabinsk-65 also contains facilities for tritium production, waste vitrification, plutonium weapon component fabrication, storage of separated civilian plutonium, interim storage of plutonium weapon components,

---

10. An eleventh facility near the city of Angarsk in the Lake Baykal region containing an uranium enrichment plant has never been described as one of the closed cities, though it certainly played an integral role in the weapon complex.

11. Konovalov and Sutiagin, "Nuclear Weapons on the Territories of the CIS States," p. 144 and note 44.

12. When such facilities are described as having a capacity of x thousand weapons per year, this means that they can conduct any combination of assembly, disassembly, maintenance, repair, or surveillance operations as long as the cumulative total does not exceed x.

and mixed oxide (MOX) fuel fabrication, and it is the site for new construction of a long-term storage facility for fissile material from dismantled weapons. (Subsequent references to Chelyabinsk are to Chelyabinsk-65 except where otherwise specified.)

The FSU's first major uranium enrichment facility is at Sverdlovsk-44. This facility provides HEU (highly-enriched uranium) weapon component fabrication, interim storage for HEU weapon components, and will also be involved in blending down weapon-grade HEU into LEU (low-enriched uranium) for sale as reactor fuel as part of the U.S.-Russian uranium deal, should that deal ever be consummated.

Krasnoyarsk-45 and Krasnoyarsk-26 contain uranium enrichment and plutonium production facilities respectively. Krasnoyarsk-26 is also used for civilian spent fuel storage. Tomsk-7 has uranium enrichment and plutonium production facilities, as well as uranium hexafluoride production facilities and weapon component production and storage facilities for both plutonium and HEU. Tomsk has also been suggested as a second site for construction of a long-term storage facility. Finally, uranium enrichment and hexafluoride production facilities are also located at Angarsk.

THE WEAPON PRODUCTION PIPELINE

During normal Cold War operations and, on a much smaller scale today, weapons production involved a series of steps. Natural uranium, mined in Russia, Kazakhstan, Uzbekistan, and Eastern Europe, was purified and converted into metal at the Glasov Metallurgical Plant. The uranium ingots were then sent to the Novosibirsk fuel fabrication plant where they were clad in aluminum and fashioned into fuel rods for plutonium production reactors at Chelyabinsk, Tomsk and Krasnoyarsk. After irradiation, the fuel rods were chemically reprocessed at Tomsk and Krasnoyarsk,[13] and the plutonium and uranium separated. The bulk Pu-239 was then sent to weapon component assembly facilities at Chelyabinsk-65 and Tomsk.

In a separate stream, the bulk irradiated natural uranium was sent to Tomsk or Angarsk for conversion to uranium hexafluoride, and then to enrichment facilities where it was enriched to 90+ percent U-235 in several stages.[14] According to one account, the enrichment facilities at Tomsk,

---

13. The reprocessing facility at Chelyabinsk is devoted to separating plutonium produced in some civil reactors (the 440-megawatt light-water power reactors, VVER-440) and in all naval and research reactors.

14. Because the bulk natural uranium feed to the enrichment facilities had already been irradiated in plutonium production reactors, their HEU product contained uranium isotopes, particularly U-232, which are not present in HEU produced from

Krasnoyarsk, and Angarsk produced LEU of several different concentrations of U-235, a portion of which served as feed for the Sverdlovsk facility, which was the sole location where uranium was brought to enrichment levels greater than 90 percent of U-235.[15] More recent information indicates that Angarsk was the only enrichment facility that never produced HEU, that the other three all produced HEU at one point, but that Sverdlovsk was the only facility where HEU or LEU was ever made from unirradiated natural uranium.[16]

Highly enriched uranium weapons components were fashioned at Sverdlovsk and at Tomsk, and these components together with the Pu-239 components described above were shipped to one of the four weapon assembly facilities, along with a variety of other components. Assembled weapons were then transferred from Minatom to MOD control at locations analogous to the "military first destination points" where this transfer of custody occurs in the U.S. complex between the Department of Energy (DOE) and the Department of Defense (DOD).[17]

PEOPLE

No discussion of Minatom's nuclear complex would be complete without some reference to its human element. Minatom employs about one million people. The complex of closed cities for designing, testing, and producing weapons has a total population of 700,000 people including

---

unirradiated natural uranium, as in the United States. This makes HEU produced in this way easy to identify. See Steve Fetter and Frank von Hippel, "Measurements of Radiation from a Soviet Warhead," *Science and Global Security*, Vol. 1, Nos. 3–4 (1990), p. 325.

15. Oleg Bukharin, "Integration of the Military and Civilian Nuclear Fuel Cycles in Russia," *Science and Global Security*, Vol. 4, No. 3 (1994), p. 395.

16. I am indebted to Oleg Bukharin for this more recent information. For further information about the Russian enrichment enterprise, see Thomas Cochran, Robert Norris, and Oleg Bukharin, *Making the Russian Bomb: From Stalin to Yeltsin* (Oxford, U.K.: Westview, 1994).

17. In the United States, these military first destination points are storage sites physically separate from the assembly/disassembly facility at Pantex. For example, the U.S. Air Force's Strategic Air Command had three military first destination points at Kirtland Air Force Base (AFB) in New Mexico, Lake Mead at Nellis AFB in Nevada, and at Barksdale AFB, Louisiana. Thomas K. Longstreth and Richard A. Scribner, "U.S. Strategic Bombers and their Weapons," in Frank von Hippel and Roald Z. Sagdeev, eds., *Reversing the Arms Race: How to Achieve and Verify Deep Reductions in the Nuclear Arsenals* (New York: Gordon and Breach, 1990), p. 217. Storage positions at Pantex are under DOE control. In Russia, the military first destination points are at the assembly/disassembly facilities themselves. There are no weapon storage positions at these facilities under Minatom control. Konovalov and Sutiagin, "Nuclear Weapons," p. 142.

both workers and their families. Minatom continues to be responsible for the social welfare of the inhabitants of these cities. A much smaller number of people — maybe 2,000 — possess extensive knowledge of the details of modern nuclear weapon design. As many as 5,000 other individuals possess extensive knowledge of the design and operation of one or several of the various technologies for fissile material production used today and in the past by the Soviets.

The Non-Weapon Nuclear Complex

Besides the closed cities, weapon storage and deployment sites, and the transportation links, are many less obvious places in need of safeguards to protect bulk fissile materials. HEU in quantities greater than needed to make simple bombs is used as fuel for naval reactors, civilian merchant ship reactors (icebreakers), space reactors, some research reactors, tritium production reactors; as start-up fuel for breeder reactors; and is interspersed throughout the natural uranium cores of plutonium production reactors to stabilize power output. Equally dangerous amounts of plutonium in the non-weapons complex are produced by and recycled into breeder reactors, are separated and stored for future recycling into MOX fuel elements, and are used for other research purposes.

The reactors in question need to be safeguarded while in use, and so do a whole series of other fuel cycle facilities where fresh fuel is fabricated; where fuel cores are stored prior to installation in a reactor; where propulsion reactors are stored prior to installation in a ship, submarine, or satellite, and where spent fuel is stored or recycled. These facilities, described in this section, comprise a whole series of closed nuclear reactor fuel cycles that make use of insecure Minatom facilities at their front and back ends.

HEU FOR NAVAL REACTORS

The naval fuel cycle draws HEU, enriched from 50 to 90 percent, from enrichment facilities or existing stocks of bulk material. Naval fuel fabrication is done at several production lines at the Electrostal plant in Moscow. Fresh fuel rods are stored at Murmansk, Archangel, and Vladivostok. They are installed in reactor cores at these shipyards or transported to naval bases where they are installed directly aboard ships, submarines, or icebreakers. After years at sea, reactors are refueled with fresh fuel, and the spent fuel is stored prior to shipment to Chelyabinsk-65, where it is reprocessed, the remaining HEU separated for reuse, and the relatively small amounts of plutonium separated and stored onsite at Chelyabinsk.

HEU FOR FAST REACTORS

Another, smaller HEU fuel cycle also begins at Electrostal. This one supplies 20–25 percent enriched HEU fuel for the cores of the fast reactors at Beloyarskaya, Russia, and Actau, Kazakhstan. These reactors produce plutonium both in their fuel assemblies, and in their uranium oxide jackets. Spent fast reactor fuel assemblies and jackets are returned to Chelyabinsk-65 for reprocessing, HEU recycle, and plutonium storage.

HEU FOR PRODUCTION AND RESEARCH REACTORS

HEU enriched to 90 percent is used in the plutonium production fuel cycle, in the tritium production fuel cycle, and in the research reactor fuel cycle. HEU is used in rods surrounding the natural uranium fuel elements of plutonium production reactors to stabilize power output. HEU is also used as fuel in special reactors that bombard separate targets of lithium with neutrons in order to produce tritium. Finally, much smaller quantities of HEU fuel (in kilograms) are used in more than a dozen research reactors throughout the former Soviet Union.

Highly enriched uranium for these fuel cycles is fabricated at Novosibirsk and shipped to the plutonium production reactors at Tomsk, Krasnoyarsk, and (during the Cold War) to Chelyabinsk; to the two tritium production reactors at Chelyabinsk; and to the various, widely dispersed research reactor facilities. The spent HEU fuel from all of these reactors is shipped back to Chelyabinsk-65 for reprocessing, plutonium separation and storage, and HEU recycling.

Aside from these HEU fuel cycles, there are also a number of non-weapon, nuclear research centers with more than 100 kilograms of HEU. An institute at Podolsk, near Moscow, designs HEU-fueled reactors for use in space to provide power to satellites, like the radar ocean reconnaissance satellites (RORSATs) that were designed to track U.S. Navy ships during the Cold War. The Kurchatov Institute in Moscow has a variety of small research reactors with HEU fuel that, among other missions, assist in the design of a new generation of low-powered, unmanned, inherently safer reactor designs. The Obninsk and Dimitrovgrad research institutes use HEU fuel in experimental fast reactors. These institutes probably fabricate their own fresh fuel from HEU supplied by Minatom, but their spent fuel is probably returned to Chelyabinsk-65.

PLUTONIUM FUEL CYCLES

The Obninsk and Dimitrovgrad institutes are also centers of research on plutonium use as fuel in fast reactors and in light water power reactors. Thus they, along with several other Russian research institutions, support the development of four new plutonium fuel cycles that Minatom plans to complete by the end of the decade.

The first involves twenty-six older 440-megawatt (electric) (MWe) light water power reactors (LWRs), known as VVER-440, located in Russia, Ukraine, and throughout Eastern Europe. Beginning in 1978, their spent fuel was returned for reprocessing to Chelyabinsk-65 and separated in anticipation of its eventual use as start-up fuel for breeder reactors. The plutonium produced by reprocessing the spent fuel of these older VVER reactors constitutes the bulk of the more than 30 tons of separated plutonium stored at Chelyabinsk-65. Russia still plans to reuse this plutonium, but its fast reactor program has been delayed and it is now considering recycling it as MOX uranium-plutonium fuel in LWRs.

The second involves the already operating fast reactors at Beloyarskaya and Actau and the two new ones planned for Chelyabinsk and one at Beloyarskaya. Rather than using the current HEU cores, or plutonium fuel from LWRs, Minatom still plans eventually to fuel these reactors with plutonium bred in and recycled from their natural uranium jackets. Such recycling is, of course, the whole purpose of any fast reactor fuel cycle. The plutonium reprocessing, recycling, and fuel fabrication for this closed fast reactor cycle would be at a new, yet-to-be-built facility at Chelyabinsk-65.

The third and most recent plutonium fuel cycle is planned for Russia's most modern class of LWRs, the VVER-1000s. There are eighteen VVER-1000s, now operating in Russia, Ukraine, and Bulgaria, and at least seven more are under construction. Currently, the spent fuel from these power reactors is shipped back to Krasnoyarsk and stored. Russia still plans to complete a long-delayed reprocessing plant at Krasnoyarsk and construct a MOX fuel fabrication plant in order to recycle plutonium separated from spent VVER-1000 fuel as MOX fuel for those same reactors.

The fourth potential plutonium fuel cycle is less well defined. It would involve the construction of one or several new design reactors, probably of the type known in the West as a high temperature gas reactor (HTGR), for the purpose of burning excess plutonium from dismantled weapons. Such plutonium disposition options are also being discussed in the United States, but planning has not advanced beyond this stage in either country.

Thus, Russia already has an extensive set of different reactor fuel cycles using HEU fuel, and has plans for several massive plutonium fuel cycles that are already in various stages of implementation. These HEU and Pu reactor fuel cycles, and the research institutes that support them, are somewhat of an anomaly: they are not a direct part of the weapon production complex, but they use large amounts of weapon usable fissile materials.

Many of these stockpiles contain enough weapons-usable fissile material to rival the entire fissile-material stockpile of any other nuclear weapon state, declared or undeclared, except that of the United States itself.

Inventorying, Securing, and Safely Transporting Fissile Material in Russia: The Unfinished Denuclearization Agenda

Today, vast, uninventoried quantities of Russia's 1,200 tons of weapons-usable materials are being transported and stored throughout Russia under conditions of great vulnerability to theft or diversion. This is because the security of Russian storage facilities and transportation assets, as well as the accuracy of the inventories of fissile materials, are inadequate to the challenge of preserving control in the midst of revolution.

THE RUSSIAN FISSILE MATERIAL ACCOUNTING SYSTEMS

Project Sapphire involved the discovery and successful retrieval from the fuel fabrication plant at Ust-Kamengorsk in Kazakhstan of 600 kilograms of HEU left over from an experimental Soviet naval reactor program (see Chapter 3). This is cause for both celebration and great concern. The good news is that 600 kilograms of HEU is now safely secured at the Oak Ridge storage facility in the United States. The bad news concerns what it shows about the Russian system for inventorying fissile material.

First, this system lost track of 600 kilograms of HEU. This cache of HEU fell through the cracks of the nuclear material control and accounting system of the FSU and remained in limbo for years.[18] If responsible Kazakh officials had not discovered it, it could have disappeared without a trace at some future date. The odds are that there are other Ust-Kamengorsks that remain to be discovered.

Second, even when the fissile material control system knows of an

---

18. This HEU was not entirely forgotten, however. Well before Project Sapphire was publicly revealed, Oleg Bukharin wrote that Ust-Kamengorsk "was involved in fabrication of berylium-HEU alloys for naval reactors fuels." Bukharin, "Integration of the Military and Civilian Nuclear Fuel Cycles in Russia," p. 397. The reactors in question were experimental, liquid metal designs with very high power densities of the type used in Alpha class attack submarines. Because this program was experimental and because of the different technology, the normal fuel fabrication line for naval reactors at the Electrostal plant in Moscow was not employed.

inventory of fissile material, the margins of error in the accounting techniques are wide. In the Ust-Kamengorsk case, using standard former Soviet assaying, or measurement, techniques, Kazakh officials understated the amount of material involved in Project Sapphire by 4 percent.[19] That is an understatement of 24 kilograms, almost enough for two simple bombs. A 4 percent inventory error at every Russian facility with stocks of fissile material translates into a truly prodigious quantity of weapon-usable material that could be diverted or stolen without detection by Russian fissile material accounting methods.

The lack of an accurate accounting system is particularly dangerous because the physical security of the materials in question is also inadequate. The lack of security at Russian research institutes has already been noted by both Russian and American authorities, but the lack of security for the thousands of dismantled weapon components piling up in improvised Minatom facilities is even more disturbing.

SECURE STORAGE FOR EXCESS WEAPON COMPONENTS

One of the great denuclearization successes of the emerging post–Cold War era has been the rapid and safe dismantlement of thousands of excess nuclear weapons in both the United States and in Russia. At the same time, these unprecedented rates of dismantlement have flooded the two nuclear complexes with thousands of excess fissile weapon components in need of safe interim storage.

In the United States, these components are being stored in highly secure, unused weapons storage bunkers. In Russia, they are being stored in converted warehouses with much less security. The difference between the two cases seems to be the simple consequence of a bureaucratic boundary that was drawn differently in the United States and in the former Soviet Union when both countries began producing weapons in dedicated industrial facilities some 45 years ago. The security at these improvised Minatom storage facilities is hardly better than the security at non-weapons nuclear research facilities, and far below the standards applied by the MOD to weapons storage.

Weapons pass out of MOD's and into Minatom's hands when they enter one of the four weapons assembly/disassembly facilities located at Sverdlovsk, Zlatoust, Penza, and Arzamas. The weapons dismantlement process under Minatom in those facilities produces on average, more than

---

19. Communication to the authors by Martin Marietta personnel involved in Project Sapphire.

one multi-kilogram fissile weapon component per retired weapon, and further dismantlement of those components is not occurring.[20]

Since 1986, Soviet and now Russian weapons have been drawn from MOD weapons storage facilities and dismantled to the pit level at the rate of at least 2,000 a year. The two fissile components taken from each dismantled weapon also need to be stored in highly secure facilities. If these components had been returned back to excess weapons storage facilities, as the pits are in the United States, and if these two components took up, at most, one weapon storage position, then the problem of storing components securely would have solved itself. Each weapon would create storage capacity for its two fissile components when it was removed from its storage position for shipment to the dismantlement facilities.[21]

---

20. A generic thermonuclear weapon has a primary and a secondary stage, each of which contains fissile material. An average primary might contain 4 kilograms of plutonium and a secondary might contain 15 kilograms of HEU. Very low yield weapons (tens of kilotons) have only a primary, while very high yield weapons (multi-megatons) have an additional tertiary stage. These components, once separated from the dismantled weapon, are put into transportation containers and stored until component dismantlement facilities are ready to accept them. At this point, in the nuclear vernacular, weapons have been dismantled to the "pit" level: the fissile shell inside the implosion assembly mechanism of a primary is called a pit. Component dismantlement facilities take multi-kilogram fissile weapon components and reduce them to several small, highly subcritical pieces of pure U or Pu metal. This step takes the dismantlement process beyond pit level and involves different storage facilities from weapons and components. On dismantling to and beyond the pit level, see Ashton B. Carter and Owen Coté, "Transport, Storage, and Dismantlement of Nuclear Weapons," in Graham Allison, Ashton B. Carter, Steven E. Miller and Philip Zelikow, eds., *Cooperative Denuclearization: From Pledges to Deeds*, CSIA Studies in International Security No. 2 (Cambridge, Mass.: Center for Science and International Affairs, 1993) pp. 93–97. The United States is currently incapable of dismantlement beyond the pit level because of the closure of DOE's Rocky Flats plutonium processing facility, and Russia also has apparently chosen not to dismantle beyond pit level. See testimony given by Lawrence Gershwin, *House Committee on Appropriations*, DOD Appropriations for 1993, Part 5, May 6, 1992, p. 498.

21. Much weapon storage capacity was lost to Russia when the Soviet Union broke up. During the peak of the tactical nuclear consolidation campaign, when the rate of weapon consolidation greatly exceeded the rate of dismantlement, it appears that shortages in weapon storage capacity occurred. One estimate is that the FSU had eight central storage sites and 67 field storage sites, and that three central and 42 field sites are now unavailable to Russia. Thus, nearly 50 percent of the central storage capacity and nearly 66 percent of the field storage capacity is irretrievably lost. The same source quotes General Zelentsov, head of the General Staff's 12th Main Directorate, as saying that "some nuclear stores are already overloaded" in the summer of 1992. Konovalov and Sutiagin, "Nuclear Weapons," pp. 144–145 and note 42. Over the last three years however, the consolidation campaign has slowed considerably while dismantlement

Unfortunately, Minatom has chosen to store dismantled weapon components in improvised facilities at the component assembly/disassembly
sites where they were produced, rather than using the more secure,
surplus weapons storage positions under MOD control. This means that
in each year since 1986, roughly 4,000 Pu and HEU weapon components
have been shipped from the weapons disassembly sites to one of the four
component storage sites described above. A recent report by an advisor
to President Yeltsin described one of these interim storage facilities at
Tomsk-7 as "an old warehouse not built for such a use."[22] Another
Russian account of this storage site said that "in [this] plant's storage are
accumulated 23,000 containers with nuclear materials from obsolete warheads: plutonium and enriched uranium."[23] Other interim component
storage sites like this one are at Chelyabinsk and Sverdlovsk.[24]

These descriptions of the interim storage facility at Tomsk echo descriptions of another interim storage facility for 30 metric tons of civil
plutonium at Chelyabinsk-65. The bulk plutonium is stored in an old
warehouse with glass windows and a padlock on the door.[25] Inside this
forty-year old building, formerly used to store chemicals, are over 10,000
thermos bottle–sized containers, each with a 2.5 kilogram ingot of separated plutonium.[26] On a smaller scale, the same conditions of inadequate
security exist at research facilities like the Kurchatov Institute, where "the
wall around the institute is falling down, and until recently there was no
fence around building 116 [containing 70 kilograms of HEU] and no
sensors within it that could detect unauthorized entry or removal of the
material."[27]

The lack of security for 70 kilograms of HEU at Kurchatov provoked
an ultimately successful, cooperative Lab-to-Lab program designed to
improve security there. There is no sign of such a program to improve

has continued. This has apparently eliminated the shortages in weapon storage capacity that emerged in 1992. Thus, MOD now has surplus secure weapon storage capacity.

22. Margaret Shapiro, "Russia Orders Tightened Security to Protect Nuclear Materials," *Washington Post*, February 24, 1995, p. A15.

23. Alexander Bolsunovsky and Valery Menshchikov, "Nuclear Security is Inadequate and Outdated," *Moscow News*, No. 49 (December 9–15, 1994), p. 14.

24. There is some dispute over whether Krasnoyarsk is also used for component
storage.

25. The authors are indebted to Frank von Hippel for providing them with a description of his recent visit to this facility. See also Frank von Hippel, "Fissile Material
Security in the Post–Cold War World," *Physics Today*, June 1995, pp. 26–31.

26. Ibid., p. 26.

27. Ibid., pp. 26–27.

the security of the hundreds of tons of plutonium and HEU stored in component or bulk form at Sverdlovsk, Chelyabinsk, Tomsk, and Krasnoyarsk.

A final aspect of the weapon component storage problem is that it gets worse before it will begin to get better, toward the end of the decade at the earliest. Every year between now and the turn of the century, 2,000 weapons will be removed from secure MOD storage bunkers and dismantled, and the 4,000 or more fissile components that emerge will be shipped to insecure, improvised storage facilities under Minatom control. At the turn of the century, at the very earliest, a new dedicated, purpose-built storage facility at Chelyabinsk may finally be ready to accept all dismantled weapon components.[28]

Thus compared to the Cold War, when the vast bulk of fissile material was in weapons and therefore stored under conditions that approximated the weapons standard of safe and secure storage, now the largest portion of the fissile material stockpile is in Minatom's hands, stored in improvised facilities whose security does not even approach the weapons standard and is little better than the level of security characteristic of non-weapons research and fuel cycle facilities. Furthermore, this shift in custody, and the ensuing loss of security that results from it, will continue to advance at the rate of 2,000–3,000 weapons per year through the end of the century.

This is a non-proliferation nightmare of epic proportions. It is all the more frustrating that the mere existence of a bureaucratic boundary seems to have been largely responsible for creating a large part of it. The secure weapons storage bunkers through which Russian nuclear weapons pass before entry into the Minatom weapons dismantlement facilities are steadily emptying out. In the United States, such bunkers are, in turn, being refilled with dismantled weapon components. In the United States, Minatom's counterpart, the Department of Energy (DOE), owns the secure weapons storage facilities near its weapons dismantlement facility and is free to use them for this purpose without losing custody of the material as a result. In Russia, those bunkers belong to MOD, and Minatom is therefore apparently unwilling to use them.

SECURE TRANSPORTATION FOR FISSILE MATERIALS

Russia's weapons, weapon components, and bulk fissile materials are transported at a much greater rate than in the United States. There are at least four reasons. First, the Russian consolidation campaign is much bigger than its U.S. counterpart. Second, because Minatom is storing all

---

28. The completion of this storage facility is far from guaranteed.

dismantled weapon components away from its weapons disassembly facilities, this creates traffic that does not exist in the U.S. complex, where pits are stored onsite at the weapons disassembly facility. Third, the maintenance needs of Russian weapons create two-way traffic between these Minatom assembly/disassembly facilities and MOD deployment or forward storage bases. Fourth, Minatom continues to produce new fissile material and new weapons, although it has agreed not to produce new weapons from new fissile material.

During transportation and while they are deployed in forward storage areas, weapons are under the control of the MOD's 12th Main Directorate. Once they are placed on a launcher, the weapons come under the physical control of the military unit that owns that launcher, although the MOD retains operational control through the use of coded locks and other safeguards against unauthorized use. At the other end of the pipeline, the weapons come under the control of Minatom during maintenance at assembly/disassembly facilities. Thus, any given weapon experiences multiple changes of custody. The risks of diversion grow when weapons pass through the borders separating different organizations, especially when those organizations are at odds with each other over budgets, roles, or missions as MOD and Minatom appear to be.

The weapon transportation requirements depend on a troubled Russian rail net, and they generate numerous periods of physical vulnerability when weapons and/or components are transferred at the various hand-off points between the rail net and local road transportation. They also generate numerous changes in custody at the organizational hand-off points both between MOD and Minatom, and between different branches of MOD.

The Russian rail net is deteriorating physically, and the links it provides between Russian nuclear installations pass, of necessity, through urban areas and through regions unsettled by ethnically based movements for local political autonomy. Proof of the physical decay of the rail net comes from the U.S. Cooperative Threat Production (CTR) program, whose mission is to improve the safety and security of Russian rail cars used for weapons transportation. One option considered by this program was the provision of fire suppression equipment for these cars, but the offer was rejected by Russian authorities because of concerns about the added weight the modified cars would place on the railbed. These same Russian authorities requested that the CTR program provide equipment for installations to detect defective track.[29]

---

29. "Weapons of Mass Destruction," *GAO/NSLAD-95-7*, p. 8.

Nuclear transportation routes that pass through large urban areas increase the consequences of an accident, decrease the capabilities of any defensive troop escorts, and reduce the probability that weapons, once lost or stolen, could be recovered. Routes that pass through regions of ethnic unrest expose nuclear weapons to the additional risk of becoming embroiled in local political or military conflicts with the central government.

Weapons being shipped from assembly facilities to disassembly facilities or to and from maintenance facilities often must travel by road between their forward deployment or storage area and a railhead. At either end of this trip is a period of acute vulnerability to theft when the weapons are out in the open being loaded or unloaded and are thus away from the physical protection of a bunker or special transportation vehicle. Huge uninventoried quantities of weapons-usable material are stored and transported under conditions of extreme insecurity, while Russia undergoes convulsive change. Without U.S. assistance, trouble is virtually certain.

Comparing the Russian and American Nuclear Archipelagos

One of the ironies of the denuclearization process in Russia after the Cold War has been that the transfer of custody of thousands of weapons between MOD and Minatom and their dismantlement has moved their fissile material from conditions of relative security to conditions of great insecurity. On a larger scale, there is another irony: It is the larger, more active, and more dispersed nuclear complex in Russia that now faces the task of denuclearization in the midst of revolution. In the United States, a smaller nuclear complex was, in many respects, already out of business before the end of the Cold War and faced fewer denuclearization challenges, as this section describes.

DOD WEAPONS

Between 1945 and 1990, the United States produced some 70,000 nuclear weapons. The stockpile reached its peak of about 30,000 weapons in the early 1960s and stabilized at about 20,000 weapons during the 1970s and 1980s. While stockpile numbers remained relatively constant over a long period, new weapons were constantly being produced, old ones were being dismantled, and fissile materials recycled. In 1985, more than 6,000 tactical weapons out of the total stockpile were deployed overseas in Germany, England, Turkey, Italy, Greece, Netherlands, Belgium, South Korea, and Guam at 125 different bases. In the United States, some 14,000 weapons were deployed at 39 bases and aboard many ships and attack submarines.[30]

The U.S. DOD controlled a nuclear stockpile approximately half the size of the Soviet MOD's in the mid-1980s, and the two military nuclear complexes differed in other ways. Although the U.S. military deployed weapons and launchers of various types in all four services, and also controlled a number of central storage facilities, the weapons deployment and storage bases were under a single military chain of command. There is no equivalent of the Russian MOD's 12th Main Directorate in the United States. This distinction extends to the U.S. military nuclear transportation system, in which weapons were mostly transported by air in U.S. Air Force C-141 cargo aircraft. Finally, unlike their Soviet and now Russian counterparts, U.S. weapons require only field maintenance while deployed or in storage. This field maintenance mostly involves periodic replacement of external gas initiators and boosters.

Since 1992, there has been considerable consolidation and dismantlement of the DOD nuclear stockpile. After the rapid implementation of President Bush's unilateral initiative of September 1991 to reduce and consolidate tactical nuclear weapons, only some hundreds of weapons remained deployed overseas in largely token numbers at 16 bases in Germany, England, Turkey, Italy, Greece, Netherlands, and Belgium. No nuclear weapons were deployed on ships and attack submarines, and the balance of the nuclear stockpile had been consolidated at 34 bases in the United States.[31] Looking ahead to the implementation of unilateral pledges and the START I and II agreements, the United States plans to maintain an operational stockpile of 3,500 strategic weapons, 500 to 1,000 tactical weapons (tactical air-delivered bombs and sea-launched cruise missiles), and 3,500 reserve weapons into the next decade.[32] Large scale dismantlement of U.S. nuclear weapons began only in late 1992. Given the plans described above, that means that about 10,000 weapons needed to be dismantled.

DISMANTLING DOD WEAPONS

Weapons scheduled for dismantlement are flown by DOD to military "first destination" points of the operating service. These three Air Force,

---

30. See "Where the Weapons Are," *Bulletin of the Atomic Scientists*, September 1992, pp. 48–49.

31. Ibid., p. 49.

32. "U.S. Strategic Nuclear Forces, End of 1994," *Bulletin of the Atomic Scientists*, January/February 1995, p. 71.

two Army, and nine Navy central weapons storage sites hold the weapons in heavily guarded underground concrete bunkers until similar bunkers at the Pantex weapons dismantlement facility in Amarillo, Texas, are ready to accept them. Pantex is part of DOE's weapons design and production complex. The change in custody between DOD and DOE occurs at the military first destination points. From there, DOE is responsible for transporting the weapons to Pantex. This is now done with special trucks, disguised to look like commercial vehicles. In earlier years, special DOE weapons transportation trains linked the military first destination points to Pantex.

Once at Pantex, the weapons are placed in weapons storage bunkers until the dismantlement facility is ready to accept them. Weapons are dismantled to the pit level at Pantex. Non-nuclear components are destroyed, returned to their place of manufacture, or analyzed under the DOE's stockpile surveillance program. Thermonuclear secondaries are trucked to DOE's Y-12 plant in Oak Ridge, Tennessee, where they were manufactured and where the U.S. HEU and lithium deuteride stockpiles are located. There, the secondaries are dismantled and the HEU is placed in storage. Plutonium pits were formerly shipped to DOE's Rocky Flats plant in Golden, Colorado, where they were manufactured, but Rocky Flats has been closed since 1989 and no other DOE facility has a large-scale plutonium processing capability. As an interim measure, complete pits have been stored in their shipping containers in excess weapons storage bunkers on site at Pantex. Up to 17,000 pits can be stored at Pantex in this fashion.[33]

The Department of Energy planned to have Pantex dismantle 2,000 weapons a year starting in 1992, but there have been problems and the rate has been closer to 1,500 weapons a year with operations on a single-shift, five-day work-week basis. Consolidation and dismantlement operations have not created the storage problems that Russia is experiencing for at least two reasons. First, DOD enjoyed a great surplus of weapons storage capacity in the United States when the weapons consolidation campaign began.[34] Second, DOE also controlled a substantial surplus of

---

33. Ashton B. Carter and Owen Coté, "Disposition of Fissile Materials," Graham Allison, Ashton B. Carter, Steven E. Miller, and Philip Zelikow, eds., *Cooperative Denuclearization: From Pledges to Deeds*, CSIA Studies in International Security No. 2 (Cambridge, Mass.: Center for Science and International Affairs, 1993), p. 131, note 10.

34. Consider that the United States had 30,000 weapons in the early 1960s, and substantially fewer weapons were deployed overseas then. At that time, therefore, the continental United States (CONUS) possessed at least 30,000 weapon storage positions. In the late 1980s, the United States had 20,000 weapons and more than 6,000 were deployed overseas. Thus, there was a surplus of at least 15,000 storage positions on

secure weapons storage bunkers at Pantex. Thus, even though the Rocky Flats plutonium weapon component dismantlement plant was closed, DOE did not need to resort to improvised storage of dismantled weapon components in converted warehouses. Instead, the components were placed in the secure weapons storage bunkers at Pantex. When DOE finishes dismantling excess weapons at the end of this decade, 20,000 fissile weapon components will have been removed from 10,000 widely deployed weapons and safely stored in two facilities that meet the weapons standard of security. In the best-case scenario in Russia, the end of the decade will have seen 30,000 weapons removed from secure MOD storage, dismantled, and the resulting 60,000 fissile weapon components put in improvised facilities located at each of four closed cities spread across Russia, none of which come close to meeting the weapons standard.

THE DOE WEAPONS DESIGN AND PRODUCTION COMPLEX

There is no analog to Minatom's complex of closed nuclear cities in the United States. The Department of Energy did run a weapons design and production complex that performed similar functions, but only the industrial facilities themselves had a fence around them: the workers and their families lived outside the fence wherever they wanted.[35]

Weapons were designed at the Los Alamos, New Mexico, Livermore, California, and Sandia, New Mexico, laboratories. Los Alamos and Livermore designed the "physics package," or the nuclear and thermonuclear components of a weapon, and Sandia designed the non-nuclear components. Non-nuclear components were produced at the Mound (Ohio), Kansas City, and Pinellas (Florida) plants. Nuclear components were produced at Rocky Flats, Colorado, and Oak Ridge, Tennessee.

Nuclear materials for weapons were produced at five sites. An older reactor/reprocessing complex at Hanford, Washington, produced pluto-

---

CONUS. The opposite situation obtained in the former Soviet Union, where the stockpile reached its peak just before the Soviet Union disintegrated. Soon after, thousands of nuclear weapons were consolidated in Russia, which had far less central weapon storage capacity than did the Soviet Union, let alone the entire Warsaw Pact.

35.   For a concise guide to the American weapon design and production complex, see: "Appendix B: The DOE Nuclear Weapons Complex: A Descriptive Overview," in Committee to Provide Interim Oversight of the DOE Weapons Complex and Commission on Physical Sciences, Mathematics, and Resources, *The Nuclear Weapons Complex: Management for Health, Safety, and the Environment* (Washington DC: National Academy Press, 1989), pp. 102–112. For more detailed information on this complex, see Thomas B. Cochran and Robert S. Norris, *Nuclear Weapons Databook*, Vol. II: *U.S. Nuclear Warhead Production* (Cambridge, Mass.: Ballinger, 1987).

nium, and a somewhat newer one at Savannah River, Georgia, produced both tritium and plutonium. Three gaseous diffusion plants at Oak Ridge; Paducah, Kentucky, and Portsmouth, Ohio, produced HEU. Highly enriched uranium fuel for naval reactors was also produced at these three enrichment plants, and spent naval fuel was reprocessed and the HEU recovered at a third reprocessing facility in Idaho Falls. This plant also reprocessed spent research reactor fuel. The recovered HEU was shipped to Oak Ridge and fabricated into fuel for the production reactors at Savannah River.

The United States stopped producing HEU for weapons in 1964. It continued to produce special supergrade HEU (97 percent U-235) for naval reactors until the late 1980s, when the Navy converted to normal HEU with 93 percent U-235, thus allowing the naval fuel cycle to live off of existing stocks of HEU produced for weapons. The gaseous diffusion plant at Oak Ridge has been mothballed, and the Paducah and Portsmouth plants produce only LEU for power reactors. These latter two plants are leased to the U.S. Enrichment Corporation, which is in the process of being privatized. Also, since the late 1970s, U.S. supplied research reactors have been switched away from HEU to LEU fuels.

The United States also ceased producing plutonium and tritium in 1989. The reactors and reprocessing plants at Hanford and Savannah River have all been closed and there are no plans to restart them. Because the Savannah River reactors are closed, there is no longer any need for the Idaho facility to reprocess spent naval fuel, and that fuel is now simply stored in cooling ponds in Idaho Falls. Apart from Hanford and Savannah River, the United States has not developed any other major plutonium fuel cycles like the Russian MOX and breeder fuel cycles described above, and has no plans for any in the future. The long-term plutonium disposition option most likely to be pursued in the United States is glass vitrification with high-level waste stored in a geologic depository.

Just as the production stream of new fissile materials has dried up completely, so has the recycling of materials from dismantled weapons. In the past, the component fabrication facilities at Rocky Flats and Oak Ridge produced new weapon components out of old ones, as well as from newly produced plutonium and HEU. Rocky Flats has been closed since 1989 and no new weapons have been produced by the United States since that date. Without a substitute for Rocky Flats, the United States will remain incapable of producing new weapons on any appreciable scale because it lacks large-scale plutonium processing facility for pit fabrication.

Thus the sum total of the activity involving fissile materials in DOE's weapons production complex lies in the dismantlement and storage activities conducted at Pantex and Oak Ridge. The rest of the complex lies dormant. Stockpiles of bulk fissile material, particularly plutonium, exist at Hanford, Savannah River, and Rocky Flats in dedicated bulk storage facilities. The naval fuel cycle continues to generate a relatively small, one-way flow of HEU out of the national stockpile at Oak Ridge into commercial fuel fabrication facilities, and onward to shipyards and refueling facilities. Other than the naval fuel cycle, which is smaller than Russia's, the United States will cease all process operations and movements involving fissile material when it is done dismantling excess weapons in or about the year 2000. The U.S. stockpile of fissile materials will remain in a few dedicated, secure storage facilities until decisions concerning long-term disposition are made and implemented.

The Russian Denuclearization Challenge

It is estimated that the Soviet Union and now Russia have produced about twice as much fissile material as the United States. For separated plutonium, the numbers are about 100 metric tons for the United States and 200 metric tons for Russia.[36] For HEU (90 percent enriched), it is about 500 metric tons for the United States and over 1000 metric tons for Russia. In the Russian case, these numbers represent twice as much as western analysts, in and out of government, estimated during the Cold War.[37]

When the Soviet stockpile reached its peak of 45,000 weapons in 1986, these weapons contained on the order of 180 tons of plutonium and 675 tons of HEU.[38] Other than the civil plutonium accumulating at Chelyabinsk, Minatom probably put plutonium in weapons as fast as it could be produced throughout the Cold War. Of the remaining 325 tons of HEU, about 100 tons had been burned in some 325 naval reactors, about 35 tons had been burned in tritium production reactors, 25 tons had been burned in plutonium production reactors, 10 tons had been burned in research reactors, 10 tons had been detonated in weapons tests, 40 tons had been lost or written off during processing, and the rest — some 100 tons — is in process somewhere in the Russian nuclear archipelago or in bulk

---

36. This includes the 30-plus tons of separated plutonium stored at Chelyabinsk-65.

37. See, for example, Cochran, Norris, and Bukharin, *Making the Russian Bomb*, p. 189; and Thomas Cochran, William Arkin, Stan Norris, and Jeff Sands, *Nuclear Weapons Databook*, Vol. IV: *Soviet Nuclear Weapons* (Cambridge, Mass.: Ballinger, 1989).

38. These numbers assume an average of 4 kilograms of plutonium and 15 kilograms of HEU per weapon. In practice most plutonium and more than half the HEU was in weapons.

storage.[39] Russia has stopped producing HEU for weapons but may continue to produce it in relatively small quantities for other purposes. Russia definitely continues to produce and separate plutonium: one ton a year at Chelyabinsk-65 and 1.5 tons a year at Tomsk and Kransnoyarsk combined.

Beginning in 1986, a massive shift in custody of fissile material between MOD and Minatom began, and it continues today. Each year, 2,000–3,000 weapons have been retired by MOD and dismantled at Minatom weapons assembly/disassembly facilities. This constitutes an average annual transfer from MOD to Minatom of as much as 12 tons of plutonium and 45 tons of HEU in the form of dismantled fissile weapon components.

During the Cold War, these components would have been refurbished, recycled into new weapons, and returned to the MOD. Such recycling may continue today on a small scale, but the bulk of the components, numbering now in the several tens of thousands, are simply piling up in the improvised Minatom storage facilities at Sverdlovsk, Chelyabinsk, Tomsk, and Krasnoyarsk. Newly produced plutonium is also accumulating at the latter three facilities. In the case of Tomsk and Krasnoyarsk, 1.5 tons of plutonium a year would have gone into weapons during the Cold War but is now joining other stockpiles of bulk plutonium at storage facilities separate from those containing dismantled weapon components. Substantial quantities of fissile material are also located at non-weapons nuclear research and fuel cycle facilities.

In the case of the naval fuel cycle, there were about 160 nuclear-powered vessels in 1990, each with two reactors, and each with a core containing about 100 kilograms of HEU enriched to between 50 and 90 percent, for 32 tons of HEU actually aboard ships. Another 32 tons of fresh fuel would be in fuel fabrication or in storage, and somewhat less than 32 tons of spent fuel would be in reprocessing or in storage. The security of fresh naval fuel storage facilities is terrible.[40] Less is known about the naval fuel fabrication line at the Electrostal plant in Moscow, but security and material accounting is apparently very weak there as well.[41] We know

---

39. David Albright, Frans Berkhout, and William Walker, *World Inventory of Plutonium and Highly Enriched Uranium 1992* (Oxford: Oxford University Press, 1993), p. 60.

40. Oleg Bukharin and William C. Potter, "Potatoes were guarded better," *Bulletin of the Atomic Scientists*, Vol. 51, No. 3 (May/June 1995), pp. 46–50.

41. Electrostal's commercial reactor fuel fabrication line is serving as a pilot project under the Nunn-Lugar program for a new Russian material control and accounting system.

nothing about the storage conditions for reprocessed and separated naval HEU at Chelyabinsk-65.

The same concerns apply to the research, fast breeder, plutonium production, tritium production, and space reactor fuel cycles. The reactors themselves contain weapons-usable fissile materials, but they are also supported by fuel cycle facilities at their front and back end that also contain fissile materials. The Electrostal and Novosibirsk fuel fabrication facilities and the Chelyabinsk-65 reprocessing facility are deeply involved in these fuel cycles, but other facilities not known in the west are, or once were, involved as well, such as Ust-Kamengorsk.

Finally, the larger, stand-alone Russian nuclear research facilities such as Kurchatov in Moscow, Obninsk, and Dimitrovgrad store quite substantial balances of fissile material with an almost complete absence of security. Obninsk reportedly possesses 750 kilograms of plutonium for experimental purposes. Dimitrovgrad operates six research reactors, three of which are significantly larger than either Israel's Dimona reactor or North Korea's Yongbyon reactor.

Thus, Russian fissile material accounting systems are inadequate, the physical security for these inadequately accounted-for materials is inadequate, and these materials continue to be transported and used in large quantities throughout the Russian nuclear archipelago. There has been a radical reduction in overall security for Russian fissile materials resulting from the end of the Cold War and the breakup of the Soviet Union. Nevertheless, Russia's total stockpile of fissile material is twice as large as the U.S. stockpile (1,200 versus 600 tons). Both these stockpiles are at least an order of magnitude larger than the fissile stockpiles of the other declared nuclear weapons states, the United Kingdom, France, and China (hundreds versus tens of tons), which are in turn an order of magnitude larger than the holdings of the so-called threshold states, India, Israel, and Pakistan (tons versus hundreds of kilograms).

These facts and their inescapable consequences can be illustrated by the following examples:

- More fissile material is now stored in improvised, insecure facilities at Sverdlovsk (or at Chelyabinsk, or Tomsk, or Krasnoyarsk) than is contained in the entire stockpiles of Britain, France, and China combined. Measured in terms of fissile material, the Russian administrative units that contain these facilities are, respectively, the second, third, fourth, and fifth largest nuclear powers in the world.

- Every year, even more fissile material is transferred from Russian MOD weapons storage bunkers into Minatom's improvised storage facilities at these sites. This is an annual movement of fissile material larger than the total stockpile of Britain, or France, or China.

- More plutonium is used for research at the Obninsk research institute than has been produced by either India or Israel. Obninsk is one of six nuclear facilities with substantial fissile material balances that Russian authorities have admitted lack adequate security and material accounting systems.

- At Ust-Kamengorsk, more HEU slipped through the cracks in the Russian material accounting system than has been produced by either Pakistan or South Africa.

- Even if 99.99 percent of Russia's fissile material stocks remained secure, but the other .01 percent leaked, more than ten North Koreas worth of fissile material would be loose and nobody would know until. . . .

Appendix B

A Primer on Fissile Materials and Nuclear Weapon Design

By Owen R. Coté, Jr.

What are fissile materials? How are they made? What quantities of these materials are necessary to produce a bomb? How do different designs affect a weapon's size, yield, and fissile material requirements? What are the differences between advanced thermonuclear weapons, advanced fission weapons, and crude fission weapons? When does testing become necessary? Given an understanding of these basic concepts, what can we assume about the bombs that might be designed by nuclear terrorists given a supply of fissile material? This appendix provides answers to these questions and shows why nuclear leakage from Russia is so dangerous.

Simple nuclear weapons are easy to design, make, and deliver, assuming an adequate supply of fissile material. It is the difficulty of obtaining fissile material that provides one of the major defenses protecting the international community from a major surge in nuclear proliferation. Fissile materials and their means of production will continue to be difficult to obtain if excess fissile materials do not leak from Russia. If, on the other hand, fissile materials do leak from Russia, then the supply of nuclear weapons in the world will soon equal the demand.

This appendix is organized as follows: First, I outline briefly the physics involved in a nuclear detonation and discuss the fissile materials required. Then I describe the design of an advanced thermonuclear weapon; almost all simpler weapons, which I next describe, are a special case of an advanced design.

Having demonstrated that design is not a major obstacle, I turn to what is the major obstacle: production of fissile materials. To summarize: since a simple weapon is not difficult to design, since expertise is available, and since testing is not necessary, all that stands between proliferants and nuclear weaponry is the difficulty of obtaining fissile materials.

FISSION AND FUSION

The simplest and lightest element — hydrogen — consists of a nucleus with one positively charged particle, the proton, and a negatively charged particle, the electron, in orbit around that nucleus. Elements are distinguished from each other by the number of protons in their nuclei. This number is their atomic number, and hydrogen's is one. Almost all nuclei also contain a second kind of particle, the neutron, which has nearly the same mass as the proton but no electrical charge. Together, protons and neutrons are known as nucleons, and the total number of nucleons in a nucleus is known as the atomic weight or mass. Hydrogen, with one proton and no neutrons, has a mass of one.

A given element generally occurs in several forms, called isotopes. Different isotopes of an element are distinguished by the number of neutrons in their nuclei. Hydrogen has three isotopes: hydrogen, with one proton and no neutrons; deuterium, with a proton and a neutron; and tritium, with a proton and two neutrons. Isotopes can be referred to symbolically by element and mass. For example, the three hydrogen isotopes can be represented as H-1, H-2, and H-3.

Uranium and plutonium have atomic numbers of 92 and 94 respectively. Uranium isotopes range from U-232 to U-238. Plutonium isotopes range from Pu-238 to Pu-242. The isotopes of most concern to this discussion are U-235 and Pu-239. They have an odd number of neutrons in their nuclei.

When nuclei of the isotopes U-235 and Pu-239 are struck by neutrons, they sometimes split, or fission. They fission into two lighter elements, or fission fragments. The sum of the atomic masses of the two fission fragments is always less than the total atomic mass of the original U or Pu nucleus. The size of the difference determines the amount of energy released in the form of neutrons, light, and other forms of radiation as a result of the fission.

Under certain conditions of high density and intense heat, the nuclei of hydrogen isotopes can come close enough to fuse despite the repulsive force of their like-charged nuclei. The atomic mass of the new element, always an isotope of helium, is always less than the sum of the two hydrogen isotopes that fused to form it. Again, this mass difference determines the amount of energy released in neutrons and other forms of radiation.

A fissioned uranium or plutonium nucleus releases roughly ten times the energy created by the most energetic of the various fusion reactions between different hydrogen isotopes. On the other hand, a single fission reaction requires on the order of 236 to 240 nucleons (protons and neutrons), while a single fusion reaction requires as few as four or five. Thus, per nucleon, fusion produces five to six times more energy than fission.

FISSILE MATERIALS

Fissile materials consist of isotopes whose nuclei fission after capturing a neutron of any energy. Fissionable isotopes fission only after the capture of neutrons with energies above some threshold value. Many heavy isotopes are fissionable, but many fewer of them are also fissile, and almost all of these are isotopes of uranium or plutonium. All fissile materials and some fissionable materials are usable in weapons. It is the odd-numbered isotopes of uranium and plutonium that are fissile: U-233,235 and Pu-239,241. U-235 and Pu-239 are the most common and are the best weapon materials.

The probability that a nucleus will fission when struck by a neutron of a given energy is expressed in terms of its fission cross-section. Cross-sections, expressed as an area, are measures of the probability that a given neutron will fission a given nucleus. Isotopes with large fission cross-sections are more likely to fission than isotopes with lower cross-sections. Pu-239 has a higher fission cross-section than U-235 at all neutron energies.

Neutrons cause nuclei to fission, and neutrons are also released when nuclei fission. The average number of neutrons released per fissioning nucleus varies, depending on the isotope. Pu-239 releases 3 and U-235 2.5 neutrons per fission, on average. Because Pu-239 has a higher fission cross-section, and because it emits more neutrons per fission, it takes less Pu-239 than U-235 to sustain a fission chain reaction.

A chain reaction occurs when every nucleus that fissions causes, on average, at least one other nucleus to fission. When this occurs in a mass of fissile material, we describe it as a critical mass, i.e., one that is just capable of sustaining a chain reaction. Nuclear reactors cause sustained chain reactions by assembling a mass of fissile material whose criticality is dependent on the presence of a moderator like graphite or water that slows neutrons down, thereby exploiting the high fission cross-sections of fissile materials in the presence of low energy, or thermal, neutrons.

An explosive chain reaction occurs when every nucleus that fissions causes, on average, more than one other nucleus to fission. A supercritical mass of fissile material is necessary for an explosive chain reaction. Nuclear weapons generally assemble supercritical masses by uniting or compressing subcritical masses of fissile materials, and by reflecting neutrons back into those masses that would otherwise have escaped into free space. The better the compression and the better the neutron reflection, the fewer neutrons escape, the more fissions are caused per fission, and the greater the rate at which the chain reaction multiplies.

For these reasons, the critical mass of Pu-239 is about three times smaller than that of U-235 at normal densities, because of its higher fission cross-section and average neutron production rate per fission. Thus, less Pu-239 than U-235 is needed to make a fission weapon.

CRITICAL MASSES

All by itself, apart from any neutron reflection and at normal densities, a bare, solid sphere of plutonium with greater than 90 percent Pu-239 is critical when its weight exceeds 22 pounds. This amount is called the "bare crit." Under the same circumstances, uranium enriched to more than 90 percent U-235 will go critical when it weighs 114.5 pounds. As the percentage of Pu-239 in plutonium is reduced, the bare crit goes up slowly. High burn up (or recycled) reactor plutonium with 60 percent Pu-239 has a bare crit only 25–35 percent higher than plutonium with 90 percent Pu-239. The rise in critical mass is much greater as U-235 enrichment levels are lowered. Uranium enriched to 50 percent in U-235 would have a bare crit three times as high as uranium with 90 percent U-235.[1]

Critical mass requirements drop steeply in the presence of neutron reflection. Reflectors made of heavy metals can reduce the bare crit to half, while reflectors made from the lightest metals can cause a threefold reduction. High explosive compression to twice normal density can reduce bare crits by half again. Thus, a highly conservative implosion weapon might use a fissile core that was large enough to be barely sub-critical at normal density when surrounded by a reflector. The detonation of the high-explosive shell and the compression of the barely sub-critical core could hardly avoid producing some nuclear yield. Once a supercritical mass has been assembled by whatever means, the yield of the resulting explosion will be increased if the explosion can be contained or tamped for several microseconds before it disassembles. Tampers can be made from any heavy metal. Therefore, in some weapons, the tamper and the reflector are the same component.

The Fat Man design tested at Alamagordo and used over Nagasaki was a simple weapon that used all these techniques. It was an implosion weapon that used a massive quantity of high explosive to implode a very heavy, spherical uranium/tungsten reflector/tamper enclosing a solid sphere containing 12 pounds of plutonium. The resulting explosion had

---

1. Paul Leventhal and Yonah Alexander, eds., *Preventing Nuclear Terrorism: The Report and Papers of the International Task Force on Prevention of Nuclear Terrorism* (Lexington, Mass.: Lexington Books, 1987), pp. 56–57.

a yield equivalent to 20,000 tons (20 kilotons) of high explosive. The same assembly mechanism would have required 30 pounds of highly enriched uranium (HEU) to produce the same yield.[2]

More sophisticated designs use even less fissile material. Current U.S. weapons use advanced fission weapons to begin a thermonuclear detonation. These use 9 pounds or less of plutonium. Fractional crit fission weapons producing low kiloton yields can be made with as little as 2.5 pounds of plutonium or 5.5 pounds of HEU.[3] On the other hand, as we will see below, advanced thermonuclear weapons use fissile materials in significant quantities in more than one place.

From Advanced Thermonuclear to Simple Fission Weapons Designs

In this section I discuss weapons design, beginning with a description of the configuration and detonation of an advanced thermonuclear weapon.[4] Almost all other simpler designs, discussed below, are a special case of an advanced design.

First, there is the trigger, or primary stage. Imagine a sphere consisting of a series of concentric shells of different materials nested together. The core of the sphere is hollow, and there is an air gap that separates the outer shells of the sphere from the inner ones. Along the outside of the sphere is a thin metal casing. Then, moving inward, one finds a high-explosive jacket, a heavy metal tamper, and a light metal reflector. These parts comprise the assembly mechanism.

Next is the air gap that separates the assembly mechanism from the fissile shell, or pit. The pit rests on a pedestal inside the air gap and is itself a hollow sphere of plutonium clad with a metal plating. The pedestal supporting the plutonium pit also serves as a tunnel connecting the

---

2. Thomas Cochran and Christopher Paine, *The Amount of Plutonium and Highly-Enriched Uranium Needed for Pure Fission Weapons: Nuclear Weapons Databook* (Washington DC: The Natural Resources Defense Council, April, 1995), p. 5 and Figures 1 and 2.

3. Ibid., Figs. 1 and 2.

4. The following discussion depends heavily on Chuck Hansen, *U.S. Nuclear Weapons: The Secret History* (Arlington, Tex.: Aerofax, 1988), especially pp. 11–41. See also Charles S. Grace, *Nuclear Weapons: Principles, Effects and Survivability* (London: Brassey's, 1994), pp. 3–24; Hans A. Bethe, "Comments on the History of the H-Bomb," *Los Alamos Science*, Vol. 3, No. 3 (Fall 1982), pp. 43–53; and "Appendix E: Physics of Nuclear Weapon Design," in Committee to Provide Oversight of the DOE Nuclear Complex and Commission on Physical Sciences, Mathematics, and Resources, *The Nuclear Weapons Complex: Management for Health, Safety, and the Environment* (Washington, D.C.: National Academy Press, 1989), pp. 123–128.

outside of the assembly mechanism to the pit's hollow core. At the other end of this tunnel are two containers of tritium and deuterium gas, one much smaller than the other. The whole assembly is called a primary, as in primary stage.

Physically separate from the primary is another component, the secondary. A cylindrical shape, rather than a sphere, it too consists of layers of different materials, but it is solid and has no air gaps. The outside layer in this notional design is natural uranium, but it could be any number of fissile, fissionable, or other heavy metals. This outer layer, or pusher, encloses a layer of lithium deuteride, a very light compound comprising isotopes of lithium and hydrogen. The lithium deuteride, in turn, encloses an innermost layer of fissile HEU, also known as the sparkplug.

Finally, a heavy casing shaped like a large watermelon contains the primary at one end and the secondary at the other. Assume that all the batteries, cables, capacitators, detonators, safety devices, fuses, radiation shields, and so on are in place, and that the fusing and firing systems work as intended, and the weapon detonates.

The detonation begins in the high-explosive layer surrounding the primary. It explodes, imploding the tamper/reflector shell. The tamper/reflector is driven inward through the air gap, picking up momentum while facing no resistance. It slams into the plutonium pit, crushing it. The pit is compressed to two or three times its normal density, driving its nuclei closer together, while remaining enclosed by the imploding tamper/reflector. Through compression and neutron reflection, a supercritical mass of plutonium is formed in the pit. This is the primary assembly phase.

As the pit approaches its maximum compression, the smaller of the two external tritium-deuterium gas containers, the initiator, uses an electric charge to compress its contents; the tritium and deuterium nuclei fuse, and emit high-energy neutrons through the tube leading into the hollow core of the imploding pit. Some of these neutrons strike plutonium nuclei and fission them. This initiates a larger number of parallel chain reactions in the pit. This is the primary ignition phase.

After ignition a race develops between the fission chain reaction propagating through the fissile pit, and the rate at which the pit blows apart by disassembly. The more generations of the chain reaction before disassembly, the more material is fissioned, and the larger the yield. Therefore, at this point, the chain reaction receives a boost. The much greater quantity of tritium-deuterium gas in the larger of the two external containers — the booster — is now injected at high pressure into the fissioning pit. There, the intense pressures and temperatures cause the hydrogen isotopes to fuse and a much larger burst of high energy neutrons is released than during the initiation phase. These high-energy neutrons boost the fission chain reaction, by greatly increasing the number of fissions in each succeeding generation of the reaction. The primary boost phase increases the energy release prior to the explosive disassembly of the plutonium pit.

The primary stage has now detonated. It first emits a burst of intense X-ray radiation. The X-rays travel at the speed of light, some thirty times faster than the nuclear particles released by the exploding primary. They are absorbed by the interior of the weapon casing and re-radiated onto the outer shell of the secondary. Thus, X-ray radiation transports, or couples, the energy of the primary to the secondary.

The secondary shell is turned into a dense plasma. As this plasma ablates, or burns off, it exerts an implosive force inward on the rest of the secondary that is a thousand or so times greater than the pressure created by high explosives. The shell pushes inward and compresses the secondary.

As the secondary is compressed, the innermost layer of fissile material at its core begins to fission. The lithium deuteride between the imploding shell and the exploding core is now being compressed even further. Neutrons from the fissioning core bombard the lithium deuteride; lithium nuclei capture neutrons, emit an alpha particle (a helium nucleus), and become tritium. At this stage, the secondary has been compressed, its fissile core has fissioned, and tritium has been bred in the lithium.

Now the two hydrogen isotopes most prone to fusion reactions — deuterium and tritium — are present in the fusion fuel capsule of the secondary. They have been compressed by the imploding shell and heated by the exploding core. They fuse under the intense pressure and temperature. The heat produced increases the temperature of the secondary further, causing more fusions of the hydrogen isotopes, and the hydrogen fuel burns, releasing thermonuclear energy in a manner analogous to the sun.

As part of this tremendous energy release, the fusing hydrogen isotopes are also producing highly energetic neutrons. These cause the imploding shell of fissionable U-238 (or fissile U-235) to fission. The fissioning of the secondary shell, in turn, simultaneously boosts and tamps the energy release in the burning fusion fuel capsule. This completes the detonation of the secondary.

Thus, the detonation of a modern two-stage thermonuclear weapon actually involves many more than two distinct stages: high-explosive detonation, primary assembly, primary ignition and fissioning, primary boosting, primary detonation, radiation coupling from the primary to the secondary, secondary implosion, secondary core ignition and fissioning, tritium breeding, thermonuclear burn, and secondary shell fissioning. It is more accurate to think of the detonation of a thermonuclear weapon as a series of mutually reinforcing fission-fusion-fission reactions, begun with chemical high explosives in a primary, and continued in secondary and, in some cases, tertiary stages via radiation coupling.

Thus one can think of the primary stage of a thermonuclear weapon as simply an advanced fission (atomic) weapon. Even though some of its explosive yield results from fusion reactions due to tritium-deuterium gas boosting, none of it depends on X-ray radiation coupling between physically separate stages.

Let us now take this advanced thermonuclear weapon, whose design we have already described, and progressively simplify it.

SIMPLE WEAPONS

The most advanced designs emerged out of the ballistic missile era that began in the United States in the 1950s. Ballistic missiles created a demand for weapons with high yield-to-weight and yield-to-volume ratios. Before the ballistic missile era, thermonuclear weapons were designed to maximize yield-to–fissile material ratios. These criteria influenced both the primary and secondary stages.

Modern primaries use as little high explosive and fissile material as possible, and rely heavily on tritium boosting to produce yields sufficient to compress and ignite secondaries. This minimizes volume and weight. Modern secondaries often use considerably greater amounts of fissile material for the same reason. For example, using fissile rather than fissionable material in the shell of a secondary substantially increases yield without increasing weight or volume. Expanding the diameter of the heavy, cylindrical fissile or fissionable components of a secondary at the expense of the diameter of the much lighter lithium deuteride component within a given overall volume increases yield, but also increases weight.

Before the advent of ballistic missiles, weapons were delivered primarily by aircraft capable of lifting large, heavy payloads. U.S. fissile material stockpiles were also smaller then, and designers built large weapons which maximized yield for a given amount of fissile material. Primaries were much larger and heavier even when they used boosting, because high-explosive jackets were larger and heavier: with more high explosive, the same pit will be compressed more and produce more yield. Secondaries were larger, but contained less fissile material. Most of their volume, and therefore more of their yield, derived from fusion. During this first phase of thermonuclear design, very large weapons were deployed with tertiaries, or third stages that brought yields into the ten-megaton range.

Prior to the development of multi-stage thermonuclear weapons, U.S. designers experimented with high-yield single-stage fission weapons. They used very large quantities of HEU in an implosion design. Plutonium could not be used because, in large quantities, its high spontaneous neutron emission rate made pre-detonation likely even in an implosion device. Even without boosting, such high-yield HEU implosion designs approached half a megaton in yield. With boosting they could approach a megaton. On the other hand, they were very heavy, they used enormous amounts of HEU, and they were very hard to make safe from accidental detonation due to shock or fire.

Concerns about accidental detonation were a major issue for weapon designers early in the Cold War because U.S. Strategic Air Command aircraft flew peacetime training and alert missions with weapons aboard. Prior to the widespread adoption of tritium boosting, single-stage implosion weapons or primaries of a multi-stage weapon were designed with two-piece cores, one piece of which was stored separately and inserted just prior to use. In the event of an accident causing detonation of the high-explosive assembly mechanism, core detonation would be impossible due to the missing piece of the pit. With boosting, sealed pit weapons were developed with less fissile material in the core. These weapons depended on a tritium-deuterium gas injection to produce an appreciable yield even if the assembly mechanism worked perfectly. In an accident, when the high explosive would detonate unevenly, and without gas boosting, such a device would produce no appreciable nuclear yield.

As we have seen, boosting was also used to maximize yield while preserving scarce fissile material. Two other innovations designed to achieve the same objective preceded boosting. One involved "levitated pits," or the separation of the pit from the tamper by an air gap. Levitated pit designs increased the efficiency of assembly mechanisms by allowing them to develop more kinetic energy before they struck the pit.

The other involved "composite pits," or pits that consisted of a mix of both plutonium and HEU. Composite cores were developed by the United States during a period immediately after World War II when it was producing eight times as much HEU as plutonium per ton of natural uranium feed. HEU could be used much more efficiently in an implosion weapon than in a gun weapon. Furthermore, as long as plutonium was scarce, a given quantity of HEU and plutonium could be used more efficiently if combined in individual weapon pits than if the two fissile materials were used separately in different weapons.

Levitated pits and composite cores, used together or separately, greatly increased the efficiency of the first postwar generation of fission weapons in the United States. Prior to the introduction of these advances in the late 1940s and early 1950s, fission weapon design had not advanced much beyond the first generation of fission weapons developed in wartime at Los Alamos.

Another early postwar innovation involved a change in the means of initiating the fissile chain reaction. Prior to the development of external deuterium-tritium initiators, internal initiators were used. Located at the core of the fissile pit, these used polonium, which is a strong alpha emitter, and beryllium, which emits neutrons in the presence of an alpha source.[5] Normally separated by a thin screen in a small, bimetallic, golf ball–sized container, these elements, when crushed together by the imploding pit, became a strong neutron source. The drawbacks to this early practice were twofold. Polonium has a very short half life of 138 days and therefore early weapons had very short shelf lives. They could not be deployed in the field for long. In addition, internal initiators tended to detonate weapons too early, causing less-than-optimal pit compression.

This simplification takes us essentially to the Trinity-Nagasaki "Fat Man" implosion design. Fat Man used a lot of plutonium packed solidly inside a massive assembly mechanism of high explosive and a very heavy tamper. The advanced neutron reflecting properties of beryllium were not exploited to reduce critical mass requirements, and the polonium/beryllium initiator needed to be inserted into the core shortly before use. Fat Man was a very conservative design, and it remains the simplest implosion weapon design available. It worked on the first try both at Alamagordo and at Semipalatinsk.

Implosion was itself a wartime Los Alamos innovation that solved the first major nuclear weapon design challenge. To explain this challenge, it is useful to consider some history. The first fissile material to be discovered was the isotope Uranium 235. Since U-235 is rare in nature (.072 percent of natural uranium), it must be enriched (concentrated). This requires that it be separated from other non-fissile uranium isotopes, primarily U-238. Isotope separation remains today a very sophisticated technology. In the late 1930s, it seemed impossible on the scale needed for a weapon.

At first, therefore, the discovery of plutonium seemed to get around this problem. Plutonium could be produced in the nuclear reactor when U-235 fissioned and emitted neutrons that were captured by U-238, producing Plutonium 239. After removal from the reactor, the Pu-239 could be chemically separated from the uranium because it was a different element. Chemical separation was much simpler than isotope separation,

---

5. On various neutron sources, see Robert Mozley, "Particle Sources and Radiography," *Science and Global Security*, Vol. 1, Nos. 3–4 (1990), pp. 291–293.

and plutonium production reactors using natural uranium fuel could be designed as soon as a moderating material of sufficient purity was found to slow fission-induced neutrons enough to sustain a thermal neutron chain reaction. Very pure graphite solved this problem for the United States, and it appeared that weapons would now be easier to produce, especially since an even simpler design than Fat Man had already been developed by Los Alamos.

This initial fission weapon design was not an implosion device. Rather, it was really just a glorified cannon. In such a "gun type" design, a shell of fissile material is fired down a gun barrel into a hollow fissile target fastened to the other end of the barrel. Once united, the two sub-critical pieces form a supercritical mass and detonate. Since no compression of the fissile material occurs in such a design, it requires a lot of fissile material, and what it uses, it uses inefficiently. Nevertheless, it was clear in 1943 that a gun-type weapon would work.

Shortly after the first plutonium emerged from the pilot scale X-10 reactor at Oak Ridge in the summer of 1944, the existence of another plutonium isotope, Pu-240, was confirmed. It was formed in the reactor when Pu-239 captured a neutron but did not immediately fission. Pu-240 spontaneously fissioned at a rate much greater than Pu-239. Thus, Pu-240 proved to be a potent neutron source, as some had anticipated.[6] More importantly, the supercritical mass in a gun weapon is assembled at a rate which turned out to be too slow to allow a gun weapon to be made with plutonium, because it spontaneously emits neutrons at a rate likely to cause predetonation. Implosion solved this design challenge at the cost of some increase in complexity. Implosion assembly of a supercritical mass occurs much more quickly than gun assembly, allowing the use of plutonium.

Thus the first design challenge of the nuclear age involved a choice between a very simple gun weapon using HEU which was very expensive to produce, and a more complicated implosion weapon using plutonium which was somewhat less difficult to obtain. In the event, the Manhattan Project pursued both options. Alongside the Fat Man plutonium weapon, Los Alamos also designed an HEU gun bomb called Little Boy. Its designers were confident enough of success on the first try that Little Boy was "tested" over Hiroshima. Gun-type weapons using HEU remain the simplest of fission weapons. Early postwar air-delivered, earth penetration bombs used gun designs because their simple assembly mechanism could function even after the shock of a high velocity impact. Later, certain

6. See Richard Rhodes, *The Making of the Atomic Bomb* (London: Penguin, 1980), pp. 548–549.

nuclear artillery shells used a gun design both because of the shock of firing the shell, and because such weapons could be made with small diameters. However, the main attraction of a gun weapon remains its simplicity. The likelihood of success without testing, combined with an indigenous source of HEU, made a gun design the weapon of choice for the South Africans some thirty years after Little Boy.

Thus we see that there are very simple nuclear weapon designs available to a potential proliferator. Weapons based on these designs would bear little resemblance to the more advanced weapons deployed by today's nuclear powers, but that is beside the point, since even simple weapons could reliably produce an explosion equal to hundreds or thousands of tons of TNT. That is a much easier task than most people think; the main obstacle has been the difficulty of securing an adequate supply of fissile material. Producing fissile materials is, however, *more* difficult than most people think, and it is to that subject I now turn.

Producing Fissile Materials

HEU is produced at enrichment plants using one of several isotope separation technologies.[7] All of these technologies exploit the small differences in atomic mass to separate different isotopes of the same element from each other. The most widely used isotope separation technique today uses centrifuges. Uranium hexafluoride gas is fed into a connected "cascade" of centrifuges. The centrifuges are spun at very high rates. The heavier U-238 gravitates toward the rotating outer wall of the centrifuge, while the U-235 remains closer to the axis. At each stage of the cascade, uranium depleted in U-235 is collected and separated. After many repetitions, what is left is run consisting primarily of U-235, or enriched uranium.

Before centrifuges, most industrial scale enrichment plants used a gas diffusion process. In a gaseous diffusion plant, uranium gas is pumped at high pressure through a series of cylinders with porous walls, or diffusion barriers. Lighter isotopes pass through the barriers at slightly greater rates. Again, after passing through a cascade of many barriers, the U-235 content is enriched and the U-238 reduced. A gas diffusion cascade is much larger than a centrifuge cascade, and consumes more electrical

---

7. See Alan Krass, Peter Boskma, Boelie Elzen, and Wim A. Smit, *Uranium Enrichment and Nuclear Weapons Proliferation* (London: Taylor & Francis, 1983); and Robert F. Mozley, *Uranium Enrichment and Other Technical Problems Relating to Nuclear Weapons Proliferation*, Center for International Security and Arms Control, Stanford University, July 1994.

power by an order of magnitude. Diffusion plants are larger because gas barriers give less enrichment, or separative work, per stage than centrifuges, and they consume more power because the gas pumps that fill the cascade need to be much more powerful than the small motors that spin centrifuges. Large gas diffusion plants still operate in the United States, France, and China. Most of the rest of the world's enrichment capacity uses the more modern centrifuge technology.

There are other enrichment technologies. The South Africans, probably with German assistance, developed an aerodynamic enrichment technology that exploits the different paths followed by different isotopes in gaseous form as they flow at high speeds around a curved nozzle. The United States developed and later abandoned an enrichment technology that used high-current cyclotrons (calutrons). Calutrons ionize uranium gas and pass the positively charged ions through an intense magnetic field that acts more strongly on the lighter isotopes. The Iraqis later adapted this inefficient method as a part of their enrichment enterprise. Laser isotopic enrichment technologies have been developed and may be used in the future, but they are probably too sophisticated for any but the most advanced nations. They also exploit the behavior of positively charged, ionized isotopes, but do so selectively and with much greater efficiency than do calutrons.

Plutonium is produced in nuclear reactors.[8] The energy produced in a reactor results from the chain reaction that begins when a critical configuration of U-235 is created in its core. As we have seen, such chain reactions are carried by neutrons. When a nucleus fissions, it produces several neutrons in addition to the fission fragments. Only one of these, on average, needs to fission another nucleus for the chain reaction to be sustained. Of the other neutrons, some are captured by "fertile," as opposed to fissile, materials in the reactor's fuel elements. A fertile isotope (U-238) is one that, upon capturing a neutron, becomes a fissile isotope (Pu-239).

Most reactors use uranium fuel with U-235 enrichment levels ranging from 0.72 percent (natural uranium) to 5 percent (low-enriched uranium, or LEU). In other words, reactor fuel usually consists mostly of fertile U-238. When U-238 nuclei capture neutrons, they decay rapidly through a two-stage process to become Pu-239. Pu-239 is both fissile and fertile. When Pu-239 captures a neutron, instead of fissioning, it can become Pu-240. When Pu-240 captures a neutron, it can become Pu-241, and Pu-241 can, in turn, become Pu-242. In fourteen years, half the Pu-241

---

8. On reactors, see Anthony V. Nero, Jr., *A Guidebook to Nuclear Reactors* (Berkeley, Calif.: University of California Press, 1979).

decays into the element Americium, but the other isotopes last for thousands of years. All of these plutonium isotopes, and Americium as well, are fissile or fissionable as well. Therefore, as plutonium is produced in a reactor, some of it also fissions. Thus, over time, the total amount of plutonium produced in the reactor fuel elements ceases to increase. On the other hand, the higher-number plutonium isotopes become a larger and larger percentage of the total plutonium produced. When reactor fuel is used in a reactor for a long time, it is called "high burn up" fuel, and the plutonium produced from it will be less concentrated or enriched in the isotope Pu-239 than if it were "low burn up" fuel that was in a reactor for a comparatively shorter period.

When fuel elements are removed from a reactor, the plutonium and uranium still present can be separated chemically in what is usually called a "reprocessing" facility. Reprocessing separates elements from each other, but not different isotopes of the same element. Thus, the plutonium is separated from the other elements, but its isotopic composition remains the same. In principle, plutonium isotopes could be separated from each other in enrichment facilities, but this is not done, at least on anything more than a laboratory scale, for several reasons.

First, the main reason to enrich plutonium would be to separate Pu-239 from Pu-240. Pu-240 is a strong neutron emitter. Its presence in all plutonium is the reason why plutonium cannot be used in simple gun-type weapons; it might cause pre-initiation. The atomic weights of these two isotopes differ by only one neutron. It would take much more enrichment capacity, using existing methods, to separate Pu-240 from Pu-239 than it takes to separate U-235 from U-238. Second, enrichment cascades used to process plutonium would be permanently contaminated with it. Third, it has generally been simpler for the weapon states to simply produce low burn up plutonium in dedicated reactors, and to treat the plutonium in higher burn up power reactor fuel as material to be recycled, or as waste.

WEAPONS GRADE VERSUS WEAPONS USABLE MATERIAL

Many confuse the concept of weapons-grade plutonium with the much more inclusive concept of weapons-usable plutonium. From a weapon designer's point of view, it is best to use plutonium and uranium that are as pure in the isotopes Pu-239 and U-235 as possible. This reduces critical mass requirements to their minima, and reduces the difficulty of making reliable plutonium weapons that remain easy to handle throughout a long stockpile life. The nuclear weapon states have established tacit standards defining weapons grade materials. In the United States, HEU for weapons is generally at least 93 percent U-235, and weapons grade plutonium is at least 94 percent Pu-239. These standards do not in any way constitute the dividing line between what is and is not usable in weapons; they simply reflect what is optimal. It is possible to form a supercritical configuration using uranium enriched to as little as 20 percent, though such a device would require a massive assembly mechanism.[9] Likewise, plutonium of any isotopic content (burn up level) is usable in a weapon.[10] High burn up plutonium simply changes the probability distribution between the "fizzle" yield and the "nominal" yield, making yields closer to the former value more likely than yields closer to the latter. The fizzle yield for the Fat Man design was about one kiloton, and the nominal yield was 20 kilotons. Thus, Fat Man's fizzle yield would have been four thousand times more powerful than the 500-pound general purpose bombs in use both then and today. Such plutonium will also produce more heat and radioactivity, but heat sinks and shielding can be included in a design, if necessary, as compensation.

DEVELOPING OR OBTAINING TECHNOLOGY TO PRODUCE WEAPONS-USABLE
MATERIALS

The United States, the Soviet Union, Great Britain, France, China, Israel, India, South Africa, Pakistan, Brazil, Argentina, Iraq, and North Korea have all developed or obtained the means of producing fissile material in programs designed at least to provide a nuclear weapons option, if not in an explicit weapons program.[11] Some of these countries successfully pursued plutonium and HEU simultaneously (the United States, Soviet Union), some developed or obtained one first and the other later (Great Britain, France, China), while the rest have, for the time being, achieved only one.

Since the early days of the Manhattan Project, the plutonium route has been perceived as the simpler technology. All other things being equal, it is technically simpler to develop and build a reactor/reprocess-

9. Mason Willrich and Theodore Taylor, *Nuclear Theft: Risks and Safeguards* (Cambridge, Mass.: Ballinger, 1974) pp. 16–17.

10. The definitive statement on this point is J. Carson Mark, "Explosive Properties of Reactor Grade Plutonium," *Science and Global Security*, Vol. 4, No. 1 (1993), pp. 111–124.

11. The following discussion uses: Joel Ullom, "Enriched Uranium versus Plutonium: Proliferant Preferences in the Choice of Fissile Material," *The Nonproliferation Review*, Vol. 2, No. 1 (Fall 1994), pp. 1–15; David Albright, "A Proliferation Primer," *Bulletin of the Atomic Scientists*, Vol. 49, No. 5 (June 1993), pp. 14–23; David Albright, Frans Berkhout, and William Walker, *World Inventory of Plutonium and Highly Enriched Uranium* (New York: Oxford University Press, 1993), especially pp. 153–194; and Leonard Spector and Jaqueline Smith, *Nuclear Ambitions: The Spread of Nuclear Weapons 1989–1990* (Boulder, Colo.: Westview, 1990).

ing facility than it is to develop and build a uranium enrichment facility. In fact, the discovery of plutonium was the event that made nuclear weapons a practical rather than merely theoretical prospect in the eyes of many physicists in the early 1940s.[12] Great Britain and France began their weapon programs with plutonium forty or more years ago largely because they were more confident in their ability to quickly, and at a reasonable expense, develop an indigenous reactor/reprocessing enterprise than an enrichment enterprise. Today, North Korea pursues plutonium presumably for the same reason.

Of course, all other things are never equal. For many states, neither route lies within the abilities of their domestic industrial base. This was China's situation in the late 1950s, but the Soviet Union planned to simply give China both a plutonium and an HEU production capability. When cooperation between these two states abruptly ended in 1960, the enrichment plant was much further along than the reactor facility and so HEU initially became the basis for the early Chinese weapon program. Most less-developed aspiring nuclear states are not offered plutonium or HEU production capabilities as a gift. The question for them becomes which technology is easiest to purchase.

Until the 1970s, for states like India, Israel, and Iraq, reactors were easier to purchase. Over time, though, these calculations have changed as the non-proliferation regime has grown in strength. Since the late 1970s, the question for less-developed states concerns the comparative ease of covert purchase. Pakistan and Iraq, and perhaps South Africa, found it easier to covertly purchase or gain assistance in developing uranium enrichment technology. Ironically, in the case of Pakistan and Iraq, it proved easier to covertly purchase components of the most advanced uranium enrichment technology, the gas centrifuge. This is because centrifuges are now in wide use in Europe where the nuclear industry has historically had more freedom than the U.S. or Soviet nuclear industry to sell its wares to all buyers.

The North Korean program is, in many ways, the antithesis of the Pakistani and Iraqi programs. It is almost completely indigenous. There has been no covert North Korean purchasing campaign of dual-use technologies, and there has been no flood of North Korean graduate students in the physics departments of western universities. It uses the oldest and simplest of fissile material production technologies, the natural uranium–fueled graphite-moderated plutonium production reactor, pioneered by Enrico Fermi and Leo Szilard in 1939 and utilized in one form or another

---

12. Rhodes, *The Making of the Atomic Bomb*, p. 352.

by the Soviets, the British, the French, and the Israelis. One can speculate that the North Koreans chose the plutonium route for several reasons, and despite a major drawback. It is the simplest way to a completely indigenous program, and North Korea's isolation made foreign assistance or foreign purchases of other technology unlikely. On the other hand, the plutonium route is difficult to hide, even when it is completely indigenous, because the "signature" associated with reactor construction is significant, especially in a country like North Korea which is already under close observation.

More advanced states have more choices, and a larger set of political and institutional factors to consider. Whether with German assistance or not, South Africa was the first country to develop aerodynamic nozzle technology on a commercial scale when it began enriching uranium at Valandiba in 1978, so this was an indigenous program to a considerable extent. South Africa also chose the HEU route for reasons of energy self-sufficiency and to add value to its already large uranium ore exports.

Somewhat later than South Africa, Argentina and Brazil also began relatively autonomous uranium enrichment programs. The Brazilian Navy already had an interest in developing naval reactor designs that required HEU fuel, and this provided both an organizational home and a rationale for HEU production. Argentina had a more inchoate set of motivations, and initially sought both HEU and plutonium production capabilities simply to match anticipated developments in Brazil's civilian nuclear sector. Though Argentina's nuclear power reactors use natural uranium fuel, its research reactors use HEU fuel, and these supplies were cut off by the United States in the late 1970s. This provided a rationale for continuing the HEU program.

Argentina and Brazil announced their uranium enrichment programs in 1983 and 1987 respectively, well before they were capable of producing HEU in significant quantities. Before these announcements, the enrichment facilities in question do not seem to have been detected by the rest of the world, although this was less certainly the case with the Argentine gaseous diffusion plant at Pilcaniyeu than it was for the pilot Brazilian centrifuge facility at Sao Paulo University. Thus, these two programs were more covert than the South African program, which was announced at its outset in 1970. On the other hand, both Argentina and Brazil announced these programs before they became operational, unlike the Pakistani and Iraqi programs, which sought to maintain a veil of secrecy to the end.

For the future, one can imagine a causal relationship of sorts, with the dependent variable being the choice between plutonium and HEU, and the independent variable being the level of development of a state's industrial base. To simplify the analysis, assume that the non-proliferation regime remains intact, that the nuclear aspirant has no civilian nuclear power industry as a base and desires at least a weapons option, but that it is not a state that could simply buy a reactor from a western supplier within the confines of the Nuclear Non-proliferation Treaty (NPT) without setting off some alarm from the non-proliferation community.

Up to a fairly advanced point of industrial development, such a state is likely to face a tradeoff created by the technology denial regime which is a part of the non-proliferation regime. HEU production technology is hard to develop indigenously, but centrifuge components can be bought covertly in dual-use pieces from many different western component suppliers, albeit over a considerable period of time, at great expense, and with considerable probability of eventual detection. Plutonium production technology is easier, but still difficult, to develop indigenously, and it is more difficult to purchase. Further, in neither case can these plutonium production capabilities be hidden as they take shape.

Rich but relatively undeveloped states like Iran and Iraq can continue to attempt to buy centrifuge enrichment technologies covertly, much as Pakistan first developed its nuclear capability. Such programs cannot be completely covert, but their scope and rate of progress may be masked until it is too late for the international community to respond effectively. The same countries can attempt to buy reactors, as Iran is doing now, but such purchases cannot be hidden, take years to unfold, and provide plenty of time for the international community to apply pressure or supply inducements designed to stop the purchase. Even if such purchases go through, countries like Iran must still prevent suppliers from demanding that the spent fuel be returned, as Russia may in the proposed Russian-Iranian reactor deal.

The denial regime had little direct effect on North Korea, which indigenously developed gas-cooled, graphite-moderated reactors. For isolated but somewhat more developed states like North Korea, plutonium may be the material of choice because the reactors are marginally easier to develop, and because plutonium requires less natural uranium feed. On the other hand, this has always mandated an essentially overt program, since reactors are vulnerable to overhead observation and identification as they are built. It remains to be seen whether the overtness of North Korea's program ultimately prevents its fruition, due to the response it has provoked from the international community.

Beyond a certain point, the industrial development of a state allows a range of choices based on a variety of financial, institutional, and military factors. South Africa, Argentina, and Brazil all had the technical and industrial skills to produce either plutonium or HEU. They chose HEU for reasons other than its comparative ease of development.

South Africa chose HEU production because it also had a civilian power industry that required low enriched uranium (LEU), because LEU could be sold on world markets, and because it may have had assistance in developing its specific aerodynamic nozzle enrichment technology from German companies. South Africa made no serious attempt to keep its enrichment program covert, but it did go to great and largely successful lengths to keep its HEU production secret.

Once Argentina decided to pursue HEU, it chose the older and less efficient gaseous diffusion method of enrichment because it could not indigenously develop the more modern centrifuge enrichment technology, and because it believed that an effort to purchase centrifuges or their components abroad would be detected. Argentina sought to maintain a covert development program, with apparent success between 1978 and 1983. It chose to make the program public in 1983, five years before it succeeded in producing its first HEU, enriched only to 20 percent U-235, late in 1988.

Unlike Argentina, Brazil was confident enough of its technical abilities to launch an indigenous centrifuge program. However, Brazil also followed the same path as Argentina of initial secrecy, followed by public revelation prior to completion, although the lag between announcement and first HEU production was only from 1987 to 1988.

If both countries had sought to preserve secrecy for their HEU production capabilities, Brazil would have had a better chance of success because its capability was based on modern centrifuge technology. Centrifuge facilities are not especially large and they consume very little power. A largely indigenous centrifuge program like Brazil's is therefore very hard to detect. The South African nozzle technology, along with the gaseous diffusion technology chosen by Argentina, is much harder to hide because of its size and prodigious energy consumption. Furthermore, the energy requirements of these older technologies can be used to determine whether an overt program like the one in South Africa, and now in Argentina, is secretly being used to produce HEU rather than LEU.

To summarize, the traditional non-proliferation regime seeks to control the spread of unsafeguarded facilities to produce fissile materials. This denial regime operates in several ways. It either forces states that seek nuclear weapons capability into covert, costly, and lengthy purchasing programs of dual-use technologies useful for uranium enrichment (centrifuges); or it forces them into the indigenous development of technologies that are difficult or impossible to hide (reactors, gas diffusion plants).[13] Only when a state's science and industrial base can support the indigenous development of a modern, energy-efficient uranium enrichment technology like the gas centrifuge has it crossed the threshold beyond which nuclear capability can be indigenously developed without interference from the international community. This means that even countries as advanced as Argentina and South Africa in the late 1970s and 1980s were far from immune to the direct and indirect constraints of the traditional non-proliferation regime.

Summary: Building a Simple Nuclear Weapon

The first nuclear weapon used in anger was Little Boy. Untested, it was detonated over Hiroshima with a yield equivalent to 15,000 tons of TNT, or 15 kilotons. Little Boy used 132.8 pounds of HEU enriched to a little over 80 percent in the fissile isotope U-235. It was 10 feet long, 28 inches wide, and weighed 9000 pounds.[14] During the 1980s, South Africa developed a very similar gun weapon using essentially the same technology. This design used 121 pounds of HEU enriched to over 90 percent U-235 and had an expected yield of 10–18 kilotons. It was 6 feet long, 26 inches wide, and weighed 2200 pounds.[15] Gun weapons of quite simple design were used in eight-inch artillery shells by the United States beginning in the early 1950s. These designs were made smaller while retaining yields in the ten-kiloton range by reducing barrel length and tamper bulk, and adding beryllium reflectors and more energetic high-explosive charges. One such design, the W-33, used about 140 pounds of HEU enriched to

---

13.   Calutrons of the type used recently in Iraq and earlier by the United States during the Manhattan Project are also very energy intensive, but they are easier to hide than gaseous diffusion plants because they do not have to be formed into massive cascades. On the other hand, calutrons by themselves are a very inefficient means of enriching natural uranium to levels necessary for use in a weapon. The Iraqis intended to use calutrons as part of a two-stage enrichment process in which centrifuges were used to bring calutron-enriched uranium from levels of a few percent U-235 to over 90 percent. See David Albright and Mark Hibbs, "Iraq's Nuclear Hide-and-Seek," *Bulletin of the Atomic Scientists*, September 1991, pp. 14–23.

14.   Thomas Cochran and Christopher Paine, *The Role of Hydronuclear Tests and Other Low-Yield Nuclear Explosions and Their Status Under A Comprehensive Test Ban*, Nuclear Weapons Databook (Washington DC: Natural Resources Defense Council, March 1995) p. 4.

15.   David Albright, "South Africa and the Affordable Bomb," *Bulletin of the Atomic Scientists*, Vol. 50, No. 4 (July/August 1994), pp. 44–45.

93 percent U-235.[16] It fit inside an artillery shell 3 feet long, 8 inches wide, and, when fully armed, weighing 250 pounds.[17]

The reduction in fissile material requirements and the possibility of plutonium use that an implosion design allows comes at a small price in design complexity. The implosion must be symmetrical; the high-explosive jacket must therefore be uniform in its effects when it explodes, which means that the firing system must detonate the jacket simultaneously at 50–100 points spaced uniformly about its exterior. Though complicated, such a firing system can be perfected through a series of instrumented non-nuclear implosion tests using non-fissile heavy metal cores. The increase in complexity does not put a crude implosion design beyond the reach of a terrorist or organized crime group. In addition, the benefits of an implosion design allow designers to use much less fissile material, and to use fissile material that would not be usable in a gun design, such as plutonium of any isotopic composition and uranium of less than the highest level of enrichment in U-235.[18]

Fat Man was about the same length and weight as Little Boy, but was 5 feet wide. Like Little Boy, Fat Man had an extremely heavy, bullet-proof aerodynamic casing that constituted a large portion of its weight. It was also highly conservative in its use of high explosive to ensure optimal assembly of a supercritical mass. High explosives constituted almost half its weight and most of its internal volume. Dramatic reductions in size

---

16. "Nuclear Notebook," *Bulletin of the Atomic Scientists*, Vol. 49, No. 1 (January/February 1993), p. 56.

17. Thomas B. Cochran, William M. Arkin, and Milton M. Hoenig, *Nuclear Weapons Databook*, Vol. 1: *U.S. Nuclear Forces and Capabilities* (Cambridge, Mass.: Ballinger, 1984), pp. 47–48.

18. J. Carson Mark, Theodore Taylor, Eugene Eyster, William Maraman, and Jacob Wechsler, "Can Terrorists Build Nuclear Weapons?" in Leventhal and Alexander, eds., *Preventing Nuclear Terrorism: The Report and Papers of the International Task Force on Preventing Nuclear Terrorism*, p. 61. Advocates of plutonium use for civilian power generation often argue that only plutonium enriched to more than 90 percent in the isotope Pu-239 can be used in a weapon. See, for example, Ryukichi Imai, "Can University Students Make an Atomic Bomb?" *Plutonium* (Tokyo: Council for Nuclear Fuel Cycle, Winter 1995), pp. 2–8. This contention has now been decisively rebutted in Mark, "Explosive Properties of Reactor-Grade Plutonium," pp. 111–124. Others make the same claim about HEU, i.e., that it is useful for weapons only if it is enriched above 90 percent in U-235. See, for example, Jane Perlez, "Radioactive Material Seized In Slovakia; 9 Under Arrest," *Boston Globe*, April 22, 1995, p. 4. Others, however, correctly note that while HEU enriched to more than 90 percent is desirable for weapons, it is not necessary. See Reuters, "Nuclear Contraband Intercepted," *New York Times*, April 22, 1995, p. 13.

and weight with no loss in yield and reliability or increase in design complexity could be achieved simply by taking Fat Man's design, adding several pounds of plutonium to the core and a beryllium reflector, and cutting the size and weight of the implosion assembly mechanism in half. Further, dramatic reductions in the size of the assembly mechanism (high explosives, tamper, etc.) could be achieved if the pit were levitated; a levitated pit design could be validated using non-nuclear proof tests of the assembly mechanism.

Thus we have seen that weapons can be designed very simply. They need be no more complicated than the first designs tested by Great Britain, France, China, and India; those designs all worked perfectly the first time. (Russia's first test in 1949 used a copy of the U.S. Fat Man implosion design.) Furthermore, much has changed since the summer of 1945, when the designs for Little Boy and Fat Man were frozen. Science has progressed, secrets have been declassified, and military technologies have developed commercial uses. College professors write textbooks that would have won Nobel prizes fifty years ago, governments publish primers on simple nuclear weapon design, and tritium-deuterium neutron sources are sold for commercial purposes.[19]

The recipe, as shown above, is no secret, and has not changed appreciably in many decades. Nor are the ingredients, other than plutonium or HEU, hard to obtain. For a gun weapon, the gun barrel could be ordered from any machine shop, as could a tungsten tamper machined to any specifications the customer desired. The high-explosive charge for firing the bullet could also be fashioned by anyone with access to and some experience handling TNT, or other conventional, chemical explosives. Other than the initial supply of HEU, the only possible complications are development of a neutron initiator and, if desired, a supply of beryllium for the reflector. All the information necessary to solve these problems, as well as any others that might crop up, are available in the open literature, and have been for some time. Designers of U.S. weapons have been repeating this basic truth over and over again since the early 1970s when John Foster, a former director of the Lawrence Livermore nuclear weapons laboratory, stated that "the only difficult thing about making a fission

---

19. On some of these points see Tom Clancy and Russell Seitz, "Welcome to the Age of Proliferation," *The National Interest*, No. 26 (Winter 1991–92), pp. 3–12. See also Robert Serber, *The Los Alamos Primer: The First Lectures on How to Build an Atomic Bomb* (Berkeley, Calif.: University of California Press, 1992). Tritium-deuterium neutron sources are used in oil wells to bombard materials surrounding the bore hole and induce various identifiable reactions, thereby providing a diagnostic tool for the well drillers.

bomb of some sort is the preparation of a supply of fissile material of adequate purity; the design of the bomb itself is relatively easy."[20]

Thus, given a sufficient quantity of fissile material, virtually any state and many terrorist or organized crime groups could build a simple, reliable nuclear weapon. There is an overwhelming consensus that fissile material constitutes the major obstacle to a simple nuclear weapons capability.[21] There is also a more narrowly specified consensus among U.S. weapons designers that almost any state, and many terrorist groups, could build a simple nuclear weapon given an adequate supply of fissile material.[22] If would-be proliferants want professional help, history suggests that they will probably get it. Nearly every successful national nuclear weapons program has benefited greatly from "brain drain," and weapon designers from any of today's declared or threshold nuclear states, but especially from Russia, could accelerate the pace of an existing program or hasten the creation of a new weapons program.[23]

Those who believe that knowledge and technology are so widely disseminated as to make advanced or unconventional nuclear weapon designs beyond denial to potential proliferants occasionally demonstrate,

---

20. John Foster, "Nuclear Weapons," *Encyclopedia Americana*, Vol. 20 (New York: Americana, 1973) pp. 520–522; see also Chapter 2, "Nuclear Weapons" in Willrich and Taylor, *Nuclear Theft*, pp. 5–28, esp. p. 6: "If the essential nuclear materials are at hand, it is possible to make an atomic bomb using information that is available in the open literature."

21. Michael May, "Nuclear Weapons Supply and Demand," *American Scientist*, Vol. 82 (November–December 1994), pp. 527, 530; Committee on International Security and Arms Control, National Academy of Sciences, *Management and Disposition of Excess Weapons Plutonium* (Washington DC: National Academy Press, 1994), p. 26; U.S. Congress, Office of Technology Assessment, *Technologies Underlying Weapons of Mass Destruction* OTA-BP-ISC-115 (Washington DC: U.S. GPO, December 1993), p. 3; and Peter Zimmerman, "Technical Barriers to Nuclear Proliferation," in Zachary Davis and Benjamin Frankel, eds., "The Proliferation Puzzle: Why Nuclear Nations Spread (and What Results)," *Security Studies*, Vol. 2, Nos. 3–4 (Spring/Summer 1993), pp. 345–356, esp. "Note Added In Proof" on p. 356: "Should a nation determined to build a nuclear weapon quickly be able to purchase the fissile material, the costs for its project would probably plummet, and the time needed to construct its first weapon might decrease from years to months or weeks."

22. Mark, et al., "Can Terrorists Build Nuclear Weapons?" pp. 55–65.

23. Of course, the most dramatic example of brain drain occurred in the Manhattan Project where individual European emigrés and the British government both played key roles. The Soviet program benefited from the efforts of captured German scientists and also the espionage of Klaus Fuchs. The British received significant assistance from the United States and the Chinese from the Soviet Union. Of the declared nuclear states, only France seems to have had a largely indigenous weapon design and production program at the outset.

albeit inadvertently, the opposite point. For example, Tom Clancy and Russell Seitz argued that such denial regimes would become impossible or irrelevant. One of their points involved an exaggeration of the utility for weapons of certain kinds of nuclear waste not normally considered to be weapons-usable material. Such a mistake could take a small, autonomous weapons program down a several-years-long blind alley, which a professional weapons designer from Arzamas or Chelyabinsk would know to avoid. This mistake makes the point that it is not easy to use modern sources of unclassified information to get the details of unusual or advanced nuclear weapons design exactly right; however, simple weapons using proven designs and standard materials are another matter.[24]

Some argue that inability to test weapons would hamper proliferation. Testing is indeed a big issue: the declared weapon states are in the midst of a debate on whether or not there is a need for continued testing at full or partial yield.[25] However, this debate has little relationship to the question of whether testing is necessary to confirm the design of a simple fission weapon.

In the declared weapon states, the need for testing grew out of the desire to get more and more bang for the buck out of a given supply of very expensive fissile material, using smaller and easier-to-deliver weapons. After small high-yield weapons were developed, testing was required to make them as safe as possible under the conditions they might encounter, including shock, fire, and radiation. Then, testing was required to make weapons reliable in the absence of testing. This involved confirming the performance of new, more conservative designs containing larger margins of error. Then, testing was required because the standards for safety and reliability rose, and the new standards had to be applied to the existing stockpile.

---

24. Clancy and Seitz claimed that Neptunium, a trans-uranic element contained in spent reactor fuel, would be an effective fissile material for weapons purposes. Clancy and Seitz, "Welcome to the Age of Proliferation," p. 9. For their retraction on this point in the face of comments by Leonard Spector and Peter Zimmerman, see "Nuclear Proliferation," *The National Interest*, No. 27 (Spring 1992), pp. 110–112.

25. Testing — the experimental detonation of weapons in the atmosphere and underground — has been an integral part of the nuclear weapon programs of the five declared nuclear weapon states: the United States, the Soviet Union, Great Britain, France, and China. Tests provide experimental data used to design weapons, they confirm the design of new weapons, and they confirm the reliability of old weapons, or weapons that have had to be redesigned because of some flaw discovered after their initial deployment.

Testing would be of much less concern to the designer who is happy to settle for simple gun-type or implosion weapons like Little Boy or Fat Man. Both designs could be considerably reduced in size and weight from their original 1945 configurations without nuclear testing. Such a step would risk only a small decrease in the size and predictability of their nominal yields. More significant design advances could be accomplished without testing using computerized simulation techniques and extensive non-nuclear testing. Thus, a levitated pit implosion weapon might be developed in this fashion by a small, sophisticated design group without nuclear testing. Such weapons were initially deployed in the U.S. stockpile in the late 1940s without testing.[26]

At some point during the climb up the ladder of sophistication, the simulation techniques become sophisticated enough to require the intellectual and financial resources one would normally associate only with a state, rather than a terrorist or organized-crime group. Some would place this point where one adds tritium-deuterium boosting to the design. Further demands might exhaust the simulation techniques available to even the most advanced industrial states; few would argue, for example, that even the United States would have confidence in any untested multistage weapon design without at least a full-yield test of the primary. (This, incidentally, was part of the rationale for the threshold test ban treaty, which allowed underground detonations of up to 150 kilotons.)

However, very simple weapons can be designed and used with high reliability without testing, as the United States did with the Little Boy design over Hiroshima. South Africa also developed and deployed nuclear weapons without testing. Israel and Pakistan are believed to be nuclear weapon states, and this status was achieved in both cases without testing. (India, with one test, is also believed to be a weapon state.) Even a relatively undeveloped state like North Korea, with no tests but with a small cache of plutonium, could be credited, and already is in some circles, with nuclear weapons capability. The same status would apply to Iraq, test or no test, if it ever succeeds in amassing thirty or more pounds of HEU.

States or criminal and terrorist groups desirous of nuclear capability designed to extort money or terrorize cities will not need to be concerned with testing. They will use the simplest designs possible given the nature and quantity of their supply of fissile material. Therefore, the necessary absence of testing in a covert weapons program is no defense against that

---

program. With a modicum of preparation, but without any nuclear testing, reliable weapons with kiloton yields can be quickly produced as soon as a sufficient quantity of fissile material becomes available.

Thus, the recipe for a simple nuclear weapon is not beyond the reach of most states and many groups. It is only by keeping a lid on the supply of fissile material that non-proliferation can succeed.

Appendix C

The HEU Deal

by Richard A. Falkenrath

At the end of August 1992, President George Bush made an announcement that would have been unthinkable even three years earlier, when he entered office.

> I am pleased to announce that the Russian Federation and the United States have now initialed an agreement to ensure that highly enriched uranium [HEU] from dismantled nuclear weapons will be used only for peaceful purposes. . . . Under the agreement, the United States and Russia would seek within the next 12 months to conclude an implementing contract establishing the terms of the purchase of weapons-grade uranium by the U.S. Department of Energy and the dilution of that material to reactor-grade uranium for sale as commercial reactor fuel. The contract would also provide for the participation of the U.S. private sector and the use by the Russian Federation of a portion of the proceeds to increase the safety of nuclear reactors in the former Soviet Union.

After over a year of hard-fought negotiations following up on President Bush's announcement, President Bill Clinton was able to announce on January 14, 1994, that the United States and Russia "have signed a contract to purchase $12 billion of highly enriched uranium over the next 20 years."[1]

The U.S. purchase of 500 metric tons of highly enriched uranium from dismantled Russian warheads is known as the "HEU deal," and it is one

---

1. See "Statement on the Russian–United States Agreement on the Disposition of Uranium from Nuclear Weapons," August 31, 1992, in *Public Papers of the Presidents of the United States, George Bush*, 1992–93, Vol. II (Washington DC: GPO, 1993), pp. 1453–1454; and "Press Conference by President Clinton and President Yeltsin in Moscow," January 14, 1994, in *Weekly Compilation of Presidential Documents*, Vol. 30, No. 3 (January 24, 1994), p. 61. Note that this study went to press in September 1995. It does not, therefore, reflect the subsequent developments in the HEU deal.

of the more intelligent national security initiatives in U.S. history. The security and accounting of fissile material in Russia is known to be inadequate, so the existence of a large stockpile of excess HEU in Russia poses a serious threat to the security of the United States and its allies. Given that blended-down HEU has real economic value in the energy industry (unlike plutonium), the U.S. government had the opportunity to implement a non-proliferation policy that would simultaneously improve U.S. national security and lower the energy bills for U.S. consumers, at negligible cost to the U.S. taxpayer. In the nuclear era, it is swords into plowshares.

Until mid-1995, the public statements of the Bush and Clinton administrations suggested that the HEU deal was in fine shape, on track to be implemented according to schedule, and working smoothly as intended. This was not, in fact, true.

In 1994–95, the HEU deal was not being implemented at the speed or scope envisaged by Presidents Bush and Clinton, and was in danger of coming completely undone. No HEU was purchased from Russia in 1994, and there was an ongoing dispute with the Russian government over the price to be paid for the small amount of material ordered in 1995; because of this dispute, the Russian government had threatened to cancel the HEU deal in its entirety. Unless the U.S. procedure for buying the Russian material is substantially reworked, the HEU deal will remain plagued by the possibility of collapse.[2]

In mid-1995, as the trouble with the HEU deal became publicly known, there emerged a widespread impression that the problem with the HEU deal was the result of a 1992 U.S. anti-dumping rule against uranium imports from Russia. While it was true that the anti-dumping process complicated the implementation of the HEU deal, the anti-dumping process was not the most serious problem with the HEU deal, and it distracted attention from the real flaw in how the United States sought to implement the HEU deal.

Fundamentally, the troubled implementation of the HEU deal was a result of an unsound decision by the White House to give exclusive executive control over the HEU deal to an enterprise — the U.S. Enrichment Corporation (USEC), a wholly owned government corporation in the process of being privatized — that is uniquely unsuited to that role. For peculiar and complex commercial reasons, USEC has no incentive to

---

2. One of the first widely noted public hints that something was amiss with the HEU deal was Jessica Mathews, "National Security Blunder," *Washington Post*, May 5, 1995, p. A25.

offer Russia a fair market price for the blended-down HEU so long as it alone has the right to order and market the material outside of Russia.

The two key reasons for the initial decision to give USEC control over the HEU deal appear to be, first, an inadequate analysis of the commercial implications of the HEU deal by the Bush administration's national security team, and second, a determined effort by officials in the Department of Energy (who would later become USEC's management) to use the HEU deal to enhance the competitiveness of the U.S. enrichment operation. USEC's conflict of interest in the HEU deal became more widely understood in the Clinton administration in 1995. The failure to correct this basic flaw in the U.S. implementation of the HEU deal now appears to be due to an unwillingness to challenge or undermine commercial interests of USEC for the sake of a national security initiative, though by late 1995, there were signs that this was changing.

OVERVIEW

The HEU deal began in 1991, a year which saw several unexpected events that would decisively influence the subsequent development of the HEU deal. First, with the Cold War coming to a close, President Bush and Soviet President Mikhail Gorbachev agreed to sweeping reductions in their states' nuclear arsenals, which over the next five to ten years would lead to the dismantlement of tens of thousands of excess nuclear weapons, thereby adding hundreds of tons of HEU to already large HEU stockpiles. Second, in an October 24, 1991, *New York Times* op-ed piece, Thomas Neff, a physicist from MIT, proposed that the United States should buy this excess HEU from the Soviet Union, blend it with natural uranium to produce a mixture suitable for use in power-generating reactors, and resell it to utilities. The Bush administration did not take up this elegant idea until after the third key event of 1991, an offer by the Soviet government to do exactly what Neff had proposed. The fourth event was the collapse of the Soviet Union in December 1991, which caused a serious degradation in the Soviet nuclear custodial system, heightening the risk of nuclear leakage from Russia and the other Soviet successor states.

Taken together, these four developments are usually seen as the catalyst of the HEU deal. The national security community, in particular, tended to believe that the HEU deal was driven primarily by non-proliferation concerns. Since buying Russian HEU makes so much sense, it sounded perfectly plausible to say that the enlightened self-interest of the United States was the prime motivating force behind the HEU deal.

However, this interpretation of the HEU deal is incomplete. Two other developments in 1991–92 had greater significance in the evolution of the

HEU deal than the four mentioned above. The first was a dramatic rise in U.S. imports of Soviet uranium, followed by a protectionist backlash. In 1988, the Soviet Union began to export uranium to the United States under an exclusive marketing agreement with Concord/Nuexco, a Colorado-based uranium mining and trading firm. Because of these imports, the Soviet share of the U.S. uranium market grew from zero in 1988 to about 20 percent in 1991, and the spot market uranium price fell by roughly 20 percent per year over 1988–91. Moreover, because it had little experience in free-market uranium trading, the Soviet government unwittingly became embroiled in a market manipulation scheme run by Concord/Nuexco, which used its control over Soviet uranium imports to profit from the fall in the price of uranium, disrupting the uranium market and exacerbating the price effects of the new imports of Soviet uranium.[3] This fall in the spot price of uranium prompted an ad hoc committee of 13 uranium mining companies, a labor union, and the Department of Energy to file an anti-dumping petition against Soviet uranium imports on November 8, 1991; this case resulted in the signing of "suspension agreements" with each of the uranium-exporting former Soviet republics, halting the anti-dumping investigation but seriously restricting their access to the U.S. market.

The second development was the mid-1992 decision to privatize the Department of Energy's civilian uranium enrichment enterprise. In the Energy Policy Act of 1992, Congress authorized the creation of the U.S. Enrichment Corporation (USEC), which would inherit the Department of Energy's two civilian enrichment plants in Portsmouth, Ohio, and Paducah, Kentucky. The creation of USEC, or something like it, had been discussed for many years. The Energy Policy Act specified that USEC would become a government-owned but independent company on July 1, 1993, and that USEC shares would be sold to the public some time in the future, with the proceeds of this sale (estimated at about $1.5 billion) going to the U.S. Treasury. The large implicit subsidies contained within the Energy Policy Act made USEC the lowest-cost enricher in the world, giving it a strong competitive position in the global enrichment market. Importantly, the Energy Policy Act also stipulated (somewhat ambiguously) that USEC would have the exclusive right to be the executive agent in the U.S. purchases of Russian HEU;[4] this was correctly seen as a way

---

3. The possibility of such a market manipulation scheme was first described in Thomas L. Neff, "Winning and Losing in a Trading Regime," *Nuclear Fuel Market Quarterly* (II/1991), pp. 7–14.

4. 42 U.S.C. § 1408(A)(1992). The precise language of the Energy Policy Act is as follows: "The Corporation is authorized to negotiate the purchase of all highly en-

of enhancing USEC's economic competitiveness and, therefore, its value to the Treasury when fully privatized. The price was that it placed the HEU deal on unsound commercial footing.

Since mid-1992, the commercial interests of USEC and the protectionist dynamics of the anti-dumping suit have been the dominant forces behind the HEU deal, and their effects on national security have been overwhelmingly negative.

During both the Bush and Clinton administrations, foreign-policy officials in the U.S. government have understood that buying HEU from dismantled Russian weapons serves the national security interests of the United States. Nonetheless, the government allowed the narrow commercial interests of the domestic uranium enrichment industry to cripple the implementation of the HEU deal. This central fact is not widely known, for it is hidden within a morass of technical, legal, and economic esoterica.

This study has four sections. In the first, I describe five specific ways in which the HEU deal, if executed as originally conceived, serves U.S. national interests. In my view, the HEU deal represents one of the best national security ideas in U.S. history, and I defend this proposition in the first section. In doing this, I also describe in more detailed terms some alternative ways the HEU deal could be implemented.

In the second section, I develop in detail the intertwined histories of the HEU deal, the uranium anti-dumping case, and the privatization of USEC. This history demonstrates the extraordinary extent to which the national security policies of two U.S. administrations have been dominated by an obscure trade law and the commercial interests of a government-owned enrichment monopoly.

In the third section, I present a number of policy options for establishing an effective and viable procedure for implementing the HEU deal. Because all of the options for reviving the HEU deal conflict with private interests of politically influential segments of the U.S. nuclear industry, the implementation of each option presented in section three would require commitment and courage on the part of the White House.

Finally, in the concluding section, I present and recommend a bolder alternative for implementing the HEU deal, one which goes well beyond the contemporary parameters of political feasibility. Under this alterna-

---

riched uranium made available by any State of the former Soviet Union under a government-to-government agreement or shall assume the obligations of the Department [of Energy] under any contractual agreement that has been reached with any such State or any private entity before the transition date." The important ambiguity concerns whether this provision gives USEC an exclusive authorization to execute the HEU deal, or whether the government is free to designate alternative executive agents.

tive, the U.S. government would directly purchase as much as possible of the insecurely stored fissile material in the former Soviet Union, as quickly as possible. The United States has directly purchased fissile material from the former Soviet Union once already: in a covert operation called Project Sapphire, the United States secretly bought and removed 600 kilograms of HEU from Kazakhstan. Implemented in a similar way, the HEU deal would have a greater and more rapid impact on reducing the threat of fissile material leakage from Russia. In effect, the HEU deal would become Project Sapphire writ large.

The HEU Deal

This section has two purposes. First, it presents the arguments for why the HEU deal, if properly implemented, would serve U.S. national interests. Second, it explains how the HEU deal is supposed to work without dwelling on the problems of implementing the HEU deal that have been encountered in practice.

HOW THE HEU DEAL SERVES U.S. NATIONAL INTERESTS
Most people in the national security and non-proliferation communities do not need to be persuaded of the value of the HEU deal; they understand already that it has the potential to serve multiple U.S. security interests in an elegant, revenue-neutral fashion. Nonetheless, since many of the problems encountered in the implementation of the HEU deal reflect a certain disregard for the benefits of buying Russian HEU, it is useful to summarize the five specific ways that the HEU deal advances important U.S. national interests.

INCENTIVES FOR RUSSIAN WARHEAD DISMANTLEMENT. First, the HEU deal provides a financial incentive for Russia to continue and accelerate the dismantlement of its excess nuclear weapons. The importance of this end cannot be overemphasized. Although Russia has treaty obligations to destroy thousands of nuclear weapon launchers, it has made no treaty-based commitment to actually dismantle its excess nuclear weapons. Because the United States is rapidly approaching the end of its own warhead dismantlement program, the HEU deal is essential to give Russia a tangible incentive to continue dismantling its own nuclear weapons. The physical destruction of Russian nuclear weapons is clearly in the U.S. interest. Obviously, however, it is crucial that the fissile material components resulting from the dismantlement process be stored under secure conditions; the HEU deal also serves this aim.

PERMANENT PROLIFERATION RISK REDUCTION. The HEU deal can permanently reduce the risk of nuclear proliferation by physically destroying 500 tons of fissile material, enough for 25,000 simple nuclear weapons. Enriching uranium is an extremely expensive and difficult process, but de-enriching it is as simple as mixing two substances together. Until it is blended with natural or low enriched uranium, however, HEU poses an acute proliferation risk. A simple implosion nuclear weapon can be built from less than 15 kilograms of HEU, and with 55 kilograms any state and many terrorist groups could build an even simpler gun-type weapon, which could have a 15–20 kiloton yield. The HEU deal gives the United States and Russia an opportunity to erase permanently a large portion of the proliferation risk posed by insecurely stored fissile material in Russia.

TRADE — NOT AID — WITH RUSSIA. The third advantage of the HEU deal is that it offers a lucrative hard-currency trade with Russia, which will assist Russia in its transition to a more liberal, more market-based economy. There can be little doubt that the United States has an enduring interest in Russian economic reform, since Russia will continue to be a drain on world resources and a latent threat to international security until it has a functioning market economy and a stable democratic polity. The $12 billion — a significant sum — that the HEU deal would inject into the Russian economy would assist the Russian government in servicing its international debt, moderate the deficit in Russia's balance of payments, promote the conversion of the Russian military complex to nonmilitary activities, and improve the ability of the Russian Ministry of Atomic Energy (Minatom) to guard the fissile material remaining in its installations. As the U.S. foreign aid budget dwindles, the role of trade in achieving these objectives will become more important, and in this respect, the HEU deal offers the possibility of assisting Russian economic reform at no net cost to the U.S. government or the United States as a whole.

LEVERAGE OVER MINATOM. The HEU deal gives the United States valuable leverage over Minatom. Minatom manages a sprawling nuclear complex facing a highly uncertain and troubled future, and desperately wants to carry out this HEU-for-dollars transaction. Doing so would allow Minatom to pay salaries, build new plants, and increase its political influence in Moscow. For this reason, the HEU deal offers the U.S. government an opportunity to influence Minatom's policies and behavior in other areas, the most important of which concerns the security of the fissile materials in Minatom custody. These materials, which are stored at dozens of sites, pose an extremely serious proliferation risk to the United

States and the rest of the international community. To date, Minatom has been hostile to most international or American efforts to cooperatively improve the security and accounting systems at its nuclear facilities. A realistic prospect of implementing the HEU deal should help reduce this hostility.

WELFARE MAXIMIZATION. If smoothly implemented, the HEU deal would probably have a positive economic effect on U.S. national welfare. The release of blended-down Russian HEU on the global market is essentially a supply curve shift in the natural uranium and separative work units (SWU) markets.[5] In a simple static model, this should result in reductions in the price of uranium, SWU, reactor fuel, and electricity.[6] However, the nuclear fuel market is exceptionally complex and suffers from serious market imperfections. As a result, the dynamic effects of the HEU deal on U.S. welfare are not entirely predictable.

HOW THE HEU DEAL IS SUPPOSED TO WORK

The HEU deal is, in principle, simple.[7] Russia dismantles its excess nuclear warheads, extracting the plutonium and highly enriched uranium contained within them. As Russia's stockpile of excess HEU begins to grow, the United States starts buying the excess Russian HEU. This HEU is blended with uranium that has a much lower isotopic concentration of U-235, producing low-enriched uranium (LEU), which has the correct isotopic concentration — about 4 percent on average — for use in civilian power reactors.[8] The LEU is then brought to the United States, fabricated

---

5. The standard measure of uranium enrichment is a "separative work unit," or SWU. Thus, when someone in the nuclear industry speaks of "producing SWU" or "selling SWU," they are referring to the enrichment of natural uranium and the sale of "enriched uranium product" (EUP, or "product") to utilities, which use it for power generation.

6. In the static partial equilibrium model, whether this supply curve shift increases net U.S. welfare depends on the elasticity and the values of U.S. uranium and SWU imports and exports.

7. For a helpful overview, see Oleg Bukharin, "Weapons to Fuel," *Science and Global Security*, Vol. 4 (1994), pp. 179–188.

8. The main uranium isotope that can sustain a slow-neutron chain reaction is U-235. Uranium found in nature consists of only about 0.7 percent U-235, which is insufficient to sustain a chain reaction in a normal light water reactor. Enrichment is the process of raising the percentage of U-235 in a quantity of uranium. (The percentage of uranium that is U-235 is called the "assay.") Normal light water power reactors use 3–5 percent enriched uranium, which is low enriched uranium (LEU). LEU is usually defined as uranium with an assay of less than 20 percent. Weapons and some reactors

into fuel assemblies, and sold to utilities in the United States and around the world. The utilities burn this LEU fuel in their reactors, producing energy and spent fuel. Thus, the HEU deal transforms nuclear weapons into the electric current that supplies the world's power grid.

The commercial viability of the HEU deal is closely tied to the economics of the front end of the nuclear fuel cycle, particularly the enrichment of natural uranium. Enrichment in a gaseous diffusion plant is an expensive process, requiring large amounts of electricity. There are two civilian gaseous diffusion enrichment plants in the United States, one in Portsmouth, Ohio, employing 2,600 people, and the other in Paducah, Kentucky, employing 1,770.[9] These plants supply 80–90 percent of the domestic SWU demand, most of which has historically been sold under long-term fixed-price contracts. These plants were run by the Department of Energy until mid-1993 when, pursuant to the Energy Policy Act of 1992, they were leased for a nominal fee to USEC. In a second and even more important implicit subsidy, the Energy Policy Act also transferred directly to USEC the long-term electricity contracts that the Department of Energy had negotiated with the local utilities in Ohio and Kentucky: these contracts allow USEC to purchase the electricity it needs to run its gaseous diffusion enrichment plants at less than one-half of prevailing commercial rates.[10] USEC has now replaced the Department of Energy as the dominant SWU supplier on the U.S. market.

Figures C-1, C-2, and C-3 illustrate the mechanics and the economics of the HEU deal.[11] Figure C-1 shows normal U.S. enrichment operations without the HEU deal. Utilities buy natural uranium on the open market and sign a contract with USEC to have it enriched to the appropriate level. The natural uranium, now called "feedstock," goes to one of USEC's two

---

(such as those in submarines) use highly enriched uranium (HEU), which usually has an assay in excess of 90 percent.

9. Paul Barton, "Piketon Plant's Future Could Hinge on Russian Uranium Deal," *Gannett News Service*, November 11, 1993.

10. These contracts allow the Department of Energy to buy electricity at less than two cents per kilowatt-hour. Unsubsidized electricity costs between four and five cents per kilowatt-hour. This difference represents an implicit subsidy from the government to USEC, since the Department of Energy could sell this low-cost electricity at commercial rates to earn a profit for the government. Electricity accounts for the majority of USEC's cost of production. Since each SWU produced consumes about 2,500 kilowatt-hours of electricity, with USEC producing ten million SWU per year, the U.S. government implicitly subsidizes USEC by $500–750 million per year.

11. The author thanks Thomas Neff for assistance with these figures. Any errors are the author's alone, and the values given for USEC's annual operations are illustrative only.

plants, where it is fed into an enrichment cascade. The enrichment process turns the feedstock into a small amount of enriched product, as well as a large amount of tailings, or tails, that have been depleted of much of their original U-235.[12] The enriched product is then converted from a gas to a solid, fabricated into fuel rods, shipped to reactors, and burned. Figure C-1 shows in rough terms one year's operation by USEC: utilities deliver 21,204 metric tons (MT) of natural uranium to USEC, and receive in return 2,373 MT of 4 percent enriched product. In so doing, USEC has produced 13 million SWU and will be paid a fee for that amount by the utilities. This fee varies from contract to contract, but the average price paid to USEC under long-term enrichment contracts is around $120/SWU.

Figure C-2 shows what happens if the HEU deal is executed alongside USEC's normal enrichment operations. Ten metric tons of HEU are removed from Russian nuclear weapons and blended with 295 MT of 1.5 percent enriched uranium.[13] This produces 305 MT of approximately 4 percent enriched LEU, which contains the equivalent of 1.9 million SWU and 2,979 MT of natural uranium, the latter of which is called the "feed component."[14] This LEU is then shipped to the United States, where it is

---

12. Tails are mainly a waste product. This relationship of feed to tails to product is expressed in the following equation:

$$FA \cdot FM = (TA \cdot TM) + (PA \cdot PM)$$

where: FA equals the feed assay, FM equals the feed mass, TA equals the tails assay, TM equals the tails mass, PA equals the product assay, and PM equals the product mass. The tails assay is used as a measure of the ratio of SWU to feed in LEU production.

13. Russia uses blendstock that is 1.5 percent enriched because the Russian HEU contains a relatively high amount of U-234, an undesirable contaminant. Because the 1.5 percent enriched uranium contains less U-234 than natural or depleted uranium, the U-234 content in the delivered LEU can be brought to an acceptable level by using slightly enriched blendstock. Using enriched blendstock, however, adds to the SWU content of the blended-down HEU, thereby displacing more of USEC's own production, which is a problem for reasons explained below.

14. The units of measurement in the uranium trade can be confusing because uranium can be contained in many different chemical compounds. The solid form of natural uranium used in the uranium trade is U308, which is called "yellowcake." UF6 is uranium hexaflouride, an intermediate product that is made from purified and converted U308. UF6 is a solid that is gasified for enrichment, and it is typically measured in kilograms or metric tons of uranium equivalent (MT, equal to 1,000 kilograms). Quantities of uranium are standardized as kilograms of uranium equivalent (kg. U). Every kilogram of UF6 contains 0.68 kg. U, and every pound of U308 contains 0.39 kg. U. (One kilogram equals 2.2 pounds.) For a more detailed discussion, see Thomas L. Neff, *The International Uranium Market* (Cambridge, Mass.: Ballinger Publishing Company, 1984), p. 11.

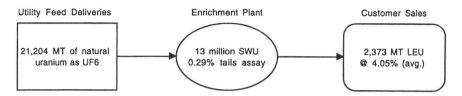

Figure C-1. Basic Enrichment Operations (No HEU Imports).

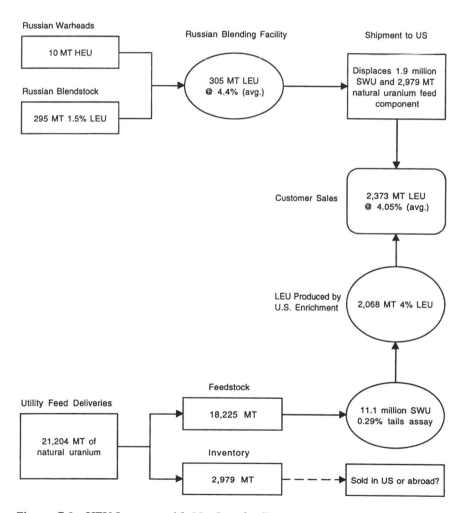

Figure C-2. HEU Imports with No Overfeeding.

to be delivered to USEC's customers in the place of new LEU from USEC's enrichment plants.

The sale of this blended-down Russian HEU to utilities will affect USEC's operations in two ways, also shown in Figure C-2. By supplying 305 MT of 4 percent enriched product for use as fuel, the HEU deal directly displaces 1.9 million SWU that USEC would normally produce each year.[15] In other words, because of the additional supply caused by the HEU deal, USEC's own SWU production would fall by 15 percent unless USEC increased its market share. Assuming that each SWU costs $60 for USEC to produce, this will allow USEC to avoid $114 million in direct SWU production costs while delivering the same amount of enriched uranium product to its customers. Note that importing Russian LEU reduces USEC's profits if it must pay Russia more than USEC's own production cost — about $60/SWU.[16] Because the United States agreed in May 1993 to pay Russia $82/SWU, executing the HEU deal displaces USEC's own lower-cost production, thereby reducing USEC's per-unit profit by roughly $22. The importance of this point is explained below.

The second part of the economic value of the blended-down Russian HEU comes from its feed component. Historically, utilities bought the uranium feed for the LEU fuel and delivered it to USEC for enrichment. Assuming that this practice continues (it may not), utilities receiving blended-down Russian HEU will still buy and deliver natural uranium feed to USEC as part of their enrichment contracts, and the HEU imports will displace a portion of these feed deliveries. As Figure C-2 shows, 2,979 MT of the natural uranium that would normally be delivered to USEC by utilities would accumulate in USEC's inventory; according to the HEU contract signed by Minatom and USEC in January 1994, Russia is not to be paid for the feed component in its blended-down HEU until this accumulated inventory is sold or consumed by USEC, or when the contract expires in 2014.

Since the utilities will not want to pay twice for the uranium feed component of the LEU fuel they receive from USEC, some other means of getting value from USEC's inventory of displaced feed must be found if Russia is to be paid for the feed component of its blended-down HEU. This can be done in one of two ways. First, the material set aside by USEC could be resold to other buyers, with the proceeds from these sales

---

15. Note that an increase in the size of the annual Russian HEU shipment to 30 MT would triple the size of this displacement effect, since 30 MT would contain 5.7 million SWU.

16. Global demand for SWU is essentially flat, and USEC cannot readily increase its market share, so importing Russian LEU necessarily displaces USEC's own production.

transferred to Russia. This approach would depress the market price of natural uranium and, as explained below, sales in the United States are constrained by the U.S.-Russian suspension agreement for uranium imports. Sales outside of the United States are legal, but Russia is already selling as much uranium on the world market as it can, which means that non-U.S. demand cannot readily accommodate the feed component of the Russian HEU. Since there is currently no viable futures market in uranium, purchasing the Russian feed in the expectation of future sales is an uncertain proposition for any market actor, even one without USEC's conflicts of interest.

Alternatively, USEC has the option of feeding this excess uranium into its enrichment cascades, which is called "overfeeding." Overfeeding increases the tails assay but decreases the amount of SWU needed to produce the same amount of LEU, which would allow USEC to avoid even greater costs. This is illustrated in Figure C-3, showing that overfeeding would save an additional 1.2 million SWU if the tails assay were raised to about 0.36 percent. Again assuming that each SWU costs $60 for USEC to produce, this overfeeding would allow USEC to avoid an additional $72 million in SWU production costs, thereby raising the total economic value of the 10 MT of blended-down Russian HEU to $184 million. Overfeeding would not depress the market price of uranium; indeed, when Thomas Neff initially elaborated the idea behind the HEU deal in 1992, he assumed that the displaced feed would be used to overfeed the U.S. enrichment cascades, thereby avoiding the uranium price-suppression problem that triggered the anti-dumping action.[17]

The problem with overfeeding, however, is that it is cost-effective for USEC only if USEC saves more from overfeeding than it has to pay for the uranium that is overfed. If this condition does not hold, then USEC will see the feed component of the Russian HEU as a liability and will resist buying it. In 1992, it was impossible to know if this condition would hold because two critical pieces of information were lacking: USEC's cost of producing SWU (which defines how much USEC could save from overfeeding) and the price USEC would have to pay for the Russian feed component.

In fact, when this information finally became known, it turned out that it would not be in USEC's economic interest to purchase the Russian feed to overfeed its own enrichment cascades. As a result of a series of implicit subsidies from the U.S. government that began to be conferred in late 1992, USEC's production cost is an inordinately low $60 or less per

---

17. See Thomas L. Neff, "Integrating Uranium from Weapons into the Civil Fuel Cycle," *Science and Global Security*, Vol. 3 (1993), pp. 215–222.

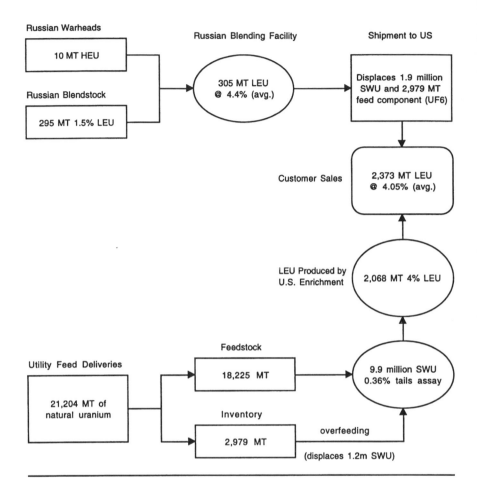

Avoided enrichment cost without overfeeding = 1.9m SWU @ $60/SWU = $114m

Additional avoided enrichment cost by overfeeding = 1.2m SWU @ $60/SWU = $72m

Cost of overfed uranium to USEC = 2,979 MT @ $28.5/kg.U = $85m

Assuming a $60/SWU marginal cost, the price of uranium for USEC must fall to $24.2/kg.U for overfeeding to be commercially viable

USEC has no incentive to purchase the Russian feed component for overfeeding when the price is $28.5/kg.U

Figure C-3. HEU Imports with Overfeeding.

SWU.[18] Because the cost avoided by overfeeding 2,979 MT of natural uranium is $72 million, it will make sense for USEC to overfeed only if USEC must pay Russia less than $72 million for the 2,979 MT of natural uranium, that is, only if USEC pays Russia less than $24.20 per kilogram of uranium (see Figure C-3). In May 1993, however, the United States agreed to pay Russia $28.50 per kilogram of uranium for the feed component in the Russian HEU. At this price, overfeeding is not cost-effective for USEC, and USEC has therefore refused to purchase the Russian uranium at the agreed price for use as overfeed.

Thus, because the implicit government subsidies of USEC's production costs meant that USEC would not voluntarily overfeed the natural uranium component of the Russian HEU, some other way must be found to compensate Russia for the full value of the blended-down Russian HEU. The obvious way to do this would be to resell the uranium component on the open market, but as explained below, the suspension agreement constrains such sales, a problem that was not widely expected when the decision to give USEC exclusive executive control over the HEU deal was made. For this complex set of reasons, finding a viable means of compensating Russia for the feed component of its blended-down HEU has proven exceptionally difficult for the U.S. government.

Implementing the HEU deal would be much simpler if it were done outside of the context of existing or traditional enrichment contracts between utilities and USEC. (USEC would not necessarily have a role to pay in the HEU deal if the sale were executed in this fashion.) If the blended-down HEU were marketed directly to utilities as LEU fuel, there would be no issue of overfeeding the enrichment cascades or displacing the feed that is normally delivered in a contract to buy SWU from an enricher like USEC. Instead, utilities would enter into contracts for LEU fuel that are different from those they historically signed with the Depart-

---

18. USEC's real production cost is not precisely known, but $60/SWU is the cost publicly quoted by the USEC management. USEC's marginal cost of production is probably closer to $50/SWU. The government has implicitly subsidized USEC in three main ways: first, the Energy Policy Act allowed USEC to inherit the very low-cost energy contracts with local utilities that were earlier negotiated by the Department of Energy; second, the Department of Energy agreed to lease its two enrichment plants to USEC for a nominal fee, which has meant that USEC has essentially no capital costs; and third, USEC is being given part of the Department of Energy's natural and low-enriched uranium stockpile, which allows USEC to cross-subsidize its SWU production. According to Klaus Messer, the CEO of Urenco — one of USEC's competitors in the enrichment market — "it is ridiculous to assume that USEC's real production costs could be below $130 per SWU." (Messer is probably referring to USEC's average cost of production, not its marginal cost.) See "Interview with Dr. Klaus Messer," *NUKEM Market Report*, June 1994, p. 20.

ment of Energy. Rather than pay USEC for the service of enriching natural uranium that the utilities procure and deliver, the utilities would be able to buy LEU as a single commodity from whomever was marketing the blended-down Russian HEU. Unless it were controlled solely by USEC, such an arrangement would run counter to USEC's commercial interests by increasing the level of competition in the SWU market, reducing USEC's market share, and probably depressing the worldwide SWU price. Such an arrangement would also increase the Russian share of the worldwide natural uranium market, and probably drive down the price of natural uranium as well. Since the authors of the suspension agreement presumed that the feed component of the Russian HEU would be handled exclusively by USEC in the context of normal enrichment contracts, it is possible that the suspension agreement as currently written would not apply to the feed component in blended-down Russian HEU marketed directly to U.S. utilities though this interpretation has not been tested. While the preceding section has explained how the U.S. purchase of Russian HEU should have worked in principle, in practice the HEU deal took a markedly different form. The actual course of events that defined the contours of the HEU deal is described below.

History: The Anti-Dumping Case, USEC, and the HEU Deal

This section develops the parallel histories of the HEU deal and the anti-dumping case against uranium imports from the states of the former Soviet Union. An understanding of the trouble encountered by the HEU deal requires an understanding of the law that permitted the 1991 suit against Soviet uranium imports, so I begin this section by briefly describing U.S. anti-dumping law as it applied against imports from non-market economies.

A chronology of the HEU deal and the uranium anti-dumping case is provided on Table C-1.

U.S. ANTI-DUMPING LAW

The historic purpose behind anti-dumping laws, dating back to the Anti-dumping Act of 1916, was to prevent predatory pricing by foreign producers. Predatory pricing refers to the attempt by one producer to drive all other producers of a certain good out of the market by lowering its prices; after its competitors are driven out, the predatory producer, now a monopoly, will be able to raise its prices and reap much higher profits, which under certain conditions can result in a net welfare loss for the United States. Under other conditions, however, predatory pricing will cause a net increase in American welfare, even if some American compa-

Table C-1. Chronology of the Anti-Dumping Case and the HEU Deal.

Anti-Dumping Case	Date	The HEU Deal
	October 24, 1991	Op-ed by Thomas Neff proposes an HEU deal
Anti-dumping petition filed	November 8, 1991	
Preliminary ITC finding of injury	December 23, 1991	
	December 25, 1991	Dissolution of USSR
Preliminary Department of Commerce finding of dumping	May 29, 1992	
Yeltsin complains about anti-dumping ruling at the G-7 summit	July 8, 1992	
Suspension agreement negotiations begin	Summer 1992	U.S.-Russian negotiations on HEU deal begin
	August 31, 1992	U.S.-Russian agreement to purchase HEU initialed
Suspension agreements initialed	September 16, 1992	
Suspension agreements signed	September 27, 1992	
	October 8, 1992	Senate passes Energy Policy Act of 1992, authorizing the privatization of USEC
Minatom voices objections to suspension agreement	October 1992	
	February 18, 1993	Russia and the United States sign the government-to-government agreement to purchase 500 MT of Russian HEU over 20 years
	May 3, 1993	HEU contract initialed
	September 9, 1993	Mikhailov announces he will not sign the HEU contracts until the suspension agreement is amended

Continued

Table C-1. *Continued.*

Anti-Dumping Case	Date	The HEU Deal
	November 18, 1993	Vote on START in the Ukrainian Rada
Amendment to Russian suspension agreement initialed	December 15, 1993	
	January 14, 1994	Trilateral Statement; HEU contract signed
Amendment to Russian suspension agreement signed	March 11, 1994	
	March 18, 1994	Transparency protocol to HEU deal signed
	November 23, 1994	Project Sapphire (Kazakhstan)
Canada agrees to drop its complaint against the amended suspension agreement	February 21, 1995	

nies are put out of business.[19] Nonetheless, predatory pricing is widely regarded as an "unfair" trading practice that should be protected against.

As currently written, U.S. anti-dumping laws have little to do with the legitimate concern over predatory pricing.[20] Instead, the U.S. anti-dumping law seeks to combat imports at "less than fair value," an ambiguous and controversial term that goes well beyond the concept of predatory pricing.[21] In practice, this has made the anti-dumping law a

---

19. The welfare gains of predatory pricing result from the fact that, in its initial phase, U.S. consumers benefit from the lower prices charged by the firm engaging in predatory pricing. A net welfare loss will occur only if these gains are outweighed by the welfare losses in the second phase of predatory pricing, when the predator raises its prices above their original level.

20. Indeed, it was the 1921 Antidumping Act that first abandoned the requirement that domestic industries seeking anti-dumping relief must demonstrate predatory-pricing intent or effect. See Peter Orszag and Joseph Stiglitz, "Dumping on Free Trade: The U.S. Import Trade Laws," Center for Economic Performance Discussion Paper No. 210, London School of Economics, October 1994.

21. The anti-dumping statute is Section 731 of the 1988 Trade Act. For a survey of U.S. anti-dumping law, see Orszag and Stiglitz, "Dumping on Free Trade"; for more detailed treatments, see Michael Kabik, "The Dilemma of 'Dumping' from Nonmarket Economy Countries," *Emory International Law Review*, Vol. 6 (Fall 1992); Richard Dale, *Anti-Dumping Law in a Liberal Trade Order* (New York: St. Martin's Press, 1980); R. Botluck and R. Litan, eds., *Down in the Dumps: Administration of U.S. Unfair Trade*

popular and effective source of protection for U.S. industries facing lower-cost foreign imports. Seeking protection against dumping enables domestic producers to brand their foreign competitors as "unfair" trading partners, and the anti-dumping statute provides them with an administrative process that almost always results in substantial anti-dumping duties. The president has no discretion to alter the size or scope of anti-dumping duties, unlike normal tariffs. Anti-dumping proceedings almost always result in very high duties because the process is heavily biased against imports in a complicated and technical way.[22] The most important source of this bias is the manner in which the U.S. government calculates the "fair value" (now referred to in the law as the "normal value") of an imported good. Furthermore, there is a special provision in the U.S. anti-dumping law that specifies how the "fair value" of imports from non-market economies should be calculated.[23]

Anti-dumping proceedings generally begin when a U.S. company petitions the Department of Commerce to initiate an investigation of a pattern of imports that appears to be dumping. The proceedings then have two strands. First, the Department of Commerce is charged with determining whether dumping has occurred, which requires it to calculate the "fair value" of the goods being imported. If the price of the import was less than the calculated "fair value," then dumping has occurred. Second, the International Trade Commission (ITC), an independent regulatory agency, is charged with determining if the imports in question have caused or are causing material injury to a U.S. producer of a similar good. Material injury is defined as "harm which is not inconsequential, immaterial, or unimportant."[24] If both findings are affirmative, then an anti-dumping duty equal to the margin between the earlier price of the import

---

Laws (Washington DC: The Brookings Institution, 1991); J.M. Finger, *Antidumping: How It Works and Who Gets Hurt* (Ann Arbor, Mich.: University of Michigan Press, 1993); P. Areeda and D. Turner, "Predatory Pricing and Related Practices Under Section 2 of the Sherman Act," *Harvard Law Review*, Vol. 88, No. 4 (February 1975), pp. 697–733; and Jeffrey P. Bialos, Randolph W. Tritell, and Martin S. Applebaum, "Trading with Central and Eastern Europe: The Application of the U.S. Unfair Trade Laws to Economies in Transition," *International Law Practicum*, Vol. 7 (1994).

22. According to one study, 80 percent of all anti-dumping cases result in findings of dumping. Orszag and Stiglitz, "Dumping on Free Trade."

23. In 1995, all of the states of the former Soviet Union were still treated by the U.S. government as non-market economies, as were the majority of the states in eastern Europe.

24. 19 U.S.C. § 1677(7)(A) (1988). See also Gregory Waddoups, "Antidumping Measure Against Republics of the Former Soviet Union: Techsnabexport, Ltd. v. United States," *Journal of Contemporary International Law*, Vol. 19 (1993).

and its "fair value" must automatically be imposed on all future imports. The Department of Commerce also has the power to impose these duties retroactively if it rules that "critical" circumstances exist.

Given that the standard for material injury is relatively easy to meet in cases like the Soviet uranium one, the key aspect of the anti-dumping process is how the Department of Commerce calculates "fair value." The most common way to calculate the "fair value" of imports from non-market economies is the "surrogate country constructed cost" method. This method combines the factor costs of one or more surrogate countries with market-based economies, with the factor-of-production ratios from the non-market economy accused of dumping or, if this information is unavailable, from other countries where such information is available. The law gives the Department of Commerce broad discretion to choose which countries to use in its surrogate cost constructions, and in fact, Commerce sometimes relies on the information supplied by the original petitioners in the anti-dumping suit, that is, from the domestic producers seeking protection against lower cost imports.[25] Because this method, on top of all of the other biases in U.S. anti-dumping law, is heavily weighted in favor of the U.S. industry seeking protection, the Department of Commerce almost always finds that dumping has occurred in cases brought against exporters in non-market economies.[26] This method also tends to result in findings of very large dumping margins, which are automatically translated into anti-dumping duties if the ITC finds that material injury has occurred.

As a way of avoiding the mandatory imposition of anti-dumping duties, the law gives the Department of Commerce the power to sign a suspension agreement with the exporters accused or found guilty of dumping.[27] A suspension agreement will stop an anti-dumping investigation, if it is still going on, and permit imports of the good in question subject to the terms of the suspension agreement, which may be highly restrictive. Commerce must determine that the suspension agreement "will prevent the suppression or under-cutting of price levels" of the goods in question; that "effective monitoring of the [suspension] agreement by the United States is practicable"; and that the suspension agree-

---

25. Bialos, Tritell, and Applebaum, "Trading with Central and Eastern Europe."

26. According to one study, the surrogate country constructed cost "approach does not result in a very accurate measure of dumping margins: the choice of a surrogate is the most significant variable and can result in a wide range of outcomes, given Commerce's discretion in this area." Bialos, Tritell, and Applebaum, "Trading with Central and Eastern Europe."

27. 19 U.S.C. § 1671c, 1673c.

ment is "in the public interest."[28] Interested parties, including the producers who bought the original anti-dumping suit, may challenge suspension agreements negotiated by Commerce in court.

THE ANTI-DUMPING CASE AGAINST URANIUM IMPORTS FROM THE SOVIET UNION

The 1988–91 developments in the uranium market that led to the anti-dumping case against Soviet uranium imports are not simple, and many of the details remain shrouded in a series of deals involving an enterprising U.S. company in Colorado, a secretive Soviet ministry in Moscow, and unsuspecting U.S. uranium miners and traders. In 1988 the Colorado-based uranium mining and trading company Concord/Nuexco signed a contract with the Soviet government that gave it the exclusive right to import Soviet uranium into the United States. This contract, and the inexperience of the Soviet government in the global marketplace, allowed Concord/Nuexco to engage in a clever market manipulation scheme that severely disrupted the global uranium market.

Concord/Nuexco's market manipulation scheme worked, in simplified terms, as follows: The Soviet Union's contract with Concord/Nuexco stipulated that Moscow would be paid according to the published forward spot market price on a specific day each quarter. Thus, Concord/Nuexco knew on exactly which day the price of the uranium it was buying from the Soviet government would be determined. Unbeknownst to the Soviet Union, Concord/Nuexco used this insider information to go short on uranium: that is, Concord/Nuexco borrowed large amounts of uranium from utilities and other firms with uranium inventories and promptly resold this material, driving down the price of uranium. Concord/Nuexco could do this safely because it knew that it would be able to cover its short position with uranium from the Soviet Union. Since the price paid to the Soviet Union would depend on the forward spot market price on a specific date that Concord/Nuexco knew in advance, Concord/Nuexco was effectively guaranteed a tidy profit (as long as no duties applied to the Soviet Union uranium). The scheme ensured that the Soviet Union's earnings from its uranium exports would steadily decrease over time. Even as the price of uranium fell from about $14 per pound in 1988 to about $7 per pound in 1991, the nuclear industry was unaware of this scheme until mid-1991.

Concord/Nuexco's manipulation of the uranium market was not clearly illegal, but, once it became known, the U.S. uranium industry

---

28. Waddoups, "Antidumping Measure Against Republics of the Former Soviet Union."

wanted to put a stop to it. This is part of the reason why the industry, with U.S. government support, decided to file an anti-dumping suit against the Soviet Union's uranium exports in late 1991. It is, of course, possible that an anti-dumping suit would have been filed even in the absence of Concord/Nuexco's market manipulation scheme, since the influx of Soviet uranium would have tended to suppress the price of natural uranium in any case. But Concord/Nuexco's manipulation of the market exacerbated this effect, thereby heightening the hostility of the U.S. nuclear industry toward the new Soviet imports.

On November 8, 1991, an ad hoc committee of domestic uranium interests asked the Department of Commerce to begin an anti-dumping investigation into uranium imports from the Soviet Union, at the time being handled exclusively by Concord/Nuexco. This committee (the "petitioners") consisted of 13 domestic uranium producers, eight of which are wholly or partially foreign owned, and the Oil, Chemical, and Atomic Workers' Union, which represents the workers at the U.S. enrichment plants.[29] The petition was also initially supported by the Department of Energy which, as the owner of the only two non-military uranium enrichment plants in the United States, supplied roughly 90 percent of the U.S. and 46 percent of the world demand for SWU.[30] On November 19, 1991, the Department of Commerce agreed to conduct this investigation.

On December 23, the International Trade Commission issued a preliminary finding that material injury had occurred as a result of the alleged dumping of uranium from the Soviet Union. Two days later, Soviet President Mikhail Gorbachev announced the formal dissolution of the USSR. This prompted the company responsible for Soviet uranium exports, Techsnabexport (Tenex), to request that Commerce's investigation be terminated on the grounds that the country against which it was directed had ceased to exist.[31] The Department of Commerce denied this request, which caused Tenex and the uranium-exporting Soviet successor

---

29. See Energy Information Administration, *Domestic Uranium Mining and Milling Industry 1992, Viability Assessment* (DOE/EIA-0477(92)), December 1993, note 37; Bialos, Tritell, and Applebaum, "Trading with Central and Eastern Europe," note 83; and "Energy Fuels Foresees Rebirth of Domestic Mining Industry," *Businesswire*, December 22, 1993.

30. The initial participation of the Department of Energy in the anti-dumping petition was described as an "exceedingly rare" occurrence, since government agencies have almost never participated in anti-dumping cases. "Maybe Good News for U.S. Producers, Maybe Not," *NUKEM Market Report*, May 1992, p. 14.

31. At the time of the original anti-dumping litigation, Tenex and the Soviet/Russian government had no lawyers of their own; they relied instead on law firms retained by Concord/Nuexco.

states to sue Commerce in the U.S. Court of International Trade. The court ruled in favor of the Department of Commerce, allowing it to continue its investigation against past uranium imports from the Soviet Union, and to apply the results of this investigation to future uranium imports from the former Soviet republics.[32] On May 29, 1992, the Department of Commerce issued a preliminary finding that sales of uranium from the former Soviet Union had occurred at less than fair value.

The Department of Commerce's calculation of the dumping margin of uranium imports from the former Soviet Union during the period under investigation illustrates the irrationality of U.S. anti-dumping law in general, and the surrogate country constructed cost method in particular. When Commerce made its ruling, the spot market price of U308 equivalent was between $7.60 and $7.85 per pound,[33] and the average price of the uranium imports from the former Soviet Union covered by the anti-dumping investigation was $9.47 per pound of U308.[34] Using Canadian data on the factors of production (i.e., labor, capital, electricity, and other inputs) for natural uranium, and factor price data from Portugal and Namibia, Commerce determined that the "fair value" of natural uranium imports from the former Soviet Union was $26.31 per pound of U308. World spot prices for pounds of U308 had been well below that level since mid-1981, when the uranium market was still in the midst of its post-1970s decline.[35] In effect, Commerce determined that to have been "fair," natural uranium imports from the former Soviet Union would have had to occur at mid-1981 price levels, or over three times the prevailing spot market price.[36]

The Department of Commerce's surrogate country constructed cost calculations for SWU imports from the former Soviet Union were similarly skewed. Using British data on the factors of SWU production, and

---

32. The Court of International Trade made separate rulings to this effect on May 21 and September 25, 1992. The sole issue on which the court ruled was "whether an antidumping duty investigation may be continued against newly-independent republics after the country named in the original proceedings has dissolved." Marion B. Schnerre, "Antidumping, A Choice Between Unilateral Duties or Negotiation of a Suspension Agreement: The Aftermath of Techsnabexport, Ltd. v. United States," *Indiana International and Comparative Law Review*, Vol. 4 (1994).

33. These prices reflected the suppressive effect of the Soviet imports and Concord/Nuexco's market manipulation scheme.

34. "A Duty. An Injunction. Or a Settlement. Take Your Pick," *NUKEM Market Report*, June 1992, p. 5.

35. "NUKEM Price Range," *NUKEM Market Report*, June 1992, p. 23.

36. "Market Overview," *NUKEM Market Report*, June 1992, p. 2.

Portuguese factor price data, Commerce determined that the "fair value" of SWU from the former Soviet Union was $141.15 per SWU.[37] At the time, the spot market SWU price was between $65 and $70.[38] In other words, Commerce determined that the fair market price for SWU from the former Soviet Union was twice the prevailing market level.

Rather than apply separate duties to the natural uranium and SWU components of uranium imports from the former Soviet Union, the Department of Commerce decided to apply a single duty to all uranium products, regardless of their chemical forms or enrichment levels. This single duty was 115.82 percent, which was the simple, unweighted average of the dumping margins calculated for natural uranium and SWU (177.87 percent and 53.77 percent, respectively). Since the SWU component has a disproportionate weight in the price of the enriched uranium (roughly two-to-one), the administrative decision to impose an unweighted average duty, applied equally to all uranium products, had the effect of yielding a substantially higher duty on enriched uranium, which served the commercial interest of the Department of Energy's enrichment operation.

Thus, on May 29, 1992, the Department of Commerce ordered the Customs Service to immediately begin levying a 115.82 percent duty on uranium imports from the former Soviet Union. Commerce also ruled that critical circumstances existed, and therefore applied this duty retroactively to all uranium imports that had entered the United States in the previous ninety days. In this preliminary decision, however, cognizant of the HEU deal, Commerce ruled that HEU and uranium derived from HEU would not be subject to these anti-dumping duties. The date for the final ruling on dumping was set for August 1992, but was later pushed ahead to October 1992.

The decision by Commerce to levy anti-dumping duties against uranium imports from the former Soviet Union provoked a harsh reaction in the Soviet successor states, particularly Russia. President Boris Yeltsin raised the issue at the G-7 summit in Munich in July 1992, arguing that the United States was being hypocritical to offer the newly independent states support, on the one hand, while denying them access to the export markets in which they are most competitive, on the other. The Russian government claimed that the uranium anti-dumping ruling would cost

---

37. "A Duty. An Injunction," p. 5.

38. This SWU price range reflected the suppressive effect of the Soviet imports and Concord/Nuexco's market manipulation scheme.

Russia 14 percent of its projected hard currency earning in 1992, which would undermine Moscow's ability to service its foreign debt.[39] In part as a response to this intervention, in the summer of 1992 the Bush administration ordered the Department of Commerce to begin negotiating a uranium suspension agreement with the former Soviet republics, in the hope of appeasing Russia by allowing it to export some uranium into the U.S. market. In a closely related move, the Bush administration began to negotiate in earnest with Moscow on the purchase of HEU from dismantled Russian nuclear weapons, which produced an initial U.S.-Russian agreement that President Bush announced on August 31, 1992.

The negotiations on the anti-dumping suspension agreement between the United States and the governments of the former Soviet republics were conducted quietly by low-level officials in the Department of Commerce in the late summer and early fall of 1992. With preliminary findings of material injury and dumping by the ITC and the Department of Commerce, respectively, and with the legal challenge to the legitimacy of an investigation against a country that had ceased to exist rejected by the Court of International Trade, the uranium-exporting states of the former Soviet Union had little choice but to accept the suspension agreement proposed by Commerce. The alternative to signing a suspension agreement was to face a prohibitive 116 percent duty on uranium exports. The Department of Commerce initialed suspension agreements with Russia, Ukraine, Kazakhstan, Uzbekistan, and Kyrgyzstan on September 16, 1992.[40]

The centerpiece of these suspension agreements was a quota for uranium imports from each country that was pegged to the price of uranium. The trigger price for these imports was set at $13 per pound of uranium: as the price of uranium rose above this level, each republic would have a progressively larger import quota. At the time, the spot market price of uranium was less than $10 per pound and, with demand flat, there was only a remote prospect that the price would rise above the $13 per pound trigger price, which meant that no imports from the former Soviet Union would be allowed. For this reason among others, Russia — the only former Soviet republic with real political leverage in Washington

---

39. Russia reportedly earned $500 million from uranium exports in 1991, and projected earnings of $1 billion in 1993. John Helmer, "West's Trade War 'Costing Russia $4b'," *Australian Financial Review*, July 16, 1992, p. 10.

40. The Department of Commerce did not reach agreement with Tajikistan, the only other uranium-exporting former Soviet republic, because Tajikistan was unable to represent itself at these proceedings.

at the time — successfully insisted on a special one-time option to sell 4.1 million pounds of uranium to the United States Department of Energy outside of its quotas in the suspension agreement.

The hope of Commerce as well as the U.S. uranium industry was that the agreement, together with the planned U.S. purchase of Russian HEU, would cause the price of uranium to rebound, thereby revitalizing the U.S. uranium industry and creating new jobs. According to Raymond Larson, the chairman and CEO of Uranium Resources Inc., a Dallas-based uranium mining company, his firm was "optimistic that the elimination of CIS [Commonwealth of Independent States] exports to the United States below $13.00 per pound selling price, plus the recently announced transaction between the U.S. Department of Energy and Russia to acquire Russian highly enriched uranium thereby eliminating the HEU overhang on the uranium market, will have a significant positive impact on market prices for uranium."[41]

The most troublesome aspect of the suspension agreement for the HEU deal, however, was that it unambiguously stated that HEU "is within the scope of this [dumping] investigation, and HEU is covered in this agreement."[42] Thus, despite the HEU deal and the earlier exclusion from the May 1992 preliminary decision, Commerce decided to include HEU within the scope of its anti-dumping proceedings and the resulting suspension agreement. One of the reasons for this inclusion was that Commerce saw no other way to avoid circumvention of the quotas if importers could easily redesignate uranium as HEU-derived uranium, a difference that Customs could not readily verify. Commerce also came under heavy pressure from the domestic uranium industry, which filed three separate legal briefs with Commerce between June and September, 1992, arguing that HEU should be included within the scope of the dumping investigation. As a result, the Department of Commerce attempted to strike a compromise between the national security interests served by the HEU deal and the commercial interests of the U.S. uranium industry by inserting a public interest finding in the suspension agreement that specifically exempts the Russian HEU or blended-down HEU from the Russian natural uranium import quota, but that prohibited the

---

41. "Proposed Settlement Agreement by Department of Commerce on Dumping Case Announcement," *Businesswire*, September 17, 1992.

42. "Agreement Suspending the Antidumping Investigation on Uranium from the Russian Federation," Section III; in *Federal Register*, Vol. 57, No. 211 (October 31, 1992), p. 49235.

reselling of the feed uranium that is delivered to USEC by utilities pursuant to enrichment contracts that were affected by the HEU imports.[43]

This complicated relationship between the suspension agreement and the HEU deal deserves further clarification. The suspension agreement required the executive agent of the HEU deal — USEC — to "quarantine" an amount of natural uranium exactly equal to the feed component of any HEU-derived enriched uranium products sold on the U.S. market. This natural uranium would be taken from the feed that utilities would normally deliver to USEC pursuant to a standard long-term SWU contract. When the suspension agreement was signed, it was assumed that USEC would use this material as overfeed, which the suspension agreement does not prohibit. As explained above, however, overfeeding is not cost-effective for USEC because of its subsidized cost of production, so USEC rejected the option of overfeeding the material, which would have obviated all problems with the suspension agreement. Thus, with USEC as the sole executive agent and overfeeding not cost-effective, the suspension agreement meant that it would be virtually impossible for Russia to be compensated promptly for the value of the uranium component of the blended-down HEU that Russia was supposed to ship to the United States.

THE HEU DEAL AND THE CREATION OF USEC
The Bush administration began to negotiate toward the HEU deal in the summer of 1992, after the Russian government protested the May 1992 decision to impose anti-dumping duties against its uranium exports into the U.S. market. These negotiations proceeded relatively rapidly, and on August 31, 1992, yielded an initial agreement for the United States to buy approximately 500 metric tons of HEU from dismantled Russian warheads over an unspecified number of years. At the time, President Bush announced that the deal would have "no adverse effect on U.S. consumers or jobs in [uranium] processing or mining," and the government indicated that it would have no effect on the U.S. budget since the purchase price of the HEU would be recouped after it was sold as reactor fuel. The president called for the conclusion of an implementing contract within 12 months."

THE CREATION OF USEC. The White House also announced in August 1992 that the U.S. executive agent in the HEU deal would be the U.S. Enrichment Corporation (USEC), a not-yet-formed government company that,

---

43. "Agreement Suspending the Antidumping Investigation on Uranium from the Russian Federation," Section IV.M.2 and Section IV.M.2(2).

assuming Congress passed the privatization legislation then under consider- ation, would inherit the Department of Energy's two civilian enrichment plants. The creation of USEC, or something like it, had been discussed for many years, the Congress finally passed the USEC privatization legislation in the fall of 1992, as part of the Energy Policy Act of 1992. This law specified that USEC would become a government-owned but independent company on July 1, 1993; then, at some point in the future, USEC shares would be sold to the public, with the proceeds of this sale (estimated at $1.5–2 billion) going to the U.S. Treasury. According to the Department of State, the HEU deal was seen as a way of making USEC more competitive in the international enrichment market, since USEC "can use blended-down HEU to replace some production at its gaseous diffusion plants, which use large amounts of electricity. About 2 million SWU would not have to be produced if 10 MT of HEU were blended down each year."[44] This, in turn, would help maximize the eventual U.S. government revenue that would result from the privatization of the government's enrichment operation. The Energy Policy Act of 1992 codified President Bush's administrative decision to make USEC the executive agent of the HEU deal, but went one step further by giving USEC an apparently exclusive right to import and market the blended-down Russian HEU.[45]

Although the decision to privatize USEC was a sound one, driven by valid concerns about the need to downsize the government and subject the U.S. enrichment enterprise to market discipline and professional management, the combination of USEC's heavily subsidized low production costs and its exclusive executive authority over the HEU deal led inevitably to problems with Russia over the planned purchase of blended-down HEU. The USEC privatization act lists 11 purposes for USEC, none of which is to implement the HEU deal; the first two of these purposes are to "operate as a business enterprise on a profitable and efficient basis," and to "maximize the long-term value of the Corporation to the Treasury of the United States." As put by Senator Wendell Ford of Kentucky, Congress "set up [USEC] to protect American jobs and America's energy security. We did not set it up to be just a broker. We expect USEC to remain a producer [of enriched uranium]. We did not set it up to finance foreign policy initiatives, or to solve budget woes of other domestic programs."[46]

44. Michael Knapik, "U.S. Agrees to Buy Russian HEU, but Details Must be Worked Out," *Nucleonics Week*, Vol. 33, No. 36 (September 3, 1992).

45. See note 4 above.

46. Pamela Newman, "Republicans Slam Clinton Nuclear Budget Proposal," *Energy Daily*, February 9, 1994.

Even while its shares were wholly owned by the U.S. Treasury, the privatization of USEC would turn it into an independent company, with its own interests and incentives that have no necessary relationship to the national interests of the United States as expressed by the president. USEC's interests, it will be recalled, were represented by the Department of Energy among the original petitioners in the anti-dumping proceedings. After July 1, 1993, the U.S. government lost its right to direct USEC's operations, and the executive branch had no formal authority over USEC except that the president can nominate and fire the members of its board of directors. For these and additional reasons that are explained in greater detail in the next section, USEC is an unsuitable exclusive executive agent in the HEU deal.

THE HEU DEAL TAKES SHAPE. In the fall of 1992, the Russian government began to complain more bitterly about the effects of the suspension agreement. Since the price of uranium did not rise above the $13-per-pound trigger price specified in the suspension agreement, no Russian uranium could be sold directly on the U.S. market. In late October, the Russian ambassador to the United States, Vladimir Lukin, wrote to the Department of Commerce asking for a series of changes in the suspension agreement. Among these, Lukin asked for the "exclusion of a paragraph in the suspension agreement that brings HEU under the scope of the agreement 'since deliveries of HEU would be covered by a separate'" agreement — the HEU deal.[47] The Department of Commerce made no effort to enact these changes, so no new Russian uranium was imported into the United States during 1992.[48]

Simultaneously, the negotiations toward a government-to-government agreement on the purchase of HEU from dismantled Russian weapons proceeded along a separate track, run on the U.S. side out of the office of General William Burns, the head of the U.S. Safe and Secure Dismantlement (SSD) delegation.[49] Burns and the Russian Minister of Atomic

47. Wilson Dizard III, "Russian Letter to Commerce Calls for 'Clarifications' of Suspension Pact," *Nuclear Fuel*, November 9, 1992.

48. Even after the imposition of the anti-dumping duties, however, substantial amounts of Soviet-origin or CIS-origin uranium continued to be sold in the United States, since some previous imports were exempt from the duties under a grandfather clause, while other importers were able to circumvent the duties by enriching the uranium in Europe.

49. The SSD delegation was created by the Bush administration in 1991 as the Soviet Union began to collapse, to provide for regular consultation with the Soviet and post-Soviet governments on issues related to the safe and secure dismantlement of nuclear weapons. The SSD delegation was responsible for, among other things, nego-

Energy, Victor Mikhailov, signed the government-to-government agreement on the HEU deal on February 18, 1993, shortly after Clinton entered office. This agreement settled the amount and the time frame of the U.S. purchase of Russian HEU: 500 metric tons over twenty years, beginning with at least 10 tons in the first five years, and rising to at least 30 tons yearly thereafter, with efforts to accelerate this delivery schedule. This agreement also specified that the blending down of HEU from dismantled weapons into low enriched uranium (LEU) would take place in Russia. Although the February agreement did not resolve the price issue, it designated Minatom and the Department of Energy as the executive agents for the HEU deal (with the understanding that the U.S. role would later be assumed by USEC). This agreement cleared the way for detailed negotiations toward a formal HEU purchase contract to implement the government-to-government agreement. Burns and Mikhailov called for the conclusion of the implementing contract within six months. February 1993 marked the point at which responsibility for the HEU deal began to shift decisively from official agencies of the U.S. government to the future USEC management team. After this point, the key figure in the negotiations on the HEU contract was Philip Sewell, a Department of Energy employee who later joined the USEC management.

A long-term contract with USEC as the sole U.S. executive agent was not the format for the HEU deal originally desired by Minatom. Rather, Minister Mikhailov first proposed the formation of a Russian-American joint venture that would combine low-cost Russian supplies with American marketing talents, allowing the two states to share in the profits of selling highly competitive LEU fuel derived from Russian HEU.[50] This approach was rejected by Department of Energy officials who would later become USEC officials. A Russian-American joint venture like the one proposed by Minatom would have had an effect exactly opposite that desired by the Department of Energy officials; it would have undermined, rather than enhanced, the future competitive position of USEC. According to the trade press, these Department of Energy officials wanted to use the HEU deal to enhance the competitiveness of the U.S. enrichment operation by buying Russian SWU at below the U.S. cost of production. Thus, the United States originally offered to buy the Russian SWU for between $30 and $40 — an "absurdly low" level.[51]

---

tiating with Russia, Ukraine, Belarus, and Kazakhstan on the umbrella agreements that were needed to use U.S. funds from the newly established Nunn-Lugar program.

50. "An Enigma Wrapped Up in a Warhead . . . (On the U.S. Side)," *NUKEM Market Report*, October 1993, p. 12.

51. "An Enigma Wrapped Up in a Warhead," p. 12.

In May 1993, Russia and the United States initialed the draft contract for the HEU purchase (identical to the final contract that was signed on January 14, 1994, in Moscow). The May 1993 draft set the initial purchase price for the Russian HEU at $82.10 per SWU and $28.50 per kilogram of uranium. At this time, the two states also announced that there would be a transparency protocol to the HEU deal to ensure that the LEU delivered to the United States came only from newly dismantled warheads in Russia, and was used solely for non-military purposes in the United States. A preliminary transparency protocol was signed by Vice President Gore and Prime Minister Chernomyrdin in September 1993.

Two key issues in the HEU deal remained unresolved by mid-1993. The first was the U.S. insistence that the revenue from the HEU sales be shared with Belarus, Kazakhstan, and Ukraine. The reason for this insistence was that the complete denuclearization of these three states was one of the highest priorities in U.S. foreign policy in 1993, and Washington wanted to provide them, particularly Ukraine, with an added incentive to transfer the warheads on their territories to Russia for dismantlement. On the other hand, the Russian government, and especially Minister Mikhailov, strongly objected to the U.S. demand that it share the HEU revenue with the other republics. Moscow charged that this demand was interference in Russia's private affairs with the other former Soviet republics, and argued that Russia would bear all of the costs associated with implementing the HEU deal, including the dismantlement of the warheads, the blending of the HEU, the internal transportation of the HEU and LEU, and the disposition of the plutonium released during the dismantlement process.

The second issue that needed to be resolved before the HEU contract could be signed concerned the suspension agreement. Minister Mikhailov insisted that the HEU implementing contract could not be signed until the United States amended its suspension agreement with Russia so as to permit at least some Russian uranium exports to the U.S. market. This demand was made clear at the April 1993 summit between Presidents Yeltsin and Clinton in Vancouver, though in all likelihood it was made earlier as well. Mikhailov went public with this demand for the first time in September 1993,[52] but in the intervening period it appears that the

---

52. In a September 9, 1993, interview with the *NUKEM Market Report*, Mikhailov stated explicitly that "We've always linked — especially me — the anti-dumping agreement to the signing of the HEU contract. . . . If the [anti-dumping] issue is resolved, we will sign the [HEU] agreement. If resolution is delayed, so will be the signing of the final [HEU] contract." Elizabeth Martin, "A Conversation with Viktor Mikhailov," *NUKEM Market Report*, October 1993, p. 25.

Department of Commerce made little if any progress toward amending the Russian suspension agreement. The two main reasons for this lack of movement appear to be the low level of attention that the HEU deal and the suspension agreement received from the Clinton administration's senior national security officials, and pressure from the domestic uranium industry, USEC, and Congress not to relax the suspension agreements. Senator Malcolm Wallop of Wyoming, for example, wrote President Clinton in September 1993 stating that while he "recognize[d] the significance of the HEU agreement to foreign policy goals of the United States, its execution cannot come at the expense of appropriate enforcement of U.S. trade law."[53] Furthermore, the domestic uranium industry's criticism of the suspension agreement became increasingly intense toward the end of 1993, since uranium importers and speculators had begun to exploit a loophole that allowed them to bypass the quotas (still set at zero) on imports from the former Soviet Union. The bypass involved buying natural uranium in the former Soviet Union, shipping it to Europe to be enriched, and then shipping the enriched product to the United States, or "swapping" it with a like amount of enriched uranium already in the United States.[54] This bypass directly affected the competitive position of USEC by helping the European enrichers.[55]

THE TRILATERAL STATEMENT

The decisive event in the final negotiations on the HEU contract happened not in Washington or Moscow, but in Kiev. On November 18, 1993, the Ukrainian parliament passed a resolution that ratified the START Treaty subject to an array of conditions. The resolution stated that the START Treaty applied only to 42 percent of the warheads and 36 percent of the launchers on Ukrainian territory; stipulated that Ukrainian President Leonid Kravchuk could exchange START I articles of ratification

---

53. Michael Knapik and Wilson Dizard III, "Spot U Price Drifts Below $10.20/lbs.; Miners, Nuexco Urge Scrapping of Suspension Pacts," *Nuclear Fuel*, November 8, 1993.

54. This loophole existed because the suspension agreement stated that the enrichment of uranium in a third country confers on that uranium a new country of origin, which was consistent with general U.S. trade practice regarding the substantial transformation of a product. For a discussion of the bypass issue, see "Clogging the Enrichment Bypass," *NUKEM Market Report*, May 1995, pp. 4–17.

55. According to USEC president Nick Timbers, buying natural uranium in the former Soviet Union and having it enriched in Europe "generally translates into a savings of $10 or more per SWU," which requires USEC "to choose between losing the sale or reducing its price by at least an equal amount to remain competitive." Michael Knapik, "Uranium Price in U.S. Moves Up Slightly; USEC Calls for Shutting Down Bypass Option," *Nuclear Fuel*, December 19, 1994.

only after gaining international guarantees of Ukraine's security; and demanded that Ukraine be given compensation for the fissile material in the nuclear warheads transferred from Ukraine to Russia. Furthermore, Ukraine's Rada annulled Article V of the May 1992 Lisbon Protocol, in which Ukraine had pledged to accede to the Nuclear Non-Proliferation Treaty (NPT) as a non-nuclear weapons state. This resolution confirmed the worst fears of the international community about Ukraine's nuclear ambitions, fears which had grown steadily since early 1992, as Kiev took every opportunity to postpone the fulfillment of its own repeated commitments to complete nuclear disarmament.

Given the importance of Ukrainian denuclearization in President Clinton's national security policy, and with the president scheduled to go to Moscow in January 1994, the vote by the Rada in November 1993 catalyzed a burst of foreign policy activism at the upper echelon of the administration. During his December visits to Moscow and Kiev, Vice President Gore played a crucial role in fashioning a trilateral agreement between Russia, the United States, and Ukraine that would put the denuclearization of Ukraine back on track. To make this agreement possible, Gore had to find a way to compensate Kiev for the HEU contained within the strategic nuclear warheads Ukraine was supposed to transfer to Russia.[56] With Russia refusing to pay Ukraine in cash, and with the Clinton administration unable to pay Ukraine directly for the fulfillment of Kiev's own disarmament commitments, Vice President Gore brokered a deal in which Ukraine would be compensated with LEU fuel assemblies for its power-generating reactors.[57]

Fuel assemblies for Ukraine had to come from Minatom, so securing Minatom's cooperation in resolving the Ukrainian nuclear problem suddenly became a high priority for the Clinton administration. For this reason among others, the White House ordered the Department of Commerce to negotiate an amendment to the Russian suspension agreement, and put pressure on USEC to finalize the HEU purchase contract.

---

56. Ukraine had also demanded retroactive compensation for the fissile material in the tactical nuclear warheads that had been transferred from its territory to Russia between December 1991 and May 1992; Russia rejected this argument out of hand, while the United States avoided taking a position on the matter. Similarly, some Ukrainians had argued that Ukraine should be compensated for the plutonium as well as the uranium in their relinquished warheads; Russia and the United States were united in their rejection of this position.

57. The idea of compensating Ukraine with reactor fuel for the warheads it was supposed to transfer to Russia had first emerged in the Russian-Ukrainian accord signed in September 1993 in Massandra, but that agreement collapsed almost immediately after it was signed when both states unilaterally rewrote its provisions.

On December 15, 1993, the Department of Commerce and Minatom initialed an amendment to the Russian suspension agreement that would allow Minatom to export substantial quantities of uranium into the U.S. market through the year 2003.[58] Then, on January 14, 1994, Minister Mikhailov and William "Nick" Timbers, the USEC transition manager, signed the HEU purchase contract. To clinch the deal, the White House persuaded USEC to make a $60 million advance payment to Minatom to cover the immediate costs of providing fuel assemblies to Ukraine, which would be credited against the bill for the first delivery of blended-down HEU to the United States. One hour later, Presidents Clinton, Yeltsin, and Kravchuk issued a "trilateral statement" which started the reciprocal flow of strategic warheads and LEU fuel assemblies between Russia and Ukraine, and which laid the basis for Ukraine's latter ratification of the START Treaty and accession to the NPT as a non-nuclear weapons state. This was an achievement of historic proportions, but in the rush and the urgency to get an agreement, the Clinton administration inadvertently allowed the HEU deal to take shape in a way which virtually ensured that it would not be implemented as originally conceived.

THE HEU CONTRACT

At the time of the Trilateral Statement, the HEU deal was publicly described by the United States government as sealed. In fact, in its details the HEU contract signed by Mikhailov and Timbers in Moscow diverges considerably from the commonly held understanding of the HEU deal. Although the HEU contract is regarded as commercially proprietary by USEC and has never been released to the public, three facts about the contract make the U.S. commitment to purchase HEU from dismantled Russian nuclear weapons substantially less ironclad than many officials in the Clinton administration seem to have believed: their public statements have offered few hints of these qualifications to the HEU deal.

First of all, the HEU contract signed by Timbers does not *obligate* USEC to purchase any Russian HEU; rather the contract gives USEC an *option* to purchase up to 500 metric tons of Russian HEU, starting with 10 metric tons annually in the first five years, rising to 30 metric tons annually for the fifteen years thereafter. This material would be blended down to an enrichment level of approximately 4.4 percent in Russia, and would then be shipped to the United States as UF6. USEC alone would decide how much HEU the United States would order from Russia each year. Thus, the HEU contract signed and negotiated by USEC differed in

---

58. The amended agreement is examined in detail below.

an important respect from the February 18, 1993, government-to-government agreement on the HEU deal, which stated that the United States would purchase *at least* 10 MT in the first five years, and at least 30 MT thereafter, with efforts to be made to increase the rate of purchase.

Second, the agreement set an initial price of $780 per kilogram of 4.4 percent enriched uranium, which would give the total deal a present undiscounted value of $11.9 billion.[59] Prices for enriched uranium products are a composite of the prices of the natural uranium feed and SWU that go into making the enriched product. In this case, the $780 price reflected a natural uranium price of $28.50 per kilogram of uranium and a SWU price of $82.10. The contract specifies that the price will be renegotiated every October to reflect inflation and changes in market conditions, but there is no provision specifying how pricing disputes will be resolved. If the two sides cannot agree on a price, then no deliveries will occur. As Nick Timbers, the president of USEC, has put it, "the Russian deal, after all, is cancelable."[60]

Third, the contract specifies that Minatom will receive payment for the SWU content in the blended-down HEU within sixty days of delivery, but will receive payment for the uranium feed component only when the material is sold or used to overfeed USEC's enrichment cascades, or at the end of the twenty-year contract.[61] The reason for this peculiarity in the HEU contract was that the suspension agreement constrained USEC from reselling the uranium feed component of the Russian HEU on the U.S. market until after the suspension agreement lapsed, in the year 2003.[62] USEC was therefore unwilling to pay Minatom up front for this

---

59. The $780 per kilogram price for 4.4 percent enriched uranium translates into a SWU price of $82.10 and a natural uranium price of $28.50 per kilogram of uranium, which equals approximately $10.91 per pound of U308 equivalent. In January 1994, the restricted market price of 4.4 percent enriched UF6 was $813 per kilogram.

60. Edward Giltenan, "A Conversation with Nick Timbers," *NUKEM Market Report*, October 1993, p. 40.

61. Since the price that Russia would receive for the uranium feed component of the blended-down HEU would be determined by USEC, as would the timing of the payment, the $780 per kilogram of 4.4 percent enriched uranium was a meaningless number, as was the much quoted $11.9 billion total value for the HEU deal.

62. Although one provision of the original suspension agreement (Sect. IV.M.2) stipulates that the uranium component of the Russia HEU sale is not subject to the suspension agreement's quotas, a different provision (Sect. IV.M.2(2)) prohibits USEC from reselling the displaced feed component that is delivered to USEC by utilities that receive LEU fuel from the Russian HEU. This second provision was designed to ensure that the HEU deal is implemented in a manner that is neutral in the natural uranium market, in other words, in a manner that does not suppress the price of natural uranium.

natural uranium portion of the HEU's value. There is a provision in the contract allowing Minatom to take back the feed component of the HEU rather than have it stockpiled under USEC's custody in the United States, but USEC has the right to override a Russian request to do so.[63]

In Moscow, Minister Mikhailov gave Timbers a written proposal repeating Minatom's offer to form a joint venture for the sole purpose of implementing the HEU deal; the joint venture would blend some of the Russian HEU in the United States. Timbers did not respond to this proposal. Mikhailov had been pushing for a Russian-American joint venture to implement the HEU deal since at least July 1992, when Minatom signed an initial agreement with Allied-Signal and Nuclear Fuel Services, Inc., two U.S. companies.[64] Allied-Signal has a plant in Erwin, Tennessee, that is licensed for HEU blending operations, and reportedly has a capacity to blend about 6–10 metric tons of HEU per year, which approximately equals the annual capacity of the one Russian blending facility at Yekaterinburg. After receiving a non-committal or negative response from USEC, Mikhailov raised the issue of a bilateral joint venture for implementing the HEU in a June 1, 1994, letter to Vice President Gore.[65] The purpose of the proposed joint venture is fairly clear: Mikhailov wants to speed the flow of revenue from the HEU deal to Russia and Minatom, and he realizes that a properly configured joint venture would have a much higher incentive than USEC does to implement the HEU deal quickly. For its part, USEC wants to keep control of the HEU deal and therefore has opposed the creation of such a joint venture. There appears to have been no U.S. government response to Minister Mikhailov's letter to Vice President Gore.

A separate point worth emphasizing about Minister Mikhailov's proposal to create a joint venture for implementing the HEU deal is that he specifically offered to sell HEU directly to the United States, to be blended down at U.S. facilities. This belies the statements made by some U.S. government officials that the decision to blend the HEU in Russia was made because of Russian concerns over the secrecy and security of their nuclear stockpile. In fact, Minatom is somewhat schizophrenic about the idea of allowing blending in the United States: Minister Mikhailov strongly favors the U.S. blending option if it speeds and increases the flow

---

63. "Weapons Dismantlement: More Details — and Controversy — Appear Concerning U.S.-Russia HEU Deal," *Nuclear Fuel*, January 31, 1994.

64. "Allied-Signal, Russian organizations plan to convert uranium," *Aerospace Daily*, July 31, 1992.

65. Wilson Dizard III, "Matek Teams Russian, U.S. Entities to Implement HEU Deal, Courts USEC," *Nuclear Fuel*, June 20, 1994.

of hard currency to his ministry, but others in the ministry would prefer to blend in Russia to provide for the continued operation of the blending facility in Yekaterinburg. It appears that the United States has not so far seriously considered Minatom's offer to allow blending in the United States.

In addition to a number of legitimate environmental and security concerns, one of the main reasons for the U.S. reluctance to allow blending in the United States is that USEC is not equipped for it. Therefore, the blending would have to be done at some other facility, such as the Nuclear Fuel Services plant in Tennessee or the Babcock and Wilcox plant in Lynchburg, Virginia. If, however, another U.S. firm were given responsibility for blending Russian HEU down to LEU for subsequent sale to fuel fabricators and utilities, then that firm would in effect become a second supplier of enrichment services (i.e., SWU) on the U.S. market, thereby breaking USEC's monopoly. USEC, with roughly 80–90 percent of the domestic SWU market, sells SWU to domestic utilities at about $120/SWU, but has a production cost of only $60/SWU.[66] Like any commercial operation, USEC wants to preserve this large profit margin and prevent the emergence of alternative suppliers. In terms of the HEU deal, however, the effect of blending only in Russia is to slow and perhaps prevent the movement of fissile material out of Russia and into safe, secure nuclear power reactors.

Finally, almost immediately after the HEU contract was signed, USEC began to complain about the price it was to pay Russia. USEC made clear that it would only execute the HEU deal if it were as profitable as any alternative business activity. According to George Rifakes, the executive vice president for operations at USEC, the "HEU deal will be viewed like the rest of our capacity; we will look at our ability to produce and our costs, and we'll look at our marketing posture, what the customer requires, and we will try to meet the requirement at the least cost. So the HEU is just going to come into the cost picture."[67] As USEC officials repeatedly made clear in nuclear industry fora until a change in corporate strategy in mid-1995, if executing the HEU deal forces USEC to accept a lower profit margin, USEC would regard this as a "national security

---

66. Ed Lane, "Uncertainty Clouds Uranium Enrichment Corporation's Plan," *Energy Daily*, March 24, 1993; Michael Knapik and Wilson Dizard III, "U.S. Weapons HEU May Be Given to USEC To Aid Economics of Russian Deal," *Nuclear Fuel*, May 24, 1993; and Wilson Dizard III, "Zarb Leaves USEC Board, Takes New Job; Corporation Issues New Pricing Policy," *Nuclear Fuel*, July 4, 1994.

67. "USEC Marketing Officials Cite Inflated Expectations as Major Challenge," *Nuclear Fuel*, January 17, 1994.

premium," and would expect the government to make up the difference.[68] The government was unwilling to provide USEC with a direct cash subsidy, though the Department of Energy has been willing to compensate USEC indirectly with free grants from the government's stockpile of excess uranium, a move that has been strongly criticized by others in the nuclear industry.[69] Nonetheless, USEC repeatedly called on Minatom to accept a lower SWU price for its blended-down HEU, and the price negotiations for 1995 broke down in February 1995 when Minatom rejected USEC's offer of $68 per SWU.

THE AMENDMENT TO THE RUSSIAN SUSPENSION AGREEMENT
The amendment to the Russian suspension agreement contained an innovation that was designed to serve the interests of Russian and American uranium producers simultaneously — no mean feat, given the nature of the uranium market. It did this by beggaring uranium producers in all other countries.[70]

The amendment to the Russian suspension agreement introduced a provision for "matched sales" of natural uranium and SWU on the U.S. market, replacing the system of import quotas pegged to the price of uranium in the original agreement. Under matched-sales quotas, Russian-origin uranium or SWU may be imported into the U.S. market if it is matched with an equal amount of uranium or SWU that is "newly produced" by domestic producers.

As the next step in a matched sale, the Russian and the U.S. products would be bundled together and sold to a utility as a single package. Although the matching ratio would be 1:1, the Russian and American producers would not split the proceeds equally; the amended agreement requires that the U.S. producer receive a higher unit price for the combined sale than the Russian producer. Consider the following illustration. A U.S. uranium producer signs a matched-sales agreement with a Russian producer to sell 2,000 pounds of uranium subject to a 70–30 revenue split. The U.S. producer would then try to find a buyer for the 2,000 pounds of uranium. If the uranium were sold to a utility for $9 per pound, giving

---

68. "Weapons Dismantlement: More Details — and Controversy."

69. See William J. Broad, "Quietly, U.S. Converts Uranium Into Fuel for Civilian Reactors," *New York Times*, June 19, 1995, p. A12.

70. The Department of Commerce has not signed similar amendments to the uranium suspension agreements with the non-Russian former Soviet republics, mainly because these states lack Russia's political and economic leverage. Another factor, however, is that the legality under international trade law of the Russian amendment has been challenged by other states, such as Canada, as noted below.

the deal a total value of $18,000, the Russian producer would receive $5,400 and the U.S. producer would receive $12,600. (The treatment of matched SWU imports is analogous but slightly more complicated.) In effect, therefore, the amended suspension agreement requires Russian producers to subsidize U.S. producers if they wish to sell uranium products on the U.S. market.[71] Nonetheless, Minatom officials acquiesced in the matched-sales agreement, not least because one company partially owned by Minatom was well positioned to reap hard-currency profits from the matched sales.[72]

The amendment imposed a new set of quotas on the amount of Russian-origin uranium and SWU that could enter the United States under matched sales. These quotas are allocated among U.S. producers on an administrative basis: that is, the Department of Commerce receives a matched-sales proposal from a U.S. firm and, if it meets minimal acceptability criteria, approves it. For 1994 and 1995, the amended agreement allowed 2,539 metric tons of uranium and two million SWU to be imported from Russia into the United States. During 1996–2003, smaller amounts of Russian-origin uranium would be allowed into the United States each year under matched sales, but no further SWU imports would be allowed, as shown in Table C-2.

The amended Russian suspension agreement generated controversy in the nuclear industry, and there are a number of problems with it. The first is that it conflicts with the principles of U.S. antitrust law by encouraging price collusion among suppliers who are supposed to be in competition with one another; for this reason, the Department of Justice is reportedly examining the agreement.[73] Second, the amended agreement violates the North American Free Trade Agreement (NAFTA), and prob-

---

71. In economic parlance, this is a "rent transfer": a transfer of wealth from one entity (Russian uranium producers) to another (U.S. uranium producers) for reasons having to do the preferential status of one of them (in this case, the greater political and legal influence of U.S. uranium producers), not with any sort of normal, productive economic activity. The value of the rent is an implicit production subsidy to the U.S. producer from its Russian partner in the matched sale. In the illustration above, the size of the rent transfer is $3,600.

72. The company was Tenex, the former Soviet uranium trading firm, which is the partial owner of Global Nuclear Services & Supply Ltd. (GNSS). GNSS had a pre-existing partnership with Concord/Nuexco. The proposal of the matched-sales scheme was first publicly made by Concord/Nuexco and GNSS in November 1993, before the amendment to the Russian suspension agreement was initialed. Michael Knapik and Wilson Dizard III, "Spot U Price Drifts Below $10.20/lbs.; Miners, Nuexco Urge Scrapping of Suspension Pacts," *Nuclear Fuel*, November 8, 1993.

73. "Clogging the Enrichment Bypass," *NUKEM Market Report*, May 1995, p. 10.

Table C-2. Annual Matched-Sales Quotas for Russian Uranium (in millions of SWU, and metric tons of uranium).

Year	SWU Quota	Natural Uranium Quota	HEU Feed Component
1994	2.0	2,539	2,970
1995	2.0	2,539	2,970
1996	0	742	2,970
1997	0	1,042	2,970
1998	0	1.385	2,970
1999	0	1,554	8,937
2000	0	1,627	8,937
2001	0	1,554	8,937
2002	0	1,881	8,937
2003	0	1,654	8,937

Note: The matched-sales uranium quotas in the amendment to the suspension agreement are given in pounds of U308. The figures listed above have been standardized in MT of uranium. The conversion factor is 1 kg. U equals 2.6 lbs. U308.

ably also the weaker General Agreement on Tariffs and Trade (GATT), by offering preferential treatment to U.S. producers at the expense of foreign sellers. Canada, the key U.S. partner in NAFTA, is the world's leading uranium exporter, and stood to suffer an economic loss as a result of the matched-sales agreement. In its economic effects, the matched-sales agreement would directly displace uranium sales in the U.S. market that could otherwise go to Canadian or other foreign uranium producers, and, if it were to encourage new production of U.S. uranium or supply of Russian uranium that would not otherwise occur, it could tend to depress the world price of uranium. Both of these effects run against the interests of uranium exporters, so Canada lodged a formal protest with the U.S. government in early 1994 and, after receiving an unsatisfactory response, began legal proceedings under Article 309 of NAFTA, which bars the discriminatory treatment of imports.[74]

The effect of the amendment to the Russian suspension agreement on the HEU deal was not immediately clear, requiring subsequent clarification by the U.S. government. The amended suspension agreement excludes the SWU content of the blended-down HEU from the matched-sales quotas, and therefore places no limit on the amount of Russian SWU that USEC can resell on the U.S. market. The amendment also did not

74. Michael Knapik, "Russians Said to Want Higher U.S. Prices; USEC Concludes Deal with Nuclear Electric," *Nuclear Fuel*, April 11, 1994.

change the original agreement's procedure for dealing with the uranium feed component of the Russian HEU, which was to require an amount of natural uranium equal to the feed component in the enriched Russian uranium to be quarantined by USEC from the U.S. market if and when USEC imports blended-down Russian HEU. Under the amended agreement, therefore, the only possible way in which this quarantined feed could be released on the U.S. market would through a matched sale.[75] The power to determine whether such matched sales will take place currently lies with USEC. As shown in Table C-2, the annual quotas for matched sales of Russian natural uranium on the U.S. market are well below the feed component of the blended-down HEU that USEC is supposed to import for the first ten years of the HEU contract, making it impossible to compensate Russia for the full value of its blended-down HEU through U.S. sales until after the suspension agreement expires.

This complex arrangement for dealing with the feed component is best understood with reference to Figure C-4. Since the feed component of 10 metric tons of blended-down HEU is 2,979 metric tons of natural uranium, USEC is required to quarantine 2,979 metric tons of its own feedstock. As Figure C-4 shows, the amended suspension agreement allows four things to be done with this material.

First, the material can be sold abroad. Unfortunately, demand for uranium is relatively flat, much of it is tied up in long-term contracts, and Russia is already selling as much uranium as it can outside of the U.S. market. Furthermore, the right to decide how, when, and at what price the feed component is sold currently belongs to USEC, which can be expected to dispose of the material in a manner that serves its own interests, not Minatom's. Second, USEC could use this natural uranium to overfeed its enrichment cascades. Because of the implicit subsidy of USEC's production costs, however, overfeeding is not cost effective at a price of $28.50 per kilogram of uranium, so USEC has refused to purchase the Russian feed component for this purpose. Third, the material can be quarantined until the suspension agreement expires, which guarantees that Russia will not be paid for it until at least 2003. Fourth, the material

---

75. Whether or not the Russian feed component can be sold in the context of a matched sale is somewhat ambiguous: there is nothing in the suspension agreement that would prohibit such sales, but it seems that Canada may have been given the impression by the Clinton administration that such sales would not take place. There have so far been no matched sales of blended-down HEU in the United States, and whether they are permissible at all seems to be up to the discretion of the Department of Commerce. In this appendix, I assume that matched sales using Russian HEU feed are in fact permissible.

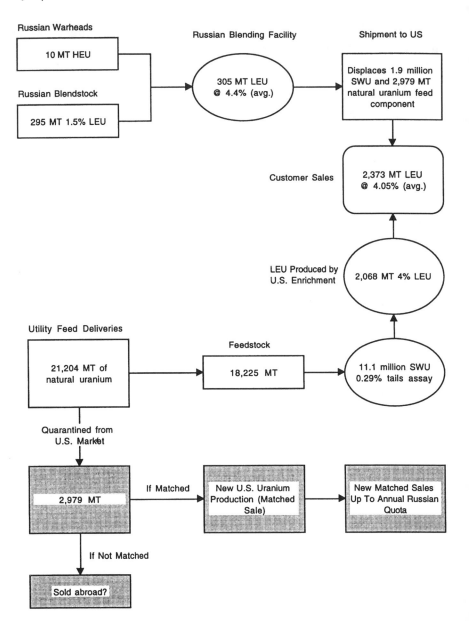

Figure C-4. HEU Imports under the Amended Suspension Agreement.

could probably be sold on the U.S. market as part of a separate matched-sale agreement.[76] Such sales would count against the annual Russian quota shown in Table C-2, so only a relatively small portion of the total uranium feed in the blended-down HEU could be released in the U.S. market in this manner. Moreover, such sales would be controlled by USEC, not Minatom. Since none of these options are particularly viable under current conditions, the amended suspension agreement ensures that Russia cannot be readily compensated for the feed component of the blended-down HEU it ships to the United States.

If there were any doubts as to the effect of the amended suspension agreement on the U.S. ability to compensate Russia for the feed component of its HEU, they were resolved in the context of bilateral trade negotiations with Canada. Canada, as already noted, protested against the matched-sales arrangement and, when that failed to resolve the issue, began legal proceedings under the non-discrimination clause in NAFTA.

Not wanting a new trade dispute with its largest trading partner, the Clinton administration worked to settle this issue with the Canadians during late 1994 and early 1995. The task was handled by the office of the U.S. Trade Representative, Mickey Kantor, and the Under Secretary of State for International Security Affairs, Lynn Davis. On February 21, 1995, Davis persuaded the Canadians to drop their year-old challenge to the amended Russian suspension agreement with an exchange of official letters that was based on a consultation between the two governments held on October 20, 1994. Although the U.S. State Department and USEC take a different view, Canada regards the Davis letter as an official assurance that the United States will allow no more Russian-origin uranium — including the feed component of the Russian HEU — to be released on the U.S. market beyond that which is already allowed by the matched-sales quota.[77] In this way, Canada was reassured that the combined market impact of the HEU deal and the amended suspension agreement would be no greater than the market impact of the matched sales of Russian natural uranium permitted by the amended suspension agreement alone. In effect, therefore, in order to protect the amended suspension agreement from a legal challenge, the United States offered its closest

---

76. See note 75.

77. According to nuclear industry sources, the reason for this ambiguity in the Davis letter is that USEC has questioned the interpretation of Section IV.M.2 of the suspension agreement that enjoins USEC from reselling utility-delivered feed that is displaced by blended-down Russian HEU on the U.S. market. "Clogging the Enrichment Bypass," *NUKEM Market Report*, May 1995, p. 13; Michael Knapik, "Analysts Expect Rise in Spot U Price," *Nuclear Fuel*, February 27, 1995.

trading partner an assurance that the sales of the feed component of the blended-down Russian HEU would be limited by the quotas shown on Table 2. This, in turn, implied a further constraint on the U.S. ability to compensate Minatom for the full economic value of the Russian HEU.

USEC'S FOUR-TIERED APPROACH AND THE $100 MILLION ADVANCE

In 1994, USEC ordered 6 metric tons of Russian blended-down HEU at the originally negotiated price ($82.10 per SWU) to be delivered in 1995. At $82.10 per SWU, the enrichment component of this 6 metric tons would cost USEC about $93 million; thus buying 6 metric tons cost USEC somewhat more than the $60 million it had already paid to Minatom in January 1994. The shipments of this material began in spring 1995, but even as the uranium was moving across the Atlantic, the two sides were still disputing how the $60 million advance would be credited against USEC's order, and how Minatom would be compensated for the feed component. Minatom wanted to credit the advance against the full value of the enriched uranium, whereas USEC wanted to credit the advance only against the value of the SWU component, not the feed component. In effect, Minatom was asking for a change in the HEU contract provision stipulating that payment for the feed component will occur only when it is sold or used as overfeed, or when the contract expires in 2014. Privately, Minatom was threatening to cancel the HEU deal unless some way around this provision in its contract with USEC was found.

At the annual price review consultations that began in October 1994, the two sides were unable to agree on the price that USEC would pay for additional deliveries of HEU beyond 1995. According to a February 1995 protocol, USEC wanted to buy Russian SWU for $68 or less, while Minatom held out for the originally negotiated price of $82.10 per SWU, as well as some sort of prompt compensation for the feed component. Because of this price dispute, USEC placed no further orders until June 1995, when it and the Clinton administration began to be criticized in the media for allowing the HEU deal to bog down.[78] On June 15, 1995, USEC informally offered to purchase (but did not formally order) 12 additional metric tons of Russian HEU at a SWU price of not less than $82.10.[79] USEC

---

78. See William J. Broad, "Deal for U.S. to Buy Bomb Grade Fuel From Russia Said to be in Peril," *New York Times*, June 12, 1995, p. A1; "An Endangered Nuclear Bargain," *New York Times*, June 13, 1995, p. A24; and "Mutually Assured Cooperation," *Boston Globe*, June 15, 1995, p. 20.

79. The original HEU contract specified a SWU price of $82.10 for 1994, and stipulated that this price would apply in 1995 if the two sides were unable to agree on a new SWU price. (The contract did not specify what would happen if the two sides

also offered to pay Minatom up front for the feed component, but linked this concession to congressional action that would give the president the authority to exempt the executive agent of the HEU deal (USEC) from the suspension agreement quotas and the anti-dumping duties, which would allow USEC to sell the material on the U.S. market without penalty.[80]

As the basis for its request for an exemption from the suspension agreement, USEC and the government developed a four-tiered approach to disposing of the Russian feed component — that is, four different and sequential means by which the Russian feed could be sold. The first tier was sales outside of the United States, which were already allowed by the suspension agreement. The second tier was a "futures" sales mechanism. The USEC proposal would create a one-month window each year in which buyers could bid for the Russian feed to be delivered five years later; USEC would have the right to reject the bids. Third, the Russian feed could be sold to U.S. uranium miners at USEC's acquisition cost, though the level of this acquisition cost could be determined by USEC. Finally, in the fourth tier, USEC would be able to sell all uranium not sold in the previous three tiers on the spot market essentially without restriction.

The main effect of the four-tiered approach would be to give USEC total control over the Russian feed and an exceptionally secure and privileged position in the global uranium market. Each of the four tiers is flawed as a means of compensating Russia for the feed component of the blended-down HEU. The first tier — sales outside of the United States — represents no improvement over the current situation. As previously noted, Russia is already selling as much uranium abroad as it can, and is limited chiefly by market conditions and the various trade barriers that Russian nuclear exports face around the world. Also, the first tier would put USEC into the position of competing with other Russian sales in the international market. The second and third tiers — forward sales and pass-through sales at cost to U.S. miners — are unlikely to work either, because of the market effects of the fourth tier.

By giving USEC the right to engage in essentially unrestricted domes-

---

failed to agree on a SWU price after 1995.) In mid-1995, however, USEC and Minatom decided to extend the start date for the contract until 1995, so that the default SWU price of $82.10 would apply for 1996 if the two sides failed to agree on a different SWU price before them.

80.   The waiver authority from Congress would allow the president to exempt any executive agent of the HEU deal from the anti-dumping duties and the suspension agreement, but since USEC is currently the exclusive executive agent in the deal, the waiver would apply only to it.

tic sales of the Russian feed component, the fourth tier would give USEC the power to severely depress short-term uranium prices.[81] Since no uranium buyer will want to pay a relatively high current price when it expects lower prices in the near future, there is unlikely to be significant demand for the Russian feed in the second and third tiers, and, even if there were, USEC would have the power to prevent the sales if it chose to do so. The four-tiered approach is effectively a license for USEC to dump Russian uranium on the spot market, a right which has already once been denied to Concord/Nuexco. More generally, the four-tiered approach would strengthen the market position of USEC to the detriment of every other firm in the nuclear industry. Uranium producers on the U.S. market; utilities, while they may temporarily benefit from lower uranium costs, fear that USEC would use its dominant position in the feed market to demand higher prices for its SWU, which accounts for two-thirds of the price of LEU fuel.[82] Moreover, continued price depression in the spot market is likely to result in a severe price rebound later if the lower spot prices discourage investment in new mines or cause more firms to leave the industry. The four-tiered approach also would seriously undermine the suspension agreement and the matched-sales concept, possibly provoking challenges from U.S. miners as well as important trading partners like Canada. Finally, since compensating Russia for the full value of its blended-down HEU ultimately depends on a healthy uranium market, the USEC four-tiered approach is likely to have a damaging effect on the long-term commercial viability of the HEU deal.

USEC's conditional offer to pay up front for the Russian feed under the four-tiered approach represented a significant change in corporate strategy for USEC. Until mid-1995, USEC treated the HEU deal as something of a liability, and claimed that it should receive a government subsidy equal to the "national security premium" contained in the politically negotiated SWU price. As it began to be criticized for allowing the HEU deal to bog down, however, USEC changed its tack. In mid-1995, USEC began to argue that the HEU deal is threatened principally by the suspension agreement's effect on USEC's ability to compensate Russia for the feed component in the blended-down HEU. This effectively turns the national security argument on its head, since it now seems to be those who resisted USEC's proposal to exempt itself from the suspension agreement that are undermining the national security benefits of the HEU deal.

---

81. Since there is relatively little uncommitted short-term demand for uranium, sudden spot sales by USEC of the Russian feed component could have an enormous effect on the spot uranium price.

82. See "Choice — The HEU Deal or USEC," *The Ux Weekly*, June 12, 1995.

In fact, USEC's four-tiered approach for dealing with the uranium feed component is both seriously flawed and plainly self-serving, and the focus of the debate on the suspension agreement issue has served mainly to distract from the more fundamental issue of USEC's own conflicts of interest as the sole executive agent of the HEU deal.

The HEU deal was one of the main items on the agenda at the meeting of the Gore-Chernomyrdin Commission in Moscow in late June and early July 1995, and, prior to this meeting, the Office of the Vice President apparently decided to support the USEC in its proposals for dealing with the feed component issue. In Moscow, USEC and Minatom signed a protocol in which USEC agreed to pay for the full value of the Russian HEU (uranium and SWU) upon delivery. However, this concession was linked to the "enactment of legislation in the United States necessary to authorize the President to waive anti-dumping duties and other trade restrictions against LEU under the HEU Contract."[83] If such legislation is not in place by November 1, 1995, Minatom will cease to regard the protocol as binding. In fact, Minatom informally let it be known that the failure to resolve the uranium feed issue by November could be the end of its relationship with USEC. This arrangement, in turn, put pressure on the Clinton administration and the Congress to do as USEC asks, since the national security benefits of the HEU deal were effectively linked to granting USEC special trade law exemptions and expanded commercial advantages.

USEC, in the protocol signed in Moscow, also offered Minatom a $100 million advance payment for future deliveries of blended-down HEU. This loan by USEC was privately guaranteed by the Department of Energy: if Russia failed to deliver $100 million worth of blended-down HEU to USEC, or if USEC cannot recoup its expenses by selling the Russian feed, then the Department of Energy will reimburse USEC in kind out of the government's uranium stockpile. Public statements by USEC and the Clinton administration suggest that the $100 million advance was needed to underwrite the continued flow of fuel assemblies to Ukraine according to the Trilateral Statement. Consistent is the fact that Minatom asked for a $400 million advance on the HEU deliveries in December 1994, and by mid-1995 had halted the delivery of reactor fuel to Ukraine.[84] The U.S. government rejected Minatom's request for $400 million when it was made, on the grounds that the reciprocal flow of warheads and reactor fuel between Ukraine and Russia is independent of the HEU deal.

---

83. Protocol between Minatom and USEC, June 30, 1995.

84. Ustina Markus, "Ukraine Accuses Russia Over Nuclear Fuel Rods," *OMRI Daily Digest II*, No. 138 (July 18, 1995).

Concern over the flow of warheads and reactor fuel between Ukraine and Russia was clearly a consideration in the U.S. decision to offer Minatom a $100 million advance in June 1995, but the dominant motive behind the $100 million advance seems to have been USEC's and the government's desire to secure Minatom's approval of the four-tiered approach for dealing with the suspension agreement problem. The $100 million advance reduced the odds that Minister Mikhailov would reject USEC's four-tiered approach out of hand. The Russians could see that the four-tiered approach was less than ideal; by giving USEC privileged control over the price and timing of the HEU feed sales, the four-tiered approach almost guaranteed that Russia would not receive a fair market price for its uranium, and that USEC would emerge with its own market position considerably strengthened. However, since a Russian rejection of USEC's proposal would have been highly damaging to USEC's political standing in Washington, securing Russia's approval was very important for USEC at the Moscow meeting of the Gore-Chernomyrdin Commission. Moreover, with a $100 million loan outstanding to Minatom, the costs of stripping USEC of its current role as the exclusive executive agent in the HEU deal were increased, making it even less likely that the government would do so.

Although the Clinton administration described the agreements on the HEU deal reached at the Moscow meeting of the Gore-Chernomyrdin Commission as a great success, in fact they amount to little more than a flawed and temporary fix to a profound problem in the U.S. strategy for buying HEU from dismantled Russian nuclear weapons. Giving the president the power to waive trade law restrictions on the executive agent in the U.S. purchase of Russian HEU would not put the HEU deal on sound commercial footing. It would, however, postpone the day on which the White House must confront the fundamentally flawed system for buying Russian HEU that the U.S. government allowed to be put in place.

Restructuring the HEU Deal

The HEU deal should be restructured in two closely related areas: the incentive structure of the executive agent and the suspension agreement. A policy change in a third area — whether or not blending is allowed in the United States — is desirable but not essential.

All of the possible policy changes described below will be legally and politically difficult to implement. Low-level national security officials in the administration are unlikely to have the clout or the authority to carry out any of these changes, as each proposal would encounter opposition from the vested interests that would be affected. The effort to repair the

HEU deal will fail unless the upper echelon of the U.S. government becomes involved and committed to the task.

The most important point to understand about the HEU deal is that it is unlikely to be implemented unless the agent given executive authority over the transaction has an incentive to carry it out. USEC has no positive economic incentive to implement the HEU deal unless Minatom agrees to reduce its SWU price from $82.10 to USEC's cost of production, which is about $60. Moreover, even if Minatom does accept the lower price, the fact that USEC and Minatom are oligopolistic competitors will work against the smooth implementation of the HEU purchase.

There were three main reasons for giving the HEU deal to USEC. First, regardless of whether or not it was the executive agent, USEC's involvement in the HEU deal was desirable, since USEC would have to overfeed its enrichment cascades for the United States to reap the full economic benefit of the HEU purchase without driving down the price of uranium. Second, because of the budget deficit, the Bush administration wanted the HEU deal to be kept "budget neutral," and one certain way to do this was to commission an organization with a separate and independent financial standing as the executor of the purchase agreement. Third, giving USEC the HEU deal was seen as a way to enhance USEC's competitiveness in the international marketplace. This, in turn, would strengthen U.S. industry, protect jobs, possibly increase U.S. export earnings, and increase the proceeds to the U.S. Treasury that would result from USEC's eventual privatization.

These were sound reasons for giving USEC the HEU deal, but if the Bush administration had looked deeper, it would have discovered that USEC would have little incentive to implement the HEU deal at the speed or scope envisioned by the president and his key advisors. The first reason for this has already been described: as a monopoly, USEC was accustomed to very high profit margins, on the order of 100 percent. "Budget neutral," therefore, has a decidedly different meaning for USEC than it does for the U.S. Treasury: whereas the government would regard anything which causes no net increase or decrease in the budget deficit as "neutral," for USEC "budget neutral" means "earning the same profit as the alternative activity." In USEC's case, the alternative activity would be to produce SWU on its own, at a (heavily subsidized) cost of $60, and sell it to utilities at a unit price of about $120. In giving the HEU deal to USEC, the Bush administration confused budget neutrality for a government with profit neutrality for a firm.

The second reason why USEC is a poor executor for the HEU deal is that USEC has an inherently adversarial relationship with Minatom. There are four suppliers of enrichment services in the world: USEC; Cogema, a French conglomerate; Urenco, a British-Dutch-German consortium; and Minatom. USEC and Minatom are oligopolistic competitors. In the enrichment sector alone, Minatom claims to have 20–25 percent of the world enrichment capacity, but only 5 percent of the world enrichment market, a percentage that Minatom desperately wants to increase.[85] USEC has no incentive to be a mere broker for its competitors, especially when that competitor has a dire shortage of hard currency. By funneling hard currency to Minatom through the HEU deal, USEC would be helping its commercial rival become more competitive in the international marketplace, thereby increasing the risk that USEC will lose market share or be forced to accept lower prices in the future. Not surprisingly, Minister Mikhailov has discerned this conflict of interest, which is part of the reason why he and his ministry have always pushed for the creation of a separate U.S.-Russian joint venture to implement the HEU deal.

Third, by reselling Russian HEU on the U.S. and world market, USEC inevitably accentuates its own problem with excess production capacity. USEC's two gaseous diffusion plants have an annual production capacity of 19.2 million SWU, but, as the global SWU market is beset with excess supply, they are together producing only about 13 million SWU per year. A decision to close one of the plants has long been described as inevitable, but USEC has no interest in doing this any sooner than absolutely necessary. Certainly, so long as its privatization legislation is before Congress, USEC will postpone its plant-closing decision, which would inevitably alienate legislators from either Ohio or Kentucky. Since 10 metric tons of HEU contains 1.9 million SWU, and 30 metric tons of HEU contains 5.7 million SWU, it is easy to see that implementing the HEU deal conflicts with USEC's political interest in keeping both of its enrichment plants open for as long as possible.

Finally, USEC is an inappropriate government executor of the HEU deal because USEC has not been subject to conventional governmental control. Even though it is wholly owned by the U.S. Treasury, the president has not been able to easily order USEC to take actions which USEC regards as against its economic interest. And, once USEC goes public, the government will have no more formal authority over USEC than it does over any other publicly held company. Although the Clinton administration has sought to define the HEU deal as "strictly commercial," in fact the HEU deal is an initiative whose value is measured primarily in terms

---

85. Ann MacLachlan, "Euratom Has Approved Some CIS U Contracts Under $13/lb. to Block 'Undue' Trader Profits," *Nuclear Fuel*, June 7, 1993.

of national security. As such, it is irresponsible to relegate its implementation to a private actor that the highest authority in the United States cannot easily and directly control, and which has incentives that do not coincide with the national security interests of the United States. That the Bush administration permitted an initiative as important to U.S. security as the HEU deal to be implemented by just such an entity was a major intellectual failure with damaging policy consequences.

There are five ways to create incentives for the HEU deal to be implemented by its U.S. executor. The first is for the U.S. government to subsidize USEC's purchases of blended-down Russian HEU. The second is for the Congress, when it passes the final privatization legislation for USEC, to create a statutory requirement for USEC to fully and faithfully implement the HEU deal. The third is to designate an alternative executive agent (or agents) for the HEU deal, which can be done in a variety of different ways. The fourth option is to reduce the government subsidies of USEC's production, which could make the importation of Russian SWU profitable for USEC. The fifth option is to cancel the privatization of USEC, leaving it a government-owned and -controlled company. Each of these options is described and evaluated below, though this discussion defers for the moment an analysis of how the amended Russian suspension agreement would need to be changed to make any of these options fully viable.

SUBSIDIZE USEC. A key obstacle to USEC's implementation of the HEU deal is that unless Minatom accepts a SWU price of $60 or less, it is more profitable for USEC to produce its own SWU than to import it from Russia. Minatom has thus far refused to go this low in price, which is unsurprising since the long-term SWU prices worldwide tend to be in excess of $100. One solution to this problem, therefore, is for the U.S. government to pay USEC the difference between its cost of production — $60 — and the lowest price Minatom will accept. In this case, if Minatom accepted a SWU price of $75, the purchase of 10 metric tons of HEU from Russia would cost U.S. taxpayers about $27 million, giving the HEU deal a total cost to the government of $1.35 billion.

This is a very bad option for salvaging the HEU deal, for three reasons. First, a U.S. government subsidy for implementing the HEU deal would be pure profit for USEC, which monopolizes the U.S. enrichment market and already demands profit margins of close to 100 percent from its domestic customers. With USEC simultaneously gouging U.S. consumers and the Russian government, it is absurd to hold that USEC deserves further government assistance. Second, if it is known that the U.S. government will make up the difference between USEC's cost of production and the price paid to Russia, Minatom will never agree to a lower price. Third, and most importantly, *the HEU deal does not need to be subsidized.* There is more than enough economic value in the HEU from Russian warheads to allow the HEU deal to be fully implemented at no net cost to the executor. The only reason why this issue has arisen at all, in fact, is that the U.S. government decided to give executive authority over the HEU deal to an entity with a serious conflict of interest that wants to implement it on a profit-neutral, rather than budget-neutral, basis. Rather than compound this mistake by further subsidizing USEC, another solution to the problem should be found.

STATUTORY REQUIREMENT.　In mid-1995, Congress had before it legislation to allow the public sale of USEC shares, the proceeds of which would go to the U.S. Treasury. Congress could insert a provision into this legislation stipulating that USEC must fully and faithfully implement the HEU deal, and this provision could set specific and detailed criteria for full and faithful implementation. Among other things, for example, Congress could require that USEC import 10 metric tons of Russian HEU annually for the first five years of the HEU, rising to 30 metric tons annually for the following 15 years.

However, this alone cannot solve the problem. USEC is virtually certain to find a way around this stipulation if the implementation of the HEU deal is not in its economic interest. This would be different if USEC were a government agency, but it is not: USEC is a government corporation that, for the moment, happens to be solely owned by the U.S. Treasury but could well become publicly held sometime in the future. Thus, no matter how carefully Congress writes the mandate to implement the HEU deal, the issue would almost certainly become mired in the judicial system, freezing out the HEU deal. Therefore, simply mandating that USEC implement the HEU deal is insufficient.

DESIGNATION OF A DIFFERENT EXECUTIVE AGENT.　The analysis in this study leads to one obvious option for salvaging the HEU deal: strip USEC of its executive role, and designate in its place some other entity with a more appropriate incentive structure. There is much to commend this idea, but there are several problems with it as well.

First, it is important to understand that keeping exclusive control of the HEU deal is very important to USEC. Giving executive authority to some other entity — be it a private company, joint venture, or government agency — would create an alternative SWU supplier on the U.S. market, which would erode USEC's monopoly, reducing its market share and probably forcing it to accept lower domestic prices for its SWU. USEC does not want this to happen. Thus, USEC is certain to oppose any initiative to appoint an alternative executive agent for the HEU deal. It is also important to recall that the Energy Policy Act of 1992 transferred responsibility for implementing the HEU deal to USEC. This provision in the law might need to be changed if any of the options outlined below are to succeed.

The key advantages to appointing an alternative executor are three. First, most firms in the nuclear industry — indeed, in any industry — are willing to operate at profit margins far lower than USEC's. Second, the nuclear-industry firms that are best suited for implementing the HEU deal — firms such as Allied-Signal, Nukem, Babcock & Wilcox, and Nuclear Fuel Services — are not currently SWU producers, which means that they, unlike USEC, do not regard implementing the HEU deal as merely displacing production they would otherwise undertake. For every other U.S. firm but USEC, implementing the HEU deal offers an opportunity for a major expansion of its business in a lucrative new market; for USEC, implementing the HEU deal imposes an obligation to funnel hard currency to a competitor and to close one of its own plants sooner than would otherwise be necessary. Thus, firms other than USEC would have a powerful incentive to initiate and expand the flow of HEU from dismantled Russian nuclear weapons into civilian reactors, since this means new business, greater revenue, and probably increased profits; USEC has no such incentive. Finally, none of these other firms is locked into an oligopolistic competition for global market share with Minatom, which means that they, unlike USEC, have no disincentive to transfer hard currency into Minatom's bank accounts.

There are four basic ways of changing the executive agent for the HEU deal. The first and most simple would be to strip USEC of its role as exclusive executive agent and transfer that right permanently to a state-sanctioned joint venture, which is the option Minatom has preferred since 1992. This option would likely be a highly effective one for implementing the HEU deal, but it would also create the greatest challenge to USEC's commercial interests. Importantly, this option would give the purchasers of Russian-origin SWU a relatively high degree of confidence in the certainty of their supply over the long term.

The second, third, and fourth options would involve systems of competitive bidding. Under one system, the HEU deal would be changed to allow firms other than USEC to bid for the right to import Russian HEU into the United States. This would force USEC to offer Minatom the full market value of the Russian HEU, since if it did not, another firm would gain access to the material and reduce USEC's share of the U.S. SWU market.

Under a third option, the U.S. government (probably the Department of Energy) would designate one or more alternative executors for the HEU deal if USEC and Minatom fail to agree on a price for the Russian HEU at their annual review consultations each October. This option would give USEC an incentive to offer a higher price, but it would also lower Minatom's incentive to accept USEC's bid.

Finally, the government could designate alternative importers for any amount of the Russian HEU that USEC chooses not to purchase. Under this system, USEC would have the first right to import 10 (or later 30) metric tons of Russian HEU into the United States. USEC would have the option to import the full amount of Russian HEU each year if it so desired. At the beginning of each year, USEC would have to declare how many tons it would purchase in the coming year, and would then be obligated to import no less than that amount of HEU. If USEC elected to import less than the full 10 (or 30) metric tons of HEU in that year, then the rights to import the difference between the amount USEC ordered and the amount Russia was supposed to ship would be tendered to private industry and allocated on the basis of competitive bidding. USEC would not have the right to prevent these sales from occurring. This option would give USEC an incentive to place orders for Russian HEU so that other firms could not become alternative SWU suppliers, but would do so without denying USEC its special role in the implementation of the HEU deal. However, like the previous proposal, this approach would undermine the ability of USEC's competitors to offer reliable long-term contracts to their clients.

All these competitive options have virtues and disadvantages, and each deserves to be carefully studied by U.S. officials involved in the HEU deal. What is clear, however, is that any of them would be preferable to perpetuating USEC's exclusive executive control over the HEU deal.

REDUCE THE IMPLICIT SUBSIDY OF USEC'S ELECTRICITY. One of the central reasons why USEC is an appropriate executive agent for the HEU deal is that it can produce SWU at a cost lower than that which must be paid to Russia. But the only reason why USEC's production costs are so low is that the government is implicitly subsidizing USEC's cost of production. Reducing the level of this subsidy would raise USEC's production costs, thereby increasing its incentive to purchase Russian SWU.[86]

---

86. Much of the technical analysis that lies behind this argument draws from Thomas L. Neff, "How Changing the U.S. Enrichment Cost Structure Can Make the HEU Deal Work," unpublished paper, 1995. A related argument was also made in Mozelle W. Thompson, "Comment on the General Accounting Office Draft Report Entitled *Ura-*

As already noted, USEC receives electricity to power its gaseous diffusion plants under long-term contracts that were negotiated by the Department of Energy. These contracts allow the Department of Energy to purchase large amounts of electricity from two utilities at an average price of about two cents per kilowatt-hour, which is less than half the commercial rate of 4–5 cents per kilowatt-hour. An agreement between USEC and the Department of Energy allows USEC to purchase this electricity at the Department's cost. Since the production of each SWU requires about 2,500 kilowatt-hours of electricity, at an average electricity cost of two cents per kilowatt-hour, the power component of USEC's marginal cost of production is $50/SWU. (Tails disposal, the other main component in the *marginal* cost of SWU production, probably costs around $10/SWU, giving USEC a total marginal cost of about $60/SWU.) Since Minatom wants at least $82.10/SWU for the blended-down HEU it sells to the United States, USEC's marginal costs of SWU production must rise above that level for it to have a strong incentive to buy Russian HEU rather than produce its own. If the Department of Energy were to sell electricity to USEC for three cents per kilowatt-hour — a rate which is still well below commercial rates and replacement costs — then USEC's marginal cost of production would rise to $85/SWU, and buying Russian SWU would suddenly become more profitable for USEC than producing its own.

Raising USEC's electricity costs by fifty percent would severely impact its competitiveness in the international enrichment market, since USEC's inefficient gaseous diffusion technology cannot compete with the other enrichment technologies used by Urenco, Eurodif, and Minatom (principally centrifuges) unless its energy costs are heavily subsidized. Because a fifty-percent cost increase would reduce USEC's future profitability, it would also reduce the revenue the government would earn from privatizing USEC. However, this reduction in privatization revenue would be at least partially compensated for by future revenue resulting from the government's above-cost electricity sales to USEC. (If the government bought its electricity for two cents per kilowatt-hour and sold it for three cents per kilowatt-hour, the Treasury would earn one cent per kilowatt-hour, or about $25 for every SWU produced by USEC.) Since the successful privatization of the government's enrichment enterprise is a major bipartisan political objective, resolving the executive agent problem

nium Enrichment: Process to Privatize the U.S. Enrichment Corporation Needs to Be Strengthened," reprinted in U.S. GAO, *Uranium Enrichment: Process to Privatize the U.S. Enrichment Corporation Needs to Be Strengthened,* RCED-95-245 (Washington DC: U.S. GAO, September 1995), p. 68.

in the HEU deal by substantially increasing USEC's electricity costs is probably politically non-viable. It is also not strictly necessary, since the executive agent problem in the HEU deal could also be resolved at lower political costs by appropriately introducing competition into the U.S. procedure for buying Russian HEU.

After this issue was raised by several government agencies in mid-1995,[87] a new provision was inserted into the Senate's draft of the USEC privatization bill that would lock in USEC's electricity subsidy by requiring the Department of Energy to resell its electricity at cost. This provision would make it impossible for the government to modify USEC's incentive structure by manipulating the electricity costs.

CANCEL THE PRIVATIZATION OF USEC. Finally, the U.S. government could resolve many of the long-term problems with the U.S. purchase of Russian HEU if it were simply to cancel the privatization of USEC. Under this option, USEC would remain the executive agent in the HEU deal, but the U.S. Treasury would remain USEC's sole owner. As a government-owned corporation, USEC could be instructed to accept lower profits for the foreign policy gains associated with the purchase of Russian HEU — a trade the corporation would resist making if it were owned by normal, profit-maximizing investors. This solution, of course, would work only so long as the government exercises more effective oversight of USEC's purchase of HEU from Russia than was the case during 1994–95.

Canceling the public sale of USEC is a less radical idea than it may seem. Most if not all of the efficiency gains associated with private-sector management were achieved in July 1993, when USEC was established as a government-owned corporation out of the highly inefficient government enrichment operation run by the Department of Energy. Few if any additional efficiency gains can expected by transferring the ownership of USEC from the government to the private sector. Indeed, there are at least two reasons why the public sale of USEC may be a poor choice for the government. The first reason has already been noted: the White House could compel a government-owned USEC to accept the lower profits associated with buying Russian HEU, whereas a publicly owned USEC would resist this pressure.

The second argument against privatizing USEC is that the net present value of USEC as a government-owned corporation exceeds by a substantial margin the net expected proceeds of the sale of USEC. In a September 1995 report, the U.S. General Accounting Office estimated that the net

---

87. Thompson, "Comment on the GAO Draft Report," p. 68.

present value of USEC's future cash flows would be $2.8–3.5 billion, but that the total return from privatizing USEC would be only $1.7–2.2 billion.[88] In other words, according to the GAO, the sale of USEC would waste between $600 million and $1.8 billion.[89] Moreover, the public sale of USEC would involve transaction costs of "about $100 million,"[90] which would be paid as fees to lawyers and investment bankers involved in the sale. In other words, about 5–7 percent of the total privatization value of the corporation would be a direct transfer of wealth from the Treasury to Wall Street. For many, these facts alone probably constitute a sufficient reason to cancel the privatization of USEC.

Thus, there are sound public-policy reasons to cancel the sale of USEC to be public, a decision that the president has the authority to make. To date, however, the wisdom of privatizing USEC has not been seriously questioned by the public or the Congress. Yet when the foreign policy costs of allowing a privatized USEC to execute the HEU deal are added to the economic costs of selling off a government corporation for less than it is worth, the case against privatization becomes compelling. At the same time, it is important to emphasize that even if the government decides not to sell USEC to the public, USEC will be an effective executive agent of the HEU deal only so long as the government exercises effective oversight.

THE SUSPENSION AGREEMENT

As far as the HEU deal is concerned, the most damaging aspect of the suspension agreement is that it currently allows the sale of the Russian HEU feed component on the U.S. market only in the context of a matched sale and subject to Russia's annual matched-sale quota for natural uranium imports.[91] Thus, the suspension agreement requires USEC to quar-

---

88. Ibid., p. 48; p. 2. The investment bank J.P. Morgan estimated that the proceeds from privatizing USEC would be $1.5–1.8 billion, but the GAO modified this estimate to calculate the total return from privatization by subtracting transaction costs and cash transfers, and by adding future tax revenues.

89. The most important source of difference between net present value of USEC as a government-owned corporation and the market value of USEC if it were sold is the use of a discount rate that is based on the government's cost of borrowing rather than a private corporation's rate of return. Ibid., pp. 48–49.

90. Ibid., p. 5.

91. See note 75. This interpretation of the suspension agreement is held by most relevant agencies of the U.S. government, though there is some ambiguity on precisely what the suspension agreement says about this point. This interpretation is clearly held by the U.S. enrichment workers' union (the petitioners in the original anti-dumping suit), the government of Canada (based on the results of its October 20, 1994, consult-

antine an amount of feed material equal to the feed material in the blended-down HEU that USEC sells on the U.S. market. This quarantined material would come from the uranium feed that utilities normally deliver to USEC pursuant to their enrichment contracts, thereby making the blended-down HEU imports "market neutral."[92]

The suspension agreement currently allows the natural uranium feedstock to be disposed of in one of three ways: first, it can be used to overfeed USEC's enrichment cascades, in which case USEC would pay Russia directly for the feed; second, it can be sold outside of the U.S. market; and third, it might be sold inside the U.S. market in a matched sale and subject to the matched-sales quota. Since USEC does not currently regard overfeeding as cost effective, and since Russia's sales of natural uranium on the world market are already close to the maximum possible level given demand considerations and other countries' barriers to Russian uranium imports, the only currently viable option for reselling the feed component of the Russian HEU is in the context of matched sales, which itself is not clearly legal. But, as shown in Table 2, even if the entire matched-sales quota were given to USEC to allow it to sell the feed component of the Russian HEU on the U.S. market, it would still be too little to permit the reselling of the full feed component. Thus, as it currently stands, the suspension agreement in effect requires USEC to stockpile Russian uranium feed until it can sell the material, which will occur at the earliest when the amended suspension agreement expires in 2003 (assuming, of course, that no new protectionist measure emerges).[93]

These provisions in the amended Russian suspension agreement are an obstacle to promptly compensating Russia for the natural uranium component of its blended-down HEU sales to the United States, and Minatom has threatened to cancel the HEU deal unless it is paid up front

---

ations with the U.S. Trade Representative and the State Department), and apparently also the Department of Energy. See the written testimony by Dale L. Alberts, President of the Uranium Producers of America, before the Senate Committee on Energy and Natural Resources, June 13, 1995.

92. The suspension agreement does not specify how the feed component of the blended-down Russian HEU would have to be handled if an entity other than USEC — that is, one that had no "utility-owned uranium products delivered pursuant to enrichment contracts affected by purchase of HEU or HEU products" — were responsible for importing the Russian HEU. In a literal sense, it appears that the suspension agreement as currently written would not apply to the feed component of the Russian HEU if some entity other than USEC were importing it. This interpretation has not, however, been tested.

93. The agreement does not explain what would happen if utilities stop sending USEC uranium feed for the LEU fuel derived from Russian HEU.

for the uranium component as well as the SWU component of the blended-down HEU. In mid-1995, the U.S. government began to devote considerable energy to finding a solution to this particular problem in the HEU deal. There are basically three options for dealing with this problem: (1) altering the matching ratios and/or quotas for the blended-down Russian HEU; (2) allowing the Russian feedstock to be sold in the U.S. market through a schedule of forward sales, a proposal known as the "Domenici approach"; and (3) slightly altering USEC's cost structure to make overfeeding commercially viable. Each of these ideas is described below.

ALTER THE MATCHING RATIOS OR QUOTAS. The administration could try to amend the Russian suspension agreement once again by inserting a new provision designed to allow the resale of more Russian feedstock than currently allowed. There are many different ways that this could be done, but the most obvious ones are changing the matching ratio for blended-down Russian HEU (e.g., by allowing one ton of U.S. uranium to be matched with more than one ton of Russian uranium), or by creating a separate and substantially higher matched-sales quota for the natural uranium in the blended-down Russian HEU.

The principle advantage of this option over the four-tiered approach is that it could have a less severe impact on the domestic price of uranium, since there would be greater certainty in the market with a quota system than there would be with a simple exemption. Its disadvantages are: (1) the resale of the Russian uranium would still be dependent on USEC; (2) the quotas would have to be raised quite substantially if they were to accommodate the full amount of the uranium component of the blended-down Russian HEU; and (3) such a substantial increase in the allowable level of Russian-origin uranium imports into the U.S. would probably incite a new legal challenge from the U.S. uranium industry, and would probably also cause Canada to reopen its case against the amended Russian suspension agreement.

THE DOMENICI APPROACH. In an approach proposed by Senator Pete Domenici (R-N.M.), Russia would be given title to the feedstock in USEC's custody displaced by the blended-down HEU imports and a legislated guarantee that it could sell this material on the U.S. market in the future.[94] This arrangement would have two major advantages. First, it would allow Russia to offer forward contracts for the material, which

---

94. See "Domenici Bill a Winner," *The Ux Weekly*, June 5, 1995; and "Some Additional Observations," *The Ux Weekly*, June 19, 1995.

in turn would allow Minatom to receive immediate compensation for the natural uranium component of its HEU sales. Second, it would have a predictable effect on the near-term price of uranium, which would tend to make this option more acceptable to the U.S. uranium industry and to Canada. In an October 17, 1994, letter to U.S. Under Secretary of State Lynn Davis, Minister Mikhailov expressed his support for the forward sales approach.

Senator Domenici's proposal would allow deliveries of Russian uranium to take place after 2002, though the U.S. nuclear industry has proposed moving this date forward. Under Domenici's proposal, Russia could sell up to 10 million pounds of UF6 equivalent annually between 2002 and 2011, and up to 20 million pounds of UF6 equivalent each year thereafter. This would allow Russia to receive immediate compensation for some or all of the natural uranium component of the blended-down HEU it delivers to the United States; the size of this compensation would depend on the price that uranium buyers offer Russia for promised deliveries early in the next century. If the permissibility of such sales were guaranteed by Congress, it is possible and perhaps even likely that uranium buyers would be willing to buy forward contracts for all of the Russian feed at a price acceptable to Minatom. Because it would deprive USEC of control over the Russian feed, USEC opposed the Domenici approach.

Senator Domenici's general approach is, however, supported by most of the rest of the U.S. nuclear industry. According to one trade press editorial:

The USEC [four-tiered] proposal is bad for all the reasons the Domenici bill is good. . . . If one thinks about the problem of selling uranium contained in the HEU as bringing a large uranium mine into production, maximum revenue would be obtained by selling this material forward into a period where there is a large uncommitted demand, rather than in the near term where demand is much thinner and the capability for sales to depress price is much greater. To put this another way, Western producers who do not face sales restrictions do not bring on new mines without contracting forward because they realize that sales opportunities in the spot market are limited. The Domenici bill best captures this type of sales behavior while at the same time slightly relaxing existing trade restrictions.[95]

In other words, it is possible to serve the national security interest in removing HEU from Russia without necessarily undermining the com-

---

95. "Choice — The HEU Deal or USEC," *The Ux Weekly,* June 12, 1995.

mercial interests of the wider U.S. nuclear industry, and without unduly enhancing USEC's already considerable market power.

The concept of forward sales is a sound one, and it deserves the support of the Clinton administration.

MAKE OVERFEEDING COMMERCIALLY VIABLE. If USEC were to overfeed the natural uranium component of the Russian HEU, the problem with the suspension agreement would disappear. The trouble with this approach is that USEC's low production costs mean that overfeeding is cost-effective only if it can buy the Russian uranium for about $24 or less per pound rather than the $28.50 per pound that was originally agreed with Minatom. As shown in Figure C-3, overfeeding 2,979 metric tons of uranium allows USEC to avoid the costs of 1.2 million SWU, which at a production cost of $60/SWU equals an avoided cost of $72 million. However, if USEC must pay $28.50 per pound for that 2,979 metric tons of uranium, the cost of the overfeed will be $85 million, so overfeeding the uranium would produce a $13 million loss for USEC. (In fact, the economic loss resulting from overfeeding this amount of uranium is probably slightly larger than this estimate, but the total annual loss is certainly less than $50 million.)

It is perhaps worth noting that the U.S. government accepted at face value the argument that USEC could not overfeed the Russian uranium, and went to great lengths to try to resolve the suspension agreement problem with the HEU deal in order to save USEC somewhere between $13 and $50 million. In fiscal year 1994, USEC had $1.4 billion in gross revenues, $377 million in profits, and was receiving an implicit electricity subsidy worth well over $500 million. At least in the near term, therefore, the government could have required USEC to overfeed the Russian uranium since the only consequence would have been a slight reduction in the profits of a heavily-subsidized government-owned company.

A slight reduction in the implicit subsidy of USEC's production costs would make it cost-effective for USEC to overfeed the Russian uranium, which would eliminate the problem with the HEU deal caused by the suspension agreement.[96] If USEC's production costs were to rise to $71/SWU, the costs avoided through overfeeding would be large enough to justify buying the Russian uranium at a price of $28.50 per pound. At a SWU production cost of $71, producing 1.2 million SWU costs $85.2 million. USEC's production cost could be increased to $71/SWU if the average price at which it purchased electricity from the Department of

---

96. See also Thomas L. Neff, "How Changing the U.S. Enrichment Cost Structure Can Make the HEU Deal Work," unpublished paper, 1995.

Energy was raised from two cents per kilowatt-hour to 2.45 cents per kilowatt-hour, which is still far below commercial rates. Of course, this would reduce USEC's future profitability and, therefore, the government's privatization revenue, but this reduction in privatization revenue would be mitigated by future government earnings from its higher cost electricity sales to USEC (roughly $11 per SWU produced).

This solution to the suspension agreement problem in the HEU deal would become less feasible when the United States begins to purchase more than 10 metric tons of Russian HEU per year. There are technical constraints on how much uranium USEC can overfeed. Thus, when the United States begins to purchase 30 metric tons of Russian HEU per year, much of the uranium component of this material would either have to be stockpiled for future overfeeding, or it would have to be sold in some fashion. For this reason, the overfeeding solution to the suspension agreement problem is fully compatible with the forward sales approach for dealing with the Russian feed.

THE BLENDING QUESTION

Finally, as noted earlier, the U.S. government should revisit the idea of importing HEU directly from Russia and blending it in the United States. The national security advantages of this option, as opposed to blending solely in Russia, are considerable: it would speed the removal of the HEU from Russia, minimize the internal movement of the material within Russia, and lower the risks of theft at the Russian uranium blending plant. Blending in the U.S. would also have the important political and economic effects of offering new business opportunities to U.S. firms other than USEC, and of allowing U.S. uranium to be used as blendstock, which would help quiet the anti-dumping complaints of the U.S. uranium mining interests. There would undoubtedly be environmental opposition to blending the HEU in the United States if this issue were ever seriously considered by the government; indeed, several local environmental groups have already expressed their opposition to blending Russian HEU at the Allied-Signal plant in Erwin, Tennessee.[97] HEU is, however, a far less hazardous material than plutonium or spent reactor fuel, so there is a strong case to be made that HEU blending would have less damaging environmental consequences than many other industrial activities.

---

97. "Transportation of Nuclear Fuel Worries Council," *Greensboro News and Record*, July 6, 1994; and Jesse Tinsley, "Erwin Firm to Process Uranium from Russia; Transport Secrecy Worries State Council," *Knoxville News-Sentinel*, July 5, 1994.

A Bolder Alternative

Beyond the policy options described in the preceding discussion, there is one final possibility for salvaging the HEU deal, a bold option which to date has received almost no official attention.

The U.S. government could simply execute the HEU deal by itself just as it did in Kazakhstan with a Project Sapphire. The U.S. Treasury would buy as much Russian HEU as possible, as quickly as possible, and ship it directly to the Department of Energy's weapons-grade uranium facility at Oak Ridge, Tennessee. The material would be stockpiled there for later gradual release into the uranium economy. In this way, the market effects of the HEU deal could be carefully regulated by the government. Exactly how and when the material would be resold in the civilian economy could be determined ad hoc, based in part on proposals submitted by industry. The cost of the transaction would initially be borne by the U.S. Treasury, but there are a number of creative financing options that could be used to lessen the budgetary impact of the purchase. First, like private industry, the government could finance the deal by borrowing against the value of the uranium. The government should have no trouble securing such loans because the uranium clearly has market value, and because the government can exercise great influence over the legality of the sale of Russian-origin uranium products. Second, the U.S. government may be able to finance part of its purchase of Russian HEU by relieving part of Russia's debt to the United States, though admittedly, this is little more than a budgetary subterfuge because the loss of future revenue is analytically equivalent to a new outlay.

Regardless of how Washington finances the deal, however, the important point is that the Russian government should receive prompt compensation for the HEU it ships to the United States. This influx of hard currency into the Russian nuclear complex would increase Russia's incentive to continue or accelerate its dismantlement of nuclear weapons and the shipment of the resulting HEU to the United States, and would give the United States invaluable leverage over Minatom, which it should use to persuade Minatom to enact comprehensive improvements in its nuclear security and accounting systems.

This option is inconsistent with the notion that the HEU deal should be executed on a strictly commercial basis. But the HEU deal is above all else a tool for promoting the national security interests of the United States. The reasons for direct government execution of the HEU deal are no less compelling than they were in Project Sapphire, in which the U.S. government acted with great initiative, secrecy, and speed to extract six-tenths of a ton of HEU from an insecure location in Kazakhstan. Why the removal of 500 tons of HEU from Russia, where it is stored in only marginally more secure conditions than was the material in Kazakhstan, merits such low priority for the U.S. government has never been clear. The U.S. government could quickly and effectively improve the security of the United States and its allies if Washington were to take control of the HEU deal, dramatically accelerate the speed and scope of the annual HEU transfers from Russia, and begin accepting normal HEU as well as blended-down HEU. Those responsible for the finances of the federal government should rely on the premise that when the material is ready to be resold commercially, and the government is ready to resell it, a determined White House will be able to find a way to recoup most if not all of its initial expenses.

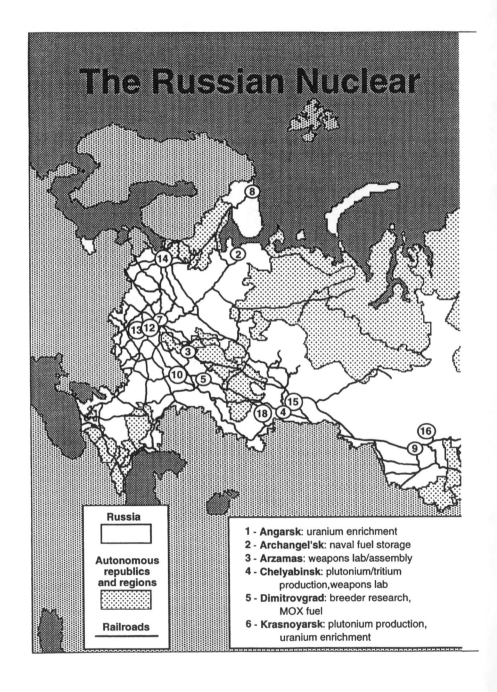

The Russian Nuclear

Russia

Autonomous republics and regions

Railroads

1 - **Angarsk**: uranium enrichment
2 - **Archangel'sk**: naval fuel storage
3 - **Arzamas**: weapons lab/assembly
4 - **Chelyabinsk**: plutonium/tritium
   production, weapons lab
5 - **Dimitrovgrad**: breeder research,
   MOX fuel
6 - **Krasnoyarsk**: plutonium production,
   uranium enrichment

Archipelago

7 - **Moscow**: 2 research reactor facilities, 1 fuel fabrication
8 - **Murmansk**: naval fuel storage
9 - **Novosibirsk**: fuel fabrication
10 - **Penza**: weapon assembly
11 - **Petropavlovsk**: naval fuel storage
12 - **Podol'sk**: research/space reactors
13 - **Obninsk**: research reactors
14 - **St. Petersburg**: research/naval fuel

15 - **Sverdlovsk**: uranium enrichment, weapons assembly
16 - **Tomsk**: plutonium production, uranium enrichment
17 - **Vladivostok**: naval fuel storage
18 - **Zlatoust**: weapons assembly

Copyright 1995 - John F. Kennedy School of Government; Map by Jeffry Pike

Center for Science and International Affairs

Graham T. Allison, Director
John F. Kennedy School of Government
Harvard University
79 JFK Street, Cambridge MA 02138
(617) 495-1400

The Center for Science and International Affairs (CSIA) is the hub of research and teaching on international relations at Harvard's John F. Kennedy School of Government. CSIA seeks to advance the understanding of international security and environmental problems with special emphasis on the role of science and technology in the analysis and design of public policy. The Center seeks to anticipate emerging international problems, identify practical solutions, and encourage policymakers to act. These goals animate work in each of the Center's four major programs:

- The International Security Program (ISP) is the home of the Center's core concern with international security issues.

- The Strengthening Democratic Institutions (SDI) project works to catalyze international support for political and economic transformations in the former Soviet Union.

- The Science, Technology, and Public Policy (STPP) program emphasizes public policy issues in which understanding of science, technology, and systems of innovation are crucial.

- The Environment and Natural Resources Program (ENRP) is the locus of interdisciplinary research on environmental policy issues.

Each year CSIA hosts a multinational group of approximately 25 scholars from the social, behavioral, and natural sciences. Dozens of Harvard faculty members and adjunct research fellows from the greater Boston area also participate in CSIA activities. CSIA also sponsors seminars and conferences, many open to the public; maintains a substantial specialized library; and publishes a monograph series and discussion papers. The Center's International Security Program, directed by Steven E. Miller, publishes the CSIA Studies in International Security, and sponsors and edits the quarterly journal *International Security*.

The Center is supported by an endowment established with funds from the Ford Foundation and Harvard University, by foundation grants, by individual gifts, and by occasional government contracts.